THE SECURITY ENVIRONMENT IN THE ASIA-PACIFIC

Studies of the Institute for National Policy Research

Established in 1989, the INPR is the leading private think tank in Taiwan. It focuses on democratization, public policy, security affairs, and economics in the Asia-Pacific region.

**TAIWAN'S ELECTORAL POLITICS
AND DEMOCRATIC TRANSITION**
Riding the Third Wave
Hung-mao Tien, editor

**THE SECURITY ENVIRONMENT
IN THE ASIA-PACIFIC**
Hung-mao Tien and Tun-jen Cheng, editors

THE SECURITY ENVIRONMENT IN THE ASIA-PACIFIC

Hung-mao Tien and
Tun-jen Cheng,
Editors

AN EAST GATE BOOK

Routledge
Taylor & Francis Group

LONDON AND NEW YORK

An East Gate Book

First published 2000 by M.E. Sharpe

Published 2015 by Routledge
2 Park Square, Milton Park, Abingdon, Oxon OX14 4RN
711 Third Avenue, New York, NY, 10017, USA

Routledge is an imprint of the Taylor & Francis Group, an informa business

Library of Congress Cataloging-in-Publication Data

The security environment in the Asia-Pacific / edited by Hung-mao Tien
and Tun-jen Cheng.
    p.   cm. — (Studies of the Institute for National Policy
Research)
    "An East gate book."
    Includes bibliographical references and index.
    ISBN 0-7656-0539-2 (hardcover : alk. paper). — ISBN 0-7656-0540-6
(pbk. : alk. paper)
    1. Asia—Foreign relations.   2. Pacific Area—Foreign relations.
3. Security, International. I. Tien, Hung-mao, 1938–   II. Cheng,
Tun-jen. III. Series.
JZ1980.S43 1999
355'.031'091823—dc21   99-37176
                                CIP

ISBN 13: 9780765605405 (pbk)
ISBN 13: 9780765605399 (hbk)

Contents

List of Tables and Figures

Tables

Figures

Preface

The growing economic importance of Asia has generated steadily increasing concern about its security environment. But although measures to strengthen security cooperation in the Asia-Pacific region have been explored by numerous organizations and forums, the development of regional "track one" programs to facilitate official discussion and analysis of major security issues has been limited by several key factors—the absence of effective multilateralism, lack of effective leadership, and the unwillingness of participating governments to alter attitudes and policies toward regional cooperation. Another major limitation is the incomplete membership of many regional organizations due to disputes about which countries should be included, and at what levels.

Perhaps as a result of the failure to establish effective "track one" institutions, non-governmental or "track two" programs have proliferated. These organizations vary in degree of policy relevance, inclusiveness, breadth of definition of security, extent of original research and conceptualization, and comfort level for new forms of intellectual exchange. Few programs have acquired all the desirable elements.

The Institute for National Policy Research (INPR), the leading independent, non-partisan public policy think tank in Taiwan, long has been engaged in raising the level of discourse on security issues in the region. One of its most noteworthy recent efforts was a joint-conference in the spring of 1995, entitled "Asia-Pacific Collective Security in the Post-Cold War Era," which was sponsored by the INPR and the European-based ISODARCO. The conference discussed issues ranging from the Korean Peninsula, South China Sea and Taiwan Strait issues to recent developments in European collective security as they relate to Asia-Pacific security. Although the discussions included many topics that were critical to the region, it was clear by the end of the meetings that a conference of this nature should be only a beginning, not an end.

Further discussions with James A. Kelly, Ralph Cossa and Yun-han Chu led to the establishment of a new "track two" security organization, the Asia-Pacific Security Forum (APSF), to fill some of the gaps in the existing structure. The concept underlying the APSF is a regional grouping consisting of a core group of research institutes, of all types, broadly representing the major countries both located and interested in the region, along with leading individual security analysts and practitioners.

The primary purpose of this forum is to provide a distinctive new venue for multilateral discussion. It promises a high comfort level for ground-breaking dialogue, a broad definition of security, a high degree of inclusiveness, and new levels of original research and conceptualization. This new venue will fully incorporate into its deliberations Taiwan-based scholars and intellectual resources, which often are barred from other "track two" fora. Also, it will bring the participation of European-based scholars and experts into the fold. To keep the APSF flexible, open, and able to accommodate change, including the incorporation of prospective participants while avoiding a rigid governing structure, the organization was to have neither formal memberships nor a secretariat. The aim is to operate a highly developed, flexible, effective program with the minimum amount of bureaucracy.

The organizational plan for the ASPF calls for a thematically structured international conference to be held every two years in Taipei, with issue- or situation-specific roundtables to be held in alternate years in other regional capitals. While the primary focus of the major conference will be the most salient and pressing security issues, such as territorial disputes, nuclear proliferation and the arms race, transparency of military expenses, confidence building mechanisms, and preventative diplomacy, the APSF will also deal with long-range security issues such as collective security mechanisms and global security regimes. It may also choose from time to time to deal with other broadly-conceived security issues such as energy dependency, ecology, terrorism, drugs, immigration, human rights, religious and ethnic conflict.

Eventually, four leading institutes in the field of Asian security decided to become the founding members of the APSF: the INPR, the Pacific Forum CSIS (USA), the Institute for Strategic and Development Studies (ISDS) (Philippines), and the *Institut Français des Relations Internationales* (IFRI) (France).

On September 1, 1997, the plan became a reality. The three-day inaugural conference of the APSF opened in Taipei, organized around this theme: "The Impetus of Change in the Asia-Pacific Security Environment." Eighteen papers were delivered and discussed by over forty leading scholars and practitioners from Taiwan and eighteen other countries. Among the highlights of the conference were keynote speeches by former United States Secretary of Defense William J. Perry, Taiwanese Vice-President Lien Chan, and former South Korean Minister of Foreign Affairs Sung-Joo Han.

The present volume is the outgrowth of that event. Our distinguished authors have refined and updated their arguments, and we have edited and arranged them in a format that we hope will be useful to a broad audience of people living in, and interested in this region. In this way, the APSF will be able to expand its function of raising the level of dialogue on Asian security issues.

In the meantime, the APSF has continued to grow and develop. Its second event, a roundtable entitled "Security Implications of the Asian Financial Crisis," was held on December 19 and 20, 1998, and was hosted in Manila by the ISDS. This event underscored our determination to regularize the APSF's activities and make it a viable and important component of the regional "track two" security structure. The second international conference, "The Dynamics of Asia-Pacific Security: A *Fin-de-Siècle* Assessment," was held in December 1999, and preparations are underway for the second roundtable to be hosted by IFRI in Paris.

In conclusion, I wish to thank all those who have made the APSF, and therefore this book, possible. I would especially like to thank my colleagues in the founding member institutes, especially François Godement at IFRI, Carolina Hernandez at ISDS, and Jim Kelly and Ralph Cossa at Pacific Forum CSIS. Without their help, we never could have gotten the APSF off the ground. In addition, I would like to thank all my colleagues and staff at the INPR who have provided invaluable support and advice on the substance of the APSF and who have done a superb job organizing its events. Finally, let me express my thanks to the people at M.E. Sharpe, who have provided us with this opportunity to turn the results of this first APSF conference into a resource for future researchers.

Hung-mao Tien
President and Chairman of the Board
Institute for National Policy Research
Taipei, Taiwan
May 1999

THE SECURITY ENVIRONMENT IN THE ASIA-PACIFIC

1

Introduction

Tun-jen Cheng and Hung-mao Tien

The international security environment in the Asia-Pacific region has many intractable problems but few tested building blocks. While confrontational alliances are being transformed into some sort of collective security system in Europe (Snyder 1996), the shadow of the Cold War still lingers in the Asia-Pacific region. The North Korea nuclear crisis in 1994, the Mischief Reef incident in 1995, and the missile firings in the Taiwan Strait in 1996 remind us that the impulse for territorial conquest is potentially strong in this part of the world. No nation in the Asia-Pacific is immune from territorial disputes with its neighbors, and as Friedberg (1996) contends, for some powers, perceived benefits from military actions still outweigh costs. Culturally diverse, politically heterogeneous, and uneven in economic development, this region is neither endowed with benign conditions nor prepared for regional integration or collective efforts to maintain security.

Shifting Ground, Weak Foundations

Conceivably, democratic change can hold some promise for international security. As scholars from Immanuel Kant to Michael Doyle have pointed out, liberal democracies are prone to peace among themselves. These regimes protect human rights, respect the authority of an independent judiciary, and require a variety of public oversights over government decisions and policies, especially those related to taxation and conscription. The republican form of government, the democratic process, political representation, separation of powers, transparent policy-making, and accountability are thus prudential mechanisms against the irresponsible exercise of state power to betray the popular will. History indeed shows that democracies rarely go to war with one another.[1]

The prospects for building international security on the bedrock of democratization are becoming brighter in Europe (Van Evera 1990/91). New Eastern European democracies are queuing up for membership of an enlarged North Atlantic Treaty Organization (NATO), while Russia may become an associate of the organization, albeit with reluctance and indignation. By comparison, the hope for international security based on the emergence of a democracy-based community must wait in the Asia-Pacific region. Although the third wave of democracy has reached other regions (Southern Europe, Latin America, and Eastern and Central Europe, in that order) with desirable results, there were no democratic sweepstakes in the Asia-Pacific region, which still houses several authoritarian states, as well as all the remaining socialist states except Cuba. In this region, the "iron curtain" did not fall and the colors of authoritarian regimes are not fading away. Indeed, before the recent Asian financial crisis, the defenders of Asian values had even preached the virtues of political authoritarianism in promoting economic development.

Another foundation of regional security is economic prosperity. As Joseph Schumpeter argued, and the idealists in the interwar era had hoped, international trade helps to alleviate conflict and even prevent war; and the more trade, the better the chance for order and peace. Capitalist democracies pacify, for the main preoccupation of the people is with production, market exchange, and profit, rather than with conflict and war. The liberal trade regime in the postwar era initially was envisioned to dampen political and military conflicts (Penrose 1953). As economies become more interdependent, the opportunity costs of military conflict increase. Thus, throughout the postwar era, trade disputes have rarely spilled over into the political domains of Western international relations. After the Cold War ended, the enlargement of the European Union to encourage collective prosperity underpins the transformation of NATO from a defense alliance into a sort of collective security system.

In the Asia-Pacific region, ideological animosity is also receding, and economic development and competition have emerged as the overriding goal of nearly every nation in the area; even North Korea and Burma (Myanmar) show some signs of becoming "trading states." As in many parts of the world, economic integration in the Asia-Pacific has accelerated. Economic interaction is no longer limited to trade. Foreign direct investment is on the rise in the region, especially in the wake of the 1985 Plaza Accord, driving Japanese capital and subsequently the capital of newly industrializing countries to Southeast Asia and the People's Republic of China (PRC). Trade patterns tend to follow investment patterns, and the intraregional trade in the Asia-Pacific now exceeds trade with other regions.

If one expects economic interdependence and region-wide prosperity to be a problem-solving instrument for security issues, however, this hope has been dampened at least temporarily by a regionwide financial crisis, an issue that warrants another volume. More fundamentally, the pursuit of prosperity is premised on benign security environments. Instability arising from friction, such as skirmishes over a South China Sea islet, border clashes in Southeast Asia, or missile firings in the Taiwan Strait, can dim the economic prospects of the parties concerned and cast a shadow over the regional economy.

In addition, as Joan Gowa (1994) argues, trade and investment thrive most vividly only within the parameters of political alliance. In the absence of a functioning regional security framework, economic interdependence by itself does not ameliorate conflict or guarantee peace. Before World War I, Britain and Germany traded heavily. So did the United States and Japan on the eve of the Pacific War. As Copeland (1996) and Papayoanou (1996) argue, dense trade ties may imply a higher opportunity cost for conflicts. In addition, they also may imply the danger of overdependence on others, leading some or even all parties concerned to conclude that potential costs may outweigh actual gains from trade. The fear of "being entrapped" is even stronger in the case of foreign direct investment, which can easily be held hostage when conflict occurs. In brief, in the absence of a collective security arrangement, the economic cobweb alone is no guarantee for peace and stability.

The construction of multilateral security frameworks in the Asia-Pacific region has lagged behind the development of regional economic institutions. With economic takeoff, private sector-led regional economic cooperation began to shape up, and at the turn of the 1970s it became institutionalized in the form of the Pacific Basin Economic Council (PBEC). The PBEC then inspired the formation of a tripartite, quasi-official institution, called the Pacific Economic Cooperation Council, or PECC, in the 1980s. The PECC, in turn, laid down the foundation for an official forum, called Asia-Pacific Economic Cooperation, or APEC, a ministerial level forum that was launched at the turn of the 1990s and transformed into an economic summit in 1992. The evolution of economic institutions in the Asia-Pacific region in no way compares to the self-reinforcing process of European integration. Nonetheless, APEC has evolved gradually from a talking shop to a goal-oriented, and in some sense, rule-making body. Moreover, the institution-building for the economies in the Asia-Pacific region has at least been a cumulative process, initiated from below by the private sector, becoming semi-public and then formalized as an official forum. In addition, the Asia-Pacific region remains an open economic grouping rather than a closed fortress; hence, it serves as a building block rather than a stumbling block of the world trade regime (Hellman and Pyle 1997).

Multilateral security frameworks in the Asia-Pacific are, in comparison, slow to start, hard to come by, and noncumulative in terms of their impact on the regional order. In the Cold War era, conventional, dyadic security pacts between the United States and many nations in the region constituted the prevailing mode of defense arrangements. The NATO-like, multilateral organization did not come into being, nor was there any attempt at establishing a cooperative framework similar to the Council on Security Cooperation for Europe (CSCE). With the end of the Cold War, leaders of the region did commence dialogues on regional security issues in multilateral settings. In 1991, the Association of Southeast Asian Nations (ASEAN) sponsored an official Post-Ministerial Conference (PMC), which developed into the Asian Regional Forum (ARF) in 1993. As many sensitive issues were precluded from the ARF official agenda, a semi-official Council on Security Cooperation in the Asia-Pacific (CSCAP) was created as a second-track mechanism for dialogue. As this semi-official channel becomes ensnared by membership issues and begins to preclude sensitive issues from reaching the table, there have been calls for new avenues of interaction based on the association of regional think tanks ("third-track" interactions or another second-track interaction).

In this manner, the growth of security forums in the region has reversed the order by which its economic organizations developed. New fora had to be created as the existing ones revealed themselves as flawed or inflexible. Existing fora have not served as building blocks for new ones, but rather as organizations that the new ones were created to fix.

Rising Powers, Existing Powers, and Their Neighbors

In postwar Europe, major powers long have been subsumed under well-developed multilateral security frameworks, but in the Asia-Pacific region, the problems of integrating rising powers into the region continue to unfold. Although previous discussions about incorporating rising powers into the security system focused on Japan, the discourse now centers on the PRC, as most chapters in Part I explain. The debate is two-dimensional, discussing the capability of the rising power relative to existing powers, versus the ascending power's intentions and ambitions. Here the contrast between the PRC and Japan is sharp and vivid. Japan, an accomplished economic power, was often criticized for doing too little too late in assuming its political and security duties. That is, the wary was faulted for failing to share the burden with the weary (Osgood 1972). As its economic capabilities expand, the PRC's emerging political hegemony and its military prowess have already begun to alarm its neighbors and the existing powers.

China's economic growth record since the end of the 1980s has been remarkable indeed, but the size of its economy had been previously underestimated. There have been tremendous efforts to reassess China's gross national product (GNP) based on purchasing power parity (PPP) rather than nominal exchange rates, for a more accurate picture of its economic growth. In the early 1990s, many observers assumed that China's GNP would surpass Japan's in the first decade of the twenty-first century and that of the United States in the subsequent decade. With the 1995 publication of a World Bank report on the Chinese economy, however, many experts began to revise their predictions downward, whereas several scholars, notably, Japan's Professor Watanabe (1996), have recently questioned the importance of PPP. According to these experts, it may take more time for China to overproduce Japan and the United States than was previously forecast. Interestingly, while the calculation of China's economic capability has become more realistic and modest, China's "conceptual boundaries" have expanded. With the reversion of Hong Kong to Chinese sovereignty, the former British colony has been added to the equation of power. If Taiwan were also subsumed under the rubric of China, then the aggregate GNP (based on PPP) of the so-called Greater China and its defense implications would become almost incomprehensible, as Byron Weng shows in chapter 7.

Whichever measurement one chooses, the sheer size and sustained high growth rates of China's economy lead to the conclusion that China will achieve great power status in due course. This naturally leads any China watcher to ask: How will China use its newly acquired capabilities? Based on historical observations, some scholars depict China as a misunderstood bona fide player rather than a source of threat (Byron Weng, chapter 7; Richard Grant, chapter 17). In modern times, China has not been an imperialist power in the European and prewar Japanese sense, but instead has been a victim. Essentially a reactive, nonprovocative and nonthreatening power, China probably only wants to be a normal and respected nation.

Richard Grant quotes a Ming dynasty founder as evidence that all China wants is to be left alone and to coexist peacefully with others, in contrast with Japan, which invaded others in the prewar era. Underlying this view is a Western legal presumption that China should receive the benefit of the doubt during its ascent to great power status and that it should not be stigmatized a priori as a troublemaker, or as a new source of threat. Indeed, many have observed that at this point, China's primary goal is economic development and that it lacks the military capability to be really aggressive in the foreseeable future. Moreover, China has also begun to show its willingness to take part in regional collective efforts—for example, subscribing to a multinational joint venture for an oil pipeline and supporting the rescue package for Thai currency. In addition, a year after Hong Kong's reversion to China's sovereignty, one seems to find the PRC honoring its promise to allow the Hong Kong Special Administrative Region to function as a quasi-state possessing positive sovereignty (Byron Weng, chapter 7). In brief, one should accept the emergence of China as a great power without qualms.

Other scholars are more cautionary about the impact of a rising PRC on regional security (Harvey Feldman, chapter 2; Carolina Hernandez, chapter 8). To them, history serves as a lesser guide than does contemporary behavior, when it comes to assessing the intentions and motivations of an emerging great power. In the contemporary era, China supported Communist insurgency in Southeast Asia and clashed with India, Russia and Vietnam, the last two cases not merely for territorial reasons. And its recent arms buildup is more than a catch-up game. All these should place China on probation for the time being. The new power that shows signs of irredentism must satisfy the burden of proof before it can claim to be a bona fide player. As Akio Watanabe argues in chapter 5, the ball is in the PRC's court, and it is natural for others to monitor her deeds carefully and continuously. It is risky to use simply one test case, such as Hong Kong, to assess China's commitment to international norms and rules, as a nation's reputation is cumulative and nondivisible.

Indeed, one needs to look at the emergence of a great power from the perspective of those countries that are likely to be affected most directly. Small powers in China's vicinity simply cannot afford to give it the benefit of the doubt, as a misjudgment in the security environment can have fatal consequences. Traditionally, many Chinese dynasties, such as the Qin, Han, Tang and Qing, were imperialistic and threatening toward their neighbors, such as Vietnam and Korea. In the eyes of Southeast Asians, the PRC's behavior in the South China Sea and on Sino-Vietnam borders is symptomatic of hegemonism. Carolina Hernandez (chapter 8) illustrates how ASEAN crafts various security-enhancing mechanisms to cope with the rise of the PRC. Members of ASEAN do not speak with one voice, and some members may be more willing to pin China down on international norms than are others. But as Douglas Paal (chapter 6) argues, every member of the organization realizes the imperative of "going along" with other members rather than "going alone" in dealing with China.

For great powers, taking precautions against a hegemonic PRC is also understandable. As Akio Watanabe (chapter 5) notes, the rise of China certainly has "externalities," just as the rise of any great power would. Its abrasive behavior can, intentionally or not, trigger regional conflicts, while its conciliatory behavior can contribute to regional stability. Cooperation among great powers, new and old, is a requisite to the making of a stable and peaceful regional order. Until China proves to be a constructive actor, the "externalities" it creates will remain "a source of anxiety rather than reassurance."

Containment and engagement are two different ways of coping with the anxiety entailed by China's rise to power. Most observers, however, have looked beyond that dichotomy (Harvey Feldman, chapter 2; Ralph Cossa, chapter 3; Douglas Paal, chapter 6; Jean-Marie Guehenno 1998). Although there is a need to accommodate China's interests and to socialize it into the international community, there is also a need to deter China if other efforts fail (Paal, chapter 6). One should engage, but should not appease (Guehenno 1998). It seems that engagement and deterrence will have to coexist. To the prevailing powers, bringing China into the international community to become a norm-abiding player is a matter of course.

This strategy already dictates the terms of China's entry into the international power game, while carrying a hidden agenda—namely effectuating incremental democratic change inside China and consequently undermining the incumbent elite's power monopoly. In the eyes of the existing powers, China needs to buy time to realize its own potentiality and to become a full-fledged power. Thus, China's commitment to legal and procedural arrangements is mainly tactical, expedient and not credible, and deterrence as a safety device should not be discarded yet.

It is in the balancing act of engagement and deterrence that the United States and Japan, the two regional powers, fine-tune their security postures. American security interests and security policies relating to the Asia-Pacific region are not always coherent or clearly articulated, though admittedly, policy-making structures for these issues are more centralized than for domestic policy issues. But the ambiguity is gradually giving way to clarification, thanks to the rise of China (Cossa, chapter 3). Similarly, the operational guidelines for the U.S.–Japan Security Treaty of 1951, which Koji Murata (chapter 4) argues have been long overdue and should have been set forth when the treaty was inked in the 1950s, were hammered out in 1997. Previously afraid of being dragged into regional conflicts, Japan is now obsessed with the idea that the United States may abandon Asia. The codification of the operational rules, though couched in deliberately vague language regarding the targeted states, helps reduce the uncertainty and miscalculation that may surround U.S. commitments to maintain regional security (for a theoretical discussion on clarification versus ambiguity, see Kegley and Raymond 1990).

Beyond Bilateralism

Like the U.S.–Japan security pact, other dyadic alliances were also updated or even newly forged, indicating the centrality of bilateralism in maintaining security in the Asia-Pacific region. Refining and reinforcing bilateral security ties flies in the face of multilateral frameworks. Desmond Ball (chapter

9) and Paul Evans (chapter 10) thus assume the task of judging the performance of the two most significant, newly emerged security forums in the
region, namely the ARF and CSCAP. Ball evaluates their progress and
achievement in terms of the goals, purposes and agendas that the leaders
inaugurating the institutions have set forth for themselves. In addition to this
criterion, Ball also suggests a comparison of the security architecture (institutional arrangements) the region has or may acquire with the security concerns (or problems) the region must face. The balance sheet—or rather the
imbalances between the architecture and the problems—leads him to express pessimism.

According to the ARF and CSCAP, adopting confidence-building mechanisms (CBMs) is the first step toward preventive diplomacy, which in turn
should lay the foundation for conflict resolution. But the reality check is
disappointing: The first step remains to be taken seriously. Various concepts
and devices for CBMs are now familiar to all parties concerned, and include
transparency (such as defense white papers), maritime cooperation (codes of
conduct and engagement rules), mutual visits, joint exercises and observation of exercises. These CBMs have been implemented on an ad hoc basis
rather than regularized; thus, the scope of the CBMs is only beginning to
expand, barely able to catch up with the development of such problems as the
arms race. The praxis of CBMs, in short, is utterly inadequate to cope with the
mounting challenges.

Paul Evans is more optimistic, however. While cautioning us not to in-
dulge in a leap of faith in the stability and peace in the region based on
institutionalized dialogues, he asserts that ARF and CSCAP "are not preordained to failure." Regional institutional leaders are blending, if not fusing;
consultation is in order, though dispute resolution has yet to surface. In addition, an epistemological community on regional security seems to be emerging, and the learning process is discernible. Evans is particularly impressed
by the evolution of CSCAP, a forum in which academicians play a crucial
role in promoting ideas, enhancing mutual learning, and, indeed, educating
officials from their own countries. This sanguine view of CSCAP is embedded in the constructionist school of international relations thought, which
argues that norms can be internalized, rules abided by, behavior altered, eventually alleviating and even solving problems and conflicts. Of course, we
should not be carried away by academic excitement. Evidently, the high frequency of meetings and demonstrated willingness to confer under the auspices of ARF and CSCAP are good points of departure for harmonizing
policies to foster a regional security system. Talking is not a powerful indi-
cator of learning. In the end it is the deeds, not the words, that count. As a
Chinese authority itself says, "Heeding one's words is fine, but action is

what counts." Both ARF and CSCAP have a long way to go in inducing cooperation among member countries.

Would APEC, as a successful scheme for regional economic cooperation, generate positive spillover effects for regional security? Dewi Fortuna Anwar (chapter 11) argues that it depends on whether one subscribes to realism or functionalism. Taking the realist view, Robert Gilpin (1997, 34) observes that "[the] three dominant APEC powers (the United States, Japan, and China) are too divided among themselves politically to provide the necessary leadership to make APEC a powerful force in Asian-Pacific affairs." Without strong leadership, APEC cannot assume tasks that it was not set up to handle. Indeed, Drysdale and Elek (1997, 65–66) submit that "consultative and confidence-building processes on economic and security issues will evolve more effectively on parallel tracks." But if we follow functionalist logic and use European experience as a guide, then trade and economic ties might mitigate political tensions. This may explain why President Clinton, at the first APEC summit meeting in 1993, suggested that the function of this regional economic forum be expanded to cover security affairs as well. It is noteworthy that this proposal was spurned not so much because of the aversion of APEC members to allow linkage between economy and security, as because of the distaste of some Asian members for U.S. roles in Asian security.

But if APEC is not expanding to cover security issues, another subregional organization is branching out into economic issues. ASEAN has been transforming itself from a vintage 1970s anticommunist device into a multifunctional 1990s organization. Aside from becoming the most coherent subset of APEC and an interlocutor for ARF, ASEAN has embarked on trade and investment liberalization among its members. Owing to the so-called ASEAN way of decision making (characterized by informality, vagueness and tacit coordination as against formal commitment), however, economic cooperative schemes are easier to frame but difficult to execute. Undertaking collective defense efforts in the post–Cold War setting is an even more daunting task. As Bantarto Bandoro (chapter 12) argues, ASEAN is in theory a "security-oriented regional grouping," but military action is not a rational option. Governed by the necessity for maintaining harmony among members, ASEAN is essentially a forum for dialogue, trust enhancement, and information sharing, rather than a policy-coordinating multilateral organization for common defense, and will remain so even as its membership continues to grow.

The birth of the Asia–Europe Meeting (ASEM) in 1996, a biannual summit for Asian and European leaders, adds a new dimension to the Asia-Pacific security system. This forum enables Asia and Europe to pursue their mutual interests without any American presence. As Gerald Segal (1997,

127) puts it, "one of the most important rationales for ASEM is to maximize European and Asian relations with the United States, and to keep the Americans honestly committed to multilateralism." The primary motivation for the formation of ASEM is economic: Europe eyes the Asian market while Asia covets European investment capital. Thus, ASEM is a perfect cooperative setting for corporate leaders to cope with *la defi Americain* and for government officials to curtail American unilateralism, such as the passage of the Helms-Burton Act, the invocation of the Trade Act of the United States, article 30.1 and other applications of the extraterritorial principle in international trade.

Of interest to us here is whether ASEM can serve as a venue for dialogue or even policy coordination on security and political issues. Francois Godement (chapter 13) suggests that as ASEM was just recently launched, nothing is predetermined. Unlike APEC, ASEM's name bears no adjective that would prevent it from addressing security and political issues that may concern Europe and/or Asia, including foreign aid, the United Nations Security Council reform, human rights, and peacekeeping. The problem with determining ASEM's role in security has less to do with finding parallel or conflicting interests between Asia and Europe than with the decision-making mechanisms that ASEM may adopt. The emerging pattern of interaction within ASEM is "for Asians and Europeans to caucus as separate groups and then try to find a common approach among two groups." Such a mechanism is, in Gerald Segal's (1997) words, the best way to proceed but a sure way to accomplish nothing. So although ASEM's first two meetings have yielded vehement discussions on all sorts of ideas for cooperation, and some reassurances were made to keep markets open even in the midst of the financial crisis, no binding decisions have been yet undertaken. Thus, ASEM appears to be another socializing forum for building confidence rather than a multilateral rule-making and conflict-resolution institution.

Flash Points and CBMs

Building confidence between potentially conflicting parties is essential to stability and order in any region, especially in the Asia-Pacific, which has more flash points than any other part of the world. Confidence-building mechanisms (CBMs) help to correct misunderstanding and misperception, and thereby minimize miscalculation, accidents and preemptive strikes. Moreover, CBMs might also induce cooperation, as regular meetings, the requirement of transparency, and the pressure generated by multilateral surveillance help to "lock in" commitment and dissuade defection.

Although CBMs are badly needed they are in short supply in the Asia-

Pacific region, as illustrated by several recent conflicts in the three most contested flash points of the region—namely the Korean peninsula, the Taiwan Strait, and the South China Sea. As Choi and Kim (chapter 14) explain, the four-party talks regarding the Korean peninsula have been slow to start and progress has been difficult. The Korean peninsula is perennially volatile. The rules on cease-fire are nebulous and ineffectual. Codes of conduct for official exchanges and citizen visits between the two Koreas barely exist. And international agreement on the Korean Energy Development Organization (KEDO)—a pact used to stifle the birth of the nuclear weapons project in North Korea—was reached only after numerous bouts of intimidation and threats. The deficit of trust between the two Koreas is so severe that international actors (the United States, China, and even Japan) have become "surrogates" for any CBM-related activities. Choi and Kim weigh the PRC factor heavily in the resolution of conflicts, given its rising political influence in the region in general and its role as the main supplier of oil to North Korea after the collapse of the Soviet Union in particular. The effectiveness of China's leverage over North Korea has been disputed (Cotton 1997). Moreover, as Oberdorfer (1997, 320–21) hints, China's willingness to cajole or discipline North Korea is linked to U.S. trade concessions to China. Nonetheless, China seems to be forthcoming in stabilizing the situation on the Korean peninsula, if only to prevent the possible influx of refugees from across the Yalu River.

China has not been supportive of CBMs, however, because of the other two tension points in the region. In managing potential conflict in the South China Sea, a multilateral workshop has been established and numerous sessions held (chapter 16). But this did not prevent the PRC, a participant in those meetings, from undertaking unilateral actions against Vietnam and the Philippines. Naval clashes have subsided and some basic rules of maritime engagement are being observed, as various conflicting parties assess the proposal to "shelve the problem of sovereignty, and explore the sea bed collectively," an idea proffered by smaller powers in the game. But the development of China's blue water capability, aggressive oil exploration by some claimants, and ASEAN's collective action all could easily upset this fragile, de facto truce.

Similarly, in the Taiwan Strait, CBMs were proposed but not adopted. China resorted to a strategy of coercion, triggering the 1996 crisis—the third one since 1949. There is some controversy about the origin of this crisis. Some attribute it to the "provocative" nature of President Lee Teng-hui's visit to Cornell University, his alma mater, where he admonished Taiwan not to provoke Beijing again (chapter 6). This flawed view implicitly defines provocation in terms of outcomes, which only can be known *ex post*, rather than some objective criteria, such as rules that both sides of the dispute should follow and that are known *ex ante*. Others believe the crisis is rooted in the military adventurism of the radical leadership wing in Beijing, and that it represents the cost of its coercive strategy toward Taiwan (chapter 15). The coercive strategy backfired, as live-ammunition maneuvers by the People's Liberation Army (PLA) alarmed all other nations in the region and elicited a firm response from the United States. A report recently released by the U.S. Department of Defense shows that PLA leaders tend to overestimate U.S. hostility, U.S. economic decline and the PRC's economic growth, and to underestimate U.S. military strength, to overlook the anxiety of China's neighbors, and to exude confidence that war is a feasible instrument for conflict resolution (*Nikkei Shimbun*, February 25, 1998).

China has responded positively to CBM initiatives by the United States in the wake of the Taiwan Strait crisis. However, these are rudimentary CBMs, involving personnel exchanges and official visits between Beijing and Washington, rather than advanced ones such as prior notice, observation, or even joint sponsorship of military exercises. As Richard Grant (chapter 17) points out, there is an asymmetry between China's willingness to engage in CBMs with Central Asian republics and Russia, and its hesitancy to embrace CBMs on the maritime front, especially those anchored in multilateral frameworks. It may well be that China perceives most CBM proposals on its maritime front as devices of containment and a violation of its sovereignty (chapter 17). As Cheng-yi Lin (chapter 18) observes, CBMs in Beijing's view can be negotiated only between states and thus cannot be negotiated across the Taiwan Strait, unless they are defined so broadly as to include both military and political aspects of interaction between both sides.

These observations spell out the chicken-and-egg problem in engaging China in CBMs. Reciprocity being one of the paramount and defining principles of CBMs, they are designed to constrain all parties concerned and thereby incrementally nurture trust and confidence among all. But if CBMs are politically construed as a Trojan horse targeted at a particular participant, then CBMs themselves will be regarded with suspicion and rejected, and the total stock of faith may be consumed rather than restored. In this case, trust-cultivating mechanisms themselves become a problem rather than a solution. In addition, it is precisely because sovereignty disputes are so intractable and inflammable that one hopes CBMs can arrest the thrust toward the eruption of conflicts. Declaring a CBM as a sovereignty-violating ploy will not only discredit the CBM but also harden the sovereignty dispute.

Wariness and even aversion to CBMs are probably a general phenomenon in Asia, where the concept of security was historically understood more in absolute terms than in relative terms, and international relations took the form of domination and subordination rather than a balance-of-power game among equals. The recent history of colonization has made nations in this region extremely sensitive to any international legal and procedural obligations. Thus, CBMs tend to be interpreted through a Machiavellian perspective, or in the logic of deception spelled out by Sun Tsu in *The Art of War*. It took centuries for European nations to learn that security is a collective good, a process facilitated by the U.S. sponsorship of a multilateral security framework. The learning process for the Asia-Pacific region has just begun.

Conclusion

The security environment in the Asia-Pacific region remains precarious and as fragile as ever. In this region, as nondemocratic regimes still outnumber the democratic ones, the Kantian "Pacific Community" among liberal states has yet to emerge. Intraregional trade and capital flow have increased drastically, but, to paraphrase Richard Rosecrance (1996), the territorial state never really gives way to the trading state (which values prosperity more than armed conflict), not to mention the virtual state (under which state sovereignty may be more apparent than real). Multilateral security forums have emerged, but preexisting bilateral defense alliances continue to form the principal pillars of national security for most nations in this region. As if this were not enough, the recent, regionwide financial crisis has added another element of uncertainty to security systems—a matter to be taken up later. The Asia-Pacific region rivals the Middle East and South Asia as the most insecure region on earth today.

Note

1. The Fashoda crisis was a notable exception, but even here the crisis did not escalate into a war. This case, nonetheless, calls our attention to public opinion and state structure, variations among democracies, and so on. (See Peterson 1995.)

Bibliography

Copeland, Dale C. "Economic Interdependence and War: A Theory of Trade Expectation." *International Security* 20, no. 4 (Spring 1996).
Cotton, James. "Mixed Signals on Korean Security." *Contemporary Southeast Asia* 18, no. 4 (1997): 400–16.
Drysdale, Peter, and Andrew Elek. "APEC: Community-Building in East Asia and the Pacific." In Donald C. Hellman and Kenneth B. Pyle, eds., *From APEC to Xanadu: Creating a Viable Community in the Post-Cold War Pacific*. Armonk, NY: M.E. Sharpe, 1997.
Friedberg, Aaron L. "Ripe for Rivalry: Prospects for Peace in a Multipolar Asia." In Michael E. Brown, Sean M. Lynn-Jones, and Steven E. Miller, eds., *East Asian Security*. Cambridge, MA: MIT Press, 1996.

Gilpin, Robert. "APEC in a New International Order." In Donald C. Hellman and Kenneth B. Pyle, eds., *From APEC to Xanadu*. Armonk, NY: M.E. Sharpe, 1997.

Gowa, Joan. *Allies, Adversaries and International Trade*. Princeton, NJ: Princeton University Press, 1994.

Guehenno, Jean-Marie. "The International System After the Cold War." Paper presented at the Warsaw Conference on International Relations and Democracy, June 26–28, 1998.

Hellman, Donald C., and Kenneth B. Pyle, eds. *From APEC to Xanadu: Creating a Viable Community in the Post-Cold War Pacific*. Armonk, NY: M.E. Sharpe, 1997.

Kegley, Charles W. Jr., and Gregory A. Raymond. *When Trust Breaks Down: Alliance Norms and World Politics*. Columbia: University of South Carolina Press, 1990.

Oberdorfer, Don. *The Two Koreas*. Reading, MA: Addison Wesley, 1997.

Osgood, Robert. *The Weary and the Wary*. Baltimore: Johns Hopkins University Press, 1997.

Papayoanou, Paul A. "Interdependence, Institutions and the Balance of Power: Britain, Germany and World War I." *International Security* 20, no. 4 (Spring 1996).

Penrose, E. *Economic Planning for the Peace*. Princeton, NJ: Princeton University Press, 1953.

Peterson, Susan. "How Democracies Differ: Public Opinion, State Structure, and the Lessons of the Fashoda Crisis." *Security Studies* 5, no. 1 (Autumn 1995): 3–37.

Rosecrance, Richard. "The Rise of Virtual State." *Foreign Affairs* (July–August 1996).

Segal, Gerald. "Thinking Strategically About ASEM: The Subsidiary Question." *The Pacific Review* 10, no. 1 (1997):124–34.

Synder, Craig. "Emerging Regional Security Cooperation in Europe and the Asia-Pacific." *The Pacific Review* 9, no. 4 (1996): 553–76.

Van Evera, Stephen. "Primed for Peace: Europe After the Cold War." *International Security* 15, no. 3 (1990/91): 1–57.

Watanabe, Toshio. "Kyomo no chukoku keizai daikoku lun." *Chuo koron* (November 1996): 38–51.

Part I

Great Powers and Their Neighbors

2

The United States-PRC Relationship

Engagement Versus Containment, or Engagement with Containment

Harvey J. Feldman

"Engagement Versus Containment": The Making of a False Dichotomy

The title of this chapter hints broadly at its conclusion, which is that U.S. policy toward the People's Republic of China (PRC) cannot be contained in one or the other of these pigeonholes. The proposition "engagement vs. containment" represents a rather shallow dichotomy, essentially an artifact of our television age in which issues are presented to an underinformed public in easily swallowed capsules of two- or three-minute durations. One result is indigestion, in the form of bad policy; another is a coarsening of discourse even among foreign policy analysts and operators.

That "discourse," which probably does not merit so dignified a name, is characterized on both sides of the engagement/containment spectrum by slogan-mongering, even among those who should know better, and has only a tenuous connection with reality. Instead, it is replete with what is little more than pro-PRC apologia from those whose business or academic pursuits depend upon favorable treatment at the hands of the Beijing leadership; or rhetorical excess from those whose political careers can benefit from painting the PRC as the new evil empire.

As examples, we have on the one hand Henry Kissinger telling the American people one day after the event that they should forget about the massacres at Tiananmen Square, because the PRC relationship is too important strategically to become emotional about student bloodshed on the streets of Beijing, and besides Deng Xiaoping is "a man who chose a more humane and less chaotic course" for China (Kissinger 1989). On the other hand we have the Minority Leader in the House of Representatives, Richard Gephardt, exclaiming during the 1997 congressional debate on the extension of most-favored-nation treatment that America's adverse trade balance with the PRC results from the toil of "two million slave laborers in China" (*Washington Post* 1997).

There is also a false analogy problem, with the "Wilhelmine" being the most fashionable at the moment—a comparison to Germany under Kaiser Wilhelm II at the beginning of the twentieth century. It argues that World War I resulted from Germany's arrival on the scene as a "great power," and its exclusion from that club by the other "great powers" of the time: France, Britain, and Russia. This exclusion made Germany nasty and aggressive, whereas kinder treatment could have resulted in a cooperative, if not necessarily benign *Reich*. The lesson, say Dr. Kissinger and others, is to treat China with the deference due a great power on the rise, and so avoid the mistakes that led to World War I.

Of course there are other equally poor analogies as well. Japan, after its victory over Russia in 1905, entered into an alliance with Great Britain, which certainly provided a key to the "great power club." But this hardly prevented Japanese aggression in Manchuria in 1931, and throughout China later in that decade.

Then there is the most exquisite bad analogy of all. This is the one that insists that just as capitalism "inevitably" triumphed over and led to the demise of Soviet Communism, "the best way to encourage reform and democratization is to strengthen China's trade and investment with the rest of the world" (Tyson 1997). Not since the nineteenth century has international trade been so applauded as the single best cure for all of mankind's ills, from tyranny to international disputes to open warfare. Along the way, proponents of this happy view ignore the many complex and unique factors that came together to produce the Soviet collapse: the war in Afghanistan; the pressure of the Reagan arms buildup; the sudden death of Yuri Andropov; the rather odd behavior of Mikhail Gorbachev; and finally the coup against Gorbachev that led to the triumph of Boris Yeltsin.

In fact, as Robert Kagan pointed out in *The New Republic*, it is peace and stability, protected by American power, that made possible the enormous explosion of trade and development seen over the past five decades, and not the other way around. It is important to distinguish between cause and effect. The technological innovations of recent years are no more a guarantee of peace than was the invention of the telegraph cable or the steamship a hundred years ago. "Now, as ever," Kagan points out, "the wealth and power produced by trade and economic development can be used for bad ends as well as good." And the PRC provides a perfect example of this (Kagan 1997).

Indeed, whether sloganeering or using absurd analogies, these varying types of reductionism are problematic because they create a kind of verbal or written static that obscures more reasoned argument. In such an environment, those who criticize almost any aspect of China's behavior are accused of "demonizing China" and told to sit back and await the historical inevitability of a flourishing democracy built upon trade with the world outside. Meanwhile, from the opposite corner, any attempt to look at how matters are viewed in Beijing is denounced as special pleading. Therefore, we ought to take a closer look at reality and try to reach more thoughtful conclusions about where the PRC is headed and what might be an appropriate China policy for the United States.

Looking at Reality: Is There a PRC Threat?

In their book, *The Coming Conflict with China*, which has done so much to frame the current debate, Richard Bernstein and Ross H. Munro state at the outset:

> The People's Republic of China, the world's most populous country, and the United States, its most powerful, have become global rivals, countries whose relations are tense, whose interests are in conflict, and who face tougher, more dangerous times ahead. (Bernstein and Munro 1997, 3)

And again a few pages later:

> China is an unsatisfied and ambitious power whose goal is to dominate Asia, not by invading and occupying neighboring nations, but by being so much more powerful than they are that nothing will be allowed to happen in East Asia without China's at least tacit consent. (Bernstein and Munro 1997, 4)

Conversely, in their book, *The Great Wall and the Empty Fortress*, Andrew J. Nathan and Robert S. Ross argue:

> But China's strength on mainland Asia does not constitute a threat to re-

gional stability. On the contrary, the current balance of power is widely accepted as an appropriate foundation for building a stable post-Cold War regional order. In order for China to become a threat to the regional balance of power, it would have to develop the military strength to contend with the other great powers and the power projection capabilities to influence developments across the open seas. In the ability to project power, China remains by far the weakest of the four great powers in Asia. (Nathan and Ross 1997, 229)

Some analysis is needed to decide which statement—or either, or both—is true.

PRC Behavior

That Chinese behavior either threatens or adversely affects American interests in a number of areas can hardly be denied. Here are a few quotes from recent reports dealing with that most important of strategic concerns, exports of weapons of mass destruction, or the techniques for building them, and the arming of present or potential enemies of the United States:

Reporting to Congress on February 22, 1996, then Director of Central Intelligence John Deutch said China continues to export "inappropriate nuclear technology to Pakistan, M-11 missiles to Pakistan and cruise missiles to Iran." (*Washington Times* 1996)

U.S. intelligence officials have concluded that companies in China are providing Iran with several virtually complete factories suited for making deadly poison gases, an act that may violate a U.S. law as well as China's pledge to abide by a global treaty banning such assistance, according to U.S. officials. (*Washington Post* 1996)

The U.S. attorney's office in San Francisco announced on May 23 that federal agents had seized 2,000 Chinese-made AK-47 assault rifles and arrested seven California residents in connection with an arms-smuggling racket allegedly run by China's two flagship armament companies. It was the biggest haul of automatic weapons in U.S. history. (*Far Eastern Economic Review* 1996)

A Federal criminal inquiry has uncovered new evidence, including American satellite photos, suggesting that a state-owned Chinese company had all along intended to divert American machine equipment to a military plant that builds missiles and fighter aircraft, intelligence officials say. (*New York Times* 1997)

Three Chinese missile engineers were caught by the Ukrainian Security Service (SBU) trying to smuggle out ICBM engine plans sold to them at the Yuzhnoe missile plant in Dneprpetrovsk. The missile in question was later revealed by the *Washington Times* to be the 10-warhead SS-18, with a range of 6,000 to 8,000 miles. (Fisher 1997c)

The Senate yesterday passed a resolution calling upon the Clinton administration to impose sanctions on China for selling advanced cruise missiles to Iran. . . . Passage of the resolution followed disclosure by Defense Secretary William S. Cohen that Iran has tested a new air-launched version of the Chinese anti-ship missile known as the C802K. The U.S. military's top admiral in the Middle East disclosed last year that Chinese C-802 cruise missiles were deployed for the first time by Iran aboard several fast patrol boats. (*Washington Times* 1997a)

China is upgrading its medium range missile forces with newer mobile systems designed to hit targets in Russia, India, Taiwan, Japan and other parts of East Asia, according to a classified Pentagon report. Details about China's intermediate-range ballistic missile (IRBM) nuclear forces, including numbers of launchers and deployment areas, have never been made public before. Currently China has about 40 CSS-2 refire capable launchers at six field garrisons and launch complexes, according to the report by the National Air Intelligence Center. (*Washington Times* 1997b)

Even if there were no serious difficulties with Beijing over human rights violations, trade issues, the protection of intellectual property, the use of force in the South China Sea, and threats to Taiwan, PRC behavior with respect to weapons and weapons technology sales would raise disturbing questions about the overall thrust of Beijing's policies and its intentions. Taken together with the rest of the list, China's actions do raise substantial questions about the leadership's view of its world role.

Still, China is not the only country that sells arms to rogue states in the Middle East and elsewhere, and of course it is hardly the only country to pursue essentially mercantilist trade policies, or to be less than rigorous in living up to its commitments to protect intellectual property. So, in deciding whether the PRC pursues policies that indicate it sees itself as an enemy of the United States, actual or potential, we need to look a bit further. More specifically, we need to examine the PRC military posture to determine whether it appears to be arming itself for a future confrontation with the United States.

PRC Military Arms, Acquisitions, and Trends

In sheer order-of-battle numbers, the People's Liberation Army appears quite formidable: an army of 2.2 million, which possesses 8,000 main battle tanks;

strategic missile forces including 17 ICBMs, 70 land-launched and 12 submarine launched IRBMs; 63 submarines, some of which are armed with Russian wake-homing torpedoes; 54 principal surface combatants (mostly destroyers and frigates); an air force fighter inventory of 4,000 planes, including about 50 advanced SU-27s.[1]

At the moment the PLA is far less impressive than these numbers would suggest. Its navy, despite the submarines, lacks a true blue-water capability, and most surface combatants lack air defenses. Its air armada is, for the most part, made up of very short range aircraft, most of them copied from Soviet designs of the 1950s and 1960s. The number of pilot training hours is, by all accounts, well short of what NATO would consider necessary. The U.S. Defense Department says "China's long-term goal is to acquire one or more aircraft carriers and it has an active program to develop a design." But that same report goes on to say that "it remains unclear whether Beijing has reached a firm decision on the kind of carrier it will have, given budget constraints and naval funding priorities" (United States Department of Defense 1997, 9).[2] Finally, we should note the many deficiencies of the Chinese army, especially in the realm of communications and intelligence—the famous "C-Four-I" (command, control, computers, communications, and intelligence).

In today's world, few military establishments remain static, and that certainly is true of the PLA. As the U.S. Defense Department notes in the report referred to above, "as an emerging great power, China will probably build its military power to the point where it can engage and defeat any potential enemy within the region with its conventional forces and can deter any global strategic threat to China's national security" (United States Department of Defense 1997, 1). As we will see below, as far as the PRC military are concerned, the United States is seen as the primary "potential enemy." Moreover, the PRC is already more powerful than any of its land neighbors, including Russia—if the Chechen war is any example—and surely would prevail in an all-out attack against an unassisted Taiwan. We therefore should look closely at the dimensions of the PRC's ongoing arms buildup for clues as to where it is headed.

1. Former Defense Secretary William Perry took note of Chinese attempts to acquire SS-18 MIRV technologies for its intercontinental and intermediate range ballistic missiles in May 1996 congressional testimony. The SS-18 missiles China sought from Ukraine have this capability (Fisher 1996a, 24). There can only be one reason for acquiring this 6,800-mile missile with its multiple independently targeted warheads—possible use against the U.S. (Gertz 1996)
2. There is evidence that China's Han class submarines are being modified to carry the C-802 anti-ship missile. (Fisher 1996a, 25ff.)

3. China is experimenting with battlefield laser weapons and particle beam weapons for disabling satellites. (Fisher 1996a, 29) Only the U.S. now uses satellites for battlefield intelligence.

4. At the Zhuhai Air Show in November 1996, the Heritage Foundation's senior PRC military analyst, Richard D. Fisher, Jr., was told by an engineer from the Beijing Research Institute for Telemetry that Global Positioning Satellite Technology is being used to increase substantially the accuracy of the DF-15 and DF-21 intermediate range ballistic missiles (Fisher 1996b). Potential targets would be Japan, including U.S. bases there, Taiwan, and Southeast Asia.

5. According to the U.S. Defense Department, "China is developing land-attack cruise missiles (LACMS) for theater warfighting and strategic [emphasis added] attack." (United States Department of Defense 1997, 4)

6. China has embarked upon a major program to upgrade its C-Four-I capabilities, concentrating on development of what the Pentagon refers to as an "integrated battlefield area communications system" based upon digital networks and "application specific integrated circuit design." It is automating its Air Defense Command and Control System and attempting to acquire AWACS type aircraft from Russia and Ukraine. (United States Department of Defense 1997, 5ff.)

7. According to the *Financial Times,* the PLA will host an electronics warfare trade fair intended to attract international suppliers of these kinds of equipment in May 1998. According to Vice Chairman of the Central Military Commission Liu Huaqing, this will lead to "strengthening international military-related electronic technology exchanges and upgrading China's military electronic equipment." (Harding 1997)

8. In addition to the 46 Su-27s purchased from Russia and now being integrated into the PLAAF, in 1996 China entered into an agreement to co-produce up to 200 Su-27s at a cost of $2.2 billion. The Su-27 is about the equivalent of the American F-15 air superiority fighter. Together with the Su-27s, China apparently also secured the Russian AA-11 Archer air-to-air missile, which is cued by a helmet-mounted sight. By simply turning his head, the pilot confers a 90-degree field of view for the 12.6 mile, infrared homing missile (Fisher 1997a). At the moment, no other air force in East Asia, including the American force, fields such sighting equipment.

9. In January 1997, China purchased two Sovremenny-class destroyers from Russia (*Jane's Defence Weekly* 1997; Gertz 1997). These are 7,600-ton vessels, almost twice the size of China's Luhu-class destroyers, and were designed to attack America's Aegis-class missile cruis-

ers. As fitted out for the Russian fleet, these destroyers carry an ASW helicopter, 130-mm guns, and anti-aircraft missiles; but their main armament is the SS-N-22 "Sunburn" anti-ship missile, which travels at twice the speed of sound, skims as low as 23 feet above the water's surface, and has a range of 150 miles. (Fisher 1997b)

The list could be extended, but I think the point is clear.

All these things take quite a lot of money, and it is obvious that Chinese military spending has increased very substantially during the present decade. Officially, the Chinese military budget amounts to about $9 billion, but as a 1995 General Accounting Office (GAO) study pointed out, "China's official defense budget does not include in its total defense profits from weapons and services sales, or PLA commercial activities, nor does it include costs of major weapons acquisitions funded from other budget accounts" (Bernstein and Munro 1997, 70, citing the GAO report). The budget also does not include weapons research, pensions, nuclear weapons development, or the cost of the People's Armed Police, which functions as a ready reserve for the PLA. The International Institute of Strategic Studies estimates the actual budget at five times the official figure, which would make it roughly equivalent to the Japanese defense budget. Using a purchasing power parity correction based on what similar items cost the Pentagon, the figure for comparison purposes would be about $85 billion. This may seem small in comparison with a United States defense budget of $265 billion, but the United States has worldwide responsibilities, including 150,000 troops in Europe as part of the NATO contingent, 37,000 in South Korea, and 45,000 in Japan; there are also peacekeeping troops in Bosnia and the Sinai, and units stationed in Saudi Arabia and Turkey (International Institute for Strategic Studies 1996). NATO-associated costs by themselves are estimated at $25 billion to $30 billion annually. The PRC military budget has had yearly increases averaging 15 percent through the 1990s.

The View From Beijing

If one took at face value repeated Chinese statements, going back to Mao Zedong's time, that "China will never seek hegemony" and is interested only in defense of its territory, one would have to ask—why a military budget this size, and why acquisition of these kinds of equipment? Those who form what Bernstein and Munro have called "the new China lobby" insist that China has no aggressive intentions. They believe that its military posture is essentially defensive and, despite the buildup, it remains inferior to Japan, let alone America; that all China wants is a seat at the great-power table; and it is a mistake to condemn China for breaking rules—that is, international nonproliferation agreements—which it took no part in making. Others, like former Assistant Secretary of Defense Joseph Nye, argue that treating China as an enemy becomes a self-fulfilling prophecy. Still, there are many voices in the PRC, including some senior officials of the PLA, who already have declared publicly that China and the United States are enemies.

In the view of these PRC officials, the United States has quite deliberately followed policies intended to humiliate China and prevent its development as a great power. These include opposition to awarding the year 2000 Olympic Games to Beijing; introducing or backing U.N. resolutions condemning PRC human rights practices; pursuing a "one China, one Taiwan" policy in violation of its pledged word to Beijing, as evidenced by the issuance of a visa to Lee Teng-hui; selling arms to "prop up" the Republic of China government and thus prevent reunification; attacking or condemning PRC arms sales abroad while itself selling massive armaments; conducting an inaccurate propaganda campaign against China's trade practices; interfering in China's internal affairs with respect to Tibet by having President Bill Clinton meet with the Dalai Lama; interfering in China's internal affairs generally and seeking to replace the ruling Communist Party by supporting political dissidents and attacking efforts to suppress these "counterrevolutionary elements."

It is precisely this supposed American strategy, say these officials, that has called forth the PRC arms buildup. For example, at a conference in early 1994, then Chief of General Staff General Zhang Wannian said: "Facing blatant interference by the American hegemonists in our internal affairs and their open support for the debilitating activities of hostile elements inside our country and hostile forces outside the mainland and overseas opposing and subverting our socialist system, we must reinforce the Armed Forces more intensively" (Lo and Li 1994). At about the same time, Hu Jintao, a member of the Politburo Standing Committee, was quoted as saying, "According to the global hegemonist strategy of the United States, its main rival at present is the PRC. Interfering in China, subverting the Chinese government, and strangling China's development are strategic principles pursued by the United States" (Lo and Li 1994).

Statements such as these are far more significant than books like *The China That Can Say No*, which essentially attempt to reap financial rewards by playing to nationalist sentiment through attacks on the United States. As Nathan and Ross point out in *The Great Wall and the Empty Fortress*, the student and worker demonstrations of May and June 1989 convinced the Chinese Communist leadership that their political survival depended far more on suppressing dissent than on maintaining good relations with the United

States (Nathan and Ross 1997, 72). Shortly thereafter, the Soviet empire and the Soviet Union itself collapsed, removing the very strategic threat that had brought Beijing and Washington so close together in the 1970s and 1980s. Now neither needed the other as a strategic counterweight against the Soviet Union. As far as Beijing was—and remains—concerned, with the demise of the USSR, the principal threat to its continued rule came from what it began to call the insidious American policy of "peaceful evolution." Moreover, the execution of the Ceaucescus in Romania brought home to the Chinese Communist leadership the possible consequences of losing political power.

Toward a Realistic China Policy

There can be no doubt that much of Chinese behavior and in the rhetoric of party organs is highly disturbing. Similarly, large parts of recent PRC arms procurement and military exercises not only appear offense-related, but seem intended to acquire the capacity to engage American forces in the region. Nevertheless, we should bear in mind that the PRC military, like their counterparts in every country, look out for potential enemies, then plan and train for how best to cope with them. And while many voices declare that the United States is China's enemy, there are also those within or close to the PRC leadership who seem to hold a different view.

For example Qian Ning, the 37-year-old son of Vice Premier and Foreign Minister Qian Qichen, has recently published in China a book called *Studying in America* (still the goal of much of the Chinese intelligentsia, for themselves or for their children), which describes the United States as a land of great opportunity, deliciously free and full of "real people." Qian, who now works in Beijing for the American accounting firm Coopers and Lybrand, found the United States endlessly fascinating and his book portrays a very positive and balanced image (Tyler 1997). One cannot believe that the publication of Qian Ning's book did not have his father's approval, or that Qian Qichen did not have President Jiang Zemin's consent to give that approval.

In 1979, Deng Xiaoping viewed a cooperative relationship with the United States as an essential ingredient in his country's economic development. For all the trade friction that exists, it is hard to believe that PRC economic planners today do not still share that view of a country which remains China's single largest market, and a principal source of foreign investment and infusions of technology. And for all the political frictions that exist, there remains an underlying respect for American idealism. Wang Jianwei, a Chinese scholar educated at Fudan University and the University of Michigan, now a Senior Fellow at the Atlantic Council, quotes an unnamed "well-known scholar" as saying,

The United States is not necessarily a hegemonic country by nature. The United States is the best power compared with Britain, France and Japan. The style of its international behavior is similar to China's rule of the East in history. Before the industrial revolution, China was the most benign power, whereas the United States is the most benign power since the industrial revolution. (Wang 1996, 136)

In any case, as stated at the outset of this chapter, containment versus engagement is a false antithesis. One way or another, positively or negatively, we have been engaged with the PRC ever since its founding, and we will remain engaged. The question is, engaged how, and in pursuit of what goals?

The "engagement policy" of the Bush and Clinton administrations was based on two assumptions about China's future development: The first was that as China opened its economic system and participated in international trade, it necessarily would adhere to international legal norms; second, this would cause the seeds of democracy and proper international behavior (in American terms) to become established in Chinese soil. The Bush-Clinton assumptions rely upon a kind of built-in automaticity. Trade, talk, invest— and all will be well. But, as we might say in Chinese, *"chi shih bu ran,"* or, loosely translated, "it ain't necessarily so." To cite just one historical example among many: The growing wealth and power of Bismarckian Germany led to the Austro-Prussian War of 1866, the Franco-Prussian War of 1870–1871, colonial adventures in Africa, the South Pacific and China, and finally World War I.

Does that mean we should try containment? And if we did, would it work? China today is not the USSR of the 1940s and 1950s. The Soviet Union was a clear and present threat not only to the United States, but all of Western Europe and many other countries across the globe. Given that threat, it was not difficult to build a stable coalition against Moscow. At the same time, the Soviet Union was an autarky, closed to trade and investment outside its own empire. It was a region of growing economic and financial backwardness that collapsed, finally, when faced with the strains of trying to match America's military buildup while at the same time trying to find a way of responding to the pent-up economic demands of its own people. In the end, it could do neither.

China hardly fits that description. While it may well be a source of future danger to the United States or to its neighbors, it is a present threat to none of them except Taiwan. Nor is it perceived as such a threat by any of those neighbors, again except for Taiwan. These countries know that while America is far away and its mood is changeable, geography is a permanent reality. Moreover, national rivalries among our Asian friends, most notably between Japan and South Korea, predict the difficulty of drawing a *cordon sanitaire* around China. Meanwhile, far from being an autarky, China is the world's third largest economy, open to foreign trade and inviting to foreign investment. Foreign competition for China's markets is intense, and the Chinese know how to use that competition in their own interest (Glain 1997).

If the kind of containment strategy used against the Soviet Union is not responsive to the challenges posed by Chinese policy and behavior, neither are the flabby engagement policies pursued by the Clinton administration. When faced with a challenge to perceived American interests—for example, by PRC export to Iran of chemical weapons precursors, or perhaps even whole manufacturing facilities—the Clinton administration calls for "dialogue." There is nothing wrong with dialogue, provided it is ordered toward clearly defined ends and embedded in an effective strategy for persuasion. Unfortunately, most of the time the Clinton administration has had neither. Instead, the American side proffers a carrot of one sort or another to get the talks going. But the only stick considered available is some congressionally mandated horror, such as complete disruption of trade, leading to a result so dire that each side knows the stick will never be used. So the carrot becomes, in effect, a preemptive concession offered in return for promises—or sometimes nothing more than hope—of future good behavior. But even this tactic may be preferable to the other characteristic typical of Clinton administration policy—turning a blind eye to PRC misbehavior.

The October 1997 summit between President Clinton and President Jiang is illustrative in that none of the fundamental problems of the Sino–American relationship were resolved or even bargained out in meaningful ways. Instead of attempting to resolve contradictions in national policies, the basic goal for each of the two leaders was to score points for a domestic political audience. Jiang's chief goal was to show both allies and rivals that he, and through him China, was being treated as an equal by the president of the United States, and that he therefore was the leader China needed. Clinton's chief goal was to have the media report that he demonstrated the ability to manage the difficult and sensitive United States-China relationship without appearing to kowtow to Jiang. In this, he was greatly assisted by his unrehearsed press conference statements on human rights and Chinese behavior.

Although the national-level agreements they reached were a secondary consideration for both Jiang and Clinton—important primarily as a demonstration that something more than smiles and handshakes took place—over time they nevertheless can prove helpful. Rebuilding military ties through personnel visits and exchanges can give the PLA a better understanding of American military capabilities and so dissuade Beijing from aggressive adventuring in the Taiwan Strait or elsewhere. The programs for judges and legal personnel can have a modest effect on moving China in the direction of becoming a nation governed by law. The Maritime Communications Agreement can help prevent accidental confrontations between U.S. and PRC naval vessels.

The most questionable of the summit agreements was precisely the one that Jiang and Clinton decided to make the capstone of the visit—the president's decision to certify that Beijing is not helping others acquire nuclear weapons, in return for PRC promises to end nuclear cooperation with and sale of antiship missiles to Iran. It is the most questionable because Beijing has a 25-year-long record of ignoring agreements to restrain proliferation of weapons of mass destruction. As the *New York Times* remarked in an editorial on October 26, 1997, "Beijing has been the world's most reckless exporter of nuclear and missile technology."

But if summits such as these accomplish little of substance, what then, as Lenin so famously asked, is to be done? The answer, I believe, is a much more muscular diplomacy that seeks areas of cooperation, but knows how to combine dialogue—"engagement" if you prefer the term used by the Bush and Clinton administrations—with deterrence when that becomes necessary.

In the book *Weaving the Net*, which he edited, and to which he contributed substantially, James Shinn called for "conditional engagement" with China, and laid down ten principles for that policy:

1. No unilateral use of offensive military force
2. Peaceful resolution of territorial disputes
3. Respect for national sovereignty
4. Freedom of navigation
5. Moderation in military force buildup
6. Transparency of military forces
7. Nonproliferation of weapons of mass destruction
8. Market access for trade and investment
9. Cooperative solutions for transnational problems
10. Respect for basic human rights (Shinn 1996, 12).

Shinn says these ten principles "can serve as the basis for the text of joint communiqués or other formal agreements with China." But it is hard to imagine that the United States and the PRC could come easily to agreement on the specific content of many of his principles. For example, with regard to Shinn's sovereignty principle, Beijing is bound to argue that Taiwan is a matter wholly within its sovereignty and therefore outside the ambit of the nonuse-of-force principle. America, for its part, could hardly concede that point. Doubtless there also would be arguments about what constitutes military transparency and market access. In short, the sticky points in the relationship would remain sticky.

What is useful here is not Shinn's proposal for an overall framework agreement on relations that would have to be negotiated with the PRC, but rather the notion that the United States must itself have in mind a fixed set of principles for conducting relations with China. Viewed in this way, Shinn's ten principles become the spine for a more coherent policy, rather than a mere wish list. On the tactical, or operational level, we also can make use of Shinn's remarks about "tit-for-tat" carrots and sticks in responding to PRC behavior:

> Economic engagement calls for what is described as symmetric tit-for-tat, and security engagement for asymmetric tit-for-tat. A symmetric response is one that counters a move by China in the same place, time, and manner; an asymmetric response might occur in another place at another time, and perhaps in another manner. A symmetric tit-for-tat would be for Washington to counter a Chinese tariff of 10 percent on imports for the United States with a tariff of 10 percent on imports from China. An asymmetric tit-for-tat would be for the United states to counter a Chinese shipment of missiles to Iran with an American shipment of F-16s to Vietnam. (Shinn 1996, 11 n. 8)

While Congress is hardy likely to approve the sale of F-16s to Vietnam any time soon, the idea of "asymmetric tit-for-tat" is well worth exploring.

Although dialogue with the PRC obviously must continue, and with it high-level visits, summits have to be understood as something more than the usual attempt of American presidents to "achieve a personal relationship" with their Chinese counterparts. All too often summits, such as the most recent one, become shows of false bonhomie that the Chinese exploit to obtain political or economic goals, and which the American side exploits only as a photo opportunity. Using something like the above principles as the underpinning for American behavior, future high-level meetings might well achieve something beyond another communiqué to paste in the incumbent president's scrapbook.

To be useful in this way, the American interlocutors will have to rid themselves of the tendency to be tentative and halting, tied to the oblique niceties and conventions of diplomatic discourse. The Chinese, for their part, do not shrink from stern lectures about the deficiencies of American policy and behavior, but I am not suggesting high-level, or even low-level, shouting matches. Rather, it is necessary to be firm and unequivocal about our principles, whether it is a matter of nonproliferation or of market access, or nonuse of force, because they are our principles and are important to us. There are two areas in which Washington has been notably successful in dealing with the PRC: the negotiations conducted over the past few years by the Office of the United States Trade Representative (USTR); and the dispatch of aircraft carrier task forces to the vicinity of Taiwan in March 1996.

Although the PRC continues to stall, and occasionally even backtracks, the USTR negotiators have pried open some markets and have laid down a series of objective benchmarks against which Beijing's behavior can be measured. They have been successful for three reasons:

1. Instead of being open-ended, the negotiations are conducted against known deadlines, and the PRC (rather than the United States) pays a price if the deadlines are passed.
2. There is a threat of highly specific, named sanctions in terms of denying access to named sectors of the U.S. economy, which tracks with James Shinn's "tit-for-tat" idea.
3. The American negotiators unmistakably are backed by the will of the Congress and the American public.

Chinese military behavior in the Taiwan Strait in February and March 1996 posed a direct challenge not only to Taiwan but also our commitment to peaceful solutions, and to America's enduring interest in freedom of the seas. Had this challenge gone unanswered, as a lower level of military maneuvers had in the summer and fall of 1995, there can be little doubt that key elements in the PRC ruling group would have tried to push the envelope further still. Dispatching carrier task forces ended the threat to further escalation and underscored the American principle that force may not be used to "settle the Taiwan question."

These two examples demonstrate the need for clarity in American policy—the need to set very specific goals when our principles are challenged (intellectual property antipiracy laws; an end to the military threat to Taiwan), and adopt policies (announcing a tariff hit list; sending aircraft carriers to Taiwan) that persuade China to moderate its behavior. China needs to understand our view of the situation and our expectations of Chinese actions. When possible, these can and should be framed in diplomatic language, but must be unambiguous nevertheless.

Overall, our goal should be a China that does not threaten its neighbors, including Taiwan; a China that avoids actions likely to destabilize key strategic regions like the Middle East; a China that will work cooperatively with appropriate countries and institutions to ameliorate conflict in the East Asian region; a China that acts to resolve boundary and territorial claims in a peaceful manner—in short, a China that is prepared to live by the same rules of international political and economic life as those observed by the world community at large.

Notes

1. Numbers are taken from the International Institute of Strategic Studies publication, *The Military Balance 1996/97*, pp. 179ff., and may be slightly out of date.
2. This is the unclassified version of a longer, classified document, and was made public by Floyd D. Spence (R-S.C.), Chairman of the House of Representatives National Security Committee.

Bibliography

Bernstein, Richard, and Ross H. Munro. *The Coming Conflict with China.* New York: Alfred A. Knopf, 1997.

Far Eastern Economic Review. "Guns and Money," June 6, 1996, p. 16.

Fisher, Richard D., Jr. "China's Missiles over the Taiwan Strait: a Military and Political Assessment." Paper delivered at the Conference on the People's Liberation Army. Washington, DC: The American Enterprise Institute and T.M.I. Asia, September 6–8, 1996a.

_____. "China's Missile Threat." *Asian Wall Street Journal*, December 11, 1996b.

_____. "The Accelerating Modernization of China's Military." In *Between Diplomacy and Deterrence: Strategies for U.S. Relations with China.* Washington, DC: The Heritage Foundation, 1997a.

_____. "Dangerous Moves: Russia's Sale of Missile Destroyers to China." *Asian Studies Center Backgrounder* (February 20, 1997b).

_____. "Unilateral Armament." *The National Review*, June 2, 1997c, p. 46.

Gertz, Bill. "Russia, Ukraine Get Stern Missile Warning." *Washington Times*, May 21, 1996.

_____. "Pentagon Says Russians Sell Destroyers to China." *Washington Times*, January 10, 1997.

Glain, Steve. "How Beijing Officials Out Negotiated AT&T on Marine Cable Plans." *Wall Street Journal*, July 23, 1997.

Harding, James. "China Courts Arms Suppliers." *Financial Times*, July 14, 1997.

International Institute for Strategic Studies. *The Military Balance 1996/97.* Oxford: Oxford University Press, 1996.

Jane's Defence Weekly. January 15, 1997, p. 5.

Kagan, Robert. "The Money Trap." *The New Republic*, April 7, 1997, p. 30.

Kissinger, Henry A. "For China, Economic Reforms Spark Eruptions." *Los Angeles Times*, June 4, 1989.

Lo Bing and Li Tzu-ching. "Military Leaders Pursuing Hard Anti-USA Stance." *Cheng Ming*, May 1, 1994. Cited in *BBC Summary of World Broadcasts*, May 13, 1994.

Nathan, Andrew J., and Robert S. Ross. *The Great Wall and the Empty Fortress.* New York: W.W. Norton, 1997.

New York Times. "Officials Say China Illegally Sent U.S. Equipment to Military Plant." March 23, 1997, p. 1.

Shinn, James, ed. *Weaving the Net: Conditional Engagement with China.* New York: Council on Foreign Relations Press, 1996.

Tyler, Patrick E. "America the Beautiful? (A Rare Rave)." *New York Times*, July 21, 1997.

Tyson, Laura D'Andrea. *New York Times*, March 30, 1997.

United States Department of Defense. "Selected Military Capabilities of the People's Republic of China." *Report to Congress Pursuant to Section 1305 of the FY97 Defense Authorization Act*, 1997.

Wang Jianwei. 1996. "Coping with China as a Rising Power." In James Shinn, ed., *Weaving the Net: Conditional Engagement with China*. New York: Council on Foreign Relations Press, 1996.

Washington Post. "Chinese Firms Supply Iran with Gas Factories, U.S. Says." March 8, 1996.

Washington Post. June 25, 1997.

Washington Times. "China's Illegal Actions Detailed," February 23, 1996, p. A3.

_____. "Senate Asks for Sanctions on China," June 18, 1997a.

_____. "New Chinese Missiles Target All of East Asia," July 10, 1997b.

3

The U.S. Asia-Pacific Security Strategy for the Twenty-First Century

Ralph A. Cossa

Overview

Let me start with the bottom line: The United States remains committed to Asia—politically, economically, and militarily—because it is in its vital national security interest to remain fully engaged in this vibrant region. It was American vital interests that brought us to Asia in the first place, and it is American vital interests that will keep us fully engaged there in the future.

This is not to say that the nature of the U.S. commitment will remain static. It is destined to change as the regional security environment changes. The end of the Cold War made it possible for the United States to draw down from over 165,000 troops forward-deployed in Asia to about 100,000 during the last decade, without any real loss in relative power or advantage given the considerably diminished threat. So too will future changes in the security environment no doubt prompt future adjustments—downward or upward—depending on the nature of the changes.

The continued streamlining of U.S. military force structure and the enhanced rapid response and power projection capabilities that were forecast in the U.S. Defense Department's May 1997 "Quadrennial Defense Review" (QDR) also are likely to have an impact on the form and structure of the future U.S. commitment. The eventual and, it is hoped, peaceful reunification of the Korean peninsula will also affect the regional security equation, and no doubt will prompt a reassessment of U.S. forward-basing requirements. In addition, recent efforts to revitalize the all-important U.S.-Japan alliance, which serves as the linchpin of U.S. security strategy in Asia, have come under increasing attack, especially in China, but also to a lesser degree in Korea and among certain elements in America, Japan and elsewhere in Asia. Although the release in late September 1997 of the new "Guidelines for U.S.-Japan Defense Cooperation" was a positive step toward increasing the future relevancy and transparency of the U.S.-Japanese alliance, it has not stemmed these concerns. It also raises questions, at least in my mind, about whether Japanese politicians will stand behind the proposed steps to make Japan a more equal partner and help promulgate the new policies and procedures necessary to enact the proposed guidelines.

All these factors raise questions about the form that the future U.S. commitment to Asia will take as we enter the twenty-first century. So too does the need to balance America's continuing security partnership with Japan with the need by both the United States and Japan to improve their respective relations with China, to avoid the prospect of a new bipolar confrontation centered around Asia. This chapter will address the evolving U.S. Asia-Pacific security strategy for the twenty-first century in light of these various countervailing pressures. Before discussing the strategy per se, I will briefly review the geopolitical environment in which it must operate and, most importantly, discuss the long-term strategic vision that this strategy should support.

Current Security Environment

In my personal assessment of American policy and strategy, this evolving security strategy will continue to augment and reinforce the positive trends emanating from the region while also minimizing and, it is hoped, overcoming areas of conflict or uncertainty.

Positive Trends/Continued Uncertainty

The end of the Cold War has coincided with the dawning of a new, more peaceful, and generally prosperous era in Asia. Democracy has taken root in the Philippines, South Korea, and most prominently in the Republic of China, and continues to evolve elsewhere. The nations of Southeast Asia continue to sweep most of their historic rivalries under the rug in the name of ASEAN unity,[1] and have created the ASEAN Regional Forum (ARF) to engage most of their Asia-Pacific neighbors for the first time in structured dialogue on broad-ranging Asian security issues.[2]

Japan has demonstrated an increased willingness and capability to take a more active leadership role in multilateral forums such as the Asia-Pacific Economic Cooperation (APEC) group of regional economies, the nongovernmental Council for Security Cooperation in the Asia Pacific (CSCAP),[3] and the previously mentioned ARF.[4] The 1996 U.S.-Japanese Joint Declaration and the 1997 "Defense Guidelines" also demonstrate Japan's increased willingness, within the confines of the U.S.-Japan alliance, to become a more equal and active security partner.

China's emergence, politically and economically, also contributes to a general sense of well-being in the region, although this is tempered by growing uncertainty about China's long-term intentions and future stability, as well as Beijing's ability to sustain current rates of economic development while managing growing corruption and other systemic problems. The successful reversion of Hong Kong (thus far) also provides reason for cautious optimism. Furthermore, China has taken a generally positive approach toward such multilateral forums as CSCAP, APEC and the ARF, although there are concerns that China seeks to use these venues to marginalize existing U.S. bilateral alliances.

Although the Soviet military threat dominated Asian thinking during much of the Cold War, today the terms "Russian" and "threat" are seldom used in the same sentence. Even the Kremlin's once-mighty Pacific Fleet today appears to threaten only the sailors that man its ships and the personnel involved in protecting or dismantling its nuclear warheads and propulsion systems. Instead, Russia seeks to play a positive role in the ARF, and it hosted an ARF track two conference in Moscow in April 1996 aimed at developing a Statement of Basic Principles for Security and Stability. In addition, President Boris Yeltsin's joint decision with Japanese Prime Minister Ryutaro Hashimoto to settle the Northern Territories dispute and craft a peace treaty before the turn of the century augurs well for future Northeast Asian security. So too does the historic November 1997 Sino-Russian border demarcation agreement, which removed a major centuries-old irritant between the Kremlin and Beijing. Russia is politely knocking on APEC's door while also seeking a more active role on the Korean peninsula.

Meanwhile, although tensions have yet to fully subside on the Korean peninsula, the immediate nuclear crisis has at least temporarily been defused. North Korea seems willing, if not eager, to improve relations with Washington and Tokyo, even as it remains reluctant to renew its once-promising dialogue with South Korea. And now that North Korea has finally agreed to come to the bargaining table in Geneva to discuss replacing the 1953 armistice with a long-overdue formal peace treaty, cooperation between the United States, Seoul, and China in offering to engage North Korea in four-party talks also holds out promise for future progress.

Most significantly, with the long overdue initiation of regular Sino-American summits, frequent and fruitful meetings involving the leaders of all the major Asia-Pacific powers have become a reality. For example, between September and November 1997, Japanese Prime Minister Hashimoto visited with Chinese President Jiang Zemin in Beijing and with Russian President Yeltsin in Krasnoyarsk, while Jiang met both with U.S. President Bill Clinton in Washington and with Yeltsin in Beijing. Meanwhile, Chinese Premier Li Peng travelled to Tokyo to meet with Hashimoto. Also, Hashimoto, Jiang, and Clinton all met along with other regional heads of state at the 1997 Vancouver APEC leaders' meeting. Such meetings increase understanding and promote confidence among the four major Asian powers.

On the surface, the security situation in Asia has seldom been better. Beneath the surface, however, a great deal of uncertainty remains. While the prospects for conflict seem low, the potential for conflict exists and could grow.

Maintaining Regional Equilibrium

The greatest challenge facing the United States in Asia is balancing the critical need to sustain the U.S.-Japanese security alliance with the equally compelling need to improve Sino-U.S. and Sino-Japanese relations to avert a new Cold War in Asia. Taiwan remains a critical variable in this equation. If the "one China" formula to which all four parties still profess to subscribe (although with differing definitions) was officially discarded by any one of the players, regional equilibrium would quickly be destroyed. This, despite the fact that "one China" is widely recognized as a convenient (if essential) fig leaf, rather than an accurate description of geopolitical fact.

Future long-term stability in the Asia-Pacific region, if not globally, rests in large part on the maintenance of harmonious relations between the United States, Japan, and the People's Republic of China. To the extent these three key actors can cooperate, a generally benign security environment can emerge, in which the challenges sure to develop in the region can be managed. Conversely, tensions and conflict among the three will have a profoundly destabilizing effect regionwide. This is not to imply that other states are not important. The future course and behavior of the two Koreas, individually and together, certainly will have an influence. And, while the United States, Japan, and China individually and collectively have the ability to influence events on the Korean mainland, it is equally true that actions by the Koreas can force policy choices by the three larger states that they otherwise might not pursue.

Likewise, we ignore Russia only at our own peril. Russia is less significant a player in Asia today than at any time in the twentieth century, but it still retains the ability to play a disruptive or spoiler role. Though concerns of a Russia-China "strategic partnership" are, in my view, overblown, the fact that both sides see the political value in periodically hinting that such an arrangement is necessary to adjust the balance of world power raises the possibility of future problems. Historic Russo-Japanese animosity also cannot be ignored, although the informal "shirt sleeves" Hashimoto-Yeltsin Krasnoyarsk summit has helped to improve this relationship.

Also, ASEAN has proven a major player in the region and two of its members, Indonesia and Vietnam, are large enough in their own right to also have a major impact on regional events. At the far reaches of the region, India's future course and its relations with its Asian neighbors, especially China and the ASEAN states, will also help shape the Asia-Pacific geopolitical environment.

Having said all this, however, I return to my basic proposition: that the security environment of Asia in the new millennium will be most influenced by the ability—or inability—of the United States, Japan, and China to interact positively and peacefully with one another. The interrelationship I am describing is neither a three-way strategic partnership nor a big power condominium; nor is it an equilateral triangle. Amicable, harmonious, and non-threatening do not mean equal. The strongest, most important leg of this relationship is, and must continue to be, the U.S.-Japanese relationship.

When we view the three sets of bilateral relationships today, the U.S.-China link is the most troubled. It is also the one that is most likely, if not given proper attention, to plunge the region into another bipolar confrontation that would serve no one's long term security interests—not America's, not Japan's, and certainly not China's. But if efforts to improve Sino-American relations imperil U.S.-Japanese relations, we end up worse off. Even more foolish, and futile, would be an attempt to shift or tilt U.S. policy away from Japan and toward China as the central U.S. relationship upon which to build regional stability.

Let me hasten to add that I do not believe this is likely to happen. For reasons detailed below, the only thing less likely than a true Sino-Russian "strategic partnership" would be a Sino-American strategic alliance. As I understand U.S. policy toward China, the objective is to develop a more cooperative friendship and to avoid confrontation and crisis to the maximum extent possible, consistent with our own national security interests and principles.

While the Clinton-Jiang Joint Statement issued at their October 1997 summit did state that both leaders were "determined to build toward a constructive strategic partnership," the nature of this partnership has been left undefined. My own discussions with U.S. officials suggest that they hope for cooperation on issues that are strategically important to the United States (i.e., controlling weapons of mass destruction, counterproliferation, etc.). It appears doubtful that this coincides with Beijing's definition of this term.

For reasons that will be discussed shortly, it is difficult for me to envision a Sino-U.S. relationship similar to the one that exists today between Washington and Tokyo. It is even less likely—not to mention ill-advised—that the United States would attempt to replace the existing U.S. Asia-Pacific strategy with one that is China-centric. At any rate, U.S. relations with China do not constitute, and should not be viewed as a "zero-sum" game. When one side of the three way relationship improves, all three sides benefit, as does Taiwan.

Long-Term Strategic Vision

The United States, Japan and China all have certain interests and objectives in common. These include a common interest in promoting peace and stability regionally and globally; seeing an end to ethnic, religious or territorial disputes; halting the proliferation of weapons of mass destruction on the Korean peninsula and elsewhere; maintaining a generally benign Northeast Asian security environment; and continued economic progress and reform. I believe all three also hope for a peaceful settlement of the China-Taiwan issue. If harmony is to be maintained over the long term, all three nations must concentrate their efforts on building upon these common objectives.

While this range of common objectives provides both the basis and the necessary incentive for three-way cooperation and confidence building, China's views on democracy, human rights and other basic freedoms show that its values remain fundamentally dissimilar to, and often incompatible with those of the United States. More importantly, our hopes—our long term visions or aspirations—differ.

Long-Term Vision of the United States

I believe when American policymakers envision East Asia twenty years hence, they hope to see a stable, prosperous region in which the United States is still a primary (although not necessarily the only) stabilizing factor and is so regarded by most of the regional states. I believe they hope for an Asia in which the United States remains fully engaged politically, economically and militarily; an Asia where stability is underwritten in no small part by the continued security partnership between the United States and Japan.

Futurists also envision a Japan that is a more equal security partner with the United States, but that continues to prefer a complementary military force to a "stand-alone" force that could prove destabilizing. They foresee a Japan that is an accepted political as well as economic leader in Asia and globally; that is more willing and able to play a positive but clearly defined role in promoting and protecting regional security; and whose markets are considerably more open and integrated than they are today.

I believe American policymakers also seek a peaceful, prosperous, reunified Korean peninsula that continues to view America both as an ally and as a regional balancer, and as an honest broker promoting improved relations between Tokyo and Seoul as well. Few Koreans residing south of the 38th parallel would argue about the desirability of a peacefully reunified peninsula under Seoul's rule, although convincing their brothers to the north that this is a good idea remains a significant challenge. Of course, Seoul will be at the center of this reunified Korean peninsula, the Republic of Korea's (ROK) political and economic system having already clearly prevailed over that of North Korea. The advisability or feasibility of a continued U.S.-Korean security relationship or U.S. military presence on the peninsula after reunification is more open to debate, although many ROK policymakers profess a preference for a continuation of this particular status quo.

American policymakers also aspire to a prosperous, cooperative, more politically tolerant China that continues to see its fortunes inextricably intertwined with the rest of Asia and the West. This China will be as much a partner in peace in Asia as America hopes Russia will be in Europe. Although China may not joyously welcome a continued American security role in the region, it at least accepts and does not actively work against that role, enhanced by a revitalized U.S.-Japanese relationship whose objectives (continued regional peace, prosperity and stability) complement China's own future hopes for the region. This is the case even though China may prefer that it and not the United States, plays the primary regional balancer role, where Seoul looks to Beijing for its security guarantees, where U.S. military forces no longer reside on the Korean peninsula, and where Japan's regional leadership role (politically and economically, as well as militarily) is kept to a minimum.

My crystal ball becomes less clear as I try to envision Taiwan twenty years hence. Clearly, the United States wants Taiwan to remain prosperous, democratic and at peace with its brethren in China. I can personally envision a "one nation, one country, two states, two governments" formula[5] that keeps the Chinese nation intact and recognizes Beijing's sovereignty concerns, while still respecting the hopes and aspirations of the Taiwanese. Getting there from here remains a formidable challenge, however. Whatever the solution, it can best—and perhaps only—be developed through frank and direct cross-strait dialogue.

I hesitate to speak for my Asian colleagues, but I believe that the long-term vision of most Japanese policymakers closely coincides with the U.S. vision just described. At a minimum, this vision does not appear to contradict Japan's long-term interests or aspirations. I believe most Southeast Asian policymakers also feel comfortable with this vision. My view of the future is also one that Beijing should not regard as threatening, even if Chinese leaders, perhaps understandably, might prefer a different Asia. China's view of itself as the primary future regional balancer is not necessarily threatening, although it may become so if Beijing tries to force this role on the region rather than letting it evolve (or fail to evolve) naturally. If China's preferred end state is substantially diminished U.S. presence and influence in the Asia Pacific region, however, this vision clearly runs counter to American interests and places the two countries on a potential collision course.

Let me hasten to add that I do not subscribe to the "Coming Conflict with China" school of thought. I do not believe a United States–China collision is inevitable or unavoidable. I do believe, however, that both sides must acknowledge their different strategic perspectives and long-term vision and move toward a common ground where their aspirations and objectives can coexist. Further, I would argue, Chinese recognition that the United States has permanent interests in Asia and is intent on defending them—and that Japan and others share this desire for active U.S. engagement—lies at the base of future Sino-U.S. cooperation.

For this reason, I do not view a United States-China strategic partnership as either desirable or sustainable and see little prospect for a significant shift in American strategic thinking vis-à-vis Asia. From an American perspective, "the world's most important bilateral relationship" will remain anchored in Washington and Tokyo. America's Asia-Pacific security strategy into the twenty-first century will continue to build on this base.

America's Asia-Pacific Security Strategy

America's past leadership in—and security commitment to—the Asia-Pacific region has been instrumental in maintaining the current equilibrium and in creating the present relatively secure environment. The United States has a particularly important role to play in the future as well. If the United States fails to properly exercise the leadership role it has earned and enjoyed thus far in Asia, or if the current relatively benign security environment lulls Americans and Asians into a false sense of complacency, this could sow the seeds for future instability. The frequency of challenges to regional peace and prosperity and the region's ability to overcome these challenges will be determined by a variety of factors, but paramount among them is the extent of America's future commitment to Asia. This commitment will not be pursued to the exclusion of other important regions; America's interests have been, are, and will continue to be global. But Asia will continue to play an increasingly prominent role in U.S. security thinking.

Current Asia-Pacific Strategy

The Pentagon's "East Asia Strategy Report" (EASR), which remains the most current and definitive pronouncement on overall U.S. Asia-Pacific security strategy, recognizes this basic fact. Although published by the U.S. Department of Defense, it represents the fully coordinated views of both State Department and National Security Council policymakers and enjoys broad bipartisan support in the Congress. The EASR lays out a three-part U.S. security strategy for the Asia-Pacific region, based on engagement, enlargement, and exploration of new multilateral security initiatives. Engagement focuses on modernizing and strengthening U.S. alliances and friendships. Enlargement entails reaching out beyond traditional U.S. friends and allies to China, Russia and Vietnam. Multilateral security initiatives are addressed as potentially important complements to existing bilateral relationships. All presuppose and require a healthy, solid U.S.-Japanese alliance.

Most importantly, EASR identifies a continued forward military presence in Asia—specifically, the continued stationing of U.S. military forces in both Korea and Japan—as the "bedrock of America's security role in the Asian-Pacific region." Maintaining the alliance was also a key component in then-Defense Secretary William Perry's concept of "preventive defense" (Perry 1996, 72). This commitment to maintaining a strong defensive posture in East Asia was reaffirmed in the Defense Department's 1997 "Quadrennial Defense Review" and was underscored in the latest version of the White House's basic national security document, *A National Security Strategy for a New Century*.

Forward Deployed Forces

The current largely benign Asian security environment, while a product of many factors, has as its single largest determinant an American forward military presence and the sense of security commitment that this entails. Such forces serve a number of goals. They help promote regional stability; guard against a resumption of hostilities on the Korean peninsula; increase America's ability to respond to crises throughout the region; demonstrate a U.S. commitment to its friends and allies; serve as a hedge against uncertainty; and prevent a "power vacuum" that others who do not necessarily share our interests might be tempted to fill.

America's national self-interest ensures that the continued presence of forward-deployed U.S. military forces will continue at least through the end of this decade, although it appears unrealistic to expect that the 100,000 troop-level forecast in the EASR and QDR will be sustainable or necessary over the longer term. This is particularly likely if there is a significant cooling of tensions between North and South Korea. Presence and commitment can be demonstrated in a variety of ways, and the size of military forces can and should be adjusted as threat perceptions change and as the regional military capabilities of friends and potential foes evolve. Even under the most benign security environment, however, one can argue that some level of forward-deployed forces will remain desirable.

Engagement

If the key to future stability in Asia is a continued American military presence, then the keys to assuring this presence are maintaining the long-standing U.S. bilateral alliances, not just with Japan, but with Australia, the Republic of Korea, the Philippines and Thailand, as well as improving defense relationships and limited access agreements with nations like Singapore—that is, nations willing to demonstrate the degree of importance they attach to a continued U.S. presence.

Added to this, of course, is the de facto U.S. security "alliance" with Taiwan. While security guarantees are not spelled out and would no doubt be situational rather than absolute, Beijing must factor the possibility of a U.S. military response into the equation whenever it contemplates a military solution to the "Taiwan problem," especially if Beijing's actions are seen as unprovoked. Conversely, Taiwan should not assume that U.S. security guarantees are assured, especially if the fig leaf is precipitously removed.

Each U.S. security relationship underwrites the other. The EASR underscores the importance to future U.S. security strategy of all U.S. bilateral relationships, and especially the existing security alliances "that have been at the heart of United States strategy for more than forty years" (Department of Defense 1995, 3).

Enlargement

The EASR also stresses the importance of improved relations between the United States and the People's Republic of China (PRC). Nonetheless, some in China have viewed this as an attempt to brand the PRC as the next enemy or as a justification for an emerging "containment policy" directed at the PRC. My discussions with defense officials involved in the preparation of these documents have convinced me that this clearly was not the intent.

The EASR stresses the critical importance of enhanced military-to-military dialogue between the U.S. military and the Chinese People's Liberation Army (PLA), so as to promote better mutual understanding. The EASR also notes that, "absent a better understanding of China's plans, capabilities, and intentions, other Asian nations may feel a need to respond to China's growing military power" (Departmentof Defense 1995, 15). The intent underlying the EASR is to underscore the need for greater transparency in China's defense programs, strategy, and doctrine.

Multilateral Initiatives

American security strategists also recognize that emerging multilateral security mechanisms provide additional opportunities for cooperation and constructive dialogue aimed at building confidence and promoting stability in Asia, provided that they complement and do not seek to replace America's vital bilateral alliances in Asia. As noted earlier, several successful multilateral initiatives are currently underway, including the ARF, APEC and CSCAP. The inaugural Asia-Pacific Security Forum also promises to add to the regional security debate in a constructive manner, filling the dialogue gap caused by PRC insistence that certain topics are off limits for multilateral dialogues— at least for those involving PRC officials or scholars.

I am a strong proponent of multilateral approaches to regional security, but with an important caveat. It must be understood that they do not now, and perhaps never will, represent collective or cooperative security arrangements or alliances aimed at countering or redressing specific acts of aggression. This is not to demean their importance. But these emerging regional organizations are no substitute for the series of U.S. bilateral security alliances that continue to undergird regional security today.

Simply put, bilateralism and multilateralism are not mutually exclusive, but mutually supportive. Without solid bilateral relationships, few states would have the confidence to deal with each other in the broader context. Conversely, some problems can best, and perhaps only, be solved bilaterally. Nonetheless, multilateral security forums hold great promise for enhancing regional security, provided their limitations as well as their benefits are fully recognized.

The U.S.-Japanese Security Alliance

Central to U.S. engagement in Asia today and into the twenty-first century is the continued viability of the U.S.-Japanese security alliance. As the EASR notes, "there is no more important bilateral relationship than the one we have with Japan. It is fundamental to both our Pacific security policy and our global strategic objectives." The Pentagon report further identifies the U.S.-Japanese alliance as "the linchpin of U.S. security policy in Asia," (Department of Defense 1995, 10).

The United States-Japan Treaty of Mutual Cooperation and Security commits both sides not only to the defense of Japan but also to the promotion of regional stability. With the significant reduction, but not elimination, of external threats to Japan's security, the alliance's focus today must shift from defense of Japan to the broader regional goal. Keeping the alliance robust and relevant will require a greater willingness on the part of Japan to share increasingly in the risks and responsibilities. Also necessary is greater trust and understanding on the part of Japan's neighbors, and an increased acceptance in Japan and in the region of a more active, responsible Japanese security role.

The April 1996 Clinton-Hashimoto Joint Declaration was a significant step forward both in informing the general publics about the importance of the security relationship and in paving the way for greater defense cooperation. It recognized close bilateral defense cooperation as a "central element" in the security relationship and went on to state:

> The two leaders agreed on the necessity to promote bilateral policy coordination, including studies on bilateral cooperation in dealing with situations that may emerge in the areas surrounding Japan and which will have an important influence on the peace and security of Japan.

Japan can and should accept more of the defense burden, and is in the process of doing so, but in a gradual, responsible manner consistent both with its own psychological and constitutional restrictions and with its neighbors' concerns. This effort is not aimed toward any third country and especially not against China. In fact, the Joint Declaration stressed the need for close cooperation with the People's Republic of China. "The two leaders . . . emphasized that it is extremely important for the stability and prosperity of the region that China play a positive and constructive role, and, in this context, stressed the interest of both countries in cooperating with China" (Clinton and Hashimoto, Joint Declaration, Section 7).

Defense Guidelines Review

The 1997 Guidelines for U.S.-Japan Defense Cooperation represent a praiseworthy attempt by military planners in Japan and the United States to find common ground between the type of support U.S. planners desire from

Japan, and the level of support Japan is willing and feels constitutionally capable of providing. Their common goal is enhanced defense cooperation in the maintenance of peace and stability.

It is useful to note that the Guidelines do not obligate Japan or the United States to do anything new. Nor does it guarantee that Japan will provide the envisioned support under any and every conceivable circumstance. The new Guidelines merely provide "a general framework and policy direction." To emphasize this point, a line in the most controversial section dealing with "situations in areas surrounding Japan" notes that "in responding to such situations, measures taken may differ depending on circumstances." In other words, there is no guarantee that steps outlined in the Guidelines will ever be taken; they are, after all, only suggestions aimed at providing a "framework" for defense cooperation. They clearly delineate what Japan should not be expected to do, but provide no guarantees of Japanese support under any and all circumstances. Japanese participation requires "a common assessment of the state of each situation."

In response to the concerns of Beijing and others, the Guidelines also specifically state that "Japan will conduct all its actions within the limits of its Constitution and in accordance with such basic positions as the maintenance of its exclusively defense-oriented policy and its three non-nuclear principles."[6] The framework's boundaries are clearly marked. Only defensive actions in accordance with "relevant international agreements such as the Charter of the United Nations" are envisioned. Japanese forces will not participate in direct combat operations beyond the immediate vicinity of Japan and are not expected to conduct rear area support or even search and rescue operations in "areas where combat is being conducted." The Guidelines also stress the importance of diplomatic efforts to prevent conflict.

These caveats are aimed at allaying the fears and suspicions of Japan's neighbors, while assuring maximum transparency as to the purpose and intent of the new Guidelines. The Guidelines' review is not a cover for Japanese remilitarization. The review will be conducted in accordance with Japan's November 1995 National Defense Program Outline, which, among other things, called for a 25 percent reduction in the level of Japan's armed forces.

The Guidelines' review effort constituted an attempt by Japan to set forth what it can and will do, given the United States-Japan treaty, Japan's Peace Constitution, and Japan's current force structure, to enhance defense cooperation with the United States in the event of an attack against Japan or during "situations in areas surrounding Japan that will have an important influence on Japan's peace and security." If a crisis were to erupt in the region that threatened U.S. and Japanese interests—conflict on the Korean peninsula being the most obvious example—and Japan were to refuse to adequately support U.S. efforts, this would tear away at the fabric of the alliance. Defining "adequate support" to the satisfaction of both nations, and in a manner not threatening to Japan's neighbors, remains the goal of the revitalization effort.

Some have argued that the United States and Japan should state unequivocally in advance that the guidelines do not apply in certain areas or under certain circumstances. Given the above comments about the Guidelines' functional rather than geographic or situational nature, such demands appear inappropriate. Such assurances could be viewed as a Japanese or American "green light" for others to conduct military operations in certain areas, or could be interpreted as a declaration that certain areas automatically fell outside our sphere of strategic interest or concern. Recalling the consequences in 1950, when the United States seemed to be giving assurances that South Korea fell outside its area of security concern, demonstrates that this is politically impossible and strategically unwise.

The principal focus of Chinese concerns is the response of the United States and Japan, in the unlikely event that hostilities erupt in the Taiwan Strait or elsewhere. America and Japan must decide, both separately and collectively, how they will respond, based on their individual national security interests, their perceptions regarding the nature and intention of the conflict, and the party whose actions are most responsible for prompting the confrontation. For others to dictate the U.S. or Japanese response in advance constitutes interference in their internal affairs.

A revitalized or redefined alliance does not assure that the United States and/or Japan will respond in the event of any specific contingency, nor is there any guarantee that either or both would not respond to such contingencies under the old Guidelines. As long as all sides remain committed to a peaceful resolution and all honor the "one China" principle, there should be no problem in the first place.

Conclusion

America's security strategy in the Asia-Pacific region, based upon strong bilateral alliances and a credible forward military presence, has played a positive role in establishing the benign security environment enjoyed in Asia today. But the end of the Cold War has not meant an end to potential security challenges, and serious questions remain regarding long-term stability in this politically dynamic, economically vibrant region. The United States appears committed to remaining engaged in Asia and to maintaining its alliances and forward presence, even as it reaches out to enlarge its circle of friends and opens the door to all-inclusive multilateral security dialogue.

The challenge for both the United States and Japan, in each nation's individual dealings with China, is to ensure that Beijing understands that the Sino-U.S. and Sino-Japanese relationships are built on the foundation provided by the U.S.-Japanese alliance. This alliance should not threaten China as long as Beijing is also willing to maintain and improve upon the current equilibrium, instead of striving for a position of predominance, or that China would consider threatening U.S. and Japanese interests.

I am frequently asked, "How can we get China to embrace and support the U.S. military presence in general and the U.S.-Japan alliance in particular?" The answer: We probably can't, and we shouldn't try. China will decide what is and what is not in its interest, based on its own perception of how particular actions or activities relate to China's own goals and aspirations.

Finally, what we must convince China of is the durability of the alliance. The Chinese do not have to embrace the U.S.-Japanese alliance; they just have to accept it as part of the geopolitical landscape. I view the Chinese as essentially pragmatic; if they are convinced the alliance is enduring, they will accept it and adjust to it. As we enter the twenty-first century, the United States must focus on defining and then pursuing its long-term strategic vision in a nonthreatening manner that focuses on our traditional friends and allies, even while extending the hand of friendship to all nations that are willing to share this vision.

Notes

1. ASEAN, the Association of Southeast Asian Nations, was formed in 1967 by Indonesia, Malaysia, the Philippines, Singapore and Thailand, to accelerate economic growth, social progress, and peace and security in Southeast Asia. It was later expanded to include Brunei and Vietnam and, most recently, Laos and Myanmar (Burma). Cambodia was scheduled to join in 1997 along with Laos and Burma, but its entry was delayed owing to political turmoil in Phnom Penh.

2. The ARF consists of the nine ASEAN states plus Australia, Cambodia, Canada, China, India, Japan, Papua New Guinea, Russia, South Korea, New Zealand, the United States, and the European Community. Regrettably, Taiwan continues to be excluded.

3. The CSCAP member committees have been established in Australia, Canada, Indonesia, Japan, Malaysia, Mongolia, New Zealand, North Korea, the Philippines, the PRC, Russia, Singapore, South Korea, Thailand, the United States, and Vietnam. A European Community consortium and an Indian institute have joined as associate members. Member committees are comprised of academicians, security specialists, and former and current foreign ministry and defense officials. Government (including uniformed military) participants take part in their private capacities. While Taiwan has not been granted any type of formal institutional affiliation to date, scholars and security specialists from Taiwan participate in all CSCAP International Working Group activities in their private capacities.

4. For example, Japan hosted the 1996 APEC conference and leaders' meeting and

co-chaired the ARF's 1995–96 Intersessional Support Group on confidence-building measures. In addition, Ambassador Nubuo Matsunaga of the Japan Institute of International Affairs serves as co-chair of CSCAP's International Steering Committee.

5. A formula currently being put forth by Pyongyang, without any detailed explanation, as their preferred (interim) solution for Korean peninsula reunification.

6. Japan's three non-nuclear principles prohibit the manufacture, possession, or introduction into Japan of nuclear weapons.

Bibliography

Clinton, William. Press release. *A National Security Strategy for a New Century.* Washington, DC: White House, May 1997.

Clinton, William, and Hashimoto, Ryutaro. "U.S.-Japan Joint Declaration on Security Alliance for the Twenty-first Century." April 17, 1996. For a copy of the complete text, see PacNet, no. 17–96, "U.S.-Japan Joint Declaration," April 26, 1996. PacNet is a weekly publication of the Pacific Forum CSIS.

Clinton, William, and Jiang Zemin. *Joint US-PRC Statement.* October 29, 1997.

Cohen, William S. *Quadrennial Defense Review.* Washington, DC: U.S. Department of Defense, May 19, 1997 (available from the U.S. Defense Department or from the World Wide Web at http://www.dtic.mil/defenselink/).

Cossa, Ralph A. "100,000 Troops: About Right . . . For Now." *The Korea Times,* May 30, 1996, p. 6.

————. "Everybody Benefits from Washington's Commitment to Asia." *Asia Times,* June 3, 1997, p. 9.

Department of Defense. *United States Security Strategy for the East Asia-Pacific Region (East Asia Strategy Report [EASR]).* Washington DC: Office of International Security Affairs, February 1995.

Japan Defense Agency. *National Defense Program Outline in and After FY1996.* Press release, Government of Japan, November 28, 1995.

Perry, William J. "Defense in the Age of Hope." *Foreign Affairs* 75, no. 6 (November/December 1996): 64–79.

4

Japan's Military Cooperation and Alliances in the Asia-Pacific Region

Guidelines for U.S.-Japanese Defense Cooperation

Koji Murata

Introduction

The U.S.-Japanese alliance is unique for three reasons. First, it is a bilateral alliance between the victor and the vanquished of a major war. Although Germany and Italy did join the North Atlantic Treaty Organization, NATO is a multilateral alliance where relations among former enemies are more relaxed than in a bilateral one. And although the United States has formed bilateral alliances with the Republic of China (Taiwan), the Republic of Korea (South Korea, or ROK), and the Philippines in postwar Asia, those countries were not vanquished in the Pacific War. Second, Japan and the United States do not have common historical and cultural backgrounds. Third, and most importantly, the U.S.-Japanese alliance, unlike many major U.S. postwar alliances, has lacked a substantive military structure. "Substantive military structure" refers to the existence of organization and procedures to discuss and implement joint military actions. One Japanese scholar points out that the avoidance of joint military action is common to Japan's alliance behaviors in the Anglo-Japanese, the Tripartite, and the United States-Japan alliances (Tsuchiyama 1993).

Despite these potential sources of tension and weakness, the U.S.-Japanese alliance has survived for four decades thanks to the Cold War. As we look for ways to maintain and to develop further this historically unique alliance in the volatile post-Cold War world, however, we should try to create a substantive military structure for the alliance. The revision of the "Guidelines for U.S.-Japan Defense Cooperation" in September 1997 was an important step toward this goal. This chapter will compare the Guidelines in 1978 and in 1997 and examine the progress that the two countries have made in advancing a substantive military structure.

Implications of the 1978 Guidelines for the U.S.-Japanese Alliance

The United States-Japan Security Treaty of 1951 permitted the United States to use its troops in Japan for regional security in the Far East and against internal riots in Japan, but did not automatically obligate it to protect Japan. In stating only that the U.S. forces in Japan could be used to contribute to the security of Japan against external military attacks, the treaty set forth a function, not an obligation, of the U.S. forces.

When the treaty was revised in 1960, the "internal riots" clause was deleted, and a new "prior consultation" clause was introduced. This clause provides that the United States will seek Tokyo's formal approval before American troops are redeployed from Japanese soil to Asia Pacific conflict zones (whether Tokyo has veto power, however, is unclear). The revised security treaty also provides that "the parties will consult together from time to time regarding the implementation of this treaty" (Article 4), and that "each party . . . declares that it would act to meet the common danger in accordance with its constitutional provisions and processes" (Article 5). Under Article 4, major forums for U.S.-Japanese security consultations were established: the Security Consultative Committee (SCC) at the ministerial level; the Security Subcommittee at the vice ministerial level; and the Security Consultative Group at the deputy vice ministerial level among others.[1]

There are crucial definitional differences between the U.S.-Japanese treaty and other major U.S. treaties. In terms of its response formula, the U.S.-Japanese alliance is less automatic than the NATO alliance. The North Atlantic Treaty regards an armed attack against one as "an attack against all," instead of as the "common danger" named in Article 5 above, and does not have the condition mentioned in Article 5. Also, while the North Atlantic Treaty defines "an attack" to include an attack upon the armed forces, public vessels, or aircraft of the parties, the United States-Japan Security Treaty does not have such a structured definition of attack.

In addition, in terms of its scope, the U.S.-Japanese treaty is wider than the U.S.-ROK alliance. Japan interprets the term "provisions" in Article 5 to mean that because Japan cannot execute the right of collective defense, in case of emergency, it will act in accordance with the provisions of Article 76 of the Self-Defense Forces Act. For example, Article 3 of the U.S.-ROK Mutual Defense Treaty states that each party "would act to meet the common danger in accordance with its constitutional processes." Article 6 of the revised United States-Japan Security Treaty states that "for the purpose of contributing to the security of Japan and the maintenance of international peace and security in the Far East, the United States of America is granted the use by its land, air and naval forces of facilities and areas in Japan." The U.S.-ROK Mutual Defense Treaty lacks such a "Far East" clause.

Despite revising the treaty in 1960, Japan and the United States did not try to develop any substantive military structure until late 1978. For one thing, Japan's ruling political party, the Liberal Democratic Party (LDP), was unwilling to take steps that might provoke opposition parties, especially the Japan Socialist Party (JSP). In fact, in 1963, the public and the opposition parties heaped criticism on the Japan Self-Defense Forces (JSDF) for its so-called Mitsuya Study of contingency measures, which was conducted without the government's knowledge. Since that incident, the Japanese government has been hypersensitive about anything that could be called "contingency studies." Second, Tokyo did not wish to provoke the Communist camp, especially Beijing, by strengthening its military ties with Washington. As long as U.S. nuclear deterrence functioned and the Pacific was an "American lake," Japan could enjoy "free security" just as the United States had done for a long time under British hegemony, whether or not Japan strengthened its military ties to the United States.

Glenn Snyder has described a typical security dilemma in alliance politics: the dilemma between "abandonment" and "entrapment." The former is the fear that an ally may leave the alliance or may not fulfill its obligation, whereas the latter refers to "being dragged into a conflict over an ally's interests that one does not share, or shares only partially" (Snyder 1984, 467). In the U.S.-Japanese alliance, Japan was for a long time more concerned about being entrapped into a U.S. war than being abandoned, because it did not perceive direct external military threats to its security until the late 1970s or the early 1980s. In contrast, South Korea was for a long time more worried about being abandoned than being entrapped, given the North Korean, Soviet, and Chinese threats to its security.

The U.S. military continued for some time after 1954 to think of the JSDF as little more than a large-scale constabulary, and required some time to adjust to Japanese sovereignty after the end of the Occupation. Japanese rear-area logistical support during the Korean War had been open-ended, and Article 6 of the United States-Japan Security Treaty left the impression that such support would automatically be forthcoming in future regional contingencies.[2] In essence, the U.S.-Japanese treaty was actually nothing more than a base-leasing agreement: The United States would defend Japan in return for being provided with bases.

Since the late 1970s, however, Tokyo and Washington have tried to establish the alliance's substantive military structure. Because Asia experienced a sense of division following the Nixon Doctrine and the end of the Vietnam War, Tokyo grew more concerned about being abandoned. Furthermore, the search for autonomous defense under Defense Minister Yasuhiro Nakasone had failed in the early 1970s owing to public negative reactions and the oil crisis. It was quite logical, therefore, for new Defense Minister Michita Sakata to seek closer defense cooperation with the United States. At the same time, given the relative decline of its economic supremacy and the post-Vietnam domestic mood, the United States began to seek Japan's active involvement in regional security.

Ko Maruyama, Sakata's Vice Minister from 1976 to 1978, recalls: "In sum, the Security Treaty with the United States was already established. We only lacked how to implement the treaty, however. In principle, it was very difficult [even for the opposition parties] to be opposed to introduce such a mechanism." He also notes: "My first question when I became Vice Minister was how Japan's defense policy was linked with American policy. . . . In reality, how, when and where the U.S. would project its forces in case of contingencies in Japan and how Japan would accept them—all of them were uncertain. Everything lacked real content."[3]

The adoption of the "Guidelines for U.S.-Japan Defense Cooperation" in November 1978 thus was a turning point for security relations between the two countries. In this document, the United States explicitly pledged to "maintain a nuclear deterrent capability, and the forward deployments of combat-ready forces and other forces capable of reinforcing them." The Guidelines also provide that while "in principle, Japan by itself will repel limited, small-scale aggression...when it is difficult to repel aggression alone due to the scale, type and other factors of aggression, Japan will repel it with the cooperation of the United States." For this purpose, according to this document, the JSDF "will primarily conduct defensive operations in Japanese territory and its surrounding waters and airspace" and the U.S. forces will conduct "operations to supplement functional areas which exceed the capacity of the JSDF." Finally, the Guidelines stipulated U.S.-Japanese joint military exercises, intelligence exchanges, and joint studies on three operational dimensions (prevention of aggression against Japan, responses to military attacks on Japan, and joint cooperation in case of conflict in the Far East).

The Guidelines are often considered the third edition of the United States-Japan Security Treaty. For example, General Takehiko Takashina, then the chairman of the Joint Chiefs Council of the JSDF, has stated that "the spirit

[was] first put into the U.S.-Japan Security Treaty [in] 1960" (Taiyukai 1980, 191). It should be noted, however, that Tokyo adopted the Guidelines to maintain a credible U.S. defense commitment to Japan, with its limited defense budget. Akihiko Tanaka notes that "although the Guidelines were adopted not for the new Cold War, this document provided the framework 'to fight' it" (Tanaka 1997, 286).

Early on, the Soviet military buildup around Japan helped narrow the U.S.-Japanese perception gaps regarding a common threat. Even China, which had strongly opposed the United States-Japan Security Treaty until the early 1970s, condoned U.S.-Japanese promotion of defense cooperation in order to deter the Soviet Union. Beijing understood that the function of the Guidelines was deterrence and that their nature was defensive. The Guidelines provided the first public authorization for the JSDF and the U.S. forces to train together. This led to a much closer focus on and appreciation of JSDF capabilities in Honolulu and Washington. The Guidelines also established the first political authorization for studies in Japan, which eased the process of developing a concrete bilateral plan for the defense of Japan.

The implications of the Guidelines for the U.S.-Japanese alliance, however, should not be overemphasized. First, the Guidelines' conclusions did not obligate either government to take legislative, budgetary or administrative measures. Second, the JSDF and U.S. forces failed to establish a "coordination center" through which they were supposed to "maintain close mutual coordination on operations, intelligence and logistic support." Third and most importantly, this document did not produce any authorized joint operation plan. A joint study on the contingency in Japan was roughly completed in the summer of 1981 and submitted to Prime Minister Zenko Suzuki. This study postulated that an enemy (the Soviet Union) would descend on Hokkaido using airborne divisions and then with about two divisions of naval vessels (*Asahi Shimbun* 1996). But while this scenario was ideal for the application of Article 5 of the United States-Japan Security Treaty, it was unrealistic. For one thing, it was inconceivable that the Soviet Union would attack Japan alone. In addition, the Soviet Union lacked sufficient landing capabilities over Japan. More importantly, this joint study was just a study, and did not set forth concrete defense plans.

The joint study on the contingency in the Far East, which was the subject of much U.S. interest, was officially initiated in 1982. Unfortunately, it was not completed. Tokyo failed to establish interagency consensus that would allow contingency planning with such critical ministries as Foreign Affairs, Transportation, Construction, and Home Affairs. The late Seiki Nishihiro, former Administrative Vice Minister of Defense, commented that "it was a mistake to separate the Article 6 situation from that of Article 5, which were inseparable in nature."[4]

It took almost twenty years for Tokyo to overcome these shortcomings of the 1978 Guidelines, which were finally revised in September 1997.

Implications of the Guidelines in 1997 for the U.S.-Japanese Alliance

When the nuclear crisis in North Korea emerged in the summer of 1994, marking the first serious post-Cold War security challenge for the U.S.-Japanese alliance, Tokyo and Washington lacked concrete joint plans in case of contingencies in Korea. Although the crisis was averted, it reminded the U.S.-Japanese security community of the vulnerability of the alliance. Shortly thereafter, the tragic incident of the rape of a schoolgirl in Okinawa by three American servicemen in the summer of 1995 posed yet another serious challenge to the U.S.-Japanese alliance. Revising the Guidelines was the answer to these crises.

Because the new Guidelines define the role of U.S.-Japanese alliance in a post-Cold War era, their scope is much wider than that of the 1978 Guidelines. The new Guidelines, for example, mention the United Nations Charter, and include humanitarian activities such as emergency relief operations. They also set forth much more concrete terms. While the new Guidelines "will not obligate either Government to take legislative, budgetary or administrative measures," "the two Governments are expected to reflect in an appropriate way the results of these efforts, based on their judgements, in their specific policies and measures."

The core of the new Guidelines is the sections related to a "situation in areas surrounding Japan." They read:

> When a situation in areas surrounding Japan is anticipated, the two Governments will intensify information and intelligence sharing and policy consultations, including efforts to reach a common assessment of the situation.
>
> The two Governments will take appropriate measures, to include preventing further deterioration of situations, in response to situations in areas surrounding Japan. . . . They will support each other as necessary in accordance with appropriate arrangements.
>
> As situations in areas surrounding Japan have an important influence on Japan's peace and security, the Self-Defense Forces will conduct such activities as intelligence gathering, surveillance and minesweeping, to protect lives and property and to ensure navigational safety. U.S. Forces will conduct operations to restore the peace and security affected by situations in areas surrounding Japan. (Guidelines 1997)

The new Guidelines also make an attempt at bilateral defense planning and mutual cooperation planning. The latter aims "to respond smoothly and effectively to situations in areas surrounding Japan in peacetime." The promotion of mutual cooperation planning is a sort of overdue homework that should have taken place under the 1978 Guidelines. Although Japan should not become an "unsinkable aircraft carrier" for the United States, it can become an "unsinkable supply ship" for activities in areas surrounding Japan. The new Guidelines also establish "a bilateral coordination mechanism involving the relevant agencies of the two countries to coordinate respective activities in case of an armed attack against Japan and in situations in areas surrounding Japan."

Although some observers have asked why the Guidelines were revised in 1997, the better question is why they were not revised sooner. South Korean security provides the best explanation. Shunji Taoka has compared the current revision of the Guidelines to giving a winter coat to a girlfriend (South Korea) in the spring, even though a winter coat was necessary in the winter (Taoka 1997, 40).[5] Nonetheless, as *Aesop's Fables* remind us, basic preparation for the winter should begin in the spring. Furthermore, the mutual cooperation planning is not a gift to a friend, but a necessity for Japan. Because the peace and security of South Korea is, as many Japanese prime ministers have repeated, essential for the security of Japan, it is not a matter to be left to others.

The difficulty lies in the fact that while Japan and the United States and the United States and South Korea are, respectively, allies, Japan and South Korea are not. Although Japan may be able to assist the United States in case of a contingency on the Korean peninsula, it cannot aid South Korea directly. To the extent its constitution allows, therefore, Japan must promote policy coordination among the three countries to avoid unnecessary misunderstanding regarding Japan's intentions and capabilities.

To maximize their effectiveness, the level of public support for the revised Guidelines is as important as their content. Tokyo and Washington were wise to make public the interim report in June 1997 and thereby promote the transparency of U.S.-Japanese security talks. This review process of the revised Guidelines became the focus of public attention in and out of Japan. In contrast, when the Guidelines were adopted in late 1978, public attention was minimal. Furthermore, while the 1978 Guidelines did not give rise to any authorized U.S.-Japanese joint operation plans for Japan or even any joint studies on contingencies in the Far East, the revised Guidelines require joint plans for both types of contingencies.

Plans themselves do not automatically induce conflicts or danger. If so, many military conflicts could be avoided by abolishing military general staffs all over the world. Naturally, a highly aggressive and inflexible military plan such as the Schliefen Plan in World War I can escalate a crisis. To avoid adopting such a plan requires various in-depth studies, which the Japanese public has tended to ignore. If Japan should face a serious military conflict without the plans to cope accordingly, the results would be tragic.

The danger that a lack of planning presents to military affairs should have been one of Japan's greatest lessons of World War II. At the start of the war, General Hideki Tojo stated that "we need the resolution as if we took a leap in the dark." Beyond this resolve, however, the Japanese leadership did not have any actual plans for executing the war. Although Japan fortunately has not had the resolve for this type of rash determination since WWII, it is unfortunate that its attitude toward military planning has not changed much either. Japan today lacks the fiscal leeway to pour close to 5 trillion yen in budget funds annually into defense forces that have no plans at all.

Japan's apparent lack of military planning has been facilitated by the fear that study of responses to military contingencies inevitably will result in dangerous plans that heighten military tension in the surrounding area (the Pandora's box argument). This belief is rooted in the profound distrust of democracy and popular intelligence that have been so assiduously cultivated by postwar Japanese society, and has only exacerbated other countries' fears of a resurgent Japanese militarism. Before the Japanese public nationalistically proclaims that the true objective of the U.S. military presence is to contain Japan, they should reflect on their own motives. If the subtext of such arguments is that the United States is using the security arrangements to serve its own national interest, well, that is only to be expected. Any alliance—indeed, diplomacy itself—inevitably serves the national interest. Japan also uses its security arrangements to further its national interest, and rightfully so. The ability to define this relationship of mutually using and being used in broader terms than self-interest is surely a mark of diplomatic maturity.

The review process of the new Guidelines has impacted Japan's defense policy in several important ways. First, it reflects a greater promotion and institutionalization of the U.S.-Japanese security dialogues. It took two and one-half years from the establishment of the Subcommittee on the United States-Japan Defense Cooperation (SDC) to the adoption of the 1978 Guidelines. In comparison, the review process of the new Guidelines was completed within one and one-half years, indicating that the bilateral security talks are, albeit gradually, becoming more institutionalized.

Second, the review process has influenced relations between the Ministry of Foreign Affairs (MOFA) and the Japan Defense Agency (JDA). The JDA has long been regarded as a second-rate central agency that one cynic used to call an "appendix of the U.S.-Japan Security Treaty Division of the MOFA." Through dialogues on the detailed defense cooperation with the United States, however, the JDA has become more assertive and active in defense policy-making. It is natural and healthy that the relations between the MOFA and the JDA is moving from verticality toward horizontality.

Third, the influence of uniformed officers of the JSDF in defense policy-making also has increased. This is not a dangerous phenomenon. The uniformed officers have been long oppressed by the overly simplified antiwar public sentiment and the excessively tight supervision of the JDA Internal Bureau. Now that the dialogue has turned to operating the JSDF effectively, its professionalism and technical knowledge deserve acknowledgment. Japan's postwar democracy and civilian control system are strong enough to prevent any remilitarization. In addition, as Samuel Huntington says, a highly profesionalized military is rarely politicized (Huntington 1957).

Finally, the integration of JSDF's three service functions is progressing through dialogues with their U.S. counterparts. Because the U.S.-Japanese security system serves as the basis for Japan's defense policy, it was impossible to promote the integration of the three services without making clear the timing, scale and function of U.S. forces in case of emergency. The adoption of the Guidelines in 1978 was a breakthrough in this regard, and the integration of the three services will be further promoted under the revised Guidelines. In this connection, the role and function of the chairman of the Joint Chiefs Council of the JSDF should be clearer and stronger.

Will these structural changes in Japan's defense policy make the U.S.-Japan alliance more effective? Several further tasks appear necessary.

Further Tasks

The collective defense issue remains the major obstacle to promoting further U.S.-Japanese defense cooperation for regional security. Although Japan is a member of the United Nations, and is seeking permanent membership in the U.N. Security Council, the Japanese government remains reluctant to budge from its position that the Japanese Constitution does not allow the government to participate in collective defense.

Beyond technical legalistic arguments, it should be noted that the concept of collective defense may vary within the international realm depending on the countries involved and the security climate at the time. When the Japanese Constitution was adopted, the Cold War served as the main feature of the international system. Accordingly, the concept of collective defense at that time encompassed the right to carry out joint military actions to defeat, eliminate, and even destroy an aggressor.

In the post-Cold War period, however, both the meaning and the function of collective security has changed. Now, collective security refers to the obligation of joint military actions to prevent military conflicts and mitigate damages resulting from such conflicts. As Kuniko Inoguchi commented, the concept of collective defense can be termed one of collective crisis management.[6] The Japanese Constitution does not anticipate this concept, and therefore does not explicitly prohibit it. At the same time, however, although Japan needs further broad discussions to formulate fully the collective defense concept, collective security should not serve as an excuse for Japan to take responsibility for regional security.

In response to a recent Yomiuri-Gallup poll, which asked what Japan should do to support U.S. forces in an emergency situation, only 2.3 percent of the people in Japan supported participation in front-line operations in comparison to 38.8 percent in the United States (*Daily Yomiuri* 1997). Although neither Washington nor Seoul actually desires Japan's participation in front-line operations, this perception gap between the Japanese and the American publics may cause problems in the future.

An additional task necessary to strengthening the U.S.-Japanese alliance involves clarifying its effect on China, which seems concerned over the geographical extent of areas surrounding Japan under the revised Guidelines. Although then-Chief Cabinet Secretary Seiroku Kajiyama stated that Taiwan was included in the area surrounding Japan under the revised Guidelines, LDP Secretary General Koichi Kato stated that it was not. Both remarks are irrelevant. It is up to Beijing and, to a lesser extent, Taipei to decide whether Taiwan is included within the scope of the Guidelines, and Tokyo and Washington should respect the sovereignty of the China policy. To avoid unnecessary misunderstandings with China, both Japan and the United States must strive for further transparency of the revised Guidelines.

By the same token, Tokyo and Washington should not actively encourage Taipei's search for independence. Chinese government officials reportedly have stated that Beijing would not abandon the possibility of military force against Taipei to prevent Taiwan's independence. If Taipei should declare independence, and if it should result in Chinese military action, the ability of Japan and the United States to provide aid under the new Guidelines may be very limited. To keep China guessing, the determination whether Taiwan is included in the area surrounding Japan is a matter that must remain vague.

The goal of the revised Guidelines is to prevent military conflicts, not to invade or defeat any third party. To the extent Beijing respects regional stability, it need not worry about U.S.-Japanese defense cooperation. It is noteworthy that Beijing encouraged Tokyo and Washington to promote bilateral defense cooperation under the 1978 Guidelines that, while adopted in the new Cold War period, served a defensive rather than offensive purpose. The revised Guidelines are the logical extension of their predecessor.

A third task confronting the alliance is the improvement of the regional security structure. Although multilateral regional security cooperation cannot take the place of the U.S.-Japanese bilateral security relationship, the two are mutually reinforcing. Multilateral regional security cooperation is important for preventive diplomacy, whereas a sound U.S.-Japanese bilateral security relationship is of great importance for crisis management. Without a secure U.S.-Japanese relationship, regional cooperation will be less effective and credible; without regional cooperation, the alliance might lead to suspicion among Asian neighbors.

A final and important task is the reconstruction of civilian control in Japan, given the change in civil-military relations since World War II. It is essential to avoid generating unnecessary concerns in neighboring countries over the revival of Japanese militarism. Too much fear, however, has led the Japanese public and its political parties to avoid discussing security issues; such discussions in the National Diet still lack content. An effective and professional defense apparatus is not in itself dangerous. The danger lies in ignoring it and, as a consequence, abandoning substantial control over it.

While implementing the revised Guidelines, Tokyo and Washington must make a greater effort to address these concerns. Let us keep in mind, as Ralph Cossa notes, that even when finally agreed upon and issued, the Guidelines only constitute "guidance." Adoption of the new Guidelines is important, but it constitutes only one step toward a more credible U.S.-Japanese alliance and more stable regional security.

Postscript

The Diet finally ratified the U.S.-Japan Security Pact Guidelines in April 1998.[7] Yet, the debates on these guidelines continue, centering around three issues. First, although the JSDF is supposed to provide logistic support to the U.S. forces in rear areas, the disctinction between rear areas and active combat areas is not necessarily self-evident; thus, it is theoretically possible that Japan may be entrapped in belligerency. To avoid blurring the borderline between two areas, the right of collective defense needs to be properly interpreted.

Second, the procedures for ship inspections on the high seas are still controversial. On the one hand, the Japanese government argued that an authorization through a UN resolution should be required for the JSDF to conduct such inspections. On the other hand, the Liberal Party insisted that such authorizations were not required because of the fact that the main purpose of the Guidelines is to strengthen U.S.-Japan defense cooperation. As a consequence, this item was not included in the Guidelines-related acts.

Third, the Guidelines-related acts stipulate that in principle the Prime Minister should ask the Diet for prior consent, but that in case of emergency he could obtain consent ex post facto. Again, the scope and conditions that constitute an emergency are not explicitly defined. Hence the need for either prior or retrospective consent of the Diet remains a contentious issue.

Notes

1. As for the SCC, U.S. members were upgraded from Ambassador to Japan and Commander-in-Chief of the U.S. Pacific Command to Secretaries of State and Defense in December 1990.
2. Dr. Michael Green's observation.
3. Interview with Ko Maruyama (April 12, 1996, Tokyo).
4. Interview with Mr. Seiki Nishihiro (Tokyo, November 16, 1995).
5. Mr. Taoka's four questions are as follows. First, why should Japan have vindicated its intentions to South Korea in terms of revising the Guidelines? Second, will the U.S. forces help Japan to rescue the Japanese citizens in South Korea in case of contingency? Third, is there any guarantee for the scope of "areas surrounding Japan" not to be arbitrarily expanded by the United States? And fourth, is there any legal ground to carry out inspections and mine-sweeping out of Japanese territory?
6. Professor Kuniko Inoguchi's comment was made at the International Symposium and Lectures on "A Nuclear-Weapon-Free Zone in Northeast Asia and the Role of Japan," sponsored by *Asahi Shimbun*, Hiroshima City, and Hiroshima Peace Cultural Foundation, July 29, 1997, Hiroshima City.
7. For the process from making public the Interim report to adopting the new Guidelines, see the Research Institute for Peace and Security, pp. 60–66.

Bibliography

Asahi Shimbun, September 2, 1996.
Daily Yomiuri, November 30, 1997.
Guidelines for U.S.-Japan Defense Cooperation, September 23, 1997.
Huntington, Samuel P. *The Soldier and the State: The Theory and Politics of Civil-Military Relations*. Cambridge, MA: Harvard University Press, 1957.
Research Institute for Peace and Security (RIPS). *Asian Security, 1998–99*. Tokyo: RIPS, 1998.
Snyder, Glenn. "The Security Dilemma in Alliance Politics." *World Politics* 36 (July 1984): 461–95.
Taiyukai, ed. *Hachijunendai kiki no shinario to taio* [The scenario and response to crisis in the 1980s]. Tokyo: Taiyukai, 1980.
Tanaka, Akihiko. *Anzenhosho: Sengo gojyunen no mosaku* [National security: Search in the postwar 50 years]. Tokyo: Yomiuri Shimbun, 1997.
Taoka, Shunji. "Gaidorainnzu ni yottu no gimon" [Four questions on the Guidelines]. *Ronza*, September 10, 1997.
Tsuchiyama, Jitsuo. "Araiansu Direnma to Nihon no domei gaiko: Nichibei domei no owari?" [Alliance dilemma and Japan's alliance diplomacy: The end of the U.S.-Japan alliance]? *Leviathan* 13 (1993): 51–58.

5

The PRC-Japan Relationship

Heading for a Collision?

Akio Watanabe

Introduction

The possibility of a collision between the People's Republic of China (PRC) and Japan depends on a variety of factors. Foremost among these is China itself. Few observers would disagree that China is the single most important determinant of future international relations in the Asia-Pacific region in coming decades. What is more, both domestically and internationally, China's future is uncertain in many respects.

China's future course will be influenced by external factors, the most important of which are the attitudes and policies of Japan and the United States. Like any other actor in the international arena, China is not a self-contained entity. In fact, since at least the late 1970s, China has realized that it cannot afford to be self-contained any longer and it has sought a broader membership in the world community. Neo-liberal writers term this a world of "interdependence"[1]; others refer to it as a "globalized market." This global atmosphere requires more attention to the role that our own thinking about the future world order will play in determining China's future, rather than simply guessing about China's internal and external behavior as if it is an independent variable.

This chapter examines the relationship between China and Japan in the context of a robust alliance between the United States and Japan. This alliance is essential to a stable order in the Asia-Pacific region in the twenty-first century. The following discussion is divided into two parts. The first examines the area's more immediate problems, focusing primarily on China's reaction to the redefinition of the U.S.-Japanese alliance in recent years. The second part discusses various problems pertaining to relations among the United States, China, and Japan in the longer term, and considers Russia, albeit tangentially, in light of its increasing importance in Asian international relations.

China's Reaction to the Hashimoto-Clinton Initiative

The end of the Cold War and the collapse of the Soviet Union as a Communist regime greatly impacted the political alignments that have existed during the past several decades. The U.S.-Japanese relationship is no exception (Hogan 1992).

From the last years of the Bush administration to the early years of the Clinton administration, the relationship between the United States and Japan lost its sense of direction. Opinion polls in both countries showed a continuously worsening public image of each country by the other. As many as 61 percent of the respondents in the United States held a favorable image of Japan in an opinion poll taken in 1991, but American images of Japan began to deteriorate rather sharply since then. Japan's favorable rating dropped to 49 percent in 1993 and further to 34 percent in 1995. It was only in 1996 that Japan's image began to recover, albeit at a slow pace. A similar deteriorating trend was observed in the Japanese public image of America (Harris 1997).

This public opinion trend reflected the general direction of official relations between Washington and Tokyo, which had soured owing to deepening economic friction. The balance of trade between the two countries depicts their economic relationship. In 1992, the balance of trade favored Japan by $49.4 billion, and peaked in 1994 when the U.S. trade deficit with Japan reached $65.7 billion. Since then, it has declined little by little: to $59.4 billion in 1995 and $47.7 billion in 1996. In the meantime, the American economy was improving while Japan's suffered from severe cutbacks after the economic bubble burst. As a consequence of this shifting business trend in the two largest economies in the world, the American people found to their relief that Japan's economy was not the invincible enemy that once seemed to affect their national interest after the Soviet threat disappeared. As one American economist commented, "It is high time [to] leave off talking of 'Japanese threat, or Japan bashing'" (Alexander 1997).

Assisted by upward trends in business and the public mood in the United States, both sides of the Pacific Ocean undertook efforts to alleviate concerns about the poor state of affairs regarding their security policy in the Asia-Pacific region. Following the end of the Cold War, Japan and the United

States attempted to redefine their security partnership in the context of the emerging security environment in the region. These attempts produced such landmark efforts as the Higuchi Report (August 1994) on the Japanese side and the Nye Report (February 1995) on the American side.

The Japanese body politic showed signs of recovery from a lengthy period of political paralysis in January 1996 when Ryutaro Hashimoto, president of the Liberal Democratic Party (LDP), gained the premiership. In the meantime, the Clinton administration had to cope with three crises in East Asia. The first of these arose from North Korea's reported nuclear arms program in the spring and summer of 1994. The United States and North Korea averted a crisis by reaching an international agreement in March 1995 on the KEDO (Korean Energy Development Organization).[2]

The second tense situation involved U.S.-Japanese relations. This resulted from a rape committed by three U.S. servicemen stationed on Okinawa in September 1995, which led to the establishment of a Special Action Committee on Facilities and Areas in Okinawa to alleviate the physical and psychological burdens on the local population in Okinawa.

The third crisis, which involved the Taiwan Strait, resulted from China's military exercises in the Strait in March 1996. Contrary to China's intent, the exercises did not detract from Taiwan's democratic progression and were followed by the impressive success of the presidential election in Taiwan that July.

On top of all these developments, President Clinton and Prime Minister Hashimoto met in Tokyo in April 1996. The two leaders issued an important document, "The Japan-U.S. Joint Declaration on Security Alliance for the Twenty-first Century." The document states:

> The strong Alliance between Japan and the United States helped ensure peace and security in the Asia-Pacific region during the Cold War. Our Alliance continues to underlie the dynamic economic growth in this region. [And they agreed] that the future security and prosperity of both Japan and the United States are tied inextricably to the future of the Asia-Pacific region.

The declaration then explains the reason for the continuing alliance between the two nations as follows:

> For more than a year, the two governments conducted an intensive review of the evolving political and security environments of the Asia-Pacific region and of the various aspects of the Japan-U.S. security relationship. On the basis of this review, the Prime Minister and the President reaffirmed

their commitment to the profound common values that guide our national policies: the maintenance of freedom, the pursuit of democracy, and respect for human rights. They agreed that the foundations for our cooperation remain firm, and that this partnership will remain vital in the twenty-first century.

One of the declaration's salient points is its emphasis on the regional dimensions of U.S.-Japanese security cooperation. This theme has run through all other major agreements and official statements on Japan's defense and security policies thereafter. Most important among them are the New National Defense Program Outline (November 1995), the U.S.-Japan Acquisition and Cross-Servicing Agreement (June 1996), and the Review of the Guidelines for U.S.-Japan Defense Cooperation (June-October 1997) (Funabashi 1997; Sasaki 1997).

China reacted rather sharply to these new developments in security cooperation. Its negative attitude should be compared to its previously supportive position on the United States-Japan Security Treaty. Until recently, the Chinese tended to welcome Japan's security ties with the United States, regarding it as a constraint on a politically resurgent Japan. As long as the chief target of the treaty was Russia and not China, Beijing did not overly concern itself with the security arrangements. But now, fearing that it has replaced Russia as the focus of international attention, Beijing has begun to feel nervous about the U.S.-Japanese relationship.

Ostensibly, China objects to the enhancement of the U.S.-Japanese alliance on two grounds. First, China maintains that the concept of military alliance is anachronistic and should have disappeared with the Cold War. To support its position, China rather abruptly began advocating a multilateral security regime in the Asia-Pacific region, as evidenced by its diplomatic strategy—namely a strategy of diluting the U.S.-Japanese alliance with the ASEAN Regional Forum (ARF). In view of China's steadfast and tyrannical position on South China Sea disputes, however, it is difficult to believe that China is really serious about developing CBMs (confidence building measures) within the framework of the ARF.

Second, China argues that the United States-Japan Security Treaty was designed not to enhance regional security but was for Japan's own security alone. This argument, however, can hardly be supported by history given the role that U.S. Forces in Japan (USFJ) played in Korea and Vietnam during the Cold War. More candid remarks recently made by officials in Beijing reveal the real reason for their concern: They fear the deterrence function of the U.S.-Japanese treaty as it pertains to possible future crises in the Taiwan Strait or over control of the Spratly Islands.

While China characteristically criticizes America's "hegemonic" behavior in advancing these arguments, most of its comments on the Hashimoto–Clinton declaration focus on the expanded role of Japan in regional security. "The core of the core" of the matter is, as one Chinese commentator puts it, the ongoing review of the Guidelines for U.S.-Japan Defense Cooperation. Rather than viewing Japan as a "protectorate" of the United States, China now views Japan as an emerging active participant in regional security. Ultimately, China fears that Japan's increasing importance as a regional power will lead it down the path to nuclear armament—in fact, Japan has stockpiled sufficient uranium to produce a hundred atomic bombs.

Despite China's apparent official posture toward the strengthened U.S.-Japanese security relationship, careful analysis of Chinese public opinion leads to the conclusion that China is still internally divided on this subject and has not yet consolidated its position (Kojima 1996; Bernstein and Munro 1997). Chinese strategists, however, tend to regard the U.S.-Japanese alliance as a restraint on China rather than on Japan. The nature and degree of China's reaction to the U.S.-Japanese alliance will be determined by its implications for the disputes over Taiwan and, to a lesser extent, the South China Sea. But despite its concern over Japan's regional security role, China has remained silent about the implications of the review of the Guidelines for Korea. It is reasonably certain, however, that China would veto any United Nations Security Council proposal to send troops to the Korean peninsula. In that event, the United States and Japan would be obliged to defend South Korea and protect their interests within the framework of the U.S.-Japanese security arrangements, which incorporates Article 51 of the UN Charter (i.e., rights of collective defense).

China has to establish a strategic partnership between Beijing and Moscow to countercheck the U.S.-Japanese alliance, by making friendly gestures with regard to Russia's apprehension over the proposed extension of NATO. While Russia shares China's displeasure about the post-Cold War trend toward America's unipolar domination of international relations, Russia espouses a different position regarding security issues in the Far East. During his trip to Tokyo, the Russian Defense Minister spoke favorably of the closer security cooperation between the United States and Japan. A high-ranking officer of the Russian Far Eastern Fleet also opined that he did not object to the new guidelines for U.S.-Japanese defense cooperation. After the June 1997 Denver G7 summit, Hashimoto and Prime Minister Boris Yeltsin began to narrow the diplomatic gap between Tokyo and Moscow. The two leaders met again in Krasnojarsk in late October to discuss the establishment of a strategic partnership. As these developments show, China's prospects for playing a Russian card against Japan appear dim.

Other countries in the Asia-Pacific region, except for North Korea, have expressed support for the closer security relationship between the United States and Japan, despite the still-lingering suspicion about a remilitarized Japan in some quarters.[3]

Accordingly, China's only realistic option is to accommodate itself to the evolving security environments in the Asia Pacific region, with the U.S.-Japanese alliance as its linchpin. Determining China's place in international society, however, also requires a longer-term analysis.

China's Place in the Future International System in the Asia-Pacific Region

The general characteristics of the contemporary international system can be summarized as follows:

1. The trend is away from a tight bipolar system to a unipolar system, modified by a growing trend toward multilateralism.
2. There is more room for concerted diplomacy among the major powers in international politics, when compared to the tight bipolar situation of the past.
3. There is, however, a greater degree of unpredictability and uncertainty concerning military calculations by the major powers in crisis situations. This uncertainty will make crisis management more difficult, in comparison to the mutual assured destruction (MAD) situation in the Cold War era.

The following basic principles of international policy can be deduced from the above:

1. Efforts to encourage conditions conducive for concerted diplomacy among the major powers should be maintained, and if possible, enlarged.
2. Efforts to reduce and, if possible, eliminate conditions for inadvertent wars among major powers should be undertaken.

Enacting these principles will permit the development of diplomatic harmony among the major powers and accordingly improve the international security environment by containing regional conflicts between and within states. The success of the UN's peacekeeping and peace-building operations also depends on these conditions.

Next, let us consider application of the above framework to relations among the United States, Japan, and China in the twenty-first century.

Is Concerted Diplomacy for the Asia-Pacific Region Possible?

How well is China qualified as a constructive partner for a concerted diplomacy? In its favor, China places a high priority on economic goals. In addition, China possesses neither the urgent need to intervene militarily in external conflicts nor the capacity to do so. Finally, a minimum degree of convergence of interest exists between China and other would-be concert partners, such as the United States, Japan, and Russia, because none of them are interested in jeopardizing the generally benign international environment.

At the same time, however, China presents a number of unfavorable factors. China's policies regarding human rights and democracy are in ideological and cognitive dissonance with the two other major powers in the region. The ideological conflict with the United States is particularly important given the inevitable role of the United States as the leader of a new global concert of nations. As long as China continues to be perceived as undemocratic, it cannot be accepted as a partner in diplomacy in the eyes of the American public. China's political attempts to soften its position on human rights issues in connection with Jiang Zemin's visit to Washington have had only a minor impact in this regard (Manning 1997).

The image of the world that Chinese leaders hold also could pose a hindrance to effective diplomatic partnership. The Chinese understandably tend to view their modern history as a series of national humiliations inflicted by "modern imperial powers" (Japan included), while forgetting their own imperial past. If China aspires to a China-centered order in Asia, its anachronistic vision about the world order would be most disturbing to an emerging international system in the Asia Pacific (Kim 1994).

The partnership between Japan and the United States is and will be a most important pillar on which to build an enduring framework for regional cooperation. This bilateral relationship possesses both healthy and unhealthy traits. Most important among the healthy signs are the two countries' shared values and shared image of the future. Notwithstanding the oft-mentioned "Japanese uniqueness" with its negative as well as positive connotations, Japanese citizens are as committed to democratic values as are the citizens in North America and Western Europe. At the same time, it is true that Japanese ideas about the best approaches to human rights problems in Asia differ somewhat from those commonly held in America and Europe. For example, although the Japanese do not ignore the critical importance of individual civil and political rights that Western political and opinion leaders tend to emphasize, they also appreciate fellow Asian concerns with economic, social, and educational improvements of groups or the nation as a whole. This attitude does not, however, signify a Japanese tolerance for human rights violations by some authoritarian regimes in Asia and other developing nations (Watanabe 1997).

Japan and America also share a common vision of a new world order in that both are "status quo" powers, interested in upholding and strengthening the UN-centered system of international security and global governance. Some observers exaggerate elements of dissonance between the United States and Japan, pointing to Japan's growing inclination toward multilateral security mechanisms on both global and regional levels. To them, this movement signifies Japanese loss of confidence about the longevity of the American alliance. These observations, however, have no firm ground. No responsible Japanese leaders would dare to dismantle the time-honored alliance with the United States.

The continuation of a bilateral alliance between Japan and the United States and the existence of a regional multilateral security forum may seem contradictory, but in fact the two are interdependent. There are many tasks that must be pursued in order to ensure the robustness of the existing system of security cooperation between the United States and Japan. Most important among them are as follows:

1. Japan, in conjunction with the United States (and, it is hoped, a united democratic Korea in the near future), must assume the role of provider of public goods in the name of regional security.[4] Although Japan's defense still is, and will continue to be, the ultimate concern of Japanese security officials, Japan's pretended indifference to security issues in the region will not be tolerated as it had been in the Cold War years.

   The United States will continue to maintain security ties with Japan, in part because of their value as an indispensable device for the security of the region. Contrary to the views of some outside observers, Japan was not a free-rider of American security policy. The arrangement between the countries since the beginning of the Cold War, in which Japan provided bases and other facilities effectively and economically and the United States supplied armed forces with their worldwide capabilities, has proved to be an excellent division of resources. Essential elements of this formula will remain intact because the United States, which will still be the sole universally powerful military power in the decades to come, will need such supporting partners. The expected primary roles and missions of U.S. forces will include protection of more vulnerable portions of the globe, as well as defense of the host nations, and Japan will assume a greater role than merely a trustful and economical provider of bases and facilities. A new division of labor under which Japan takes an active defense role is clearly in order to prevent a not insignificant trend in the United States toward disengagement from international responsibilities after the Cold War.

2. The structure of the existing regional security mechanism places the United States at the hub of a wheel from which individual countries such as Japan, Australia, and Korea extend. It does not, however, connect the various U.S. partners with each other. This lack of collectivity is disadvantageous for fostering a sense of a security community within the Asia-Pacific region.

To make up for this default, such multilateral security fora as the governmental ASEAN Regional Forum (ARF) and the nongovernmental Council for Security Cooperation in the Asia Pacific (CSCAP) have been formed. In addition, a series of bilateral (and sometimes trilateral) security dialogues involving Japan are taking place more frequently in recent years than before.

Transparency and the setting of norms are the most important functions of these various forms of security dialogues. Renouncing the use of force as a means to solve international disputes has not yet become firmly established among the member countries of this region. The initiative among ASEAN countries to encourage this norm is highly commendable (Chalmers 1996).

Only when members of these regional fora come to share this perspective will they be able to foresee the birth of a true security community. To this end, an efficient device to deter possible defectors is absolutely necessary. The regional security mechanisms created in the past, almost without exception, were those for collective self-defense and did not differ essentially from alliances in the traditional sense. As John Ruggie explains, "The institutional difference between a bilateral alliance and a collective security mechanism can be simply put: in both instances, state A is pledged to come to the aid of B if B is attacked by C. In a collective-security system, however, A is also pledged to come to the aid of C if C is attack by B" (Ruggie 1993, 10). In other words, an essential requisite of a collective security system is its comprehensive membership.[5]

The North Atlantic Treaty Organization (NATO) will approach a truly collective security mechanism for all Europe if and when it includes not only Central and Eastern Europe but also the former Soviet Union. Its functional equivalent for the Asia-Pacific region would have to include at least four major partners: the United States, Japan, China, and Russia. The conditions for making this dream a reality currently do not exist, but if they did, the global scheme of the UN would also be already functioning adequately, reducing the need for an Asia-Pacific collective security system of the UN-type.

Conversely, if today's international conditions compel reliance on UN forces—which are an assembly of armed forces recruited from individual member countries—to cope with global security issues, the same conditions compel reliance on individual forces at the regional level. This is particularly true of Asian and Pacific nations because the region's three military powers (the United States, China, and Russia) and its two greatest economic powers (the United States and Japan) are destined to be involved in some sort of regional scheme. The United States will have to provide the core military forces to underwrite regional security with collaboration and support from its willing partners. Japan is one obvious candidate for this partnership; Australia is another. No other partners are to be excluded from joining this circle if they are willing to cooperate (Watanabe and Toshiya 1997).

Can We Avoid Crises in the Asia-Pacific Region?

Post-Cold War international relations are characterized by a greater degree of unpredictability and uncertainty concerning military calculations by the major powers in crisis situations. China will be the single most important variable in the military equation in coming decades, not because other nations necessarily believe that China is heading toward military superpower status, but because it needs to catch up militarily and economically with advanced nations. In other words, China is an unsettled, if not a revolutionary, power in international society. In this regard, the following items deserve special attention.

Nuclear Armament

The two Cold War superpowers had reached a sort of stalemate called MAD, which forced them to behave in an extremely cautious manner in the event of military crisis. No functional equivalent of MAD exists with regard to China's nuclear armament. A nuclear-free zone scheme may provide a good solution for ASEAN countries because they are not a likely target of nuclear attack by China, and for this reason, China supports the concept of an ASEAN nuclear-free zone.

Northeast Asia is a problematic area, however, because it comprises a number of states with competing nuclear ambitions. China is already armed with substantially powerful nuclear arsenals. North Korea is not yet completely cleared from lurking suspicions about its nuclear ambitions. Taiwan has ample reasons for going nuclear if it faces intimidation from its mainland cousin. Japan possesses the technological advancement to go nuclear, but lacks the political motivation to do so as long as it can rely on the extended

deterrence of American nuclear weapons. Russia is temporarily highly unlikely of using nuclear weapons, but its current state of disorganization might
result in the uncontrolled spill-out of nuclear materials and technology. Finally, the United States seems determined to pursue the long-term goal of a
nuclear-free world but still lacks a reliable strategy to cope with defectors in
the process of nuclear marginalization. It is impossible to construct a good
six-dimension equation that ensures nuclear stability in northeast Asia. It
seems certain, however, that the three nuclear powers—China, the United
States, and Russia (especially the first two)—have to take the initiative.

As noted above, the status of nuclear strategy in East Asia is unclear.
Given the many uncertain factors in the post-Cold War era, one of the essential roles of the United States is to uphold the alliance system if only to
prevent the East Asia situation from becoming more complex and uncontrol-
lable. Few issues in the history of nuclear policy have been more vexing than
the credibility of the nuclear guarantees at the heart of the alliance network.
The U.S.-Japanese alliance had not been undermined by this issue as NATO
had been during the Cold War. Utilizing the "three non-nuclear principles,"
Japan could afford to pretend innocence about nuclear deterrence. Ironically,
however, the nonproliferation treaty-related issues, including that of extended
deterrence, have become a real test for the viability of the U.S.-Japanese
alliance after the Cold War.

The implications of counterproliferation for China must also be taken into
consideration. Technically, China is not a target of counterproliferation strategy because it is already a declared nuclear power, whereas the purpose of
counterproliferation is to halt the emergence of a new nuclear state that is
fully equipped with nuclear arsenals. Nevertheless, China has responded rather
sharply to the suggested development of a theater missile defense (TMD) by
the United States and Japan, decrying the system as a violation of the anti-
ballistic missile (ABM) treaty, to which it is not a party (Mochizuki, 1997).
China also has criticized Japan, arguing that a country under the nuclear umbrella of another country is not entitled to criticize the nuclear policy of its
neighboring states. In a further attempt to justify its nuclear policy, China has
argued that because Japan in 1937 committed an atrocity in Nanjing that claimed
more than 300,000 Chinese lives, it deserved the atomic bombings of Hiroshima
and Nagasaki, which claimed a comparable number of Japanese lives.[6]

Would China then prefer to see Japan removed from the American nuclear
umbrella? Is it possible and desirable for Japan and China to establish a local
version of MAD of their own? What really is the merit of China's nuclear
strategy with respect to Japan? These are difficult questions, but it seems
certain that China is firmly committed to upgrading its nuclear arsenals, which
it regards as a status symbol of a great power.

The Problem of Nationhood

Unlike the former Soviet Union, today's China has neither the ambition nor the capability to intervene militarily in remote areas on the earth for its own political gain. In this regard, China is not an expansionist power. China, however, remains unsettled as a modern nation-state, and in this sense, is still a "developing" state.

Nonetheless, development need not take a form of lateral or territorial expansion. It is possible for the more than one billion Chinese people to form a community of discourse—one linguistic and cultural unit—while allowing multiple political authorities to develop and coexist within that community in the form of a confederation. In the first half of the twentieth century, the concept of "self-determination" functioned as an ideology of *decolonization*, encouraging emancipation of colonial peoples from imperial rule. It may well assume a new role in the next century by facilitating the devolution of power to local communities. Taiwan and Tibet provide possible cases in point. China is feared primarily because of its size, and if China can solve its internal problems by accepting a "United States of China," the psychological tension of its neighboring countries might be reduced.

Territorial Questions

The configuration of China also is unsettled with regard to its territorial boundaries, as its borders with Vietnam and several other ASEAN countries remain undefined. National boundaries are not determined by the divine but by politics, which is entirely human. As such, they are a product of political history and can be amenable to negotiated solutions. Territorial problems in the South China Sea are not, however, only the concern of the claimants or their proximate neighbors. Because of the public nature of the sea lane through the South China Sea, all regional members are seriously concerned not only with the outcomes of the disputes but also the means of their settlement. Failure to obtain a nonviolent solution would deal a fatal blow to the burgeoning confidence-building measures (CBM) regime of the ARF. The South China Sea problem constitutes a crucial test for the future of CBMs for Asia.

China's Place in the Region

There are a few promising signs that China is increasingly aware of its responsibility to create and uphold a regional security system. Its collaboration in the UN peacekeeping operations in Cambodia provides a good example. The Cambodian experience is, however, an isolated one. Dearth of experience prevents us from making any reliable predictions regarding China's role in future regional crises.

Unfortunately, most of the likely regional conflicts in Asia will involve China in one way or another because of its geopolitical position. But because "regional conflicts" generally denote only those armed conflicts to which none of the major powers are direct parties, and because China is a permanent member of the UN Security Council, such conflicts in the Asia Pacific involving China assume greater importance than mere regional conflicts. This has serious implications for regional security, for the "externality" of major powers is a prerequisite for their cooperation in regional conflict resolution. Only when major powers stay out of such conflicts can a multilateral scheme for peacekeeping/peacemaking, and peace building perform properly. This condition cannot be satisfied in most of the likely regional disputes to which China is a party, offering little hope for a genuinely regional solution to conflict in this part of the globe. Thus, a minimum degree of cooperation among the three major powers in the region is an essential prerequisite for crisis management in the area.

The notion of externality, as used here, holds a meaning similar to that assigned to it by economists and those political scientists of the public theory school. Great power behavior has unintended consequences or spillover effects because a great power is willingly or unwillingly factored into any equation of conflict. Likewise any reconciliation between major powers, intentionally or not, contributes to regional conflict resolution or stability. Therefore, minimum cooperation among great powers is a requisite to a stable, peaceful regional order. As China has yet to meet expectations for becoming a constructive actor in the above sense, its externality remains a source of anxiety rather than reassurance.

Conclusion

The following assumptions underlie the above discussion. First, the end of the Cold War has given rise to a new international situation with more room for concerted diplomacy among the major powers. Second, however, the new situation is accompanied by a greater degree of unpredictability and uncertainty concerning military calculations by the major powers in crisis situations.

China must be taken into serious consideration with regard to both of the above assumptions. It would make no sense to speak of concerted diplomacy in the Asia Pacific region without China, but China has not yet become a well-rounded partner for joint management of international problems on either a global or regional level. Whether China will become such an international actor depends on what emerges from the ongoing political, economic and social changes in China as well as on the ability of the international climate to accommodate China appropriately to its greatness. Outside forces can play a constructive, if subsidiary, role in China's adaptation, provided that China itself is seriously committed to that goal. This is the proper "constructive engagement" strategy for China.

Crisis management, however, is equally important. The possibility of "local" conflicts is remote in Asia, because most of the Asian nations have become sufficiently resilient, unlike many nations in Africa and elsewhere (perhaps except for Cambodia). In contrast, any crisis in the region would probably involve China as a deeply interested party because of China's very place in history and geography.

Given China's crucial importance in terms of both concerted diplomacy and crisis management, the nature of security problems in the Asia-Pacific region cannot be captured properly by the term "regional conflict." As the sole superpower in the post-Cold War era, the United States cannot disengage from this important task if it desires a leading role in shaping a new world order in the twenty-first century. Furthermore, the United States cannot perform this function without collaboration from willing partners, including Japan. Hence, the crucial importance of the continuation of a U.S.-Japanese alliance.

Notes

1. See, for example, Keohane 1989.
2. For an account of the crisis concerning North Korea's nuclear plan, see Kashiyama 1997.
3. For a Korean view, see Young-Sung Song, 1996.
4. For a similar view about Japan's security role, see Katzenstein, 1996.
5. Regional security arrangements are provided in Chapter VIII of the UN Charter, whereas the existing regional security arrangements (such as the NATO and the U.S.-Japan Security Treaty) are justified by the UN Charter's provisions for "individual and collective rights to self-defense" (Article 51).
6. This argument disturbed Japan, especially because it was advanced by the Chinese Ambassador to Geneva in his attempt to defend his country's policy of nuclear testing.

Bibliography

Alexander, A. "Nichi-bei eno teigen" [Advice to the U.S. and Japan]. *Nihon Keizai Shimbun*, April 16, 1997.
Bernstein, Richard, and Munro, Ross H. *The Coming Conflict with China*. New York: Alfred Knopf, 1997.
Chalmers, Malcolm. *Confidence-Building in South-East Asia*, Bradford Arms Register Studies, no.6. Boulder, CO: Westview Press, 1996.

Funabashi, Yoichi. *Domei hyoryu* [Alliance adrift]. *Asahi Shimbunsha*, 1997.

Harris, Louis, "A Warning from the Latest Public Opinion Poll." *Gaiko Forum*, no. 101 (January 1997): 65–68.

Hogan, J. Michael, ed. *The End of the Cold War: Its Meaning and Implications*. New York: Cambridge University Press, 1992.

Kashiyama, Yukio. "Beicho kosho no uchimaku" [An inside story of the U.S.-North Korea negotiation in 1994]. *Sankei Shinbun*, December 2–3, 1997.

Katzenstein, Peter, J. *Cultural Norms and National Security*. Ithaca, NY: Cornell University Press, 1996.

Keohane, Robert O. *International Institutions and State Power: Essays in International Relations Theory*. Boulder, CO, and London: Westview Press, 1989.

Kim, Samuel. "Chinese Perspectives on World Order." In David Jacobson, ed., *Old Nations, New World, Conceptions of World Order*. Boulder, CO: Westview Press, 1994: 37–74.

Kojima, Tomoyuki, "Nichibei anpo wo chushi suru Chugoku" [China carefully watches the review of the U.S.-Japanese security relationship]. *Toa*, no. 348 (June 1996): 49–66.

Manning, Robert. "Clinton-Jiang Summit: Toward a New Consensus on China?" Progressive Policy Institute, Policy Brief, October 1997.

Mochizuki, Mike M. *Toward a True Alliance: Restructuring U.S.-Japan Security Relations*. Washington, DC: Brookings Institution, 1997.

Ruggie, John Gerald, ed. *Multilateralism Matters: Theory and Practice of an Institutional Form*. New York: Columbia University Press, 1993.

Sasaki, Yoshitaka. "Beikoku wa naze saiteigi wo sitanoka" [Why has the United States determined to redefine its alliance with Japan?]. *Sekai*, no. 641 (October 1997): 98–116.

Song, Young-Sung, "Korean Concern on the New U.S.-Japan Security Agreement." *Korea and World Affairs*, XX-2 (Summer 1996): 197–218.

Watanabe, Akio. "Toward a Middle Path in Human Rights Policy." *Japan Review of International Affairs*, no. 2 (Summer 1997): 93–117.

Watanabe, Akio, and Hoshino, Toshiya. "Kokuren to ajia-taiheiyo no anzenhosho" [The United Nations and security in the Asia Pacific region—Between collective security and collective self-defense]. Nihon Kokusaimondai Kenkyujo (comp.), *Kokusai Seiji*, no. 114 (March 1997): 57–71.

6

The Regional Security Implications of China's Economic Expansion, Military Modernization, and the Rise of Nationalism

Douglas H. Paal

China is turning a qualitative corner in its historic quest for comprehensive power, achieving the traditional Chinese goal of "wealth and power" (*fu-qiang*). Long gone are the days when China was regarded as a basket case, inviting outside opportunistic intervention, as in the early part of the twentieth century. Gone too are the days when China's sheer size and systemic inefficiency gave it a relatively passive and dependent role in the "strategic triangle" of U.S.-Chinese-U.S.S.R. relations. Today China is poised to have an ever-larger say in the security system of East Asia in all its dimensions: political, economic and military. Yet in many ways the rapid maturation of China's capabilities has not yet been matched by development of a genuine intellectual appreciation throughout the Chinese leadership of the many membership dues, mutual obligations and rules of order that underpin the success of the Asia-Pacific region.

This is not to say there has been no progress in this dimension. China's kid-glove handling of Hong Kong ever since its reversion to Chinese rule, for example, shows that the leadership can adapt when the stakes are clearly high enough. Yet the repeated seizures of territory in the South China Sea from 1974 to 1995 serve as reminders that Beijing is also capable of proceeding according to another rule book of its own devising.

Modern Communist Chinese historiography has left a stirring nationalist legacy that, frankly speaking, borders on myth. It is a history of resentment against foreign insults, territorial seizures and repeated invasions, which, although true enough, tend to set Chinese thinking, particularly that of the powerful older generations, in a nineteenth-century mindset of *Realpolitik*. This historiography promulgated by Mao Zedong and his amanuensis, Hu Qiao-mu, ignores the sizable contribution foreigners made to China's traditional culture and modern economy and society. Foreigners for the most part created Shanghai, to take but one example. But the history books that will correct this bias toward xenophobia have not yet been published in China, and those who deal with the Chinese mainland must wrestle with these two sides of the Chinese personality.

Students of history and international relations, such as Donald Kagan and Joseph Nye, have written that ever since the era of the Greek city states, documented in Thucydides's *History of the Peloponnesian Wars*, rising powers have tended to destabilize the established international system as they seek to make the system serve their interests. Certainly, China appears to be everyone's favorite candidate for the rising power role in the early twenty-first century. Having witnessed the wasting struggles and huge human, cultural, and material losses incurred by the rise and fall of Germany, Japan, and Russia in the twentieth century, it is easy to conclude that the stakes are high in the case of China.

Naturally, the twentieth century has taught us lessons that may serve us well in attempting to avoid repeating the tragedies of that era. Better efforts to understand the intentions and fears of China, lest our actions provoke unexpected reactions, must be one such lesson. Another is to avoid stirring the resentments that result from applying double standards to the rising power and to current power holders. China's mytho-historiography suggests that these lessons are particularly important. They should inform the policymakers who must work with China and the Chinese themselves.

Thus, we confront simultaneously a need to make room for China's growing interests, to inculcate Chinese respect for our interests, and to provide for deterrence in the event our other efforts fail. Speaking at the broadest levels of generality about the region, it is fair to say that China's ascent is quietly but relentlessly forging a new entente among the states of Northeast Asia and Southeast Asia with the United States. In Northeast Asia, emblematically, Japan's government and public opinion have shifted over the past four years away from a pattern of deteriorating security relations with the United States toward strengthening ties, culminating in the April 1996 reaffirmation of the United States-Japan Mutual Security Treaty. Korea's reaction to the rise of China should be similar, but will require the more pressing immediate problems of the Korean peninsula to be resolved first. Together, the U.S., Japanese and Korean security elites are coming to the common conclusion that China is too big a challenge to be met by any one of the states, but that Beijing will treat their allied interests with greater respect.

In Southeast Asia, the nearly complete effort to draw all ten countries of the region into the Association of Southeast Asian Nations (ASEAN) reflects an implicit drive by the region's leaders to forge a multinational mass with sufficient common security interests to be taken seriously by the Chinese. ASEAN's subtle and complex strategy shuns confrontation with China and actively seeks many forms of cooperation. But history has taught this part of the region to opt for a quiet insurance policy with an outside power—today the United States—as a hedge against unwanted Chinese pressure on their interests. This strategy is further complicated by the history of outside powers, who tend not to get involved in Southeast Asia when times get tough, giving rise to a greater need for indirection and flexibility in Southeast Asian diplomacy.

Beijing's policy specialists may not unanimously agree, but I believe these broad trends in Northeast and Southeast Asia are generally positive and stabilizing developments. The emerging "blocs" are in the developmental stage of constructing a regional balance of power, which should permit these nations more self-confidently to nurture interdependency and patterns of cooperation that over time may reduce the saliency of the balance of power framework.

Before examining some of the positive implications of China's modern self-strengthening, it is important to note that Taiwan is today an outlier among these developing blocs. Even though some Japanese policy thinkers might wish to embrace Taiwan more closely, it seems clear that both Japan and Korea will shun Taiwan in their official security plans, as will the Southeast Asian states, to avoid overly provoking the mainland. Taiwan is thus likely to remain in a unique and equally complex security relationship with the United States.

Trends Toward Integration of China in the Region

In the areas of trade, finance, energy, investment, and arms sales as well as education and culture, Beijing has demonstrated evidence of moving toward a more cooperative and complementary behavior with its neighbors with each passing year. Although much is made in the United States of a bilateral trade deficit with China, I believe it is distorted, overstated and probably irrelevant. The trading pattern, more properly understood, demonstrates that in fact China is the fastest-growing export market for American producers. The rapid growth of China's exports as a share of its understated gross domestic product (GDP) indeed tells a fundamental truth about China's modern condition: that exports are vital to employ China's masses, to raise living standards, and so to preserve the regime. All other factors being equal, China needs good trade relations with its neighbors, although it is quite possible that Beijing is prepared to sacrifice trade ties with a few countries over specific issues as long as the bulk of global markets remain open to it.

In the area of finance, Beijing's international cooperation is in its infancy, but so far the indications for regional cooperation are good. China's movement to convertibility on the current account is a major first step toward overall convertibility of its currency, the *renminbi*. The developing story of China's internal banking troubles appears likely to retard this progress, as responsibility for state-owned enterprises is sorted out, state subsidies are reduced, and firms fail, in the process creating a tidal wave of nonperforming assets for China's banks. But the addition of Hong Kong's financial acumen to Beijing's arsenal and the growing skill of China's investors and the management of the People's Bank augur renewed cooperation over time. Beijing's commitment of $1 billion to the International Monetary Fund (IMF) rescue package for the Thai *baht* in August 1997 symbolized China's regional activism in this new arena. The U.S. Treasury chose not to participate in the package, sending a small, and I believe unintended, signal to the region of American disengagement.

Energy is another new area of interaction in the region that suggests growing Chinese interdependency. The visit of then-Russian Prime Minister Chernomyrdin to Beijing in July 1997 was the most prominent manifestation of this developing trend. After flirting unrealistically for years with strategies for energy autonomy and alternatives to the global energy market, China is now plunging actively into the international scene. China has become the largest investor in Kazakhstan's petroleum sector. Beijing has undertaken to construct natural gas pipelines from Russia to supply China and further export destinations. Russia and China will undertake construction of a hydroelectric grid in the Russian Far East. Beijing has been importing substantial amounts of petroleum since 1995. It is reasonable to assume that as regional gas and electricity grids exploit efficiencies of scale and develop in Northeast and Southeast Asia, China will be an ever more substantial participant.

The logic of the marketplace has similarly attracted Chinese investment into new ventures. Having accumulated ample foreign exchange to cover imports, China is now seeking to put its reserves to work. Investments as far-flung as transshipment facilities in Panama, the forests of Canada, and Southeast Asian telecommunications will give Beijing a greater incentive than before to maintain good relations with its investment partners and host governments. While a positive step toward integrating China with established interests, the Panama venture creates potential difficulties for Taiwan in its efforts to sustain diplomatic recognition by some countries targeted for mainland investment.

Until recently, China's arms sales abroad were a greater source of concern than reassurance. But as China has come to an apparent realization of its interests in a stable global petroleum market, Beijing has yielded over the past five years to a series of constraining agreements that appear to be on the verge of exhausting the long-standing U.S. agenda of proliferation worries. By signing international weapons and nuclear conventions,[1] agreeing to cooperate only in fully safeguarded nuclear facilities (significantly, in Pakistan), and restraining legitimate but unwise sales of nuclear reactors and uranium processing equipment to Iran, China needs to take but a few steps to shed its pariah image. These include: ceasing sales of C-802 cruise missiles to Iran, enacting agreed export-control legislation, and agreeing to abide by Annex II of the Missile Technology Control Regime (MTCR). This advanced stage of arms control cooperation has gone almost completely unnoticed by the news media.

Finally, in the "soft" areas of education and culture, China's expanding web of interaction is most notable in the West's universities and in the rising ranks of Chinese bureaucrats and managers educated there. The number of Chinese educated in Asia outside China remains relatively small, but tourism to China, and by Chinese to Asia, is on the rise, the latter from a small but significantly growing base. As long as Chinese universities continue to be saddled with insufficient resources, this trend to foreign education will be largely unstoppable, and judging from anecdotal evidence, a generally good thing.

By touching on these integrative factors in the rise of China, we should not delude ourselves. Europe on the eve of World War I was in many ways comparable to the prevailing situation in Asia today. Markets were growing then as the Americas opened to development, international travel and foreign direct investment reached unprecedented heights, and war seemed impossible to responsible observers as the general level of prosperity rose. Yet things went wrong then, and they can go wrong in Asia today.

If things are to go wrong in the region, they will occur in specific contexts over concrete issues. China's growing economic and military power and rising nationalism will intersect with the interests of the established order in the region in the six issue areas discussed below.

Conflict in the Korean Peninsula

The Korean peninsula remains everyone's favorite candidate for the most explosive situation in East Asia, as a failing, but heavily armed North and a successful, democratic South grind toward a common fate. It is certainly unclear how or when the two Koreas will resolve their tensions and reunify the two halves of the peninsula; at the same time, however, no one will benefit by concluding that reunification will take a long time and thus do nothing in the short term, lest it surprise everyone by occurring sooner.

The strategic issues that attend the notion of Korea's reunification are substantial. There is no regional multilateral security arrangement in place to support the transition. The prospects for reunification are hobbled by a hermetic North, whose people live in the dark about conditions in the South. Both Koreas are armed with a prickly nationalism unique to the peninsula. Without abundant resources to finance the reunification, and with neighboring states sometimes at odds with each other, the environment for Korean unity could hardly be more difficult.

China has a standing relationship with the Kim Jong Il regime in the North based on a former common ideology, a mostly former military alliance, and past economic complementarity. Today the status quo on the peninsula largely suits China's interests. The North Korean border with China remains in reasonably friendly hands, and not those of an ally of the potential rival, the United States. By aiding the North with food and fuel to stave off a disastrous collapse, the older generations of Chinese Communist leaders also forestall the embarrassing failure of another socialist regime, despite growing Chinese recognition that this is only buying time.

Shrewdly, Beijing began more than five years ago to nurture its longer-term interests and cultivate the rising power on the Korean peninsula, the Republic of Korea in Seoul, despite the discomfort and protests of officials in Pyongyang, North Korea's capital. Ties grew first economically, then diplomatically at the United Nations and then bilaterally, to the disadvantage of Taiwan. Relations today between Seoul and Beijing are robust enough to form a foundation for a dramatic shift in the status quo should the North undergo internal unrest or utter collapse. One of the few potential sources of mistrust under the stressful conditions of a transition on the peninsula will be Seoul's external security relations, including its alliance with the United States.

China's political investment in Seoul and its constructive role in resolving the nuclear weapons issue in the North and possibly the aftermath of the September 1996 submarine incident (in which a North Korean submarine infiltrated the South's waters and landed a group of commandos in the South) as well, have given it the expectation that Seoul will be solicitous of Chinese advice on sensitive security issues. In any event, China's sheer power and proximity demand serious attention to its views. By the same token, after eight tension-filled years, U.S. policymakers appear to have learned the need to consult to some degree with Beijing on issues of this magnitude. China's willing participation in the upcoming "four-party talks" with the Koreas and the United States exemplifies this trend, even if the talks prove unproductive.

Eventually, a reunified Korea will require some sort of international understanding or agreement to guarantee its territorial integrity after centuries of alienation, dismemberment, and reunification. China, Russia, Japan and the United States are the likely outside guarantors. Omission of any one could doom the process over time. Now is not too soon to begin thinking about the security requirements of a reunified Korea. I am confident China is already pondering these matters. The direction of China's thinking with respect to the peninsula has been a subject of considerable speculation, ranging from the worrisome to the reassuring. After several visits to Beijing, where I pursued these issues in depth with the relevant leaders and policy officials, I conclude that China will likely be a constructive force for stability during a transition to a unified Korean peninsula.

Beijing's leaders appear prepared to continue increasing humanitarian and energy assistance to the failing North Korean regime, although if their economy truly fails, only the North Koreans can save themselves through drastic reform. At what point Beijing will say "enough is enough" is unclear, and will probably remain the subject of some debate among the Chinese leadership. But for now, they appear to have reached a consensus that if there is a political crisis within the regime—say, between modernizers and conservatives—that threatens the survival of the North, Beijing will not intervene. At the same time, China is prepared to acknowledge Seoul's likely desire to continue its alliance with the United States, though it will not publicly endorse the alliance. It will even be prepared to accept some U.S. forces in the North, provided they are not aimed at China specifically. Beijing will be concerned, however, if the revised force structure that accompanies reunification appears to be aimed at China specifically.

Taiwan benefits from continued U.S. activity on the peninsula, which lends weight to American credibility in moments of tension between Washington and Beijing over Taipei. But if this secondary role of the U.S. presence is overplayed, Beijing can be expected to be more hesitant to acquiesce in arrangements to perpetuate the alliance. Washington, moreover, will grow weary of tensions if it believes they are sparked by incaution on Taiwan. Meanwhile, virtually all sides now recognize how unwise was the effort to ship Taiwan's nuclear waste to the North, where it would be unsafe at best, and politically provocative to South Korea and China at worst.

Russian Cooperation or Conflict

The relationship between Beijing and Moscow has mixed implications, tilting somewhat toward the positive side in the eyes of concerned outsiders. China's ambitious agenda of energy cooperation with Russia, already mentioned, offers some reassurance to its neighbors that the Chinese are learning to modify their highly traditional notions of autarky and sovereign independence. Interdependence is an emerging trend here.

Moscow and Beijing have also signed a comprehensive set of agreements demarcating all but a small, sensitive section of the Russo-Chinese border, and codifying arrangements to freeze or downsize military deployments there. Skeptics may point to the cautious wording of the agreements as an indication that the parties may want to reopen some territorial issues when the correlation of forces favors them later, but overall the trend here is also positive. The alternative to these agreements—roiling disputes with a weakened Russia in an area where central control is weak and resources rich—could well lead to a scramble for influence among China, Japan, Korea, and even the United States, with highly dangerous implications for regional stability.

Less positive is the perceived need of both Moscow and Beijing to present the appearance to the West of a "strategic partnership" that replaces their formal strategic rivalry, given their conflicting underlying motives. In the same bed, but dreaming different dreams, the Russians have used this formula to chastise the United States for pressing ahead with NATO enlargement, while Beijing also wanted to force Washington's attention *and* retard Moscow's own temptation to seek admission to NATO.

Also on the debit side of the ledger is Moscow's arms sales and technology relationship with Beijing's modernizing armed forces. After the collapse of the former Soviet Union, Russia found itself in the uncomfortable position of throwing its arms manufacturers out of work or allowing them to sell to, among others, Russia's former adversary—China. In the first few years of this new arms relationship, Moscow was too disorganized to impose discipline and restraints on the quantity and quality of arms transfers to Beijing. Since 1995, however, Russian diplomats have asserted that a review process in now in place that should keep the continuing arms sales relationship from destabilizing the situation among China's neighbors, including Russia. The outcome of this review process is not yet clear, but the price haggling for new Russian aircraft and ships that occurred during the Chernomyrdin visit suggests at least that the terms of trade are worsening for Beijing. The region's states will undoubtedly watch this arena carefully for its military implications. Here again, Taiwan is particularly disadvantaged as Russia has a bigger stake in China than across the Taiwan Strait. The new arms may find themselves opposite Taiwan's shores more often than not.

Japan

China's historically troubled relations with Japan were strained anew when the United States and Japan reaffirmed their military alliance in 1996. In a very real sense, these tensions were an accident of the diplomatic calendar. Updating the treaty became a priority largely in response to the uncertainties of U.S.-Japanese military cooperation in the event the Korean nuclear crisis of 1994 had worsened to the point of conflict. The reaffirmation of the treaty was scheduled to occur in late 1995, when President Clinton was to have visited Japan for the Asia-Pacific Economic Cooperation (APEC) leaders' summit, but it was postponed because of domestic political infighting that closed down the American government and kept Clinton in Washington. When it was rescheduled for April 1996, tension between Taiwan and China over Taiwan's presidential elections was not foreseen as a factor. Indeed, largely because of a series of missteps by all three capitals—Washington, Beijing and Taipei—the situation nearly careened out of control.

Whatever the specific origins of Beijing's renewed suspicions about Tokyo's intentions, the Chinese hammered Japan rhetorically for the following year, only relaxing this line in June 1997. Tensions subsided partly owing to the efforts of Japanese officials to explain that the guidelines for the renewed U.S.-Japan treaty did not explicitly involve planning for contingencies regarding Taiwan. Beijing may also have been affected by Japan's resumption of both its foreign assistance and its *yen* loan program to China, suspended since China's last round of nuclear weapons tests.

Although tensions abated, a sea change occurred in Japanese thinking about China. The romanticism that infused Japan's elites about China following normalization of relations in 1972 began to erode after the 1989 Tiananmen Square massacre. This erosion accelerated as China embarked on Deng Xiaoping's last wave of reforms in 1992, creating a competitior for Japan's treasured status as Asia's greatest economic power. Moreover, China had continued to acquire military capabilities that could cause the Japanese to reconsider their pacifist constitution, in the absence of a strong American military tie.

Japan today finds itself in a challenging position. It is reinforcing its American connection against possible negative Chinese trends, but is prepared to downsize it if tensions on the Korean peninsula are resolved. It aspires to a uniquely Japanese voice in Asian diplomacy, independent of America's, but it must reassure its neighbors that Japanese renewed activism will not become a threat. China will continuously test Japan with respect to its relations with Taiwan, forcing it to choose between a cooperative regional security environment (and good business), and stronger ties to Taiwan. As noted above, all things being equal, I have no doubt Tokyo will proceed with caution regarding Taiwan. Probably only in the event of unprovoked Chinese aggression against Taiwan—not now in the cards for a variety of reasons—will Tokyo debate changing its course.

Southeast Asian States

Chinese influence is growing in Southeast Asia in many dimensions. Partly this is by the design of the Southeast Asians, who are as a group genuinely attempting to stress interdependency and cooperation in all dimensions as an alternative to bloc politics, even as they implicitly form a bloc in ASEAN to hedge China's rise. Partly it is because China, in working its way out of post-Tiananmen isolation, organized a highly effective diplomatic campaign to woo its neighbors.

The two most important tests thus far of China's intentions toward the region were Beijing's behavior in Cambodia and in the Spratly Islands. An emerging test will be the character of China's relationship with Burma (now Myanmar). Chinese willingness to de-internationalize the conflict in Cambodia was demonstrated through the Paris Peace Conference, and led China to cut public links to the Khmer Rouge. When tensions rose within Cambodia again in mid-1997, China's restraint in response to appeals from Cambodia's Prince Ranariddh for support and its avoidance of contentious accusations that Vietnam was behind Hun Sen's takeover of the Cambodian government, despite appearances, was well received throughout the region. It is interesting to note that Beijing's price for its support of Hun Sen appears to have been to cut off Taiwan's influence in Cambodia, another negative among the trends for Taiwan.

The stormiest weather recently occurred over the 1995 discovery of Chinese on the Philippine-claimed Mischief Reef, in the Spratly Islands. In a departure from previous practice, the ASEAN states used their new ASEAN Regional Forum (ARF) as a venue to press Beijing to adhere to its previous pledge not to disturb the status quo in the area. The Chinese are still on the reef, and the ASEAN governments are watching the situation closely, yet they are also eager to note that China's behavior largely has been cooperative.

I believe that China's pursuit of diplomatic and economic success in Southeast Asia has long occupied one track in Beijing, and that territorial irredentism in the South China Sea has followed a separate military track. If so, the ASEAN riposte to Mischief Reef may have forced the Chinese leadership to reconcile these two tracks, even if only to be nice to ASEAN now and worry about regaining the islands later.

Given China's correct behavior regarding sensitive Southeast Asian issues, such as the role of the overseas Chinese, the effectiveness of the ARF, and the development of substantive ties between Taipei and other nations, the remaining incipient concern is with Burma's (Myanmar) relations with Beijing. ASEAN's leaders have differed for some time over the degree to which Rangoon deserves to be considered respectable company, but I believe they decided to override these qualms and admit Burma to ASEAN primarily to compete for influence there with China. There is a sense in several ASEAN capitals that China is conducting a subtle flanking maneuver around them by developing a stake in Burma so large that its leaders will not dare defy China's wishes, and that these might one day be adverse to ASEAN.

The United States

Having survived and partly recovered from their worst tensions over Taiwan in twenty-five years, China's relations with the United States now are slowly being mended. The tensions of 1996 prompted elements within the Clinton administration for the first time in four years to begin constructing and implementing priorities for the world's most prominent rising power. The managerial entropy of the administration—somewhat like herding cats—along with the unfortunate outbreak of anti-China fever in the media in late 1996 and the Senate "donorgate" hearings in 1997, combined to make the White House approach to China timid and tentative. Nevertheless, both sides are progressing slowly toward a more orderly policy, focused on summit meetings to drive the agendas of the two sides. This is a distinctly positive reversal in the trend lines, though its future remains uncertain.

Much depends on the course of China's leadership transition. With Zhu Rongji injecting his pragmatic, problem-solving approach into relations with the United States, those ties should develop positively overall. As the Tiananmen massacre recedes in memory, it will drive U.S. policy less, making room for cooperative undertakings. This impulse was on display in the generally positive exchange of state visits between Jiang Zemin and Bill Clinton in 1997 and 1998.

Yet much also depends on effective management of Washington's relations with Beijing. The American people tend to blow hot and cold toward China, and 1999 witnessed a very cold breeze, with the publication of espionage accusations against China by the Cox Commission, rejection of Premier Zhu's forthcoming bid to join the World Trade Organization by President Clinton, and the violent Chinese reaction to the U.S. bombing of Beijing's embassy in Belgrade.

Despite an apparent desire by leaders on both sides to improve relations, both have evidently found themselves constrained by worsening public attitudes toward each other's country. Ordinary Chinese have a long list of grievances against the United States, just as similar Americans harbor extensive doubts about China. Taiwan, despite a strong desire among the people to enjoy peace and prosperity, is equally driven by nationalist and independence forces to raise demands that strain U.S. and PRC efforts to make progress.

It will not be possible for either Washington or Beijing to dispel all their mutual suspicions given the nature of the process where a rising power confronts a dominant power. With clear policy purpose and steadfast implementation, however, both sides have the capacity to turn the process into a positive sum game. As generational change in China continues to soften the face of the regime, as cooperation on issues of proliferation and trade grows, and as China focuses on solving its huge problems through interdependency, the chances of catastrophic conflict should be reduced. But then, such a course of events would be only the second time in history an emerging great power would come to greatness without such a conflict. The first instance was when the United States supplanted Britain without a fight in the early twentieth century, but of course we Americans had the luxury of distance from troubling neighbors.

The Taiwan Question

What are the implications for Taiwan of China's emergence as a nationalistic economic and military power? As the above discussion suggests, Taiwan's freedom of maneuver appears to be under threat from Beijing in all of Asia's quadrants. Moreover, tensions with the United States and Taiwan in 1996 appear to have led to one clear conclusion in Beijing: that it must acquire greater military means to counter U.S. and Taiwanese capabilities in the region, should it find this necessary. Taiwan's extraordinary accomplishments in democratization and economic development have won it extensive praise, but the security implications of an increasingly powerful China occupy a higher priority among governments virtually everywhere.

Senior American officials are also quietly exasperated by the twin effects of provocative politics on Taiwan (sometimes carried out on American soil) and the lobbying to adjust U.S. policy toward Taiwan in ways that upset Beijing. Of course, the same American officials are often to blame for failing to set forth a China policy that holds the allegiance of Congress, and mistakes have been made in the treatment of Taiwan. Nevertheless, I believe the government in Taipei has learned that these tactics have imposed a cost on effective relations with Washington.

Taiwan's legitimate and extensive public debate about possible sovereign independence for the island has predictably stoked nationalist antipathy among the mainlanders, especially among the younger generation, who are technically more skilled and internationally more savvy than their elders. Whatever the domestic politics of the matter, it seems clear that the advantages of competing for diplomatic recognition have run their course. Taiwan's superb representatives run the risk of demeaning themselves in chasing after petite states. Moreover, the reversals continue to outnumber the victories. In the aftermath of last year's tensions, China has shown determination to score the big successes it did, for example, in South Africa and Cambodia.

In light of the growth of China's military, political and economic influence, Taiwan's security landscape is shifting in ways more profound than would be apparent by focusing only on the standoff between American aircraft carriers and Chinese missiles. Americans will defend Taiwan's liberties, in the event of an unprovoked attack, but the dividing line between "provoked" and "unprovoked" has become less clear and the protection less certain. The fundamental understanding between Washington and Taipei remains that Taiwan will enjoy security in exchange for refraining from disturbing the Asian security environment, while Washington contends with adjusting to China's presence.

In light of these changing circumstances, Taiwan would do well to play to its strengths. It should continue to invite the world to witness its successes. The energies and resources that are wasted, in my opinion, in diplomatic competition should be devoted to making Taiwan indispensable to the world's humanitarian agenda, such as in medical research, disaster relief, and economic and political modernization assistance. Taiwan's influence on the mainland, through investment, trade, and people-to-people exchanges, is considerable and should be bolstered, not diminished through acts that turn Chinese emotions against the island. Outright military competition is similarly a dead end. Taiwan must provide itself a reasonable capacity for self-defense through its relations with the United States and other countries, but at the present, a solely military path to resolving the issues between Taipei and Beijing plays to China's advantage over time.

Talk of independence without respect to obtaining China's agreement is unproductive and can be irresponsible, although the goal may someday prove feasible. By buying time, letting China focus on its internal development, and cultivating friends who are not asked to make a stark choice between the two capitals, Taiwan will respect the realities of its situation, reduce current tensions, head off new ones, and prepare the way for inevitable serious talks with Beijing.

China is showing a capacity for growth out of its resentment-filled nineteenth-century mindset. The regional powers are organizing to encourage it while preparing for the alternative. Leaders in Taipei should join in the effort.

Note

1. Beijing has signed the Nuclear Nonproliferation Treaty (NPT) and the Comprehensive Test Ban Treaty (CTB); has agreed to abide by Annex I of the Missile Technology Control Regime (MTCR); has joined the Chemical Weapons Convention (CWC); and has agreed to participate in the Zangger Committee of the International Atomic Energy Administration (IAEA) to control sensitive nuclear-related exports.

7

The Challenge of the Hong Kong Transition

Its Implications for Asian Security

Byron S.J. Weng

In the context of Asia-Pacific regional security, the 1997 Hong Kong transition to Chinese rule raises at least three sets of questions:

1. What is the international status of the Hong Kong Special Administrative Region (HKSAR)? What roles can it play? How will other countries in the region receive and regard it?
2. Will Hong Kong's return to China lead to the development of a Greater China? Will it affect Beijing's worldview? Is the perception of a China threat among its neighbors, if any, likely to increase or decrease?
3. What impact will the Hong Kong transition have on the development of the Asia-Pacific region? Will it bring faster and healthier economic growth? Will it significantly alter the balance of power or affect the peace and stability of the region in any way?

Not all these questions can be answered at this time. In this preliminary analysis, they will be discussed briefly under three headings: the creation of the HKSAR, the Greater China implications, and the impact on Asia-Pacific peace and security.

The Creation of the HKSAR

The creation of the HKSAR under China's "one country, two systems" policy challenges the existing concepts and theories on constitutional and international law (Weng 1985b; Weng and Chang Hsin 1994). The HKSAR amounts to a new type of local territorial unit with a unique governmental system that is different from China's provinces, autonomous regions, or centrally directed municipalities. It also differs from the Swiss canton, the German or American federal state, the Commonwealth of Puerto Rico, the Canadian province, or any other existing variant of autonomous local government known to us. Consequently, scholars of constitutional law may have to amend their relevant theories and concepts to accommodate this new type of government, while administrators may be called upon to deal with a new set of policies and laws.

In international law as well, the "one country, two systems" notion is an innovation. As espoused by Deng Xiaoping and his followers, it is a formula, hitherto unknown and untried in international relations, for resolving questions of national unification. Thus conceived, the Special Administrative Region (SAR) is effectively a quasi-state, an international personality that enjoys a status higher, and autonomous rights more substantial, than a colony or one of the American states. Though China unilaterally decides whether to consider a governmental entity an SAR, other countries are expected to follow its lead when addressing such matters as passports, visas, customs, judicial cooperation, membership in international organizations, and so on.

Two Hong Kong scholars have addressed the question of the HKSAR's international status. Roda Mushkat defines a territory as autonomous and self-governing when it possesses governmental powers comprising a locally elected legislative body capable of independent decision making on local matters, excluding matters of foreign relations and defense, a locally chosen chief executive with powers of administration and execution, and an independent local judiciary (Mushkat 1987; Hannum and Lillich 1981). Under these criteria, the British colony of Hong Kong was not autonomous because (1) its governor was not locally elected and (2) the election of the Legislative Council (Legco) members did not begin until 1991 and it only encompassed a portion of the membership. Mushkat expresses doubts about the future SAR legislature's independent law-making capability and the true autonomy of the chief executive under the Basic Law, the "mini-constitution" for the HKSAR. She sees some shadows over the future judiciary despite the many provisions that seem to suggest judicial independence, and she concludes that complex factors other than formal international legal agreements will affect Hong Kong's future, including its international status.

In contrast, James Tang appears more optimistic (Tang 1993). Tang approaches the issue through an examination of the concepts of sovereignty and state, using a theoretical model based on Robert H. Jackson's ideas of negative and positive sovereignty and quasi-states (Jackson 1990). Political entities are said to possess negative sovereignty "when the international society has conferred upon them a formal-legal entitlement for constitutional independence and freedom from outside interference." They are said to have positive sovereignty when their governments "can provide political goods for their citizens and are capable of collaborating with other governments in international arrangements and reciprocating in international commerce and finance." The former refers to a formal condition, whereas the latter refers to a substantive condition. Jackson uses the term "quasi-states" to denote those entities that possess no negative sovereignty. Using these criteria, Tang finds the future Hong Kong worthy of quasi-state status.

There is merit in both Mushkat's assessment and Tang's interpretation of the future HKSAR's international status. Mushkat is sound in judging reality: The future HKSAR can be truly autonomous only to the extent that Beijing permits. Staking all the expectations of the Hong Kong people and the other international players on the Sino-British Joint Declaration on the Question of Hong Kong (1984) and the Basic Law will undoubtedly be problematic. Even so, Tang's interpretation is at least technically correct, and until Beijing decides to do away with the autonomous arrangement, the HKSAR may prove to be unique and substantial as an autonomous entity. If matters are stretched somewhat, one may even venture that, to the extent the international recognition of its quasi-state status is routinized, the HKSAR also enjoys negative sovereignty of a sort.

If the "one country, two systems" formula remains intact, the HKSAR's autonomy is considerable. By the provisions of the Basic Law, the HKSAR issues its own currency and passports. It maintains a separate customs area. It may, "using the name 'Hong Kong, China,' maintain and develop relations on its own and conclude and implement agreements with foreign states and regions and relevant international organizations in the appropriate fields, including the economic, trade, financial and monetary, shipping, communications, tourism, cultural, and sports fields" (Basic Law, Article 151). Indeed, Hong Kong enjoys a high degree of international recognition. It is already a member of the World Trade Organization (WTO) and most of the international organizations in the United Nations family, and will qualify for membership in many others. In addition, the United States-Hong Kong Policy Act of 1992 accords the HKSAR a very special status and grants it significant rights. It is not wrong to say Hong Kong's formal authority to conduct its external economic, cultural and social relations, and to take part in regional affairs in its own right is unmatched by other substate entities.

Nonetheless, the HKSAR plays little or no significant role in the military or security sphere. The only possible exception is a secondary role in the

Asia-Pacific Economic Cooperation group (APEC), if and when APEC begins to function as a multilateral forum on security affairs. Because it is essentially an economic entity, the HKSAR by itself is not likely to become a threat to anyone. Although it is a member of APEC and the Asian Development Bank (ADB) within the Asia-Pacific region, it has not been and probably never will be a party to the ASEAN Regional Forum (ARF). Nor is it likely to be an active participant in track-two dialogue in the Council for Security Cooperation in the Asia-Pacific (CSCAP) or other similar fora. The HKSAR will still be a market for arms sales and technology transfer, an operational stop for arms smuggling, a port for supply replenishment and personnel resting and recreation of naval forces, but it will lack any independent and significant military authority.

In the past, the British government did not allow the colony to be used as a major naval port. Under Chinese rule, the same will be true. Hong Kong's role as an economic gateway and a free and open port is not compatible with military use. For one thing, the navy would find the merchant ship and civil aviation traffic too hazardous. Nor would the necessity of conforming the civilian sector to the requirements of a major navy port likely be "good for business."

What the HKSAR can be is a growth catalyst for many of its southern neighbors. Hong Kong's own economic and strategic position is and will remain important to the countries of the Asia-Pacific community. Many have benefitted and will continue to benefit from making the most of what this "pearl of the Orient" has to offer. More so than its many competitors, Hong Kong is, among other things, a free entrepôt port, an open market for trade and investment, a source of capital, technology, and managerial know-how, a financial and business center, a communication and transportation hub, and a diplomatic arena and intelligence gathering place. It is a favored corporate regional headquarters. It has served and may continue to serve as a bridge, a buffer zone, an intermediary, and even a mediator among peoples, corporations, and nations.

The HKSAR's ultimate fate, however, is closely tied to mainland China. Few can afford to belittle Hong Kong and place the China market in jeopardy or risk China's wrath. At the same time, the HKSAR's powers will derive mainly from Beijing's authorization. In the short run, Beijing will probably prove capable of making the "one country, two systems" policy work to ensure Hong Kong's stability and prosperity. Further down the road, though, Beijing may run into problems.

In a sense, the regime in Beijing is steering a ship in the capitalist sea with little knowledge of the waters. As China ventures further, there is a possibility that President Jiang Zemin and company may find themselves over their heads. China and Hong Kong may confront pressure to equalize living standards; to confront mainlander demands for freedoms and privileges enjoyed by HKSAR residents; face constant friction between mainlanders and bona fide Hong Kong residents in the HKSAR; and deal with potential emigration of disillusioned Hong Kong professionals, foreign "interference" in questions of human rights in Hong Kong, and so on. China certainly will be judged by the way it resolves these conflicts. In the long run, Hong Kong's future will depend, above all else, on its utility to China and China's own economic and political development. The efforts of Hong Kong's people will be secondary in importance, as the composition of the Hong Kong population will be subject to Beijing's manipulation through border control and other policies.

The "one country, two systems" policy is not a panacea for these problems. In fact, in Beijing's plan, it is a transitory device—that is, the HKSAR will be absorbed into the main body of the Chinese system after a certain period. Moreover, Beijing is interested more in the stability and prosperity of the HKSAR as a Chinese territory than in the autonomy or freedom of the Hong Kong people. Of course, the question of stability and prosperity depends on whether the territory will remain open and free. Without the supervision of a democratic Chinese parliament in the background, the SAR must itself become democratic to ensure this continued freedom. Unfortunately, this need is not incorporated into any known Beijing plan for Hong Kong. The Basic Law permits at best an executive-led, semi-democratic government system. The conditions for an open and free society, such as freedom of the press and the effective rule of law, are likely to suffer under any Socialist or Communist regime in Beijing. Thus, there is little ground for optimism unless China becomes much more open, democratic and free than today (Weng 1995).

Chances are that China will remain a socialist country for decades to come. China is the most prominent remaining Socialist-Communist state, and to true believers it is now the great hope of a Communist future. In due course, China will probably offer another ideological thesis and another set of political and economic doctrines. If the present trend of relative Western decline continues in economic and moral terms, the future of socialism may well improve, permitting China to guide many followers down a separate road in the coming decades.

The Greater China Implications

The reacquisition of Hong Kong probably will not lead to the development of a Greater China, if that term means a centrally controlled future superpower that includes the mainland, Hong Kong, and Taiwan. It may help boost China's economic, political, and military prowess. It may, with luck, help Beijing navigate the capitalist sea better and thereby indirectly affect the latter's worldview. It may even lead to the formation of a southern China economic community that includes Guangdong, Fujian, Hong Kong, and Taiwan. But the concept of a wholly integrated Greater China is too far-fetched and uncertain. China's relationship with Taiwan provides some insight into the prospects for integration. After the Taiwan Strait crisis of 1996, a political Greater China has become rather hard to imagine. Even the idea of an economic or ethnic/cultural Greater China is seriously challenged in Taiwan these days, as the Taiwanese people forge their own identities.

Hong Kong's importance to China is a point much too obvious to belabor. During the early Cold War period, during the era of containment, Hong Kong was virtually China's only opening to the Western world. Before Deng Xiaoping's open door policy, Hong Kong was earning 60 percent or more of China's foreign exchange needs. Politically, the British administration in Hong Kong provided a much needed place of convenience, linking China to the Western world. After 1978, Hong Kong became the largest foreign investor in China, contributing some $80.547 billion, or 60.39 percent of all foreign investments, between 1979 and 1995 (MAC 1996). Today, Hong Kong is the major entrepôt port for China's foreign trade, a financial center for *renminbi (yuan)* support, a principal source of commercial intelligence, a gateway for Chinese investment abroad, a training ground for needed personnel modernization, and so on. In addition, it will serve as a base for promoting "the three links" and other united-front work with regard to Taiwan.

It was Hong Kong's practical utility that made Mao Zedong and Zhou Enlai decide that instead of recovering Hong Kong early, the better policy was *"changqi dasuan, congfen liyong"* (take a long-term view and make full use) (Lee 1994). In fact, Deng's "one country, two systems" policy was actually a kind of admission that China would benefit most by maintaining a hands-off policy toward Hong Kong. Nonetheless, "the pearl of the Orient" has been something other than beautiful in the eyes of leftist Chinese leaders. During the Cultural Revolution, Gang of Four member Wang Hongwen encouraged the Red Guards to stir up unrest in Hong Kong and labeled it a remaining symbol of China's shame. Then minister of defense Lin Biao reportedly stated that *"xianggang buxiang"* (the fragrant harbor—the literal translation of Hong Kong's name—is not fragrant). In the Anti-Spiritual Pollution Campaign of 1983 and the Anti-Bourgeois Liberalization Campaign of 1987, Hong Kong was cited as the most prominent embodiment of the bad and the undesirable (Weng 1985a).

Whether Hong Kong is beautiful or ugly, the distinction seems to arise

Table 7.1

Selected Economic Powers, February 1997, Ranked by GNP

Countries	GNP ($ millions)	Population (millions)	Per Capita GNP ($)
United States	7,088,906	266.3	26,620
Japan	4,568,427	125.8	36,315
Germany	2,057,153	82.6	24,905
France	1,517,982	58.7	25,860
Britain	1,101,680	58.6	18,800
Italy	1,087,730	57.4	18,950
China, Hong Kong, Macau, and Taiwan	1,085,138	1,254.1	865
China, Hong Kong, Macau	818,987	1,232.4	665
China, Hong Kong	810,250	1,231.9	658
China	661,770	1,225.5	540
Canada	567,000	30.0	18,900
South Korea	453,420	45.0	10,076
Taiwan	266,151	21.7	12,265
Hong Kong	148,480	6.4	23,200
Singapore	81,840	3.1	26,400
Macau	8,738	0.5	17,475

Source: Asiaweek, February 21, 1997, p. 55

between the capitalist roaders who speak of the primacy of economics and the Socialist-Communist die-hards who cannot separate economics from politics. The former see nothing but goodness in Hong Kong, whereas the latter can see only evil and trouble. In the final analysis, Deng embodied both avenues at the same time. He was lenient and progressive in economic matters about which he knew relatively little, but rather conservative and tough in political affairs, where he was as shrewd as anyone.

With the addition of Hong Kong, China's international stature will become even more formidable, possibly taking China one step closer to becoming a superpower. Tiny Hong Kong, however, may prove a tough bundle to swallow. The problems of incorporating a free and open capitalist society like Hong Kong into a controlled and still half-closed Socialist-Communist China may well be much more complicated than Beijing understands, Deng's ingenious "one country, two systems" policy notwithstanding.

Gauging the impact of the Hong Kong acquisition also is a difficult matter. It is a simple exercise to add the GNP, trade statistics, foreign reserves, and other economic indicators of mainland China and Hong Kong and then to compare the sums with those of other major powers. The results can be variously interpreted (Tables 7.1 and 7.2). According to the economic view-

Table 7.2

Selected Economic Powers, February 1997, Ranked by GDP (PPP*)

Countries	GDP (PPP*) ($ millions)	Population (millions)	Per capita GDP (PPP*) ($)	Reserves ($ billions) (excluding gold)
United States	7,143,498	266.3	26,825	64.5
China, Hong Kong, Macau, and Taiwan	4,068,374	1,254.1	3,252	254.5
China, Hong Kong, Macau	3,758,172	1,232.4	3,049	166.5
China, Hong Kong	3,749,752	1,231.9	3,044	164.5
China	3,596,843	1,225.5	2,935	100.9
Japan	2,792,760	125.8	22,200	215.9
Germany	1,665,629	82.6	20,165	86.4
France	1,217,438	58.7	20,740	26.9
Italy	1,129,058	57.4	19,670	48.2
Britain	1,121,018	58.6	19,130	37.8
Canada	666,000	30.0	22,220	20.0
South Korea	528,750	45.0	11,750	31.0
Taiwan	310,202	21.7	14,295	88.0
Hong Kong	152,909	6.4	23,892	63.6
Singapore	73,052	3.1	23,565	74.2
Macau	8,420	0.5	16,840	2.0

Source: Asiaweek, February 21, 1997, p. 55.
*PPP = purchasing power parity.

point, China immediately became a larger economic entity with the addition of Hong Kong from both a quantitative and a qualitative standpoint, experiencing a 27 percent increase in its GNP. With the addition of the capital assets, the managerial know-how, and the marketing network of Hong Kong, this greater China has been described as a "tiger with wings" *(ruhu tianyi)* (Shao 1997). Nonetheless, the addition of Hong Kong has not transformed China into an economic giant. Although the Hong Kong addition is significant in relative terms, the resultant overall economic capacity still falls far short of the envisioned Greater China. As of the mid-1990s, serious assessments generally still describe China as an effective regional power with the potential for global superpower status. The addition of Hong Kong is not likely to change this assessment in the short term.

It is important to note that suffering foreign humiliation is much more difficult for China, a nation with an ancient, innately developed culture, than for a country that borrows liberally from others (such as Japan). Notwithstanding the opinion of some neighboring countries, China's imperialism has been more cultural, rather than territorial or economic, in the European or prewar Japanese tradition. Throughout its history, China has been more successful as a self-centered cultural imperialist, satisfied that rulers of lesser countries pay tribute to it. From the time of the Chin unification in the second century B.C. to the mid-nineteenth century, China was a middle kingdom unto itself (Fairbank 1968). Dynasty after dynasty, China's literati have claimed cultural superiority in their known world, a Sinic world. Thus, although China has expanded its territory at the expense of its smaller neighbors, such expansions usually, if not always, were justified in terms of cultural superiority.

Ever since the Opium War of 1839 to 1842, however, Western challenges have not only humbled the celestial dynasty but also ushered in modern and different ways. For a century, China struggled with itself, agonizing over the *ti-yong* question (whether to Westernize completely) without a clear and final answer. To a patriotic Chinese historian, the century spanning 1840 to 1940 was primarily an elegy, a symphony of humiliation and a tragedy for the Chinese people. The following half century has been one of revolution and prolonged struggle for national salvation *(geming jiuguo)*. It is not difficult to understand why many thinking Chinese would ask: "Having suffered more than a century of national humiliation and having endured another half century of revolutionary convulsions, will China finally become a truly strong world power? Will it become a 'normal' and respected nation in the next century? Will China finally carry out true national reforms and realize national prosperity *(gaige xingguo)*?" (Wang 1996). Again, one should not lose sight of the possibility that a strengthened and invigorated China may become a glory seeker and turn expansionist. For the time being, however, Beijing leaders have had to focus on becoming strong again and regaining wide respectability in the first place.

During the latter half of the twentieth century, China's international status has changed drastically, particularly since the Deng Xiaoping reforms. By virtue of its population, territory, history and culture, economic viability, governmental effectiveness, and potential overall capabilities, China has become a country that deserves respect. In fact, current propaganda from China wants the world to bear this in mind.

As much as other global powers, Beijing is concerned with China's national interests and its international role in shaping the post-Cold War order. In a nutshell, Beijing under Deng and Jiang has developed a view of a constantly changing world in which nations grow stronger or weaker. In the post-Cold War period, the central international contest has shifted from one of ideology and arms races to one of economic security and strength. Correspondingly, the main theme of international order has changed from war, alliance, and détente to peace, trade, and development. Accordingly, instead of military pacts, nations have busied themselves with organizations for regional economic integration such as the European Union, the North American Free Trade Area, and the forum for Asia-Pacific Economic Cooperation.

All nations vie for a desirable place in the world arena using their comprehensive national power. Comprehensive national power includes all elements of power, such as economics, history, sovereignty, national identity, and military strength. In Beijing's view, at least for now, enhancing China's national position urgently requires reform and economic growth. On January 16, 1980, when Deng elaborated on China's three main tasks for the 1980s, he already had all this in mind. He spoke then of anti-hegemonism in foreign policy, unification with Taiwan, and the four modernizations, and stressed that economic construction would lie at the core of it all (Deng 1983). The accomplishment of these three tasks will truly enhance China's security and other interests.

Throughout the entire Deng era, China's foreign policy stance was to be *duli zizhu* (independent)—that is, not dependent on or aligned with anyone—and to oppose hegemonism. Its obvious diplomatic objectives today are national modernization and national unification, which require a stable and peaceful environment. Therefore, the Deng regime constantly emphasized political stability, both domestically and internationally.

At a luncheon talk at the Forum on the Prospects for the Twenty-first Century on September 4, 1996, Hu Sheng, President of the Chinese Academy of Social Science, had this to say:

> Will China be a stable and positive power in Asia and the world in the twenty-first century? The answer is affirmative . . . [China can] promote the world's peace and development by doing at least two things: one, to provide for a reasonably good living for the people who make up one-fifth of the world's population; and two, to have the necessary defense force so that no power in the world will commit pillage or aggression against her. (Hu 1996)

At the end of the Deng era, however, something different seems to have caught the world's attention. As new waves of nationalism are rolling over China, some Chinese individuals are displaying an attitude that worries outsiders. At the center of their concern is the controversy over "the China threat" thesis, which has appeared frequently in the Japanese and Western press as well as in semi-academic articles during the past few years. The "China threat" posits that an awakened China poses a looming new threat or "new yellow peril," necessitating an international containment of China. The much-discussed book, *The Coming War with China*, by Richard Bernstein and Ross Munro, constitutes the latest example (Bernstein and Munro 1997), and Samuel Huntington's theory of a coming "clash" between Chinese and Western civilizations might have contributed to this thesis (Huntington 1993).

China has interpreted the "China threat" thesis as an international conspiracy to prevent or delay China's emergence in the world arena. Notwithstanding the Clinton administration's "comprehensive engagement" policy, China views many of Washington's moves as part of that conspiracy. That this is so is amply manifested in the many books published in China during the past few years, with nationalistic titles such as *China Can Say No*. Beijing's many rebuttals and counterattacks to the United States have produced an image of a defiant and intransigent China (Weng 1996). The debate over how to deal with China remains unsettled. Some Western observers who believe China is a putative superpower concur with Hu that China will be a peaceful force in Asia for some time to come, although their reasons are not necessarily the same. For instance, after considering pertinent scenarios, Paul Monk concluded on the basis of an "incompleteness theorem" that "China will have strong inducements to be other than a globally aggressive or threatening Titan" (Monk 1995). Andrew Nathan and Robert Ross also espouse a similar view (Nathan and Ross 1997).

Although Beijing may have accepted the concept of the modern sovereign state, it is by no means free from the belief systems of the middle kingdom. It has tended to assert its own peculiar, if not erroneous views, regarding such established concepts as sovereignty, domestic jurisdiction, democracy, and human rights. For example, during trade discussions with the United States, Beijing has countered the threat of most-favored nation (MFN) status withdrawal and Clause 301 punishment with its own threats of retaliation, forcing Washington to back down time and time again. When answering accusations of arms sales to terrorist countries, Beijing has responded by citing evidence of dubious American arms sales. In defending its position on human rights, Beijing has rejected the existing Western definition on the grounds of cultural relativism and has taken pains to detail many of America's own shortcomings, especially blatant human rights violations (*Renmin Ribao*, March 5, 1997).

China's heterodox ideas pose considerable difficulties for the international community. Its advancement of the idea that, for developing nations, human rights can only be defined as the right of collective survival and development runs counter to the very idea of human rights (State Council Information Office 1991). Even the unilateral introduction of the innovative and clever "one country, two systems" scheme is highly unorthodox and places considerable demands for adjustment on other members of the international system (Weng 1985b). China's self-serving claim that Hong Kong and Macau were simply and wholly Chinese, rather than "non-self-governing territories," was presumptuous and arbitrary.[1] In the process of recovering sovereignty over Hong Kong, Beijing had taken a firm stand and demanded that Britain avoid imposing its values on China, declaring that the days of colonial-imperial bullying were no more. These are but examples that come to mind. If China insists that other countries conform to these values, it cannot reasonably demand that they refrain from doing the same.

Hong Kong's effect on China's international status remains to be seen. If the crux of the matter is China's view of the world, then Hong Kong may have a beneficial effect, possibly helping to ameliorate the intransigence of Beijing. First, China now has a stake of honor and prestige in successfully maintaining the stability and prosperity of the HKSAR. Second, Beijing wants to ensure that the "one country, two systems" model turns out favorably for Hong Kong and that Taiwan will take note. Third, Beijing needs Hong Kong to serve as the locomotive of growth in the mainland for many more years to come. For these reasons, Beijing will have to behave somewhat more "normally" and "reasonably" in the eyes of both the Hong Kong people and the world.

If Hong Kong successfully cultivates its influence on China, then China's enhanced international role may not be as threatening in the short run as some have feared. In his time, Deng Xiaoping regarded China's national interests as national security, national modernization, national unification, and national prestige, more or less in that order. This has not changed with the Jiang Zemin regime. The notion of security encompasses more than territorial protection; it also includes economic security and the preservation and advancement of China's core culture (Shambaugh 1994). Modernization will lead to national power and a better livelihood for China's population. Unification refers mainly to Taiwan and secondarily to Hong Kong and Macau; it may also refer to such autonomous regions as Xinjiang and Tibet. Prestige enables China to shed national shame completely and become a leading nation of strength and honor. Taking back Hong Kong must provide China with real satisfaction in this context.

Whether China will remain peace-oriented in the long run remains to be seen. The resurgence of nationalism in recent years will probably recur now and then. Beijing also understands that nationalistic flare-ups can lead to anti-Beijing sentiment and problems in the autonomous regions and in Taiwan. The fear of reduced prestige may explain why any suggestion of a mass movement over the Diaoyutai (Senkaku) Islands was quickly suppressed in China during 1996. Thus, China's current leaders face the question of whether to encourage patriotic sentiment, and, if so, to what degree. Like it or not, nationalism is a double-edged sword.

Impact on Asia-Pacific Peace and Security

Will the "new China" become the dominant political and military power in Asia? Will it significantly alter the balance of power of the region? Will it help to bolster coexistence and sustainable growth in Asia? Will it be a welcome influence for the region and for the world?

This author has suggested in an earlier paper that, to the ASEAN nations and other countries of the Asia-Pacific region, the Hong Kong transition spells something uncertain but important (Weng 1997a). These countries welcome the fact that the new China, featuring Hong Kong, has become more economically oriented and more business-minded because they perceive an economically oriented China as necessarily less revolutionary and more constructive. This change signifies less support to revolutionary elements in the ASEAN countries from Beijing and more opportunities for exchanges and cooperation, which should bring mutual benefits. Taking this argument a step further, the world community may hope that China will finally join the family of nations and help build a world of peace in earnest. At the same time, however, there is a distinct possibility that a stronger and more threatening "new China" may rise out of this transition. As Napoleon said, China the giant may shake the world, once awakened. Whether a limited South China Economic Community, a more extensive "new China," or even a Greater China, the prospects are worrisome to some of China's smaller neighbors.

Since the late 1970s, China has impressed the world with a sustained two decade-long period of high economic growth. In October 1995, Jiang Zemin announced during a visit to the United States that China's GNP growth rate for the 1979 to 1994 period averaged 9.8 percent per year, with an average annual growth rate of 13.1 percent between 1991 and 1995. For a country the size of China, such high rates of economic growth inevitably attract attention; sooner or later, China will become the world leader in GNP. In fact, as early as 1989, a RAND futurist projected that China's GDP would surpass Japan and the United States by the year 2010 (Li 1996).

On May 19, 1993, London's Institute for International Strategic Studies (IISS) issued a report declaring that by 2010, China would indeed become the third largest economic entity in the world, a story that headlined in the *New York Times* the next day (*Zhonggong Nianbao* 1994). In 1995, the International Bank for Reconstruction and Development (IBRD) reported that China's GNP for 1993 totaled $577.42 billion and ranked seventh in the world. Its GDP was tenth, at $425.61 billion. Using a purchasing power parity (PPP) computation, however, China's 1993 GNP actually amounted to $2,745.67 billion and ranked second in the world, behind the United States and above Japan (IBRD 1995). In 1996, China managed a very difficult economic soft landing. The future looked promising as of mid-1997, especially with the new addition of Hong Kong.

Still, Beijing's government officials have been cautious in making economic projections. Perhaps they have been concerned more with China's need of foreign loans and investments than with its impressive economic status. World Bank and IISS reports met with rebuttals that emphasized that China is, and will be for some time to come, a developing nation. In mid-February 1995, China's Defense Minister Chi Haotian reminded the visiting Japanese Chief of the General Staff that "China is a big power but she is also a poor country. In terms of economic strength and of modernization of armed forces, there is a large discrepancy when compared to Japan. To catch up with Japan, efforts of several generations will be required" (*Yazhou Zhoukan*, March 5, 1995). Likewise, in the negotiations over China's entry into the WTO, the United States asked that China enter as a developed nation, and Beijing rejected that honor.

These displays of humility and caution provide no assurance to those wary of a potential China threat, especially given the nationalistic fervor in China during the past few years. China has become a very weighty international actor, with or without Hong Kong, and the world will benefit or suffer greatly not only from China's actions but even the nature of China's character. Its dictatorial and patriarchal rulers are in a position to make decisions with effects that reach beyond China.

For example, if Beijing were to open its gates so that Chinese people could freely emigrate, the impact on the more advanced parts of the world would become a very real concern—witness the Hong Kong experience during the last 50 years. Whenever Beijing or Guangdong authorities encouraged mainlanders to cross the borders, or ceased to cooperate in border control, the British Hong Kong Government always became rather nervous. Furthermore, several economies are already closely tied to and dependent on China. Hong Kong has quite clearly benefited from the Chinese hinterland over the past decades. Reliable supplies of water and food from the mainland have helped to keep Hong Kong competitive in the world market, and did not cease even while the mainland was suffering a famine in the aftermath of the Great Leap Forward. Likewise, Taiwan today is tied to the mainland by virtue of the huge market for trade and investment, which is increasingly becoming indispensable.

China is also involved to varying degrees with the hot spots in the Asia-Pacific region: North Korea, the Taiwan Strait, South China Sea, the Diaoyutai Islands, Cambodia, and Kashmir. In many cases, it plays a pivotal role. Beijing is a major player in security issues such as nuclear proliferation, nuclear testing, transfer of military technology, arms sales, and it often insists on playing by its own rules. China's behavior also affects domestic and international politics, economics, and military effectiveness in such areas as reasonable trade practices and investment protections, transparency, and national defense budgets, and the observance of international agreements.

Perhaps in anticipation, although few have said so publicly, some international actors in the Asia-Pacific region have targeted China in their security arrangements. The "Japan-United States Joint Declaration on Security— Alliance for the Twenty-first Century," signed by Prime Minister Hashimoto and President Clinton on April 17, 1996, is best understood in this context. As Beijing saw it, Clinton, who had been sympathetic to the Taiwan cause, did not have the time to visit China during his first term of office but found the time for an impromptu trip to Tokyo within a month after the Taiwan Strait crisis in 1996. Prime Minister Hashimoto, the most nationalistic and most conservative leader of Japan since Yasuhiro Nakasone, clearly wanted to assert Japan's power position, even if doing so required an offensive move against China. Thus, the resulting "Joint Declaration" is clearly aimed at China, because any threat against Japan in the international setting is likely to come from China. That a government spokesman would explicitly include the Taiwan Strait within the domain of the declaration—a proposition with which Beijing does not agree—was not surprising.

China's recent approaches to territorial disputes also invite critical analysis. With regard to the South China Sea islands, China's basic position has been for joint exploration with other claimant countries, shelving the sovereignty question for the present time. Despite this official position, China engaged in a naval skirmish with Vietnam over the Spratly Islands on March 14, 1988. Furthermore, the Standing Committee of the National People's Congress (NPC) adopted a territorial law of the sea on February 2, 1992, stating China's claim to the South China Sea islands in black and white. Except for Thailand, which seems to aspire to the role of mediator between China and ASEAN, the ASEAN countries have all expressed different degrees of unease over these developments. Indonesia in particular has expressed its unhappiness quite publicly, and in 1990, Jakarta started sponsoring a series of Workshops on Managing Potential Conflicts in the South China Sea. The Philippines has endeavored to garner an ASEAN common stand on the issue (Chen 1996). It is noteworthy that ASEAN accepted Myanmar (formerly Burma) as a member in June 1997 even though the military junta there was under severe international condemnation. Many observers believe that the ASEAN countries were concerned that Myanmar might fall under China's spell had it been denied membership.

The one area, however, where the Hong Kong transition has a direct and heavy impact is Taiwan, which takes the China threat very seriously, and for obvious reasons. Taipei has repeatedly stated its objection to the application of the "one country, two systems" policy to Taiwan. The Hong Kong transition clearly adds to the pressure that Taiwan feels from the Chinese mainland, compelling Taipei to deal with Beijing not only with regard to Taiwan–Hong Kong relations but also mainland-Taiwan relations, which formerly utilized Hong Kong as a convenient third party conduit. The June 1996 statement of Qian Qichen (Qian's Seven Points) has made this need amply clear (*Ming Bao*, June 23, 1995). With the creation of the HKSAR, Taipei has found it necessary to tackle difficult diplomatic cases such as South Africa and Panama. All is not lost, however. In fact, Taiwan-Hong Kong relations may improve in some ways because China has a stake in Taiwan that the British rulers of Hong Kong did not have (Weng 1997b). Interestingly, as long as the military solution remains elusive or more costly than Beijing is willing to pay, the Taiwan question may mellow Beijing. China's peaceful evolution is not only Taipei's hope but also its strategic goal.

Conclusion

In the final analysis, the peace and security of the Asia-Pacific has relatively little to do with Hong Kong per se. The challenge of the Hong Kong reversion is important only to the extent it impacts China's behavior in the international arena. The HKSAR may serve as a forum for discussion, but it has no independent and active role. Its impact on China is likely to be significant more for its effect on China's subjective worldview, and somewhat less for its impact on its objective military and economic capabilities. To have a positive impact on China, Hong Kong must maintain its continued separate existence. Countries of the Asia-Pacific will undoubtedly continue to take advantage of what Hong Kong has to offer, especially economically. Only a few need to worry about the implications of the "new China" or a Greater China. Taiwan has more to ponder, however, as the continued economic success of Hong Kong depends in part on the sustained credibility and viability of the "one country, two systems" policy.

The more things change, the more they stay the same. Strategic planners of the Asia-Pacific must continue to pay attention to China. Conventional wisdom will argue that as long as China is not powerful enough, it will grudgingly play the international game according to the rules first established by the West. But once it becomes a power capable of resisting any other power's pressure, China is likely to become not only independent but defiant and intransigent, at least in the eyes of those previously in a dominant position. And if it becomes a dominant superpower herself, China may well endeavor to reintroduce a *Pax Sinica*, a new world order incorporating some features of the tribute system, in the name of peace and harmony perhaps, in the larger world.

Note

1. On March 10, 1972, only a few months after China was admitted to the United Nations, Huang Hua, then Ambassador of the PRC, sent a letter to the General Assembly's Special Committee on Colonialism. It said the question of Hong Kong and Macau is "entirely within China's sovereign right and does not at all fall under the ordinary category of colonial territories."

Bibliography

Bernstein, Richard, and Ross Munro. *The Coming War with China.* New York: Alfred Knopf, 1997.
Chen, Xinzhi. "ASEAN Countries' Views and Responses to 'the China Threat.'" *Wenti yu Yanjiu* (Taipei) 35, no. 11 (November 1996): 15–33.
Deng, Xiaoping. *Deng Xiaoping Wenxuan, 1975–1982* (Selected works of Deng Xiaoping, 1975–1982). Beijing: Renmin Chubanshe, 1983: 203–37.
Fairbank, John K. *China's World Order: Traditional China's Foreign Relations.* Cambridge, MA: Harvard University Press, 1968.
Hannum, Hurst, and Richard B. Lillich. "The Concept of Autonomy in International Law." In Yoram Dinstein, ed., *Models of Autonomy.* New Brunswick, NJ: Transaction Books, 1981.
Hu, Sheng. "China's Role in the Twenty-first Century World." *Qiushi Zazhi* (Beijing), no. 19 (1996): 20–22.
Huntington, Samuel. "The Clash of Civilization?" *Foreign Affairs* (Summer 1993): 22–49.
International Bank for Reconstruction and Development. *World Development Report, 1995.* New York: Oxford University Press, 1995: 166–67.
Jackson, Robert H. *Quasi-States: Sovereignty, International Relations, and the Third World.* Cambridge: Cambridge University Press, 1990.
Lee, Kwok Sing. "The Past, Present and Future of Communist China's Hong Kong Policy." *Yazhou Yanjiu* (Asian studies—Hong Kong), no. 9 (July 1994): 27–69.
Li, Jingwen. "Outlook on China's Economic Development and Economic Cooperation with East Asian Countries, 1995–2010." *Kaifang Daobao* [Open tribune—Shenzhen], no. 1 (1996): 21 (citing "Forecast of Economic and Military Development Trends, 1950–2010," a RAND report, April 1989).
Liu, Baosan, and Chen Honglie. "Deng Xiaoping on China in the Twenty-first Century." *Jianghan Luntan* [Jianghan tribune], no. 2 (1996): 27–30.
MAC. *Liangan Jingji Tongji Yuebao* [Monthly statistics of cross-strait economics—Taipei], no. 48 (August 1996): Table 27.
Monk, Paul. "China: An Emerging Superpower?" *CAPS Papers* (Taipei), no. 7 (February 1995): 31.
Mushkat, Roda. "The International Legal Status of Hong Kong Under Post-Transitional Rule." *Houston Journal of International Law* 10, no. 1 (Autumn 1987): 1–24.

Nathan, Andrew, and Robert Ross. *The Great Wall and the Empty Fortress: China's Search for Security.* New York: Norton, 1997.

Renmin Ribao. *"Qing kan meiguo de renguan jilu"* [Looking clearly at America's human rights record], March 5, 1997, p. 6.

Shao, Chung-hai. "The Role of Hong Kong in Communist China's Economic Expansion and in the Development of Cross-Strait Relations." Paper delivered at the International Conference on Hong Kong-Asia-Pacific Relations After 1997, Institute for Communist China Studies, Taipei, February 20–21, 1997.

Shambaugh, David. "Growing Strong: China's Challenge to Asian Security." *Survival* 36, no. 2 (Summer 1994): 43–46.

State Council Information Office. *Zhongguo de Renquan Zhuangkuang* [Human rights in China]. Beijing: Zhongyang wenxian chubanshe, 1991.

Tang, James. "Hong Kong and the Changing International Order." *Pacific Review* 6, no. 3 (1993): 205–15.

Wang, Jionghua. "From a Philosophy of 'National Salvation' to a Philosophy of 'National Prosperity'—Views on Twenty-first Century Chinese Philosophy." *Huazhong Ligong Daxue Xuebao* [Journal of the Polytechnic University of Central China], no. 3 (1996). Abridged in *Gaodeng Xuexiao Wenke Xuebao Wenzhai* [China University periodicals abstracts (humanities)] 14, no. 1 (1997): 6.

Weng, Byron S.J. "The Integration of Outlying Areas: The Case of Hong Kong." In Harish Kapur, ed., *The End of an Isolation: China after Mao.* Dordrecht: Martinus Nijhoff, 1985a: 308–61.

———. (Weng Songran). "A Rustic Theory on 'One Country, Two Systems': Concept, Nature, Content, Obstacles and Prospects." In F.Q. Quo and Zhao Fusan, eds., *Taiwan zhi Jianglai Dierci Xueshu Taolunhui Lunwenji* [Papers presented at the 2nd symposium on "Taiwan's future"]. Beijing: Friendship Publishing, 1985b: 349–84.

———. "Hong Kong's Future: An Examination of Key Factors." Paper delivered at the 37th annual meeting of the American Association of Chinese Studies, Reno, Nevada, November 10–12, 1995.

———. "Cursory Views on the Theory of the China Threat." *Ershiyi Shiji* [Twenty-first century bimonthly] (April 1996): 18–24.

———. "Mainland China, Taiwan and Hong Kong as International Actors." In Gerald A. Postiglione and James T.H. Tang, eds., *Hong Kong's Reunion with China: The Global Dimensions.* Armonk, NY: M.E. Sharpe, 1997a: 42–78.

———. "Taiwan-Hong Kong Relations, 1949–1997 and Beyond." *American Asian Review* 15, no. 4 (Winter 1997b): 159–93.

Weng, Byron S.J. (Weng Songran), and Chang Hsin. *Yiguo Liangzhi yu Xianggang Qiantu* ["One country, two systems" and the future of Hong Kong]. Research report. Taipei: Mainland Affairs Council, 1994.

Yue, Qian. "Deng Xiaoping Willingly Sold the Diaoyutai Islands," *Kaifang* [Open monthly—Hong Kong], no. 118 (October 1996): 33–35.

Zhonggong Nianbao 1994 [Yearbook of Communist China, 1994]. Taipei: Zhonggong Yanjiu Zazhishe, book 5, chapter 5 (1994): 5-21–5-31.

8

ASEAN Responses to an Emerging China

A Philippine Perspective

Carolina G. Hernandez

Introduction

In any discussion of post-Cold War Asia-Pacific regional security, the emergence of China as a modernized regional and potential global power inevitably arises. Indeed, the rise of a power that remains largely an enigma to most of its neighbors and the rest of the world has made the security equation in the region an uncertain one.

It is easy to see why the region views an emerging China as its principal challenge in the future. It is the world's third largest conventional military power and the world's most populous country. It commands an economy that has sustained high levels of growth over the past 15 years and is projected to become the world's largest economy by 2020. Isolated from the main regional interactions during most of the postwar period, it remains committed to the use of force to achieve its goals. Its history of exacting obeisance from less powerful neighbors has not helped to dispel the concern that China, over the long term, could revert to its "Middle Kingdom" mentality, especially as its modernization goals are achieved and the U.S. influence and presence in Asia recedes.

In the absence of the Cold War's overarching influence on regional security, Asia-Pacific states needed to craft alternative mechanisms to meet their security needs. The United States and Japan, partners in the arrangement that provides much of the region's security, upgraded their security relationship, coincidentally, after the Chinese military exercises in the Taiwan Strait and shortly before the presidential elections in Taiwan in March 1996. Despite the growth of multilateral institutions for dealing with political, security, and economic issues in the region, the nations that entered into bilateral military alliances with the United States during the Cold War have chosen to maintain those arrangements, even as some consider them unsatisfactory or inadequate. The Philippines, for example, finds the Mutual Defense Treaty with the United States unable to meet its security needs, yet it remains in force even after the United States closed its military bases in the Philippines in 1992. The treaty constitutes some kind of insurance policy or safety net in the event regional security deteriorates to the point that U.S. involvement would be critical to regional stability.

The member states of ASEAN (the Association of Southeast Asian Nations), individually and as a group, have sought to develop policies designed to meet their present and future security needs, including those that could arise from an emerging China. This does not mean, however, that the members of ASEAN and the association itself currently view China as a security threat. To the contrary, they seek to engage China in constructive ways, either individually or collectively, to avert the emergence of an unreasonable and intractable China.

This chapter discusses and analyzes the measures taken by ASEAN member states, individually and collectively, to respond to the emergence of China, with a special focus on the Philippine response.

ASEAN-China Relations in Historical Context

On the whole, relations between member states of ASEAN and China have been difficult. China's imperial dominance over most of its neighbors in the ancient past was replaced in the postwar period by concern over the spread of communism emanating from the People's Republic of China. The fact that most of the ASEAN states had sizable ethnic Chinese immigrant populations that controlled large shares of wealth and wielded considerable economic power only exacerbated this concern. In the early Cold War years, these immigrant Chinese communities were regarded as veritable fifth column elements that were responsible for the growth of local Communist insurgencies in Southeast Asia.

The core states of ASEAN—Indonesia, Malaysia, the Philippines, Singapore, and Thailand—which formed the association in 1967, experienced serious Communist insurgencies that tied up their resources for most of the postwar years. These countries thus viewed domestic insurgency as the principal challenge or threat to their security. Because they regarded security as comprehensive and multidimensional, the ASEAN core states thought that resolving their domestic peace and stability problems would form the foundation for regional order, stability and security. Hence, the resolution of Communist insurgency at home was as high a priority as the achievement of harmony among their diverse ethnic communities.

Even though such domestic factors as gross inequities in land ownership and wealth led to the rise of Communist insurgency, it was also a product of external forces. The policy of the Chinese Communist Party to support local insurgencies among its neighbors strengthened the movements' capacities to challenge Southeast Asian governments. The security problem created by armed Communist insurgents consequently raised concerns over China.

In the case of Malaysia and Singapore, ethnic Chinese predominance in the economy augmented negative perceptions of China, which arose from the Malayan Communist Party's challenges to national security. In Indonesia, the critical role that the Indonesian Communist Party (PKI) played in the latter years of Sukarno-guided democracy exacerbated tensions over China. The PKI's close relationship with Sukarno became an important cause for the massacre of numerous Indonesian Chinese and Chinese nationals residing in Indonesia during the turbulent transition before the establishment of Suharto's New Order government. China interceded on behalf of its nationals residing in Indonesia, holding Jakarta responsible for the violence and even bringing the issue before the United Nations. This action did not bode well for Indonesian-Chinese relations in the post-Sukarno period. Consequently, among the original ASEAN member countries, Indonesia was the most seriously concerned over the Chinese threat and was the last among them to normalize relations with China.

In the Philippines, anti-Chinese feelings were shaped by both the dominance of the Chinese in the economy and the fear, shared with the United States and other "free-world" allies, of Communist expansion in Asia. The Philippines differs from other ASEAN countries because its initial interactions with the Chinese took place within the context of trade and commerce. In the absence of a central government, local rulers in the pre-Spanish Philippines did not have to pay obeisance to imperial China (Doronila 1997). But at the same time, as a close American ally, the Philippines firmly opposed the spread of communism. The Filipino government regarded the large presence of ethnic Chinese, many of whom remained Chinese nationals, as a matter of national security. When Filipino troops also participated in the Korean War, they fought against the North Koreans and the Chinese as part of the American-led effort to halt Communist aggression against South Korea. To most Filipinos, therefore, mainland Chinese were enemies of peace and democracy, with partners in the local Communist insurgency.

Although ethnic Chinese communities in Thailand were better integrated into Thai society (as Sino-Thais) than in neighboring societies, Bangkok also sided with the United States in the contest between the superpowers during the Cold War. Like the other members of the San Francisco network of bilateral military alliances forged by the United States as part of the Cold War containment strategy, it opposed the expansion of communism in Asia. As the ASEAN member most geographically proximate to China, Thailand only sharpened its security sensors against the Chinese Communist threat.

Thus, apart from the desire to prevent the rest of Southeast Asia from becoming an arena of superpower competition, the fear of the spread of communism in Asia inspired the establishment of ASEAN. As they watched opposing ideologies tear Vietnam apart during the Vietnam War, the original ASEAN nations sought to prevent similar tragedies in their own countries. To insulate themselves from superpower rivalry, ASEAN nations set their bilateral disputes aside to eliminate them as an excuse for superpower intervention in regional affairs, while applying their limited resources toward solving their domestic problems. Sublimating their primordial interests was a necessary precondition for achieving these goals.

Amid these circumstances, ASEAN was established in August 1967. Composed of noncommunist states, in just 30 years ASEAN member countries successfully prevented the spread of communism in their subregion, transformed themselves from poor and unstable societies into dynamic tiger economies enjoying a modicum of internal peace, and carved an important regional role for themselves. The reconciliations among member nations were extended to embrace those neighbors whose cooperation was critical to their national goals but with whom they had a history of difficult relations. These included Japan, with whom reconciliation was achieved much earlier, and China.[1]

ASEAN-China Reconciliation: The 1970s and Beyond

Until the rapprochement between the United States and China following President Richard Nixon's visit to the mainland, ASEAN member states did not maintain normal diplomatic relations with China. Like most noncommunist nations in the rest of the world, ASEAN member states continued to treat Taiwan as the successor state to the Republic of China, whose seat in the United Nations was occupied by the government in Taipei. With the admission of Beijing into the United Nations, however, many states began to normalize relations with China while maintaining economic and cultural (or nonofficial) relations with Taipei. The ASEAN nations also adopted this legal fiction in dealing with the two Chinas dilemma, as both Taiwan and the mainland were important partners in their external relations.

Several factors shaped the reconciliation between ASEAN member states and China. By the 1970s, Indonesia, Malaysia, Singapore and Thailand had already reversed Communist insurgency and influence in their countries, and the fear of Chinese influence regarding this problem had receded considerably. Nonetheless, suspicion over China's future intentions remained, particularly in Indonesia and Singapore.

Although the Communist insurgency in the Philippines continued through the 1990s, Manila decided to normalize relations with China for other reasons. It hoped that normalizing relations would make it easier to persuade China to refrain from providing material and other support to the local Communist movement. In addition, China was a potential source of crude oil, a vital source of energy for a country such as the Philippines, which was 75 percent dependent on foreign energy sources at the time of the first oil crunch in the early 1970s. The Philippines also sought to broaden its external relations, which until then had been dominated by the United States. Finally, President Ferdinand Marcos wanted to gain some leverage with the United States to assure the latter's continued support for martial law. The Philippines regarded improved relations with China as an important step in this regard.

It was also becoming apparent that China's successful drive to modernize would improve its prospects for becoming a formidable regional player. As the 1980s and the 1990s unfolded, China's modernization efforts began to show some positive results. At the same time, there was increasing regional concern that the United States would reduce its military presence and influence in the region because of increasing economic and political difficulties at home. Indeed, the drawing down of U.S. forces in Asia and the Pacific was regarded as evidence of the uncertain future U.S. military presence in the region. Consequently, normalized relations with China might serve as an important step toward promoting cooperative relations with China.

The first ASEAN member country to normalize relations with China was Malaysia in 1974, followed by the Philippines in 1975, and then by Thailand, Brunei, Singapore and Indonesia. By the early 1990s, all of the original ASEAN member states and Brunei had already established full diplomatic relations with Beijing and nonformal relations with Taipei. By mid-1990, ASEAN increasingly was becoming China's interlocutor vis-à-vis the rest of the world, a role it played in relation to Japan in the 1970s and in the 1980s.

China saw in ASEAN a valuable partner, as states in the region gained confidence in the association's credibility as a regional actor. In particular, ASEAN was becoming a major player in the resolution of the Cambodian crisis—Southeast Asia's most serious security problem in the late 1970s and the 1980s. The association's code of behavior in dealing with the outside world, as embodied in the Treaty of Amity and Cooperation, was also compatible with China's desire to avoid intrusion by outsiders into its internal affairs. Moreover, in the 1990s, the debate over democracy, human rights and "Asian values" provided China with a community of interest with many ASEAN states that did not wish for intervention on the part of Western countries, particularly on these issues (Chen 1993). The opportunity was ripe for better relations between ASEAN and China.

ASEAN Responses to an Emerging China

The fundamental changes in the regional security environment in the late 1980s and the early 1990s, particularly the end of the Cold War and the implosion of the Soviet Union, led states in the region to devise alternative mechanisms to deal with their security requirements.[2] China's rise as a great economic and political actor was another important element in this new security environment. In addition, the United States had adopted a policy of drawing down its forces in the Asia-Pacific and encouraging regional partners to share the burden of providing for their own security and the security of the region. Phase I of the 1990 East Asian Strategy Initiative resulted in the withdrawal of some 15,250 troops, representing 12 percent of U.S. military personnel in East Asia. It was followed by the withdrawal of another 8,000 troops from the Philippines in 1992, following the Philippine Senate's rejection of a new military bases treaty with the United States. The uncertainty and fluidity of this post-Cold War environment led states in the region to adopt alternative measures to deal with their security needs.

Earlier thinking about regional security led ASEAN members to aspire to make Southeast Asia a Zone of Peace, Freedom and Neutrality (ZOPFAN). As a ZOPFAN, ASEAN would endeavor to insulate Southeast Asia from big power rivalry by preventing the rise of tension and conflict. The end of the Cold War and subsequent developments only increased ASEAN's resolve to make the ZOPFAN ideal a reality while member countries adopted more specific means to promote national and regional security.

Making Southeast Asia Nuclear-Weapons Free

One of ASEAN's most important steps toward making ZOPFAN a reality was the adoption of the Treaty for the Establishment of a Southeast Asian Nuclear Weapons Free Zone (SEANWFZ) during the 1995 ASEAN ministers meeting (AMM) (Hernandez 1996). Nuclear-Weapons Free Zones (NWFZs) have been established in other parts of the world, including Latin America (the Treaty of Tlatelolco, 1967), the South Pacific (the Treaty of Raratonga, 1985), and Africa, among the members of the Organization for African Unity (Treaty of Pelindaba, 1995). The Treaty of Tlatelolco covers the Latin American continents, whereas the Treaty of Raratonga encompasses a zone stretching from Latin America to Australia's west coast and from the Antarctic to the equator. North and South Korea agreed to denuclearize their peninsula in 1992, although the agreement awaits implementation (Hernandez 1996, 8).

The end of the Cold War was regarded as an ideal time for realizing the SEANWFZ, with the removal of superpower competition and the rise of a benign peace in Southeast Asia, and the end of the permanent U.S. military presence in the Philippines. For SEANWFZ to be effective, however, nuclear-weapons states with a military presence in the region needed to sign a protocol providing for their recognition and support in the observance of such a zone. Unfortunately, the United States, China and Russia have not yet agreed to such a protocol. Without it, any hope that the treaty will succeed is futile.

Enhancing Military Security

To improve military security, most ASEAN members undertook modernization programs.[3] Establishing control over domestic insurgency gave rise to the need to restructure the armed forces, reducing the primacy of ground forces and developing the naval and air forces. In addition, as the United Nations Convention on the Law of the Sea came into force, coastal and archipelagic states acquired extended responsibilities over vast maritime areas, requiring modernization. Most military hardware stocks had to be upgraded or replaced. In many ASEAN countries, the armed forces continued to enjoy overwhelming influence in politics, and funds from their new wealth were used to finance defense modernization.

Also, ASEAN member countries decided to forge access agreements with the United States, allowing American troops port calls for repair, refueling and related activities. This policy stands in contrast to the last years of the Cold War, when the U.S. military presence was confined to Japan and South Korea in Northeast Asia and to the Philippines in Southeast Asia. It is noteworthy that states like Indonesia and Malaysia, which were strongly committed to nonalignment and opposed the stationing of U.S. troops, were now partners of the United States in these port-of-call arrangements. Despite rhetoric to the contrary, ASEAN's original member states continue to view the U.S. military presence as a positive factor for regional stability. They regard the United States as the only country in the 1990s with the capability to halt aggression by any of the major powers in the region.

Mutual defense agreements also continued to maintain relevance to regional security (Tow et al. 1997). In the fluidity and uncertainty of the post-Cold War world, states in the region use a combination of strategies to deal with their security needs (Jordan 1997). Because unilateralism and isolation are unrealistic policy options in a highly interdependent world, ASEAN countries combine bilateral and multilateral approaches to security to deal with their security concerns more effectively, and will continue to employ this strategy as long as the regional and global security order remains fluid and uncertain. Accordingly, both the Philippines and Thailand have chosen to maintain their bilateral military alliances with the United States while Malaysia and Singapore have remained partners of Great Britain, Australia, and New Zealand through the Five Power Defense Arrangement (FPDA). Despite Philippine dissatisfaction with the uncertain U.S. commitment to the defense of the Philippines under the treaty, analysts and policymakers in the Philippines believe that access to joint military exercises with the United States and other aspects of military cooperation are important and perhaps necessary to modernizing the Filipino armed forces. Moreover, the treaty affords the Philippines an opportunity to continue playing a regional strategic role.

Recently, the United States also has sought to conclude status-of-forces agreements with the Philippines and Thailand. Although agreements with the Philippines have stalled because of residual opposition to U.S. military presence in the country and the constitutional ban on allowing nuclear weapons on Philippine soil, there are those among the country's political and military leaders who believe that such an agreement benefits the country's security needs.

Indonesia, a stalwart in the Non-Aligned Movement, concluded a security agreement with Australia in 1995. This is an extraordinary development between two countries that had difficult relations stemming from territorial disputes and human rights issues in the past. The agreement was negotiated at the highest levels and in such secrecy that even the Indonesian Foreign Minister, Ali Alatas, was surprised when the agreement was finally made public. Although Indonesian sources deny that the rise of China as a regional power and concern over its future foreign policy intentions played a role in the agreement, the opposite appears to be true. Indonesia's concern over China has not been altered significantly by China's present moderation in foreign policy, and Indonesia entered into the agreement when the regional security environment had been at its most benign and relations with China were apparently improving. In addition, recent ethnic tension in Indonesia displayed an anti-Chinese element reminiscent of the transition from Sukarno to Suharto in the mid-1960s.

Finally, ASEAN members have forged closer security cooperation with one other. Beginning in the early 1990s, ASEAN nations began to conduct regular joint meetings, an initiative that contributed to policy coordination among the member states. Also, ASEAN armed forces have conducted joint military exercises, and have undertaken exchanges in intelligence, military education and officer training as part of their recent security-enhancing measures.

Expanding the PMC and Establishing the ASEAN Regional Forum

Expansion of the ASEAN Post-Ministerial Conference (PMC) also may be considered an ASEAN response to an emerging China. Members of ASEAN recognized the PMC's limitations as a vehicle for dealing with regional political and security issues, as its membership was confined to its partners in North America, Western Europe, Australasia, and Northeast Asia. Apart from being ASEAN's key aid, investment, and trading partners, these countries were also all anticommunist. The key political and security powers in the region, however, were China and Russia, neither one of which was a dialogue partner of ASEAN. Any regional political and security dialogue mechanism that excluded these two powers could not be viable.

Consequently, in May 1993, senior officials of ASEAN and the ASEAN-PMC decided to expand the PMC process despite initial hesitation on the part of Indonesia, Thailand and Japan, who were concerned about the implications of including new partners with different backgrounds in the process. In the end, China and Russia, already ASEAN consultative partners since July 1991, were invited to become full dialogue partners in the PMC, signifying the first time that the PMC included unlike-minded states. ASEAN hoped that by extending its process for dealing with security issues to China and Russia, including accession to the Treaty of Amity and Cooperation, these two major powers could be integrated into an emerging ASEAN-centered regional security structure. Thus, together with the existing dialogue partners, and with Papua New Guinea, Laos, and Vietnam as observers, China and Russia attended the 1993 Singapore AMM, which decided to convene the first meeting of the ASEAN Regional Forum in Bangkok in July 1994. Effectively, the expanded PMC became the ASEAN Regional Forum (ARF).

In conjunction with bilateral relations between ASEAN members and China, ASEAN has attempted to use the ARF to influence Chinese foreign-policy behavior to the greatest extent possible. Ever since its establishment, the ARF has sought to explore the means through which it can promote preventive diplomacy, to manage potential conflict in the South China Sea as well as on the Korean peninsula; to prevent nonproliferation of weapons of mass destruction; and to reduce tensions arising from the development of nuclear, bacteriological and chemical weapons. As the largest claimant in the South China Sea and a nuclear-weapons state committed to upgrading its nuclear capability, China occupies a key role in both regional security concerns.

To date, the ARF has not made any significant decisions regarding these two issues, in part because the participants are still learning how to work together through an expanded ASEAN process. The assistance of track-two mechanisms to develop the ARF's role in preventive diplomacy and nonproliferation, such as the Council for Security Cooperation in the Asia Pacific (CSCAP), has recently been stepped up. For example, some of the ASEAN member committees of CSCAP brokered a compromise to ensure China's participation as a full member of CSCAP, with Taiwanese scholars involved in its working groups. This was intended to ensure that China, as the most likely country to pose a security challenge to the region in the future, is engaged fully in the track two process of CSCAP, improving its transparency on security issues and encouraging its cooperation.

ASEAN Approaches to the South China Sea Issue

The South China Sea disputes have become the centerpiece of ASEAN–China security relations. Of the six claimants to the contested territories in the area, four are ASEAN member states: Brunei, Malaysia, the Philippines and Vietnam. The South China Sea forms part of the strategic sea lanes of communication (SLOC) linking the Indian and Pacific Oceans through the Straits of Malacca and the Lombok Strait. The claimants also believe that the contested areas contain energy, minerals and marine resources that are of increasing importance to their development—for example, a number of claimant states have entered into petroleum exploration agreements with oil companies in the West in recent years. China and Vietnam had engaged in armed skirmishes over these disputed territories, the last one in the spring of 1988. Starting in 1990, acting on an Indonesian initiative and with Canadian financing, ASEAN has been practicing preventive diplomacy among the claimant states through a series of workshops intended to prevent the disputes from turning into armed conflicts. The South China Sea Workshops have apparently approached the point of diminishing returns, however, and Indonesia holds China principally responsible.

Concern by ASEAN over Chinese intentions in the disputed area was heightened when the Standing Committee of China's National People's Conference approved a law regarding territorial waters and contiguous areas in February 1992. While reaffirming China extensive claim over all the islands in the South China Sea, the law's language suggested that China's claim also extended to the waters between them. This alarmed the ASEAN claimant states, particularly the Philippines, which initiated the adoption of the ASEAN

"Declaration on the South China Sea" during the AMM in Manila in July 1992. The declaration called upon the claimant states to settle their disputes peacefully, and to reject taking unilateral action that the other claimants could interpret as provocative. It also called upon the claimants to abide by the principles embodied earlier in the Treaty of Amity and Cooperation.

While China has not acceded to the declaration, it agreed in a November 1995 joint declaration that essentially the same principles will govern its relations with the Philippines. Following China's occupation of the Panganiban (Mischief) Reef in March 1995, the Philippine government protested and destroyed the markers set up by Chinese nationals suspected to be members of the People's Liberation Army (PLA). The Philippines, aware that it could not confront China militarily, sought international and ASEAN support, stressing the multilateral character of the disputes. In response to China's creeping occupation of the Mischief Reef, the AMM in Brunei in July 1995 issued a joint communiqué urging all claimants to "refrain from taking actions that could destabilize the region, including possibly undermining the freedom of navigation and aviation in the affected areas" (Valencia 1995, 42). It also urged discussion of the issue in various multilateral and bilateral settings.

Unfortunately, ASEAN could not be more forceful in its response to China's occupation of Mischief Reef. The member states of ASEAN have different interests in their relations with China, and they view China in different ways as well. Furthermore, they seek economic access to the huge Chinese market, as most major trading nations do. The ASEAN member states wish to maintain a stable regional order for economic development to continue, and they do not welcome difficult relations with China. In fact, they bank on the primacy China has placed on economic development and hope it will continue, ensuring the regional stability that their own economic progress requires. Finally, ASEAN does not wish to be seen as ganging up against China, particularly with Vietnam's entry into ASEAN. China and Vietnam bear deep suspicions toward each other, and the end of ASEAN confrontation with Vietnam over Cambodia marked the end of Chinese-ASEAN collaboration against Vietnam. Hence, ASEAN has consistently pursued the policy of constructive engagement with China in the post-Cold War era.

In addition to adopting the "Declaration on the South China Sea," including China in the PMC and ARF processes, and issuing a joint communiqué following the Chinese occupation of the Mischief Reef, ASEAN has intensified its efforts to respond to an emerging China by undertaking a number of significant steps.

On April 3 and 4, 1995, the first ASEAN-China Senior Officials' Meeting (SOM) took place, marking the first time that ASEAN and Chinese senior officials sat down to discuss the issue of conflicting claims in the South China Sea. Because China agreed to discuss the issue with ASEAN as a group, rather than with each rival claimant as it had insisted in the past, the SOM represented progress in ASEAN's relations with China and marked a clear departure from China's original position against multilateralizing the dispute. In addition, previous discussions on the issue between ASEAN and China had taken place in the nonofficial forum of the Indonesian-initiated workshops, which in contrast to the SOM were not considered binding by participants.

Next, in August 1995, during bilateral consultations between the Philippines and China in Manila, China reassured the Philippines that it would not undertake hostile acts in settling the Spratly Islands dispute, and the Philippines suggested mechanisms for defusing tension in the area on both bilateral and multilateral levels. The most important result of the meeting was the agreement on principles for a mutual code of conduct.

In addition, ASEAN was able to bring the South China Sea dispute before the summit of the Non-Aligned Movement in Cartagena, Colombia. The document released by the summit called for the resolution of all sovereignty and jurisdictional disputes concerning the South China Sea by peaceful means and urged all parties to exercise restraint. It also supported the principles enumerated in the 1992 "Declaration on the South China Sea" and the 1995 ASEAN statement on recent developments there—an apparent allusion to the Mischief Reef incident.

The ASEAN countries took the opportunity to speak with Chinese leaders on other occasions. For example, when Philippine President Fidel Ramos met with Chinese Premier Li Peng during the Asia-Europe Meeting (ASEM) in Bangkok in March 1996, he suggested the establishment of acceptable distances for ship movement in the South China Sea as a type of mutual code of conduct.

Efforts to establish positive and cooperative relations in such areas as economic and people-to-people exchanges demonstrate the constructive engagement of China even though the disputes in the South China Sea remained unresolved. In this spirit, the Philippines and China conducted bilateral consultations in mid-March 1996, reaffirming their Joint Statement on the South China Sea of August 1995 and establishing other forms of cooperation. They agreed to work toward avoiding maritime conflict and to exchange visits among military and defense officials. They also agreed to establish working groups on fisheries, marine environment and confidence-building measures.

The Philippines also welcomed China's proposal that China, Malaysia, the Philippines and Vietnam participate in a group that will develop cooperation in the areas of information network, biodiversity, and tidal- and sea-level changes. It also reiterated its proposal to establish common radio frequencies among law enforcement agencies, including detachments on islands in the disputed areas, and proposed limiting the movements of vessels to those necessary for resupplying the islands and avoiding the permanent presence of military vessels in the area. Finally, the Philippines raised the need to define areas where military exercises would be prohibited.

China proposed that ASEAN adopt an overarching political document governing ASEAN-China relations. Initially, the Philippines was the only country that favored such a document; ASEAN believes that it is in its best interest to have as many formal agreements as possible with China, including codes of conduct. Although China opposes a separate code of conduct regarding the South China Sea, it is prepared to include such a code in a comprehensive political document governing ASEAN-China relations. As this document might serve as the only vehicle to formally adopt the code of conduct outlined in the declaration approved by China, it currently is being readied for adoption at a time when the draft becomes mutually acceptable.

In addition, ASEAN welcomed China's ratification of the United Nations' Convention on the Law of the Sea (UNCLOS) in May 1996. Some members, however, expressed concern over China's definition of its baselines for delimiting its maritime boundaries, which intrude into the disputed parts of the South China Sea. In their view, China's action disturbs stability in the area, sets back the spirit of cooperation that had been developing slowly in the South China Sea, and does not contribute to resolving the area dispute. In fact, another dispute threatened to disrupt bilateral relations between China and the Philippines over the Scarborough Shoal, just a few nautical miles from Subic Bay. The Philippines claim the shoal as part of its exclusive economic zone, but China historically considers it part of China. This issue raised new regional concern over stability in the South China Sea.

These developments occurred as ASEAN and China were engaging in bilateral dialogue, in bilateral talks between claimant states, and in the multilateral forum of the ARF. Aggression by China creates confusion among its ASEAN counterparts, giving the impression that China is pursuing two divergent paths in its relations with ASEAN—a course of action that does not encourage confidence over China's real intentions.

Expanding ASEAN

The decision to expand ASEAN to include all ten countries in Southeast Asia is another response to the emergence of China as a major regional power. Although ASEAN ran the risk that Beijing would take a negative view of

Vietnam's inclusion, and although the expansion would extend ASEAN's borders to China, ASEAN nations decided nonetheless to extend ASEAN membership to Hanoi. Strategic considerations weighed heavily in this decision. Uniting all the ten Southeast Asian countries under ASEAN would signify the creation of a potential major player in the region. It would boast about a quarter of a billion people with largely vibrant economies. Moreover, it would occupy a large chunk of the Asian mainland and the major islands in Southeast Asia, in commanding position over the strategic SLOCs between the Indian and Pacific Oceans. Combined, they would be in a better position to engage China and other major powers in the Asia-Pacific. Individually, they would remain little pebbles in the Asia-Pacific terrain that could easily be ignored or missed in constructing a post-Cold War security architecture for the region.

Concern over China's dominance in Myanmar (formerly Burma) was a contributor to ASEAN's decision to extend membership to Yangon (formerly Rangoon), although the slogan sold in public is the realization of the dream that ASEAN's founding fathers were reuniting Southeast Asia. A preponderant Chinese influence in Myanmar could undermine the interest of its Southeast Asian neighbors because of Myanmar's size and strategic location, but ASEAN members calculated that bringing Myanmar within its fold could moderate this influence, if not drastically reduce it.

Surely, the expansion of ASEAN presents many problems. The inclusion of unlike-minded states complicates the development of harmonious relations, particularly among countries that used to be opponents over the Cambodian issue. In addition, the levels of economic development across these countries vary widely, from highly prosperous Singapore and Brunei, to increasingly wealthy Malaysia, Thailand, Indonesia and the Philippines to the poorest members, Cambodia, Laos and Myanmar.

The member states also operate under diverse types of political systems, which complicated bilateral relationships even among the original members of ASEAN (for example, the diplomatic row between the Philippines and Singapore that followed the execution of Flor Contemplacion in 1995). Finally, the threat perceptions, friendships, and international networks differ among ASEAN members. A key challenge in ASEAN's expansion is the ability of its members to maintain ASEAN solidarity despite these differences. This difficulty has become evident in their divergent positions regarding the Hun Sen coup d'état in Cambodia. Vietnam, Laos and Myanmar appear to take a position close to that of Malaysia, and they seem prepared to accept the fait accompli presented by Hun Sen. The other ASEAN members appear unwilling to abandon responsibility for restoring the integrity of the Cambodian constitution and the inclusion of all parties in the elections scheduled for May 1998.

Despite these differences, a two-tiered ASEAN could emerge not only across the economic divide, but also on issues such as Cambodia. A united Southeast Asia can play a more influential role in regional politics and stand in a better position to deal with China.

Challenges for the Twenty-first Century

A principal challenge facing ASEAN in its relations with an emerging China is the ability to forge a consensus on key issues and to promote ASEAN solidarity. An ASEAN divided within would be less effective in managing diplomacy with a powerful China. The membership of Myanmar, a close friend of China, could present difficulties for ASEAN in the future—particularly if Myanmar's interests diverge from those of other ASEAN members and it seeks Chinese allegiance.

Close observation of ASEAN-China relations reveals that China is engaging in some doublespeak regarding the South China Sea. Although China has taken reasonable stances on the issue in the diplomatic forum of the ASEAN-China dialogue, in the ARF, and in bilateral consultations with ASEAN countries, it concurrently undertakes actions that tend to undermine the status quo. The occupation of Mischief Reef provides a good illustration. Recent developments indicate that China could be upgrading the structures on Mischief Reef, permitting it to station troops there (*Far Eastern Economic Review* 1997). Instead of maintaining the status quo and refraining from provocative action, China has behaved in an aggressive fashion. Should China in fact become able to establish a military presence on Mischief Reef, it is certain to provoke further concern among ASEAN countries, particularly the Philippines and Vietnam, whose disputes with China have given rise to tension and armed conflict on occasion. China also has pursued what Mark Valencia calls a policy of creeping occupation or creeping assertiveness in the South China Sea (Valencia 1997). It has occupied disputed territory, undertaken probing actions and expeditions to test how far its neighbors would allow it to go, and strengthened its position in the disputed areas as each window of opportunity presents itself.

But ASEAN has not developed a common position beyond the "Declaration on the South China Sea," and it appears ill-prepared as it engages in bilateral dialogue with China. To meet the challenge of an emerging China, ASEAN must be more assertive in reprimanding China when it pursues acts of aggression. It is not enough to wait for an aggrieved ASEAN member to call on the others for support on the South China Sea issue. Because all members have agreed to the "Declaration on the South China Sea," each has a right to protest any infringement of its principles by any claimant or aggressor. Depending on the gravity of the infringement, ASEAN members individually or collectively must express concern through reprimand or even diplomatic protest. If China does not receive the correct signals from ASEAN, China is likely to exploit the lack of cohesion to its full advantage.

It is also important to highlight the strategic value of the South China Sea to nonclaimant states in the region. Any disruption of order in the South China Sea region affects the economic, military and political interests of the area as a whole. Interruptions or impediments to free navigation on the South China Sea would be particularly disruptive. Thus, ASEAN members should attempt to enlist the support of non-ASEAN states in the region to ensure that China plays according to the rules, especially those in UNCLOS and the ASEAN "Declaration on the South China Sea." Freedom of navigation can be promoted best if tension and conflict among claimants are averted. In this regard, ASEAN must define clearly each member's maritime jurisdiction in areas where ownership is a settled matter. An important first step is to convene its legal experts on UNCLOS to determine the extent to which the boundaries can be defined.[4] ASEAN members also must work more closely together to prepare for bilateral dialogue with China.

Constructive engagement remains an important policy objective, but it must take place within the parameters that the political document on ASEAN-China relations establishes. The ARF also must pursue similar goals on a regionwide basis. In addition, ASEAN must prepare for the possibility that constructive engagement may fail. This rationale underlies the varying forms of security cooperation that ASEAN countries maintain with the United States and other countries that are able to deter China from behavior that destabilizes the region. China must be made to understand that if constructive engagement does not produce positive results, its neighbors have no alternative but to pursue their interests more aggressively.

Ideally, the Asia-Pacific region of the future will craft a regional order no longer based on a balance of competing powers, but on a concert of powers governed by principles of nonaggression, peace and mutual benefit. This cannot occur, however, without the cooperation of all relevant powers, including China. In the meantime, ASEAN must continue its efforts toward enhancing and raising the level of internal cooperation in various functional areas as well as in the political and security fields. It must also ensure that it meets the challenges of an expanded ASEAN as effectively as possible, and promote the ability of the ARF to meet the reasonable expectations of its partners.

Notes

1. For a detailed discussion of this issue, see Carolina G. Hernandez, "Regional Reconciliation in the Asia Pacific Region: Challenges for the Twenty-first Century,"

a Carlos P. Romulo Professorial Chair in International Relations lecture delivered at the College of Social Sciences and Philosophy, University of the Philippines, November 1996.

2. An analysis of the post-Cold War security challenges in the Asia-Pacific region and responses to them can be found in Carolina G. Hernandez, "Peace and Security in the Post-Cold War Asia Pacific Region," in Toshiro Tanaka and Takashi Inoguchi, editors, *Globalism and Regionalism.* Tokyo: United Nations University, 1997: 42–55.

3. This issue had been raised against Southeast Asian military modernization by critics from the region and elsewhere in the form of a growing arms race.

4. The ASEAN Institutes for Strategic and International Studies has recently made this proposal to a number of ranking ASEAN officials in order to enhance the capacity of ASEAN in its consultations with China on the issue.

Bibliography

Chen Jie. "Human Rights: ASEAN's New Importance to China." *The Pacific Review* 6, no. 3 (1993): 227–37.

Dibb, Paul. "Defence Force Modernization in Asia: Toward 2000 and Beyond" *Contemporary Southeast Asia* 18, no. 4 (March 1997): 347–60.

Doronila, Amando. "RP Won't Give in to China Bullying." *Philippine Daily Inquirer*, May 25, 1997, pp. 1, 19.

Far Eastern Economic Review. "Awaiting Mischief." August 28, 1997, p. 12.

Hernandez, Carolina G. "The Southeast Asian Nuclear Weapons Free Zone: Implications for Regional Stability." Paper presented at the Workshop on Nuclear Weapons Free Zones, Peace Research Centre, Research School of Pacific and Asian Studies, Australian National University, Canberra, December 10–11, 1996.

Jordan, Amos. "Reflections on the Place of Alliances in the Post-Cold War Era." Paper presented at the 11th Asia Pacific Roundtable, ASEAN Institutes for Strategic and International Studies, Kuala Lumpur, June 5–8, 1997.

Tow, William, Trood, Russell, and Hoshino, Toshiya, eds. *Bilateralism in a Multilateral Era: The Future of the San Francisco Alliance System in the Asia-Pacific.* Tokyo and Brisbane: Japan Institute of International Affairs and Griffith University, 1997.

Valencia, Mark J. "China and the South China Sea Disputes." *Adelphi Paper* no. 298. Oxford University Press for IISS, October 1995.

Part II

Multilateral Frameworks: Evolution and Assessment

9

Multilateral Security Cooperation in the Asia-Pacific Region

Challenges in the Post-Cold War Era

Desmond Ball

Introduction

The security architecture of the Asia-Pacific region is in the process of profound transformation owing to the end of the Cold War and the dynamic economic developments in East and Southeast Asia (Ball 1996a). Economic factors, particularly the extraordinary rates of economic growth and the high degree of economic interdependence, are changing both the structure of security relations and the systemic tendencies toward conflict or peace in the region. Economic factors have also generated new or at least more engaging security concerns. For many countries in the region, economic vitality depends upon relatively long and sometimes quite vulnerable sea lanes of communication (SLOCs). The extraordinary economic growth has provided increased resources for allocation to defense programs, raising the prospect of a regional arms race. And there are concerns that the high degree of interdependence may facilitate the spread of security problems through the region. More particularly, if growth falters, or if conflict is introduced into the system, friction and disputation may quickly permeate the region.

The end of the Cold War, the collapse of the Soviet Union, and the fundamental transformation in global and regional strategic circumstances ensuing with the elimination of the superpower competition generally have been welcomed throughout the Asia-Pacific region. New and sometimes potentially very disturbing security issues, however, have arisen in their stead.

The regional security environment is now much more complex and uncertain than it was during the Cold War. There are now more major actors on the stage—in particular, Japan, China and, over the longer term, India. There are numerous disputes involving competing territorial claims and challenges to governmental legitimacy, some of which could escalate to major regional conflict. Most countries in the region are determined to enhance their defense self-reliance to enable them to rely on their own resources when dealing with regional contingencies. Many are engaged in substantial defense buildups involving the acquisition of advanced maritime and air defense capabilities. Several are acquiring new technologies (such as ballistic missiles) or weapons of mass destruction (such as nuclear or chemical weapons) that are extremely disturbing.

Multilateral security cooperation is an integral aspect of the evolving regional security architecture. At the start of the 1990s, there was almost no security cooperation in the region apart from the bilateral relationships established during the Cold War. There was no regionwide mechanism for discussion of security matters, and the prospects for multilateralism appeared bleak. The United States, and indeed most countries in the region, were firmly committed to the maintenance of the bilateral structures. Multilateral endeavors were viewed as incompatible with the fundamental aspects of Asia-Pacific strategic cultures, and even as damaging to the architecture of the bilateral arrangements that arguably had served the region well during previous decades. The Asia-Pacific region was simply too large and diverse, in terms of the sizes, strengths, cultures, interests, and threat perceptions of its constituent states, to support any meaningful regionwide security architecture.

As it turns out, however, these "realities" were not immutable, at least insofar as they ruled out the institutionalization of an active, purposeful, and productive regional security cooperation process. Mechanisms for regionwide security dialogue have now been firmly established, of which the ASEAN Regional Forum (ARF) has emerged as the centerpiece. Numerous confidence- and security-building measures (CSBMs) have been instituted or are in the process of implementation, many of which have been designed to enhance transparency throughout the region. Considerable progress is taking place with the development and institutionalization of maritime CSBMs and other maritime cooperative measures. Cooperation among regional defense forces—involving reciprocal visits of senior officers, joint exercises and joint training programs—has burgeoned. Concepts and mechanisms for conflict prevention and arms control are now receiving more serious official consideration, with a view toward institutionalizing arrangements for preventive diplomacy and conflict resolution within the next five to ten years. There is also considerable interest in the institutionalization of mechanisms to prevent the proliferation of weapons of mass destruction.

Progress in institutionalizing security cooperation in the region over the last half decade has been extraordinary. But how should it be assessed? What has really been achieved? Against which expectations, strategic contingencies, or other criteria should the progress be measured? How does it compare to the more disturbing developments in the regional security environment?

The Achievements

The areas exhibiting the most progress involve the institutionalization of a regional security dialogue; the adoption of numerous CSBMs, particularly with respect to transparency measures; various aspects of maritime cooperation; and a wide range of defense cooperation activities (such as joint exercises and training programs).

Institutionalized Regional Security Dialogue

It is generally accepted that the most fundamental building block for regional security cooperation is the institutionalization of a regional security dialogue. Such dialogue should lead to better appreciation of the concerns, interests, and perceptions of the participating countries, enhancing mutual understanding and trust, and preventing the misinterpretations, misunderstandings and suspicions likely to cause tensions and even conflict. More generally, institutionalized dialogue should serve as a mechanism for managing some of the uncertainty that presently confounds regional security planners and analysts. Nonetheless, it was unreasonable to expect too much from the dialogue process in terms of agreed solutions to regional security problems, at least through the 1990s. The task for the near term, as Mahathir bin Mohamad stated over a decade ago with respect to regional dialogue on economic cooperation, is "the tedious one of getting to know each other" (Mahathir 1980, 18). It could well take more than a decade for the developing dialogue processes within the region to produce sufficient mutual understanding, confidence, and trust to resolve or manage substantive regional security issues.

The most important development in this area has involved the ASEAN Regional Forum (ARF), the first meeting of which took place in Bangkok in July 1994. To begin with, the ARF agenda was quite modest, although as Singapore's Defense Minister Yeo Ning Hong has noted, the fact that 18 countries "at different levels of development and with different views on how to achieve regional stability and resolve security issues" could meet to discuss sensitive security matters "is by itself a significant achievement" ("The Jane's Interview," 1994). The first meeting was exploratory in nature and was concerned as much with getting the mechanics and the process of dialogue right as it was with substantive issues.

The second ARF meeting took place in Bandar Seri Begawan in Brunei Darussalem on August 1, 1995. The ministers considered and endorsed the Report of the Chairman of the ARF Senior Officials Meeting (SOM), which was prepared in May 1995. They also adopted "a gradual evolutionary approach" to security cooperation, as set out in a Concept Paper prepared by the ASEAN Senior Officials for the ARF-SOM in Bandar Seri Begawan in May (Chairman's Statement 1995, 1; ASEAN Senior Officials 1995, 1–10). This evolution is to take place in three stages:

Stage 1: Promotion of Confidence-Building Measures
Stage 2: Development of Preventive Diplomacy Mechanisms
Stage 3: Development of Conflict-Resolution Mechanisms (Chairman's
          Statement 1995, 2).

The Concept Paper included two lists of confidence building measures and other cooperative activities (Table 9.1). The first "spells out measures which can be explored and implemented by ARF participants in the immediate future"—that is, over the next couple of years, such as publishing statements of defense policy, participating in the UN Conventional Arms Register, and engaging in reciprocal high-level personnel exchanges. The second is "an indicative list of other proposals which can be explored over the medium and long-term by ARF participants and also considered in the immediate future by the Track Two process," such as cooperative approaches to SLOCs, the establishment of zones of cooperation in areas such as the South China Sea, and the development of maritime information databases (Chairman's Statement 1995, 3–4, 7–10).

It has been recognized that the Post-Ministerial Conference (PMC) and ARF processes must be supported by the development of some institutionalized infrastructure at both the official and the nongovernmental levels. At the official level, ARF has instituted a process of Senior Officials Meetings (SOM), the first of which took place in Bangkok in May 1994, preparatory to the ARF meeting in July. Various proposals for CSBMs were raised at the SOMs (CSCAP 1994; Evans and Dibb 1995), but these received only perfunctory consideration as most of the meeting concerned the protocol and organizational aspects of the first ARF.

The second ARF-SOM took place in Brunei in May 1995, two months prior to the second ARF, and was much more productive. It received for consideration the Concept Paper prepared by the ASEAN Senior Officials, as well as the products of three other "inter-sessional" meetings (on trust-building, peacekeeping, and preventive diplomacy). In addition to endorsing the Concept Paper, the ARF-SOM also recommended the establishment of an Intersessional Support Group (ISG) on Confidence Building and of Intersessional Meetings (ISMs) on Cooperative Activities (including Peace-keeping) to assist the Chairman of the ARF-SOM (Chairman's Statement 1995, 4). These intersessional mechanisms have become the most important mechanism for the development and implementation of regional CSBMs.

The Use of "Second-Track" Processes

At the same time as the ASEAN PMC process developed into a more fully multilateralized and institutionalized Regional Security Forum, nongovern-mental activities and institutional linkages, now generally referred to as the "second track" process, have burgeoned (Ball 1994). According to a recent compilation, these second-track meetings now take place at least once weekly (Department of Foreign Affairs and Trade and Strategic Defense Studies Center 1997). Some of these are small workshops involving fewer than two dozen participants, and they are designed to address specific issues (such as security of the sea lanes through the region or territorial disputes in the South China Sea). The largest and most inclusive of the meetings, however, is the annual Asia-Pacific Roundtable, now organized by the ASEAN Institutes of Strategic and International Studies (ASEAN ISIS), which involves several hundred participants from some two dozen countries in the region.

The most structured and ambitious second track initiative has been the establishment of the Council for Security Cooperation in the Asia-Pacific (CSCAP), which was formally announced at the Seventh Roundtable in Kuala Lumpur in June 1993 (Ball 1996b). The CSCAP's progress over the past four years has been quite remarkable. Four working groups, intended to serve as the primary mechanism for CSCAP activity, have been established. One con-cerns the concepts of comprehensive and cooperative security; the second con-cerns the development of regional CSBMs, especially those that enhance transparency; the third concerns maritime cooperation in the region; and the fourth concerns the promotion of security dialogue and cooperation in the North Pacific, although it is fair to say that this group has made much less progress than the other three. A Study Group has also been established to explore the security aspects of transnational crime in the Asia-Pacific region.

Transparency

Most of the CSBMs that the ARF has endorsed for immediate implementa-tion involve the enhancement of transparency. These include arrangements for dialogue on security perceptions and selected international security issues; the publication of "voluntary statements of defense policy positions" and Defense White Papers; participation in the UN Conventional Arms Register; and increased contacts and exchanges among regional defense establishments.

Maritime Cooperation

Maritime issues are at the forefront of current regional security concerns, and they mandate that the regional CSBM process be weighted heavily toward various maritime mechanisms. In fact, the salience of maritime concerns is well-reflected in current regional CSBM proposals, as evidenced in the ASEAN Concept Paper, which employs some half dozen measures to address maritime matters directly as well as others with a significant maritime dimension. For example, maritime strike capabilities not only comprise a large proportion of the new acquisitions in the region, but these capabilities are also the ones most likely to generate offsetting acquisitions elsewhere in the region and hence to trigger unanticipated and undesired arms races. It is thus particularly important that these acquisitions are accompanied by transparency and dialogue. Many of the new maritime weapons systems, such as submarine warfare systems and long-range antiship missiles requiring over-the-horizon targeting, are more prone to accidents and miscalculations; hence the desirability of instituting some mechanism to avoid incidents at sea in the region. Other concerns, such as piracy and illegal activities throughout many of the exclusive economic zones (EEZs) in the region, can best be addressed through cooperative surveillance or information-sharing efforts and arrangements.

Some of the foundations for building confidence and security in the maritime dimension have already been instituted in the region. For example, the Western Pacific Naval Symposium (WPNS), a biennial conference initiated by the Royal Australian Navy (RAN) in 1988, gathers representatives of the navies of the ASEAN states, the United States, Japan, the Republic of Korea, the People's Republic of China, Papua New Guinea, Australia, and New Zealand for a frank exchange of views on a wide range of issues, including the law of the sea and SLOC protection. It is a unique forum and a significant step toward better understanding among regional navies. The naval dialogues in the early 1990s yielded several important conclusions. Participants agreed that the focus of cooperative activities should be on operational matters, directed to very particular concerns (perhaps mostly nonmilitary in nature), and should begin with basic modes and procedures for information exchange rather than the erection of new structures for multilateral maritime surveillance efforts.

For example, a WPNS Workshop in Sydney in July 1992 produced an agreement to develop a joint "Maritime Information Exchange Directory"

(MIED), whereby information on certain maritime activities would be shared by the participating navies (MacDougall 1992, 8). A suggested list of activities requiring "time-critical" reporting included "maritime pollution/environmental concerns; high seas robbery and piracy; fisheries infringements; search and rescue; suspicious activity indicating possible narcotics trafficking; [and] humanitarian concerns" (MacDougall 1992, 8–9). The MIED will include formatting styles, addresses for reporting information, and the agreed means of communication (e.g., specific radio frequencies).

The development of common procedures for communication between regional navies and vessels provides a capability whose significance for regional confidence-building far transcends the particular purposes of the MIED itself. Similarly, the process of reaching agreement among naval staffs on the priority areas for information reporting will enhance regional appreciation of particular national concerns and interests and will increase the "understanding of navies at the working level" (MacDougall 1992, 9).

Defense Cooperation

Defense cooperation has burgeoned since the late 1980s, particularly among the ASEAN countries and Australia. In this region, cooperative defense activities—such as reciprocal visits by senior defense officers, joint exercises, training programs and personnel exchanges—now account for the great weight of cooperative activities concerning regional security. In addition, most of the ASEAN countries, especially Indonesia, Singapore, and Malaysia, are now more engaged with Australia with respect to cooperative defense activities than with any other country, including their own ASEAN neighbors, placing Australia at the center of cooperative defense activities in Southeast Asia (Ball and Kerr 1996, 58–72).

Reciprocal Visits by Senior Officers

Reciprocal visits by senior officers provide a mechanism for increasing "openness," encouraging closer personal relationships, and enhancing mutual understanding and trust. Senior Australian Defense Force and Department of Defense personnel now visit with their ASEAN counterparts more than once a month.

Training Programs

Training programs provide a very useful means of imparting much-appreciated staff and technical skills, sharing operational concepts and doctrines, creating networks of personal friendships and professional contacts, reducing the likelihood of misunderstandings and misinterpretations, and building trust.

Table 9.1

The ARF Agenda

ANNEX A: IMMEDIATE (1995–1996)
I.   **CONFIDENCE-BUILDING MEASURES**
     Principles
     1. The development of a set of basic principles to ensure a common
        understanding and approach to interstate relations in the region; and
     2. Adoption of comprehensive approaches to security.
        Transparency
     3. Dialogue on security perceptions, including voluntary statements of defense
        policy positions;
     4. Defense publications such as Defense White Papers or equivalent
        documents as considered necessary by respective governments;
     5. Participation in UN Conventional Arms Register;
     6. Enhanced contacts, including high level visits and recreational activities;
     7. Exchanges between military academies, staff colleges and training;
     8. Observers at military exercises, on a voluntary basis; and
     9. Annual seminar for defense officials and military officers on selected
        international security issues.
II. **PREVENTIVE DIPLOMACY**
     1. Develop a set of guidelines for the peaceful settlement of disputes, taking
        into account the principles in the UN Charter and the TAC;
     2. Promote the recognition and acceptance of the purposes and principles of
        the TAC and its provisions for the pacific settlement of disputes, as
        endorsed by the UNGA in Resolution 47/53 (B) on 9 December 1992; and
     3. Seek the endorsement of other countries for the ASEAN Declaration on the
        South China Sea in order to strengthen its political and moral effect (as
        endorsed by the Programme of Action for ZOPFAN).
III. **NON-PROLIFERATION AND ARMS CONTROL**
     Southeast Asia Nuclear Weapons-Free Zone (SEANWFZ).
IV. **PEACEKEEPING**
     1. Seminars/Workshops on peacekeeping issues; and
     2. Exchange of information and experience relating to UN Peacekeeping
        Operations.
V.   **MARITIME SECURITY COOPERATION**
     Disaster Prevention
ANNEX B: MEDIUM AND LONG TERM
I.   **CONFIDENCE-BUILDING MEASURES**
     1. Further exploration of a Regional Arms Register;
     2. Regional security studies center/coordination of existing security studies
        activities;
     3. Maritime information databases;
     4. Cooperative approaches to sea lanes of communication, beginning with
        exchanges of information and training in such areas as search and rescue,
        piracy and drug control;
     5. Mechanism to mobilize relief assistance in the event of natural disasters;
     6. Establishment of zones of cooperation in areas such as the South China
        Sea;
     7. Systems of prior notification of major military deployments that have
        regionwide application; and
     8. Encourage arms manufacturers and suppliers to disclose the destination of
        their arms exports.

II. PREVENTIVE DIPLOMACY
1. Explore and devise ways and means to prevent conflict;
2. Explore the idea of appointing special representatives, in consultation with ARF members, to undertake fact-finding missions, at the request of the parties involved in an issue, and to offer their good offices, as necessary; and
3. Explore the idea of establishing a Regional Risk Reduction Center as suggested by the UN Secretary-General in his Agenda for Peace and as commended by UNGA Resolution 47/120 (see section IV, operative para 4). Such a center could serve as a database for the exchange of information.

III. NON-PROLIFERATION AND ARMS CONTROL
A regional or sub-regional arrangement agreeing not to acquire or deploy ballistic missiles.

IV. PEACEKEEPING
Explore the possibility of establishing a peacekeeping center.

V. MARITIME SECURITY COOPERATION
1. A multilateral agreement on the avoidance of naval incidents that apply to both local and external navies;
2. Sea Level/Climate Monitoring System;
3. Establishment of an ASEAN Relief and Assistance Force and a Maritime Safety(or Surveillance) unit to look after the safety of the waters in the region;
4. Conventions on the marine environment
   a. Dumping of toxic wastes
   b. Land-based sources of marine pollution;
5. Maritime surveillance; and
6. Explore the idea of joint marine scientific research.

Joint Exercises

Joint military exercises can be instrumental in promoting closer defense relations. Australia now conducts an average of one joint exercise with one or more of the ASEAN defense forces every two weeks (compared to about one every two months a decade ago), along with numerous minor exercise activities (such as Passage Exercises or PASSEXs).

These joint exercises have become not only more frequent and regular, but have also increased in scope to include a broader range of force elements. In addition, they have increasingly involved the coordination of some of the most sophisticated capabilities in the respective defense forces, and the exercise scenarios have become generally more fruitful with respect to the promotion of closer cooperation and confidence building.

Observers at Exercises

Although serious resource factors inevitably limit the conduct and scope of joint exercises, invitations to officially observe a neighbor's other exercises are still a very important CSBM, especially in terms of assuaging concern about intentions.

Forming a Critique

Assessment of these achievements is extremely difficult. First, many of the conceptual variables are quite intangible, such as "confidence," "trust," "transparency," and even some of the more elastic concepts of "security" itself. Furthermore, the standards of measurement are problematic. They are conceptually embryonic, inconstant, and, indeed, are at least in part a function of the variable being measured. Nonetheless, the simplest yardstick is the schedule set forth in the August 1995 ASEAN Concept Paper. Although inherently subjective, and reflecting the drafters' views of the acceptability of particular measures as much as the significance of the measures in terms of security enhancement, it does provide a guide to the expectations at the time of the ARF's foundation.

A much more demanding standard would incorporate the structure and systemic tendencies of the regional security architecture: that is, the extent to which the cooperative ventures are keeping abreast of the changing components and configurations of security relations and of the systemic propensities for conflict or peace in the region. The difficulty is greatly compounded by the lack of any conceptual framework for addressing the interaction of institutionalized cooperation and geostrategic developments based upon power politics and national self-interest. The theoretical literature is essentially bifocused on liberal institutionalism and extreme realism, whereas most international political activity, and certainly some of the most critical security activity in the Asia-Pacific region since the end of the Cold War, involves the confluence of cooperative modalities and power relationships.

In general, the cooperative security measures that have been officially accepted and institutionalized over the past half decade satisfy one or more of the following criteria:

First, they address the real concerns of regional security policymakers and analysts regarding certain aspects of the emerging regional security environment. These include the uncertainty pervading the region; the high levels of economic interdependence and concomitant levels of vulnerability to potentially destabilizing economic forces and economically inspired political conflict; the challenge of the major Asian powers; the vigorous arms acquisition programs underway in the region; the potential for proliferation of weapons of mass destruction; a variety of important maritime issues; the existence of numerous territorial and sovereignty disputes; and the possibility that one or more of these could erupt into war (Ball 1996d).

Second, the security measures do not impinge on core national interests, such as territorial claims and other sovereignty issues, defense capabilities and operations, or internal political processes, which might be affected by more transparent policymaking.

Third, their design and their development have been in accord with "the Asian way." In other words, cooperative security measures have involved evolutionary developments from extant regional structures rather than the importation of Western modalities or the creation of new structures; decisions are made "by consensus after careful and extensive consultations" rather than by voting; and the implementation of particular measures eschews legalisms and is left to voluntary compliance (ASEAN Senior Officials 1995, 3–4; Ball 1994). According to the ASEAN Concept Paper:

> The ARF should . . . progress at a pace comfortable to all participants. The ARF should not move "too fast for those who want to go slow and not too slow for those who want to go fast." (ASEAN Senior Officials 1995, 4)

Clearly, there are strong tensions among these criteria. Measures addressing important security issues are likely to affect national interests to some degree. And measures that are relatively easy to implement because they reflect "the Asian way" are less likely to substantively address important issues. In practice, the scope for significant maneuver is fairly limited.

The institutionalization of dialogue is a necessary building block for enhanced security cooperation, but it is also easier to put into place than other "blocks" (such as preventive diplomacy, conflict resolution, and arms control). There is no guarantee that laying the foundation will lead to any further (and harder) construction.

The ARF Agenda

The Concept Paper that the ARF adopted in August 1995 covered some three dozen proposals for CSBMs, preventive diplomacy, maritime cooperation and other cooperative measures. As noted above in Table 9.1, these were divided into two lists: the first (Annex A) containing "measures which can be explored and implemented by ARF participants in the immediate future"; and the second (Annex B) "an indicative list of other proposals which can be explored over the medium and long-term by ARF participants and also considered in the immediate future by the Track Two process" (ASEAN Senior Officials 1995, 3–4, 7–10).

The terms "immediate future" and "medium and long-term" are not defined, but ARF senior officials generally reckoned in mid-1995 that Annex A should be achieved within one to two years, whereas some of the measures in Annex B could take from three to five years and others perhaps a decade or so. In terms of the progression from confidence-building to preventive diplomacy and conflict resolution, dialogue and consultations about the latter were to begin immediately, with the expectation that some preventive diplomacy mechanisms would be devised and put into place within about five years and some conflict resolution mechanisms in about ten years.

According to this schedule, Annex A should have been substantially implemented by late 1997. In fact, there has been considerable progress toward most of its 16 measures. Many of them were fairly simple, such as the organization of "seminars/workshops on peacekeeping issues," "exchanges between military academies [and] staff colleges," and "enhanced contacts, including high level visits and recreational activities." Some required novel activity on the part of many of the members, such as the preparation and publication of Defense White Papers or "equivalent documents," although some of the products have involved little transparency. An important achievement has been the Southeast Asian Nuclear Weapons Free Zone (SEANWFZ) Treaty, which became effective on March 27, 1997. Nonetheless, some of the measures in Annex A are still some years away, such as the development of guidelines for the peaceful settlement of disputes, or the adoption by all ARF members of the principle of "comprehensive approaches to security."

It is fair to say that ARF is off to a good start toward some of the 19 measures in Annex B. This is especially true of maritime CSBMs, where there has been considerable progress with the development of maritime information databases, such as the Australian-developed Strategic Maritime Information System (SMIS). In addition, the CSCAP Working Group on Maritime Cooperation currently is drafting "Guidelines for Maritime Cooperation," a multilateral agreement on the avoidance of naval incidents, for submission to the ARF in 1998; and the CSCAP Working Group on Maritime Cooperation is exploring joint marine scientific research and other aspects of oceans management. It is quite likely that other measures will be implemented over the next few years, such as a mechanism to mobilize relief assistance in case of natural disasters, and exploration of a possible regional peacekeeping center, as well as additional maritime cooperation measures.

At the same time, it is clear that some proposals have already stagnated, such as the notion of a Regional Arms Register. Others are unlikely to be implemented during the next decade, such as the "establishment of zones of cooperation in areas such as the South China Sea." More generally, the institutionalization of preventive diplomacy, conflict resolution, or arms control is unlikely to experience much progress during the next decade.

Annex B contains three specific proposals for Stage II of the ARF agenda, preventive diplomacy: first, to explore conflict-avoidance measures; second, to explore the idea of appointing special representatives to undertake fact-finding missions and to "offer their good services"; and third, to explore the idea of establishing a Regional Risk Reduction Center. The ARF has sponsored two seminars on preventive diplomacy, the first in Seoul in May 1995 and the second in Paris in November 1996. (A third, organized by CSCAP for the ARF, was held in Singapore in September 1997). The Paris meeting, which an Australian participant described as "a useful movement forward in the application of concrete measures of preventive diplomacy in the Asia-Pacific region" (Harris 1997, 11), recommended three needs to the ARF for consideration: the need for production of a regular "regional strategic outlook"; for a "core list of CSBMs specifically oriented toward preventive diplomacy"; and the expansion of the ARF Chair to include a "good offices" role. The meeting, however, also established that the ARF had no funding for any preventive diplomacy activities, and deferred consideration of an ARF Risk Reduction Center to "the longer term" (Department of Foreign Affairs and Trade 1996).

With regard to conflict resolution, Stage III of the ARF agenda, the Concept Paper stated:

> It is not envisaged that the ARF would establish mechanisms for conflict resolution in the immediate future. The establishment of such mechanisms is *an eventual goal* that ARF participants should pursue. (ASEAN Senior Officials 1995, 5, author's italics)

The ARF agenda promises little in the way of nonproliferation and arms control. Even transparency measures concerning arms acquisitions are unacceptable to most ARF members, let alone constraints on the acquisition and employment of weapons systems. Although the Concept Paper's Annexes include two nonproliferation and arms control measures: the SEANWFZ (in Annex A) and "a regional or sub-regional arrangement agreeing not to acquire or deploy ballistic missiles" (in Annex B), these measures are essentially hortatory at this time. The entry into force of the SEANWFZ in March 1997 was a major achievement, but it is essentially symbolic. None of the ASEAN countries are prospective proliferants, and current nuclear weapons states have acceded to the Protocol only because it does not interfere with their peacetime nuclear-related operations or their use of nuclear weapons in case of war in the region.

In addition, an agreement by all ARF members prohibiting the acquisition or deployment of ballistic missiles is really not possible in the foreseeable future. The United States intends to retain some 450 to 500 intercontinental ballistic missiles (ICBMs) and 14 Trident submarines equipped with submarine-launched ballistic missiles (SLBMs). China has produced a full suite of

ICBMs, SLBMs, intermediate-range ballistic missiles (IRBMs), medium-range ballistic missiles (MRBMs), and short-range, tactical ballistic missiles. At least 17 ICBMs (7 CSS-4/DF-5 and 10 CSS-3/DF-4) and 70 IRBMs (60 CSS-2/DF-3 and 10 CSS-5/DF-21) have been deployed; a MIRV (multiple independently targeted reentry vehicle) version of the CSS-4 is being tested; and two new solid-fuel mobile ICBMs (the DF-31 and DF-41) are being developed for deployment soon after the turn of the century. China also has exported some short-range ballistic missiles elsewhere in the region (for example, it exported M-11 missiles, with a range of some 300 km, to Pakistan). North Korea has some 136 Scud B/C missiles in service, and is developing the longer-range Nodong-1 (1,500 km) and Taepo Dong (2000 km) ballistic missiles. South Korea has some 12 NHK (250 km) ballistic missiles. Taiwan is developing the 950 km-range Tien Ma ballistic missile (Mack 1996; Opall 1996; Bowen et al. 1997; Moosa 1997; "One Arrow, Three Stars" 1997). At the same time, however, there is little likelihood that the Southeast Asian nations will acquire or develop ballistic missiles in the near future.

There is no mention of other categories of weapons systems or of other possible arms control arrangements. Some disturbing aspects of the current arms acquisition programs in the region that remain unaddressed are the "offensive" character of some of the new weapons systems, particularly new strike capabilities such as cruise missiles, and the implications of these acquisitions for arms race and crisis stability (Ball 1993b; 104–105; Ball 1996c, 217–219). I believe that the danger of cruise missile proliferation is more serious than that of ballistic missiles in this region. Cruise missiles are technically easier to produce and cheaper to acquire then ballistic missiles. Enabling technologies such as antiship cruise missiles (such as Exocets and Harpoons), unmanned aerial vehicles (UAVs), GPS navigation systems and small turbojet engines are now widely available. Moreover, the development and deployment of cruise missiles are also more difficult to monitor (International Institute for Strategic Studies 1997, 16–31). Several countries in East Asia have begun either to design and develop long-range, land-attack cruise missiles indigenously (e.g., China), or to consider the acquisition of such missiles (e.g., Australia).

Imbalances in the Emerging Regional Security Architecture

Self-reliance, Bilateralism, and Multilateralism

Some observers have asserted that the development of cooperative security activities represents a transformation of the regional security architecture in which national interests, power politics, and military force are being replaced by common security interests and the peaceful resolution of differences. In fact, however, the emerging regional security architecture will be firmly grounded in national self-reliance, with strong and important bilateral connections, and a gradually thickening but still very thin veneer of multilateralism.

In light of the end of the Cold War and the changing regional security environment, most East Asian countries have resolved to enhance their defense self-reliance to improve their ability to deal with regional contingencies on the basis of their own resources. Some countries, of course, such as China, Vietnam, and Indonesia, already had adopted policies of self-reliance or "national resilience" in the 1960s. As the Malaysian Prime Minister, Dr. Mahathir Mohamad, stated in July: "In the final analysis we can rely only on ourselves" (Skehan 1997).

Although much of the regional dialogue and confidence-building agenda is multilateral, most arrangements involving defense forces are bilateral. Much of the burgeoning security cooperation in the region is bilateral rather than multilateral, and some of the existing bilateral connections remain critical to the stability of the regional security architecture, especially the U.S.-South Korean and U.S.-Japanese connections.

The Relative Weight of Emergent Concerns and Cooperative Developments

It was noted earlier that the new activity concerning security dialogue and cooperation in the region was a response to the concerns of regional security policymakers and analysts over such aspects of the emerging regional security environment as pervasive uncertainty, the vigorous arms acquisition programs, the prospect of proliferation of weapons of mass destruction (WMD), maritime issues, and the numerous territorial and sovereignty disputes that cause tensions and could lead to war. It was also noted that the ability to meet these concerns constitutes the most important but also most demanding standard for measuring the recent cooperative achievements. Has cooperation kept abreast of the more disturbing developments in the regional security environment?

Two important concerns that are amenable to this evaluation are the propensity for conflict and the danger of an arms race in the region. The propensity for conflict can be evaluated in light of developments in preventive diplomacy and other conflict prevention and conflict-resolution mechanisms.

As discussed above, the ARF has been sponsoring substantial dialogue about preventive diplomacy, but no conflict prevention mechanisms are likely to be established in the foreseeable future, and the establishment of mechanisms for conflict resolution remains "an eventual goal." At the same time, however, there is much fertile ground for conflict in East Asia, and an increasing likelihood of significant war in the region over the next decade or so. The geostrategic shifts, involving immense changes in the economic strength and military capabilities of countries in the region, will be extremely difficult to accommodate peacefully. More specifically, there are more than 30 areas of simmering and potential conflict involving competing sovereignty claims, challenges to government legitimacy, and territorial disputes in East Asia.

Most of these issues are unlikely to lead to outright conflict. Some could well be resolved through negotiation, possibly involving the institution of joint surveillance and development zones encompassing the areas of disputation. Others are quiescent, such as the Philippines' claim to Sabah, and others will remain essentially internal matters, such as the insurgency movements in Indonesia and the Philippines. Nevertheless, the high proportion of issues between nations suggests that conflict is more likely in the Asia-Pacific region than elsewhere.

It is important to note that the half dozen countries in Northeast Asia figure in about a third of the conflict issues and in nearly half of the conflicts between states in the region. Further, most of the disputed issues, with more intense and more frequent crises, as well as more frequent use of force, involve the Northeast Asian countries. War on the Korean peninsula was a real possibility in May and June 1994. I believe that between now and 2010, the likelihood that at least one or more of these or some other issue will erupt into a major war is higher than the probability that substantial conflict prevention mechanisms will be established in the region.

The second area of concern is the regional arms buildup and the relative development of arms control arrangements. It is clear that at least over the next decade or so, there is very little possibility that East Asian countries will engage in arms control or even in multilateral security dialogues to constrain their force development plans and programs. Most countries in the region are committed to robust acquisition programs and can provide both the funds and the strategic justifications for them (Ball, 1996c, 210–214, 217–219).

It is wrong to characterize the current arms acquisition programs in East Asia as an "arms race." In most countries in the Asia-Pacific region, the proportions of GNP committed to defense spending were much lower in 1994 than they had been in the early 1980s—typically 30 to 40 percent lower, with the exception of China, whose spending has remained relatively constant. In Asia as a whole, the total value of arms imports (in constant dollars) was much lower in 1993 than it was in the late 1980s. In East Asia, arms imports were valued at $4.6 billion in 1993 as compared to $6.9 billion in

1988, and in Asia as a whole, arms imports were worth $7.3 billion in 1993 as compared to $14.4 billion in 1989. In addition, there has been little evidence to date of the action-reaction dynamics that are an essential feature of arms races. Rather, the current regional acquisition programs can best be explained in terms of the requirements for enhanced self-reliance in the context of a rapidly changing and increasingly uncertain regional security environment.

Nonetheless, the possibility that some regional arms race will develop around the turn of the century remains a serious concern. Because the requirements for defense self-reliance cannot be defined without reference to the capabilities of neighbors and potential adversaries further afield, there must come a point where further acquisitions begin to stimulate reciprocal or interactive dynamics. By the turn of the century, most countries in the region will face the demands not only to continue modernizing their forces but also to replace the weapons systems they acquired in such large volumes during the late 1980s. Defense budgets and acquisition programs may enter another cycle of substantial increase, but this time from a base of higher numbers and more sophisticated capabilities than during the late 1980s and early 1990s.

The "offensive" character of some of the new weapons systems being acquired is also cause for concern. Many of the new acquisitions (such as the maritime attack aircraft, modern surface combatants, and submarines, all equipped with antiship missiles) involve strike capabilities with offensive connotations. For many countries, they provide the most cost-effective basis for self-reliance; in some cases, such as that of Australia, a viable posture of self-reliance would not be possible without some minimal strike capabilities. Unfortunately, these capabilities also are the most likely to generate counter-acquisitions. This is true particularly of new fighter aircraft purchases. Not only is air power at the forefront of force modernization programs in the region, but it is also a principal means of projecting power in the region. The quantitative and qualitative enhancements of air power thus are perhaps the most prone to triggering unanticipated and undesired arms acquisition competitions.

Other acquisitions, such as submarines and long-range antiship missiles, are more disturbing in terms of their implications for crisis stability. The underwater environment is particularly opaque, and underwater operations are especially subject to uncertainty, confusion, loss of control, and accidents. Similarly, over-the-horizon targeting of long-range antiship missiles raises the prospect of errors and miscalculation, and making inadvertent escalation increasingly likely. I believe that over the next decade and a half, the probability that serious manifestations of these disturbing possibilities will occur will become greater than the likelihood that arms control mechanisms will be instituted with any capacity to assuage them.

Geostrategic Discordance

There is clear subregional discord between recent regional security cooperation efforts and the regional security developments that led to them. Whereas
the great weight of the emergent regional security concerns is coming from
Northeast Asia, the impetus for and mode of cooperation are coming mainly
from Southeast Asia (Ball 1997). The ARF evolved from the ASEAN PMC
process, and although its membership and agenda have become regionwide,
it remains very much an ASEAN creature in both substantive and procedural
terms. The ASEAN Institutes of Strategic and International Studies (ASEAN
ISIS) have been involved in the development of many of the regional CSBMs,
and are central to the second track process, including the establishment of
CSCAP. Most of the current defense cooperation activities involve the
ASEAN countries.

These cooperative mechanisms are on the whole not well suited for serious dialogue about—let alone resolution of—Northeast Asian security issues. With respect to the ARF, for example, the Northeast Asian countries
cannot be expected to pay much heed to a body in which two-thirds of the
members are extraregional, at least over issues affecting their important security interests. The ARF and CSCAP can promote cooperation in Northeast
Asia by highlighting the area's critical importance to regional security, suggesting and analyzing relevant cooperative avenues and mechanisms, and
providing political encouragement. But for matters affecting the important
security interests of the Northeast Asian countries alone, the dialogue arrangements and conflict-resolution mechanisms must be exclusive, and they
must be composed of and constructed by the countries in Northeast Asia
itself. Unhappily, however, the record for multilateral security cooperation
in Northeast Asia remains very poor.

Engaging China

Regional concerns about China are becoming manifest in several ways.
Japan's declaration that the Self-Defense Force (SDF) was upgrading its
"watch" on China (*Washington Times* 1996); Taiwan's acquisition of an
antitheater ballistic missile (ATBM) system; the Philippines' decision in February 1995 to fund extensive defense modernization; and the conduct of
Indonesia's largest-ever military exercise (involving 20,000 troops, 40 aircraft, and 50 ships) around the Natuna Islands in the southwestern part of the
South China Sea in September 1996 are several of many examples
(Richardson 1996; Hatano 1996). Nonetheless, it is imperative—as Malaysia's
leaders have argued—to avoid portraying China as a threat to the region. In

June 1993, Malaysian Defense Minister Datuk Seri Najib Tun Razak observed that China was becoming "the West's new bogeyman," and he argued that "we should not allow any country to drive a wedge between regional states and China" (Razak 1993). And Malaysian Prime Minister Mahathir has warned that to regard China as a threat "would not only be a wrong policy, but it would also be a bad and dangerous one" (Ahmad 1995). It could become, in the worst case, a self-fulfilling prophecy.

Rather, it is essential to engage China in multilateral dialogues, confidence-building arrangements, preventive diplomacy, and other forms of security cooperation in the region. This will not be an easy exercise (Shambaugh 1994, 428). Many Chinese security analysts and policymakers still regard multilateralism as either largely irrelevant or even potentially damaging to resolving regional security issues, and probably also damaging to China's national interests. China is unwilling to discuss substantive issues concerning the South China Sea or Taiwan, which it regards as "internal affairs," and it refuses either to allow Taiwanese participation in multilateral security fora or to participate itself when Taiwan might be involved. Substantial military transparency is unacceptable. Thus, to achieve success, China's leaders and security planners must be persuaded that multilateral dialogue, transparency, and cooperative activity are more likely to alleviate regional apprehensions about its defense policies and acquisition programs and thus to enhance its security interests over the long term (Garrett and Glaser 1994).

Involving Taiwan

The involvement of Taiwan in regional security cooperation poses an intractable problem. Although Taiwan's involvement is essential to both inclusive regional dialogue and the resolution of some of the most critical regional security issues, there is little prospect for Taiwan's direct involvement in these processes and activities during the foreseeable future.

With a population of only 21 million, Taiwan had a GNP in 1995 of $262 billion, or almost half that of China ($560 billion). Its foreign exchange reserves ($87.7 billion in November 1996) are the second or third highest in the world. It is the world's seventh largest source of foreign investment capital, and the twelfth largest trading country in the world. For many nations, Taiwan is a more important trading partner than is China. The United States is its largest trading partner, with Japan second and mainland China third—in fact, Taiwan may well be the largest source of foreign investment in China (Klintworth 1995, 179). The implications of these economic relationships for regional security are extremely complex but doubtless profound (Shirk and Twomey 1996; Smith and Harris 1997).

Taiwan's defense expenditure was $13.1 billion in 1995—the fourth highest in East Asia. It now has one of the most modern defense forces in Asia, supported by one of the strongest indigenous defense industrial sectors in the region. As Taiwan is in the process of acquiring some 466 new fighter aircraft (*Mirage* 2000s, F-16s, and *Ching Kuo* fighters), some 30 new destroyers and frigates, and 6 to 10 submarines, as well as various missile (and antimissile) systems, serious progress toward arms control regimes in East Asia is impossible without the involvement of Taiwan.

Beyond its defense capabilities, Taiwan is also a party to several of the territorial disputes in East Asia. The relationship between Taipei and Beijing is one of the most disturbing issues in the region, especially given Beijing's refusal to disavow the use of force against Taiwan and its propensity to practice large-scale military operations (including ballistic missile launches) in the Taiwan Strait. The general acceptance of the "one China" policy means that the ultimate resolution of the issue depends on Beijing and Taipei, but the rest of the region has direct and legitimate interests in the process and outcome of any such resolution. Taipei and Beijing are also competing claimants to the Senkaku (or Diaoyutai) islands, as well as virtually all of the islands in the South China Sea. (Indeed, the Taiwanese garrison on Itu Aba/Taiping Island is the largest in the South China Sea, and is larger than the deployments of all other countries on all the other occupied islands).

There is no question that Taiwan must be involved in regional security dialogue activities as well as any prospective regional arms control and conflict resolution mechanisms. The challenge is to design and develop arrangements that, while satisfying or bypassing conditions imposed by Beijing, provide for Taipei's meaningful involvement.

Frameworking the Korean Peninsula

The Korean peninsula is the most volatile and most serious flash point in the Asia-Pacific region. Across the Demilitarized Zone (DMZ) separating North and South Korea, only 40 km north of Seoul, South Korea faces a virtually fully mobilized, obdurate Communist regime, with an active armed force of over a million personnel, and a resolute nuclear development program. The threats to regional security that North Korea poses are manifold. They include military threats generated by its military capabilities, aggressive espionage activities, nuclear weapons program, and ballistic missile development and test program, with periodic crises involving the real possibility of war on the peninsula (as in mid-1994). But they also increasingly include concerns about potential instability arising from North Korea's economic decline, food and energy crises, and political uncertainties (Snyder 1996).

Despite these urgent concerns, there are neither well-established proce-dures for dealing with issues of economic crisis or political instability on the peninsula, nor any mechanism for addressing their implications for regional security. Indeed, in the absence of any confidence-building process that ad-dresses the fundamental sources of tension on the peninsula, such mecha-nisms would be of limited effectiveness.

Conclusion

It is extremely difficult to assess the progress of multilateral security coop-eration in the Asia-Pacific region. The progress over the last half decade has been extraordinary, and some expectations have been more than satisfied. At the same time, the impact of dialogue and other cooperative measures on the regional geostrategic architecture remains marginal, and it is quite likely that advances will fail to match some of the more negative possibilities, includ-ing major regional conflict.

The achievements of the past five years cannot be overemphasized. The progress has really been quite remarkable. Various arrangements have been established for institutionalized dialogue and confidence-building, the most important of which are the ARF and its intersessional activities, but mecha-nisms for naval cooperation, such as the Western Pacific Naval Symposium (WPNS) and some second-track arrangements, such as CSCAP, are impor-tant as well. Most of the ARF's *Concept Paper*'s Annex A has been imple-mented, and there has already been some progress with many of the measures in Annex B.

For continued progress, however, new conceptual tools must be devel-oped, especially where national interest, power politics, and institutional-ized cooperation coexist. Assessing complex, subjective, often intangible, and rapidly and profoundly changing events and processes requires clearly delineated criteria and analytical methods. More conceptual work also is necessary with respect to some of the premises of confidence-building, trans-parency, and peace and security (Ball and Kerr 1996, 91–92). For one thing, serious externalities stemming from the emergence of the defense establish-ments and armed forces as the leading edge of regional security cooperation remain unexplored (Ball 1993, 65–66). And more conceptual work is neces-sary concerning the definition and impact of "the Asian way" on regional security enhancement. For example, the importance of consensus and, in the case of the ARF, moving "at a pace comfortable to all participants" requires additional discussion (ASEAN Senior Officials 1995, 6).

The ARF could clarify matters somewhat by providing further and clearer articulation of its agenda. The *Concept Paper* was drafted in early 1996, and reflected the strategic concerns, confidence-building measures and expectations that had emerged about 1993 and 1994. As the measures contained in Annex A of the *Concept Paper* should have been explored and implemented by now, an interim stocktaking is appropriate at this time and should include the development of a new Annex for the "immediate future"; the addition of measures reflecting such imminent concerns as the proliferation of long-range, land-attack cruise missiles; and a clear explanation of ARF's expectations for key milestones. Many countries will resist more specific schedules. Many will reckon that the process is more important than the specific outcome. But without an ability to measure progress, to take stock, and to develop new initiatives, the process will succumb to inefficiency and irrelevance.

The institutionalization of dialogue is a crucially important foundation for regional security cooperation. But while necessary, its achievement implies little about the prospects for multilateralism in connection with conflict prevention, arms control and other major matters of regional security management. The process is still in its infancy, and it is simply too soon to know whether dialogue will proceed into the more consequential but more difficult realms. Already, however, some critical imbalances have become apparent.

First, the role of multilateralism in the regional security architecture will be fairly marginal, as compared to self-reliance. Second, progress with institutionalized cooperation is failing to keep pace with some of the more disturbing strategic developments (such as the acquisition of long-range cruise missile and other strike capabilities).

Third, the subregional discord caused by the virtual lack of security cooperation in Northeast Asia is fundamental to the dynamics of the security architecture of the Asia-Pacific region as a whole.

Given the overwhelming magnitude of the security concerns in Northeast Asia (amounting to more than 80 percent of defense expenditures), the impressive progress made with security cooperation among the ASEAN countries and Australia still counts for little. In other words, the enhancement of security cooperation in Northeast Asia is the most important consideration in determining the structure and operational modalities of the emerging security architecture of the Asia-Pacific region. Without enhanced cooperation in Northeast Asia, balance of power strategies based upon narrow conceptions of national interests will inevitably prevail.

Finally, the institutionalization of security cooperation in Northeast Asia must proceed on many fronts—bilateral and multilateral, formal and informal, direct and indirect. It must include mechanisms and processes designed to build trust in Northeast Asia. It must address such issues as bilateral arrangements for dealing with particular conflict issues (e.g., relations across the Taiwan Strait; North Korea-South Korea relations; and various territorial disputes); multilateral mechanisms for addressing energy and other economic problems, and political instabilities, and their regional security implications; mechanisms for subregional dialogue on security issues; arms control and disarmament agreements (with respect to both conventional armaments and weapons of mass destruction); and mechanisms designed to engage the Northeast Asian countries in the broader web of regional cooperative security activities.

Bibliography

Ahmad, Reme. "Malaysia: Malaysia PM Slams Nations That See China as a Threat." *Reuters News Service*, January 23, 1995.

ASEAN Senior Officials. "The ASEAN Regional Forum: A Concept Paper." May 1995.

Ball, Desmond. "Strategic Culture in the Asia Pacific Region." *Security Studies* 3, no. 1 (Autumn 1993a): 44–74.

———. "Arms and Affluence: Military Acquisitions in the Asia Pacific Region." *International Security* 18, no. 3 (Winter 1993b): 78–112.

———. "A New Era in Confidence Building: The Second-Track Process in the Asia Pacific Region." *Security Dialogue* 25, no. 2 (June 1994): 157–76.

———. "Introduction." In Desmond Ball, ed., *The Transformation of Security in the Asia Pacific Region*. London: Frank Cass, 1996a: 1–14.

———. "CSCAP: Its Future Place in the Regional Security Architecture." In Bunn Nagara and Cheah Siew Ean, eds., *Managing Security and Peace in the Asia Pacific*. Kuala Lumpur: Institute of Strategic and International Studies (ISIS), 1996b: 289–325.

———. "Arms Acquisitions in the Asia Pacific: Scale, Positive and Negative Impacts on Security and Managing the Problem." In Thangam Ramnath, ed., *The Emerging Regional Security Architecture in the Asia Pacific Region*. Kuala Lumpur: Institute of Strategic and International Studies (ISIS), 1996c.

———. "The Agenda for Cooperation." In Ray Funnell, ed., *Asia Pacific Security: The Challenges Ahead*. Canberra: Australian College of Defense and Strategic Studies, 1996d: 50–77.

———. "Northeast Asia and Security Cooperation in the Asia Pacific Region." In R.K. Thomas, ed., *Asia Pacific Security: Challenges and Prospects for North East Asia*. Canberra: The Australian College of Defense and Strategic Studies, 1997: 54–76.

Ball, Desmond, and Kerr, Pauline. *Presumptive Engagement: Australia's Approach to Regional Security in the 1990s*. Sydney: Allen & Unwin, 1996.

Bowen, Wyn; McCarthy, Tim, and Porteous, Holly. "Ballistic Missile Shadow Lengthens." *International Defense Review* 2, no. 2 (February 1997 suppl.): 1–3.

Chairman's Statement of the Second ASEAN Regional Forum (ARF). Bandar Seri Begawan, August 1, 1995.

CSCAP Pro-term Committee. *The Security of the Asia Pacific Region*. Memorandum no. 1, Council for Security Cooperation in the Asia Pacific, April 1994.

Department of Foreign Affairs and Trade. Second ARF Seminar on Preventive Diplomacy: Chairman's Statement. November 8, 1996. Available at http:// www.dfat.gov.au/arf/prevdihtr.

Department of Foreign Affairs and Trade and Strategic and Defence Studies Center. *Regional Security Dialogue: A Calendar of Asia Pacific Events, July 1997–June 1998.* Canberra: July 1997.

Evans, Gareth, and Dibb, Paul. *Australian Paper on Practical Proposals for Security Cooperation in the Asia Pacific Region.* Paper commissioned by the 1993 ASEAN PMC SOM and submitted to the ARF SOM in Bangkok, April 1994. Canberra: Strategic and Defense Studies Center, Australian National University, January 1995.

Garrett, Banning, and Glaser, Bonnie. "Multilateral Security in the Asia-Pacific Region and Its Impact on Chinese Interests: Views from Beijing." *Contemporary Southeast Asia* 16, no. 1 (June 3, 1994): 14–34.

Harris, Stuart. "ARF Track Two Seminars on Preventive Diplomacy." Australia and Security Cooperation in the Asia Pacific (AUS-CSCAP) Newsletter no. 4 (March 1997).

Hatano, Ruriko. "Indonesia to Stage Massive Military Drill." *Daily Yomiuri* (Tokyo), August 24, 1996.

International Institute for Strategic Studies. *Strategic Survey 1996/97.* Oxford: Oxford University Press, 1987.

"The Jane's Interview." *Jane's Defence Weekly*, February 19, 1994.

Klintworth, Gary. *New Taiwan, New China: Taiwan's Changing Role in the Asia Pacific Region.* Melbourne: Longman Australia, 1995.

MacDougall, Vice Admiral I.D.G., Chief of Naval Staff (CNS). "CNS Presentation to WPNS III on the Inaugural Western Pacific Naval Symposium Workshop." Sydney, Australia, July 9–10, 1992.

Mack, Andrew. *Proliferation in Northeast Asia.* Washington, DC: The Henry Stimson Center, Occasional Paper no. 28 (July 1996).

Mahathir, Mohamad bin. "Tak Kenal Maka Tak Cinta." In *Asia Pacific in the 1980s: Toward Greater Symmetry in Economic Interdependence.* Jakarta: Center for Strategic and International Studies, May 1980.

Moosa, Eugene. "Missile Could Strike Japan, Minister Warns." *The Sydney Morning Herald*, April 15, 1997, p. 12.

"'One Arrow, Three Stars': China's MIRV Programme—Part One." *Jane's Intelligence Review* 9, no. 5 (May 1997): 216–18.

Opall, Barbara. "Study: North Korea Can Win by Waging Bio-Chem War." *Defense News*, November 4, 1996, p. 3.

Razak, Datuk Seri Najib Tun. "Region Must Chart Its Own Destiny." *The Star* (Kuala Lumpur), June 19, 1993, p. 20.

Richardson, Michael. "Indonesia Plans War Games to Caution China." *International Herald Tribune*, August 16, 1996, p. 4.

Shambaugh, David. "Pacific Security in the Pacific Century." *Current History*, December 1994: 423–29.

Shirk, Susan L., and Twomey, Christopher, eds. *Power and Prosperity: Economics and Security Linkages in Asia Pacific.* New Brunswick, NJ: Transaction Publishers, 1996.

Skehan, Craig. "Mahathir Questions U.S. Defence Pledges." *The Sydney Morning Herald*, July 26, 1997, p. 7.

Smith, Heather, and Harris, Stuart. "Economic Relations Across the Taiwan Strait: Interdependence or Dependence?" In Greg Austin, ed., *Missile Diplomacy and Taiwan's Future: Innovations in Politics and Military Strategy.* Canberra: Australian National University, Strategic and Defense Studies Center, Papers on Strategy and Defense no. 122, 1997.

Snyder, Scott. "A Coming Crisis on the Korean Peninsula?: The Food Crisis, Economic Decline, and Political Considerations." Washington, DC: United States Institute of Peace, 1996.

The International Institute for Strategic Studies (IISS). *Strategic Survey 1996/97.* Oxford: Oxford University Press, 1997: 16–31.

Washington Times. "Japan White Paper Upgrades China Watch." July 20, 1996, p. 7.

10

Assessing the ARF and CSCAP

Paul M. Evans

> *Anarchy as such is not a structural cause of anything. What matters is its social structure, which varies across anarchies. An anarchy of friends differs from one of enemies, one of self-help from one of collective security, and these are all consti-tuted by structures of shared knowledge.*
> *—Alexander Wendt (1995, 95)*

The idea that the ASEAN Regional Forum (ARF), a formal governmental process, and the Council for Security Cooperation in the Asia Pacific (CSCAP), a nongovernmental one, should be closely connected is not uni-versally shared. Some governmental officials have stated that the ARF does not need CSCAP and can arrange its own track-two (or track-one-and-a-half) activities more effectively without it. As a corollary, some academics have stated that CSCAP is too close to government and should do more to preserve its independence and autonomy (Woods 1997).

Yet in conception, approach, intentions, and substantive activities, the two are twins running in tandem. The concept of an Asia-Pacific-wide dialogue process with both formal governmental and "track two" dimensions took root in the summer of 1991, beginning with a series of meetings in Jakarta, Manila and Bangkok, involving an overlapping cast of officials, academics, and institute directors. They were formally launched in 1993 against the back-ground of uncertainty about the post-Cold War security order in East Asia and particularly the rise of China and the regional debate over the appropri-ate response.

The two institutions are the highest profile and most ambitious of the multilateral dialogue fora that have arisen in the 1990s. Both are composed of participants from diverse nations, with varied intellectual outlooks. In both, individuals, institutes, and governments from the Association of Southeast Asian Nations (ASEAN) play a leading role. And both have established a coherent if not complete membership grouping, a regular schedule of meetings, a loose though identifiable institutional structure, and systematic work plans.

It is premature to reach a conclusion whether the two institutions can be judged successes or failures. But now that both have an identifiable character and identity, it is an opportune moment to reflect on their progress and future development. With their founding phase complete, what lies ahead? What can and should we expect them to contribute?

Against What Standards?

Identifying standards against which we can understand the character and effectiveness of the two institutions leads into some tricky terrain. Although the research on institution-building in the Asia-Pacific is growing quickly, only a few studies have examined the origins and development of the ARF and CSCAP. The most important is Michael Leifer's short monograph on the ARF (Leifer 1996). Its general conclusion is a measured skepticism about both the accomplishments of the ARF and its future prospects. While acknowledging the successes of the ARF in establishing a regional dialogue, Leifer emphasizes that the institution confronts substantial problems in extending the ASEAN style of institution building to other parts of Asia, especially Northeast Asia, and involving great powers, especially China, in substantive discussions.

Underlying Leifer's conclusions is his view, shared by several British-based writers, that the ARF is possible only because of a fortuitous moment in the regional balance of power. At best, it can serve to make the balance-of-power system work more effectively. Reflecting one stream of realist political thinking, Leifer believes that the existence of international anarchy and its solutions are universal problems of the state system. By extension, the argument goes, the ARF (and consequently CSCAP) cannot play a primary role in building peace because the only logical solutions to the problem of international anarchy are either collective security or collective defense systems. It is a "category mistake," he argues, to assume that the ARF can actually solve problems or mature into a security framework:

> The fact of the matter is that the ARF . . . is an embryonic, one-dimensional approach to regional security among states of considerable cultural and political diversity and thus suffers from the natural shortcomings of such an undertaking. To interpret its role in terms of a new intellectual paradigm

in international relations would be the height of intellectual naivete. It is more realistic to regard the Forum as a modest contribution to a viable balance or distribution of power within the Asia-Pacific by other than traditional means. Those means are limited, however, and the multilateral undertaking faces the same order of difficulty as the biblical Hebrew slaves in Egypt who were obliged to make bricks without straw. A constituency for any alternative form of security cooperation does not exist in [the] Asia-Pacific. (Leifer 1996, 59)

Others proceed from a different philosophical starting point and arrive at a more open-ended and positive conclusion, especially if the ARF and CSCAP are evaluated as part of the same process instead of as self-standing mechanisms. Among this group are Amitav Acharya (1997), Desmond Ball (1993), Mohamed Jawhar Hassan (1997), Jusuf Wanandi (1996), Yuen Foong Khong (1997) and myself (Evans 1995). Those proverbial bricks, these "measured optimists" believe, are being made in a distinctive and evolutionary way using indigenously available resources. If nothing else, this group is part of the constituency for exploring alternative forms of security cooperation beyond balance of power politics, while recognizing the enormous constraints—material and ideational—that stand in the way.

Theoretical introspection and debates have not been central preoccupations of the pragmatic individuals who have created the ARF and CSCAP. Nonetheless, arguments about the nature and prospects of these dialogue structures inevitably intersect with an academic debate about theoretical origins. In its current manifestation in the British, North American, and Australasian canon, the three contending positions of most interest and policy significance are realism, liberal institutionalism, and constructivism. The intellectual dividing points are numerous and substantial, and include disagreements about the universality of international anarchy under the Westphalian state system; the role of history and culture in shaping institutional responses to this anarchy; the character and strength of the nascent institutions emerging within Asia; the nature and even existence of international society (or community) in Asia and its subregions; and the transformative possibilities of ideas like cooperative and comprehensive security.

From a *Realpolitik* perspective, CSCAP and the ARF are limited instruments for promoting stability and reassurance by reducing anxiety and promoting exchange about security perceptions—a kind of getting-to-know-you exercise with no expectation that the interaction will change the fundamental nature or interests of the participants. From a liberal institutionalist perspective, the value of the institutions can be measured by their capacity to contribute to stability by establishing regional norms and increasing the costs of violating them. Involvement in international institutions, even dialogue mechanisms like the ARF and CSCAP, adds new multiple costs and benefits (such as side-payments, threats of sanctions, linkages to other issue areas) such that cooperation pays, even for states with opportunistic, prisoner's dilemma-like payoff preferences (Martin 1993). From a constructivist perspective, CSCAP and the ARF can be viewed as part of a process of redefining interests and identities and socializing states into new forms of behavior. They can "teach" states new interests through a complex set of ideational channels including nongovernmental institutions (NGOs), transnational coalitions, and domestic constituency building (Risse-Kappen 1995; Katzenstein 1996). Though it is only a matter of historical *possibility*, these nascent dialogue mechanisms are potential gateways to a system of cooperative or even collective security. This security may be based either on the foundations of international organizations as experienced elsewhere, or on a distinctively Asian basis reflecting the conditions of economic interdependence and cultural identity at the end of the twentieth century. At a minimum, CSCAP and the ARF are devices through which a new regional order can be conceived.

I begin with the assumption that there is no guarantee that dialogue channels like the ARF or CSCAP will produce a more stable and peaceful Asia in the decade to come. Indeed, both face serious obstacles. To extend Studs Terkel's quip that "all of life is six to five against," the odds on any institution surviving and prospering are even lower. But I am also starting from the assumption that these Asian-based institutions are not preordained to failure or irrelevance because they do not conform to a realist approach to overcoming the anarchical condition of the state system.

What Kind of Leadership?

It is widely acknowledged and frequently stated that ASEAN members are the "primary driving force" and play the "pivotal role" in both institutions. The ARF, as its name implies, is chaired by an ASEAN country on a rotational basis. Conversely, CSCAP uses a co-chair system, with one of the two co-chairs of the Steering Committee selected from an ASEAN country. At least one of the co-chairs of each working and study group, save one (the North Pacific Working Group), is co-chaired by an individual from an ASEAN country. Moreover, both institutions make explicit reference to extending the principles and practices that have been effective within ASEAN to a larger regional setting.

The "ASEAN way" has received considerable academic attention. It has been accorded a variety of characteristics, including:

- establishing a comfort level among all participants
- building cordial relations among political elites
- emphasizing inclusiveness and avoiding strategies of exclusion and isolation
- reinforcing state-enhancing principles of sovereignty and equality
- avoiding interference in the domestic affairs of other states
- emphasizing encouragement rather than punishment
- moving at a pace acceptable to all participants
- operating on the basis of consensus rather than majority rule
- fostering the habit of disagreeing without being disagreeable
- avoiding bureaucratic institutionalization through permanent secretariats
- promoting "soft regionalism" by using nonbinding and voluntary commitments rather than formal treaties and negotiations
- using multilateral processes to set the stage for successful bilateral negotiations and conflict management
- developing instruments for sublimating and defusing conflicts rather than resolving them
- building cooperation in an evolutionary, step-by-step manner rather than by grand design, and
- supporting the vocabulary and rhetoric of cooperative and comprehensive security

Mak Joon Nom has distilled these characteristics into six key features of the ASEAN approach. First, it is unstructured, with no clear format for decision making or implementation. Second, it often lacks a formal agenda; issues are negotiated as and when they arise. Third, it is a consensus-building exercise. Fourth, decisions are made on the basis of unanimity. Fifth, decision making can be a lengthy process without a fixed timetable because of the need for consensus. Finally, it is closed and lacks transparency (Mak 1995).

Although ASEAN has put an indelible and distinctive stamp on the current phase of Asia-Pacific multilateralism, the ASEAN-ization thesis can be overdrawn. First, the ASEAN approach is neither as consistent nor as static as it first appears. Despite its preference for informality, ASEAN has occasionally used formal and binding treaties (e.g., The Treaty of Amity and Cooperation, the Southeast Asia Nuclear Weapons Free Zone). Despite the commitment to open regionalism in institutions such as the Asia-Pacific Economic Cooperation (APEC) group, the ARF, and CSCAP, the ASEAN countries occasionally have championed exclusive regional processes, including the East Asia Economic Caucus (pushed principally by Malaysia), the Asia-Europe Meetings (ASEM), and its track-two companion, the Council for Asia-Europe Cooperation (CAEC), which consciously exclude North Americans even in observer or associate member roles.

Second, in the ARF and CSCAP, as in APEC, others who sit at the table, while respecting and supporting ASEAN's leading role, have their own perspectives on the pace and direction of the institutions. In CSCAP, like the Pacific Economic Cooperation Council (PECC) before it, the founding members included active and vocal participants from outside of ASEAN. Much of the security cooperation vocabulary has been borrowed from elsewhere, though, to be sure, substantially modified as it has filtered through regional discussions. Much of the intellectual legwork supporting concrete initiatives takes place outside of the ASEAN. Most importantly, many ideas about the role of international organizations in building peace have come from foreign ministries and research institutes connected to European and North American-style multilateralism. As one Canadian scholar has framed the issue, the "ASEAN way" is evolving into the "Asia-Pacific way" (Acharya 1997).

It is tempting to apply Yoichi Funabashi's term "fusion," which he has used in the context of APEC, to the ARF and CSCAP (Funabashi 1995). The APEC group is more than the sum of its parts and has developed a unique work style and approach as well as a complex language of is own, with concepts like "concerted unilateralism" and "open regionalism." Both CSCAP and ARF have not yet produced their own distinctive vocabulary, but they have developed distinctive work styles and have modified various security concepts in ways that reflect both ASEAN and Western approaches. If not "fusions," they can certainly be described as "hybrids."

Character and Accomplishments of the ARF and CSCAP

In defining the character of CSCAP and ARF, it is easiest to begin with what they are not. Neither one is a household word in Asia or across the Pacific. Neither is explicitly committed to building a system of collective defense like an Asian NATO or a collective security apparatus. The ARF is not now a mechanism for regional conflict management or resolution and shows no signs of developing into one in the near or medium future. Neither one has a well articulated or universally shared vision of its goals.

What do they do? Both institutions are primarily about dialogue and words, mainly uttered in English. They are security talk shops (the *Economist* priggishly prefers "security talking-shops"), vehicles for multilateral consultation and exchange rather than mechanisms for dispute resolution. What are they talking about, how, and to what end?

The Asian Regional Forum

With four ministerial meetings under its belt, as well as some 25 intersessional meetings and gatherings of senior officials and intersessional support groups, the ARF can be considered effectively launched. Several countries want to join the organization (including Britain, France, North Korea and Mongolia), and no member has dropped out. There have been predictable rumbles of dissatisfaction that it is moving too slow or too fast, that it has too many or too few members, and so on.

Among the ARF's principal accomplishments has been the historically rare leadership of a regional political-security by the region's medium and smaller powers. It has been able to bring all of the great powers of Asia and the Pacific—including China, India, Japan, Russia, and the United States—into the organization. Though all five countries have certain reservations about the ARF process, all are participating actively and constructively. To many, the most important success has been the engagement of China in multilateral dialogue activities. And in the past year, participants in ARF discussions have been extended to include military officials.

Operationally, the ARF actually functions as two organizations. The first is the realm of the senior officials who run the intersessional meetings and support groups and who occasionally meet among themselves on an ASEAN and ASEAN-plus basis. The second is the annual ministerial meetings.

At the ministerial level, the ARF has been rated as useful by almost all participants for the frankness and informality of discussions that take place in and outside the formal events. Discussions have been wide-ranging and occasionally pointed, as in the criticisms of the Myanmar government that took place in Kuala Lumpur in July 1997. Contentious issues have been raised, including the South China Sea problem and most recently the Cambodian crisis, where the ministers lent explicit support to the ASEAN management of the issue. Elite chemistry has not reached the proportions of intra-ASEAN meetings but has, according to most reports, been surprisingly favorable.

At the level of the senior officials, the ARF has been a more complex process. Although the process uses a three-phase conception, efforts to date have focused on the first phase, confidence building, and have involved successful exchanges on security perceptions, transparency (including the encouragement of Defense White Papers, use of the United Nations' arms registry), peacekeeping, search and rescue, disaster relief, and nonproliferation of weapons of mass destruction. As the intersessional meetings on confidence-building mechanisms (CBMs) in Beijing (March 1997), Bandar Seri Begawan (November 1997), and Sydney (March 1998) revealed, consensus has not yet developed about how to approach more demanding constraint measures including advance notification of exercises and the invitation of observers. Considerable work remains to consolidate the discussions to date and to achieve some practical outcomes, especially in the areas of peacekeeping training and preparation of Defense White Papers.

The ARF is beginning to address the second phase of its plan, preventive diplomacy. It is doing so cautiously and largely through track two instruments. Three ARF seminars have been organized on a track two basis, the first in Seoul in 1995, the second in Paris in November 1996, and the third in Singapore in September 1997. Previously, a series of three meetings organized under the umbrella of the "Workshop Series on ASEAN-UN Cooperation in Peace and Preventive Diplomacy" took place in Bangkok in March 1993, Singapore in July 1993, and Bangkok in 1994.

The list of specific preventive diplomacy (PD) proposals or suggested measures now on the table is extensive.

From the Workshops on ASEAN-UN Cooperation:
closer connection to UN efforts on PD; building regional norms on PD, especially the non-use of force; creation of an early-warning capacity in the region; including human rights issues as part of the PD discussion; discouraging the proliferation of weapons of mass destruction; using joint development approaches as a possible solution to disputes over natural resources between states; support for the UNTAC process; creating some kind of link between CSCAP and the ARF to advance discussion of PD issues. (Koh and Sarasin 1994)

From the ARF seminar in Seoul:
promote CBMs as a step toward PD; connect to the findings of track two processes like CSCAP; encourage the ARF to approve of bilateral and multilateral discussions on the nuclear issue on the Korean peninsula; develop codes of conduct along the lines of the Treaty of Amity and Cooperation; create a regional conflict prevention center; promote crisis prevention exercises; establish an ARF register of experts on PD; appoint a High Commissioner for Maritime Affairs; establish specific working groups on PD issues in the region. ("Chairman's Summary" 1995)

From the ARF seminar in Paris:
an annual security outlook through an instrument like CSCAP; creation of a regional research information center; further study of PD instruments including fact finding, good offices, mediation, moral suasion and third-party mediation; expansion of the good offices of the ARF chair, reinforcement of networks of bilateral preventive diplomacy; establishing a register of experts on PD; ad hoc procedures such as committees, working groups and special representatives; creation of regional norms; in the longer term, creation of a regional risk-reduction center and a special ARF unit on PD ("Chairman's Statement" 1996)

From the Recent ARF ISG Meetings in Bandar Seri Begawan and Sydney:

> an enhanced role for the ARF Chairman, particularly the idea of a good offices role; development of a register of experts or eminent persons among ARF participants; an annual security outlook; voluntary background briefing on regional security issues. ("Co-Chairmen's Summary" 1998)

The discussions to date indicate that preventive diplomacy (PD) will not prove an easy issue for the ARF to address. Part of this difficulty results from confusion about the meaning of the term. Although it was initially a UN-sponsored instrument intended to restrict Soviet and American involvement in regional conflicts, in the post-Cold War setting, preventive diplomacy is being interpreted differently in various regional settings. In the Asia-Pacific, the analytic distinction between CBMs and PD measures is far less clear than the original ARF concept paper suggested. Moreover, several states, China chief among them, fear that the concept can lead to extended and expensive international intrusions into domestic affairs of sovereign nations. Ideas for the creation of any kind of conflict prevention center have been rejected as premature, and there is hesitation about any special good offices role for the chair of the ARF in regional conflicts. Rather, there appears to be a preference for establishing conflict-prevention services on an ad hoc basis, as was the case in assigning three ASEAN foreign ministers the task of dealing with the Cambodian situation after the July 1997 coup. Looking beyond Southeast Asia, several Northeast Asian states, including South Korea, seem reluctant to see the ARF chair play any special role, in part because North Korea is not a member of the ARF and in part because of a perception that Southeast Asian leaders are insufficiently informed about Northeast Asian security matters.

Two promising ideas concern the preparation of an annual security outlook (Morrison 1997). One is a project underway outside of ARF and CSCAP but with close connections to them; the other is a preliminary investigation of some kind of nongovernmental resource and information center that would bolster both the CBM and PD agenda and provide a soft mechanism offering advance warning of potential conflict situations. Unfortunately, the search for a regional code of conduct or set of regional norms did not get off to a good start in Moscow. More recently, the ASEAN Institutes for Strategic and International Studies (ISIS) have investigated this code through the concept of a "Pacific Concord." Though it will need careful and sensitive handling, some kind of concord is possible and could find broad agreement without violating the sovereignty concerns of some governments or disappointing those who feel that the lowest common denominator is too low (Hassan and Raffie 1997).

Also under discussion is the creation of some kind of support unit for the ARF, possibly located within the ASEAN secretariat. The CSCAP already has a secretariat, now based in Kuala Lumpur, that coordinates steering committee meetings, oversees finances, and releases publications including a newsletter and CSCAP memoranda. Although the ARF depends on the good offices of its rotating chair, opinion is divided about how efficient these chairs have been in organizing meetings and distributing materials in a timely fashion. In addition, there is no official repository of ARF documents and papers, although a website has been created in Australia that fills some of the gap.

Council for Security Cooperation in the Asia-Pacific Region

Unlike the ARF, CSCAP does have a founding charter. It has proven surprisingly durable save for the matter of the "inclusive" nature of the institution. The idea that membership would be open "to all counties and territories in the region" did not prove workable. For almost three years, the China-Taiwan membership issue dominated discussion at the meetings of the CSCAP steering committee. It was only in December 1996 that the members agreed to a formula under which China would enter as a full member, and individual experts from Taiwan were invited to participate in working-group meetings.

In dispute is CSCAP's precise role as a "track-two" process. To many, its relationship to the ARF is its most important function, even if the formal relationship is not yet defined and even if the ARF hesitates to designate CSCAP as its official track-two instrument. In this understanding, CSCAP is a vehicle for shadow diplomacy in which influence on government policy is the principal task. Not surprisingly, many of the key players in CSCAP are former or retired officials. To others, probably a minority, the ARF relationship to CSCAP is valuable but neither essential nor of primary importance. Instead, they conceive of CSCAP as an intermediary between broader elements of society (including research institutes, universities, NGOs, and businesses) and governmental agendas. Its independence and creativity are valued as much as its connection to government.

There are several advantages to a loosely defined, even ambiguous, connection between the two institutions. One is the flexibility it gives CSCAP. For example, in the event of deterioration of the ARF process, CSCAP could serve as an independent foundation for supporting other governmental efforts. These could include analytic support for Northeast Asian track-one processes at some future point. A second is the ability to include Taiwan in the discussion. Any formal connection between CSCAP and the ARF would certainly raise Chinese objections to the presence of even individual participants from Taiwan in CSCAP events. Third, the insecurity of the current situation generates an incentive for CSCAP to compete for ARF attention, rather than to treat it as guaranteed.

The four working groups of CSCAP are at various stages of their deliberations. Three have prepared memoranda approved by all member committees. Only the North Pacific Working Group has not advanced to the point of setting forth its findings and suggestions in memorandum form. It has, however, conducted two unprecedented meetings with "full house" participation from all of the member committees in the following areas: Northeast Asia (including North Korea, China, and Mongolia); North America; Australia and New Zealand; Indonesia; the Philippines; Vietnam; Europe (as an associate member); and experts from Taiwan and the Korean Peninsula Energy Development Organization. In addition, a new study group on transnational crime has convened two meetings.

Despite its successes, however, CSCAP faces several substantial challenges. Unlike the ARF, which has a near monopoly on inclusive political security dialogue on an Asia-Pacific basis, CSCAP faces a host of competitors. There are now more than 50 track-two seminars per year, but CSCAP accounts for fewer than 20 percent of them. New networks of institutes are being created, including the Council for Asia-Europe Cooperation, that overlap with the Asian members of CSCAP. Thus, CSCAP faces pressure to produce high-quality work that is both academically respectable and policy-relevant. Unless it maintains momentum and quality, it will lose its constituency and support. Unlike the ARF, it is essentially a volunteer organization and has acute financial problems.

A distinctive feature of CSCAP is its member committees, which, according to the CSCAP Charter, are to be "broad-based." In fact, the member committees vary substantially in size and vitality, and they have been most effective *outside* ASEAN. In several instances, including the Canadian and Chinese, the member committees are proving to be useful vehicles for establishing connections among individuals who do not normally meet frequently or at all and who have an abiding interest in security matters. If the member committees are not able to capture the best available talent, other dialogue channels will.

In addition, CSCAP faces the complex challenge of balancing insiders and outsiders, generalists and specialists, those close to government and those more independent in their orientation, ideas that are ripe for policy action and those that are beyond the horizon. The vast majority of the individuals present at CSCAP meetings are selected by their respective member committees. The few additional individuals are present at the invitation of the working group chairs. The quality of the working groups is thus largely dependent on the kinds of people the member committees select. This system increases the probability that representatives will be closely informed about the positions of their respective national governments. Moreover, it now appears that many of these participants are also able to act beyond the official positions on some matters.

Can CSCAP be considered the institutional expression of what has been labeled an "epistemic community?" According to the four-point definition offered by Peter Haas—a shared set of normative and principled beliefs, shared causal beliefs, shared notions of validity, and a common policy enterprise—CSCAP obviously falls short (Haas 1992). Though academics are involved and research institutes were the founding force, they are not the majority owners, and CSCAP is not an academically driven institution. Instead, it lies somewhere between a nongovernmental and semi-governmental process. Beyond a common commitment to promoting "security cooperation," multilateral dialogue, and peaceful resolution of disputes, CSCAP participants are characterized as much by differences as by similarities. They differ not just in views on specific disputes and national interests but also more fundamentally in worldview and philosophic origins. Here there is a major difference between the political security realm and the economic one where, despite national differences, groups like the Pacific Forum on Trade and Development (PAFTAD) and APEC have a common base in elements of neo-economic theory and the virtues of market openness. The CSCAP is better conceived as the site of the intersection of differing ideas, some of which approximate the form of "epistemic communities."

The more interesting and appropriate question is whether there is evidence of convergence. It is instructive that CSCAP has been able to construct an institutional form without anything approaching a consensus on the direction of multilateral dialogue and security cooperation. Its major success has been in establishing process norms, legitimating multilateral discussion and the habits of dialogue. The CSCAP memoranda constitute a blend of lowest common denominator statements and some creative efforts to move beyond existing national positions.

Emerging Challenges

The regional dialogue processes of which the ARF and CSCAP are both a part face a myriad of challenges related to their substantive agendas and the maintenance of momentum, purpose and interest. They also face two key strategic issues, one related to changes within ASEAN that affect its leadership role, and a second concerning the engagement of the great powers.

To begin with, ASEAN is changing. Its enlargement to nine and soon ten members is altering the chemistry of the institution. How much time and energy can be devoted to ARF and CSCAP activities, as intra-ASEAN affairs become more complex and demanding, remains to be seen. This worry has been compounded by the strain on governmental attentions and resources resulting from the current financial crisis. It is far from clear that ASEAN's new members have either the interest or the capacity to play leading roles in guiding a complex and at times sensitive process. The ASEAN tradition of rotating the chair of the ARF annually compounds these expansion-related concerns. Even at the track two level, it is apparent that the quasi-familial pattern of ASEAN interaction has not yet fully absorbed Vietnam or the other new entrants to the process.

In addition, related divisions are appearing within ASEAN intellectual circles on some key issues relevant to security dialogue matters. The ASEAN countries are in a process of rapid societal change, often moving further apart on key developmental and political questions. These divisions have most recently surfaced with regard to Cambodia, pitting those advocating the traditional position of noninterference against those advocating "constructive involvement" or constructive intervention" (Ibrahim 1997). A parallel debate is taking place among ASEAN elites on the future of the institution. One view espouses a modest and limited agenda for ASEAN, focusing on reducing interstate conflict. Another view insists that ASEAN cannot survive unless it becomes involved in complex societal issues, including poverty alleviation and human rights violations, and unless it connects a broader cross section of society to the ASEAN agenda. The ferment within ASEAN promises, at a minimum, to complicate its leadership capacity. Both the ARF and CSCAP will survive and prosper only if ASEAN leadership is extended to become Asia-Pacific leadership. For the moment this appears easier in CSCAP, with its co-chair system, than in the ARF.

Engaging the Great Powers: The Case of China

As an unusual experiment in which leadership of regional processes is not directly dominated by the region's great powers, the ARF and CSCAP both face the problem of ensuring the participation and continued engagement of these great powers. The clash between American and Chinese representatives at the ARF meeting on CBMs in Beijing in March 1997, a year after the confrontation in the Taiwan Strait, underscored the complexities of reconciling competing ideas about the fit between bilateral security alliances and cooperative security systems, not to mention technical questions related to notification provisions in various CBM proposals. It also revealed that Sino-American confrontation remains a major regional worry.

The engagement of China in these regional institutions has a complicated and controversial history. Both CSCAP and the ARF were conceived as "inclusive" mechanisms in which China's participation was actively sought. In turn, they were expected to influence Chinese attitudes and behavior. The understanding of what engagement means or what it can accomplish varies widely. To some, engagement means "enmeshment" or a way of restraining or constraining China in specific conflict areas including the South China Sea. To others, engaging China is related to a deeper process of making China more comfortable in regional institutions, involving increasingly large numbers of Chinese in contact with multilateralism, and increasing the chances that China will act as a responsible regional power (Wanandi 1996).

China has had considerable influence in shaping both the terms of its entry and the operation of these institutions. Its involvement has been "conditional," meaning that certain conditions were implicitly or explicitly set before China entered each institution. In the case of the ARF, which China joined at its inception, these conditions were more implicit and included an understanding that cross-Strait relations would not be part of the ARF's discussion agenda. In the case of CSCAP, China insisted on an additional condition relating to the status of Taiwanese participation.

Chinese representatives have attended every meeting of the ARF since 1994 and every CSCAP meeting since China's entry in December 1996. Within the ARF, Beijing has hosted and co-chaired the Intersessional Support Group (ISG) on CBMs. Within CSCAP, China has established a large and active member committee, has become a co-chair of one working group, and prepared papers for at least eight meetings. Qualitatively, Chinese participation in regional security dialogue has changed substantially during the past seven years. Before 1995, Chinese officials and academics tended to be skeptical, reluctant, uncomfortable and defensive in their involvement in regional dialogue processes. By 1996, however, the Chinese approach had become more positive and sophisticated. Rhetorically, Chinese officials have increasingly championed and, when necessary, defended the multilateral dialogue process. In June 1997, for instance, Assistant Foreign Minister Chen Jian stated that "a multilateral framework seems to be the order of the day, both in the economic and security fields" and continued:

> We should judge the ARF by what it has achieved, not what it has done. ARF is the first ever collective endeavor in this region to carry out institutionalized multilateral security dialogue. It represents a regional effort to form a new security order. Its progress and success is already remarkable. (Chen 1997)

The change in approach extends beyond style into content. Chinese participants have been increasingly proactive in advancing specific approaches and positions. In the ARF, for example, these initially included general concerns about the pace and direction of regional discussions, including insistence on noninterference in domestic affairs, insistence on "consensus" interpreted to mean unanimity, and a pace comfortable to all participants. More recently, China has emphasized the distinctive characteristics of the region, which demand special approaches to CBMs. Chinese officials have repeatedly noted the success of this regionally sensitive approach, as in the border CBM agreements it has signed with Russia, Kazakhstan, Kirgizstan, Tajikistan and India.

China serves not so much as a brake on the ARF and CSCAP enterprises as it does a competitor for control of the rudder. Largely because of concerns about noninterference in domestic affairs, China is trying to steer discussion away from preventive diplomacy measures and back to the CBM agenda. China has used ARF and CSCAP channels to question and criticize the security arrangements of other ARF participants, especially the U.S.-Japan alliance. Less important than the origins of Chinese criticisms, however, is the manner in which they have been adjusted and tuned to elements of the regional discourse emphasizing multilateralism and post-Cold War thinking. The ideas of "mutual security" and "new security approaches" advanced by Chinese speakers in 1997 share similarities with the five principles of peaceful coexistence but are far more sensitive to the emerging regional style in expressing them.

With regard to concrete confidence-building measures (CBMs), China has disagreed with Americans and others on issues including intrusive surveillance and notification and observation of joint maneuvers. Instead, China has proposed several concrete measures such as ship visits, has supported several of the softer CBMs relating to exchange of information, exchange of views on bilateral and multilateral defense policies, and various nonmilitary CBMs, including exchange of personnel from defense universities and colleges.

Contrary to some expectations, China has rarely been isolated in the CSCAP and ARF debates, the ARF ISG on CBMs being a partial exception. Chinese representatives have skillfully found common cause with others while emphasizing that the principle of consensus means that all must agree. In this respect, China is more often in the mainstream of the discussion rather than an outlier on its margins.

This new approach has been accompanied by the creation of new institutional arrangements within China. Like other participants in the dialogue structures, China is not unique in being uncertain about how to manage these dialogue fora in a bureaucratic way. China worries in particular about whether these channels should be directed by geographically defined departments such as the Asia Department, or thematically defined units, such as the International Organization Department or the recently created Arms Control and Disarmament Department. In addition, it is concerned about the types of coordinating mechanisms that should be established to work with other units within the Ministry of Foreign Affairs (MFA), the People's Liberation Army (PLA), and, considering the track two nature of many of the meetings, the research institutes and universities. In an important 1996 decision, the MFA established a special unit within the Asia Department to manage regional cooperation fora including the ARF and, eventually, CSCAP and the other track-two venues.

One consequence of China's participation in an increasing number of track-one, track-two, and academic fora is the expansion of the number of Chinese representing China. My rough estimate is that fewer than 15 different individuals from China attended regional security dialogues in 1992. By 1997 that number probably exceeded a hundred, and would probably be at least double that if we also included bilateral meetings. There appears to be a systematic effort to recruit and prepare individuals who will represent China in regional meetings, if the varying ages of Chinese participants, the increasingly broad range of organizational affiliations, and their multiple capacities in English as well as the vocabulary, style, and issues of the regional discussions are any guide. The MFA and PLA have systematically expanded their training and exchange programs with several countries including the United States, Canada, Australia and Britain. China's CSCAP member committee has more than 45 members, has met on at least three occasions, and is regarded by its members as an unusual and constructive means for establishing horizontal connections among previously disparate components of the policy elite. Each CSCAP working group and study group has been assigned to an institute in Beijing that is responsible for coordinating Chinese participation and preparing papers.

It is easy to demonstrate the seriousness and sophistication with which China has engaged these regional dialogue mechanisms. It is also easy to demonstrate that China's positions on key regional security issues, including the Taiwan Strait, the Korean peninsula, and managing potential conflicts in the South China Sea, have not changed in substantial ways. But has Chinese participation changed Chinese interests or merely the style of asserting them? Does the fact that Chinese participants are acting in new ways point to simple tactical learning or a more complex process of cognitive learning that, in the longer term, will also affect interests and policy? And how much weight does the new security thinking have beyond the small group of officials in the MFA and PLA who are assigned to managing multilateral security institutions?

The answers to these questions are not yet clear. It is important, however, to note that participation in the ARF and in CSCAP is not particularly demanding of any state. Dialogues are not venues for making binding decisions, and none of the participants up to this point have made major compromises or sacrifices. The most important functions of the dialogue fora at present are not the rules they create but the suspicions they allay and the norms they reinforce. In the ARF and CSCAP, perhaps the most basic norm is the nonuse of force for settling disputes. At the level of rhetoric and practice, China has been as good a citizen in minding these norms as any other player.

On a range of issues including transparency and CBMs, Chinese thinking and positions have moved over time, though not necessarily at the pace and in the direction that all participants would wish. Participation has encouraged rethinking of Chinese interests and a normative devaluation of some of the costs of commitments. It is fair to say that Chinese attitudes have shifted further than those of almost any other participant. And for the first time in 50 years, there is a growing constituency in China, well connected to the outside world, that is rethinking the future of China's international relations.

Looking toward the early years of the twenty-first century, it is quite possible that the genuinely reluctant party in Asian multilateralism will be the United States, not China. American official positions on multilateral dialogue have moved considerably in the 1990s from initial suspicion and hostility to positive acceptance of multilateralism as a useful supplement to the strategy of forward deployment and the system of bilateral alliances. In fact, an American was a founding co-chair of CSCAP. Under the Clinton administration the level of American activity in dialogue mechanisms—bilateral, subregional (e.g., the Northeast Asia Cooperation Dialogue, the Four Party Talks on the Korean peninsula), and regional—has advanced substantially. But if the regional security agenda shifts toward substantive arms control and CBM matters that impinge upon the alliance systems or, more fundamentally, forward deployment and strategic military dominance, it is the United States that potentially could become the outlier.

Conclusion

The leaders of the ARF and CSCAP almost appear to be building a highway to an unknown destination. For the moment, the process of discussion and the engagement of China are as important as substance for this construction crew. But the critics of both institutions correctly realize that ARF and CSCAP must do more both to justify their existence and maintain momentum. Going into the next century, the most active tasks will be in the areas of transparency, confidence building, and exchange of security perceptions.

But what about the highway engineers defining the destination? Whether it takes place in official circles, track-two processes like CSCAP, or track-three processes that are even further removed from government, a systematic discussion of alternative security orders is urgently needed. This is complicated terrain because of major differences in national interests, historical experiences, and philosophical starting points. Unlike the situation in Europe for three hundred years, there is not a tradition of domestic and regional speculation on the causes of war linked to explicit prescriptions on how to build peace. One part of this project in the Asian and Asia-Pacific context will be the search for an acceptable common denominator, perhaps informed by the Treaty of Amity and Cooperation and perhaps taking the form of some kind of Pacific concord. Another will be a deeper analysis of the history and current dynamics of the region, creating a vision of where it might be going. While benefiting from a fortuitous moment in great-power relations, the greatest accomplishment of both the ARF and CSCAP at this time is a platform for engaging thoughtful people around the Pacific in such a creative process.

Bibliography

Acharya, Amitav. "Ideas, Identity, and Institution-Building: From the 'ASEAN Way' to the 'Asia-Pacific Way'?" *The Pacific Review* 10, no. 3 (1997).

Axelrod, Robert, and Keohane, Robert. "Achieving Cooperation Under Anarchy: Strategies and Institutions." *World Politics* 38 (October 1985).

Ball, Desmond. "Strategic Culture in the Asia/Pacific Region." *Security Studies* 3, no. 1, (Autumn 1993).

"Chairman's Statement." ARF Seminar on Preventive Diplomacy, November 9, 1996.

"Chairman's Summary." ARF Seminar on Preventive Diplomacy, May 11, 1995

"Co-Chairmen's Summary Report of the Meetings of the ARF Intersessional Support Group on Confidence Building Measures," Bandar Seri Begawan, November 4–6, 1997, and Sydney, March 4–6, 1998.

Chen Jian. "Challenges and Responses in East Asia." Text of speech delivered at the CSCAP Annual Meeting, Singapore, June 4, 1997.

Evans, Paul M. "The Prospects for Multilateral Security Cooperation in the Asia/Pacific Region." *The Journal of Strategic Studies* 18, no. 3 (September 1995).

Funabashi, Yoichi. *Asia Pacific Fusion: Japan's Role in APEC*. Washington, DC: Institute for International Economics, 1995.

Haas, Peter M. "Introduction: Epistemic Communities and International Policy Coordination." *International Organization* 46, no. 1 (Winter 1992).

Hassan, Mohamed Jawhar, and Sheikh Ahmad Raffie, eds., *Bringing Peace to the Pacific*. Kuala Lumpur: ISIS Malaysia, 1997.

Huxley, Tim. "ASEAN's Role in the Emerging East Asian Regional Security Structure." In Ian Cook et al., eds., *Fragmented Asia: Regional Integration and National Disintegration in Pacific Asia*. Aldershot, UK: Avebury, 1996.

Ibrahim, Anwar. "Crisis Prevention." *Newsweek*, July 21, 1997.

Johnston, Iain, and Evans, Paul. "China's Engagement with Multilateral Security Institutions." In Iain Johnston and Robert Ross, eds., *Engaging China: Managing a Rising Power.* London: Routledge, 1998.

Katzenstein, Peter J. "Introduction: Alternative Perspectives on National Security." In Peter J. Katzenstein, ed., *The Culture of National Security: Norms and Identity in World Politics.* New York: Columbia University Press, 1996.

Koh, Tommy, and Viraphol, Sarasin. "Final Report of the Third Workshop on ASEAN-UN Cooperation in Peace and Preventive Diplomacy." March 18, 1994.

Leifer, Michael. *The ASEAN Regional Forum: Extending ASEAN's Model of Regional Security.* London: Oxford University Press; London: Institute of Strategic Studies, Adelphi Paper no. 304, 1996.

Mak Jun Nom. "The ASEAN Process ('Way') of Multilateral Cooperation and Cooperative Security: The Road to a Regional Arms Register?" Paper presented to the MIMA-SIPRI Workshop. Kuala Lumpur, October 2–3, 1995.

Martin, Lisa L. "The Rational Choice State of Multilateralism." In John Gerard Ruggie, ed., *Multilateralism Matters: The Theory and Praxis of an Institutional Form.* New York: Columbia University Press, 1993.

Morrison, Charles, ed., *Asia Pacific Security Outlook 1997.* Honolulu: East-West Center, in cooperation with the Research Institute for Peace and Security in Tokyo and the ASEAN Institutes of Strategic and International Studies, 1997.

Risse-Kappen, Thomas, ed., *Bringing Transnational Actors Back In.* Cambridge: Cambridge University Press, 1995.

Segal, Gerald, and Buzan, Barry. "Rethinking East Asian Security." *Survival* 36 (1994).

Wanandi, Jusuf. "ASEAN's China Strategy: Towards Deeper Engagement." *Survival* 38, no. 3 (Autumn 1996).

Wendt, Alexander. "Constructing International Politics." *International Security* 20, no. 1 (Summer 1995).

Woods, Lawrence T. "Rediscovering Security." *Asian Perspective* 21, no. 1 (Spring–Summer 1997).

Yuen Foong Khong. "Making Bricks Without Straw in the Asia Pacific." *The Pacific Review* 10, no. 2 (1997).

11

The Role, Significance, and Prospects of APEC

Contributions to Regional Security

Dewi Fortuna Anwar

Introduction

The Asia-Pacific Economic Cooperation (APEC) group was founded in Canberra in November 1989 by a dozen Pacific Rim countries, including Australia, the United States, Canada, Japan, the Republic of Korea, the six ASEAN nations, and New Zealand. China, Hong Kong and Taiwan joined in 1991, and by 1994 the membership increased to 18, with the inclusion of Papua New Guinea, Mexico, and Chile. The APEC members are termed "economies" rather than countries or nations, in deference to China's sensitivities over the participation of Taiwan and Hong Kong.

The establishment of APEC was a direct response to the growing interdependence of the Asia-Pacific economies over the past two decades. Unlike other regions, notably Western Europe, the economic integration of key members of the Asia-Pacific region has primarily been market driven, rather than government-led. The foundations of Asia-Pacific regionalism, however, lie in the first two decades of the Cold War. As the United States provided security and substantial financial aid to the anticommunist, front-line states during the fight against Asian communism, a number of East Asian states under its influence developed along similar economic and political lines. Building on this foundation, Japanese companies have used investment and trade, and the Japanese government has employed economic aid, to define the boundaries of the region more clearly and to bring the regional economies closer together (Stubb 1990).

The importance of APEC to its member economies is clear (Table 11.1).

Table 11.1

Intraregional Trading Within APEC, NAFTA, AFTA, and EAEC (in percentages)

	APEC		NAFTA		AFTA		EAEC	
	Exports	Imports	Exports	Imports	Exports	Imports	Exports	Imports
Japan	67.1	63.9	29.2	25.8			33.0	31.8
United States	57.8	66.5	78.3	73.4				
Canada	87.6	86.2	81.6	70.5				
Mexico	86.1	86.2						
Korea	70.7	69.1					41.4	41.4
Taiwan	68.5	76.5					35.1	49.6
Hong Kong	72.6	81.6					45.8	71.6
Singapore	70.4	75.7			22.1	22.2	45.7	57.1
Thailand	65.4	76.6			22.1	16.1	45.7	61.9
Malaysia	76.7	82.5			29.1	23.2	54.6	64.6
Philippines	77.5	73.7			5.9	9.5	34.2	52.0
Indonesia	81.8	75.6			11.8	64.3	55.6	
China	77.6	78.4					65.8	65.2
Australia	73.0	67.2						
New Zealand	67.8	73.2						

Source: Nagata 1994.

Trade within APEC forms more than half of each APEC member's total trade, and these amounts continue to increase despite—or perhaps because of—deepening subregional economic arrangements such as the North American Free Trade Agreement (NAFTA), the ASEAN Free Trade Area (AFTA), and the East Asian Economic Caucus (EAEC).

A Brief History of APEC

From its modest beginnings, APEC has developed into the most important grouping in the Asia-Pacific region and has garnered increasing international prestige, not only because of the high degree of interdependency among member economies, but also because the APEC region is now considered the most dynamic center of global economic growth. Originally conceived as nothing more than a loose forum for international dialogue, APEC is definitively moving toward achieving trade and investment liberalization in the Asia-Pacific region by the year 2010 for industrialized economies and by 2020 for industrializing members. Moreover, APEC is ready to promote economic and technical cooperation to narrow the gap between the industrialized and industrializing members, a prerequisite for further trade and investment liberalization.

The development of APEC as an open regional trading arrangement, dedicated to safeguarding the multilateral economic system under the General Agreement on Tariffs and Trade (GATT), now the World Trade Organization (WTO), was spurred in part by the growth of closed regional trading blocs such as the European Union (EU) and the North American Free Trade Agreement (NAFTA), which discriminate against nonmembers. From the very beginning, considerable emphasis was placed on APEC's unique characteristic as a form of "open regionalism," which would serve as a building block, rather than a stumbling block, to global trading.

The APEC group received little attention until November 1993, when President Bill Clinton invited other APEC leaders to Blake Island, Seattle, for APEC's first informal summit. The direct involvement of its top leaders, dubbed the APEC Economic Leaders' Meeting (AELM), gave new importance and weight to APEC and generated substantial media attention that helped to promote awareness among the general public. In addition, the first AELM produced the *Vision Statement*, in which the leaders outlined their commitment to the following objectives:

- to find cooperative ways to overcome the various obstacles resulting from rapidly changing regional and global economies;
- to support the expansion of the world economy and the open multilateral trading system; and

- to continue the reduction of trade and investment obstacles, permitting goods and services to move freely among the members of APEC.

Given that APEC members include industrialized, industrializing, and transition economies, unlike other more homogeneous regional groupings, its members naturally have different interests and priorities. Predictably, ASEAN countries initially were wary of the APEC process, fearing that the larger grouping would dilute ASEAN and that the more powerful members would dominate the agenda. Malaysia was the most critical of APEC, and Prime Minister Mahathir refused to attend the leaders' meeting at Blake Island. Mahathir would have preferred to promote an East Asian Economic Grouping that excludes the non-Asian countries in the Asia-Pacific. Therefore, AELM II, which convened in November 1994 in Bogor, Indonesia, represented a significant achievement: The summit, which all member leaders attended, produced the *APEC Economic Leaders Declaration of Common Resolve*. Confounding the skeptics, APEC leaders entered into a political commitment to carry out trade liberalization in the Asia-Pacific region by the year 2010 for the developed members and 2020 for the developing economies. Although these deadlines are nonbinding in nature, trusting individual members to carry out trade liberalization unilaterally, each member is expected to feel honor-bound to conform to the agreement. The Bogor Declaration also resolved to investigate the possibility of setting up a voluntary consultative dispute mediation service as a supplement to the WTO, but agreed that the WTO remained the primary forum for settling trade disputes.

To reassure hesitant members regarding the nature and direction of APEC, the Eminent Persons Group (EPG), led by C. Fred Bergsten, introduced a set of principles that serve as guidelines for achieving the APEC vision. These principles include free trade and investment; international cooperation; regional solidarity; mutual benefits; mutual respect and equality; pragmatism; consensus decision-making process; flexible implementation; and open regionalism, and were intended to ensure that APEC would not become an inward-looking and discriminatory trading bloc or a rigid regional structure with binding authority. But despite the insistence on maintaining APEC as a loose forum, it was clear that a degree of institutionalism had taken place, as exemplified by the holding of the annual summit.

The third AELM, held in Osaka in November 1995, succeeded in developing a blueprint for carrying out the Bogor Declaration, despite initial concerns that the meeting would be a failure. Regional economic tensions had increased because of escalating trade disputes between the United States and Japan, various disagreements between Washington and Beijing, most notably involving China's desire to join the WTO; and the demands of four members—

China, South Korea, Japan and Taiwan—for special treatment for their agricultural sectors. Japan's efforts to forge a consensus, however, bore fruit. AELM III produced the *Osaka Action Plan* to carry out trade and investment liberalization and to promote economic and technical cooperation. The plan also contained a more detailed program for economic and technical cooperation, which encompasses 12 areas including human resources development, science and technology, and the promotion of small and medium-sized enterprises. The Osaka summit also agreed that trade and investment liberalization would be achieved through three simultaneous approaches: the unilateral approach, which stresses initiative by the respective members; collective action; and comparison and review, which would ensure that no member falls behind the commitment to concerted unilateral liberalization.

At the AELM IV in Subic, the Philippines, 1996, APEC leaders agreed to adopt the *Manila Action Plan for APEC* (MAPA) to implement the Osaka Action Plan. At this fourth AELM, the leaders reiterated their commitment to begin trade and investment liberalization by January 1997, to satisfy the deadlines established earlier. Although the Subic summit did not produce any new spectacular agreements, it was still very important to the momentum of APEC. Now every member has to prepare its economy to meet the demands set by APEC, and no member can retreat from the commitment to achieve a free trade and investment area in the Asia-Pacific region.

The fifth APEC Economic Leaders' Meeting took place in November 1997, amidst a deepening regional currency crisis that began in Thailand in July and spread like brush fire to the other ASEAN countries and Northeast Asia. The regional currency crisis was triggered by massive property debts in Thailand, which led to the closing of several financial institutions and to floating baht exchange rates. The currency crisis quickly engulfed Indonesia, which in turn was also forced to float the rupiah. To stabilize their rapidly depreciating currencies, both Thailand and Indonesia were forced to turn to the International Monetary Fund (IMF), which pushed both economies to reform their financial institutions, resulting in the liquidation of 16 ailing banks in Indonesia alone. The currency crisis that shook the ASEAN states also spread to South Korea, forcing Seoul to turn to the IMF for assistance, and to Japan, where a number of established banks and security houses collapsed. Within the span of a few short months, the East Asian economic miracle seemed to be coming to an end.

Given the grave financial situation in the region, it was not surprising that the AELM V primarily focused on restoring confidence in East Asian economies and averting similar crises in the future. As part of the effort to handle future currency crises, the AELM agreed to support Indonesian President Suharto's proposal to create an emergency fund to supplement IMF resources.

Despite the currency crisis, however, the APEC leaders reaffirmed their commitment to achieving trade liberalization. The meeting produced a 21-point communiqué entitled the *APEC Economic Leaders' Declaration: Connecting the APEC Community*, which proposed to liberalize trade in nine key sectors in 1999 and urged the successful conclusion of WTO negotiations regarding the financial services markets. The declaration also approved a framework for enhanced public-private partnerships in infrastructural development, encouraging voluntary principles for facilitating private sector participation by establishing a sound macro-economic environment, a transparent legal framework, and increased availability of long-term capital.

Differing Expectations of APEC

Although all APEC members have arrived at an agreement regarding APEC's vision and the means to realize it, they nonetheless hold real differences in their expectations and approaches toward the grouping that reflect the diversity of the organization. The industrialized members desire a more structured and legally binding regional organization, whereas the industrializing members insist on keeping APEC loose and informal. Industrialized members wish to focus on trade and investment liberalization; the industrializing members argue that equal weight must be given to economic and technical cooperation. Thus, the different interests that divide the North and the South generally, which can clearly lead to disagreements, disappointments or disillusionments, are being expressed in the much smaller APEC forum and pose a major challenge to the APEC process.

Nevertheless, unlike the acrimony that usually characterizes North-South relations in larger international fora, the real interdependence that binds the APEC economies provides an incentive for the members to reach a compromise, as each member believes that APEC will help it attain its individual objectives. Here we shall examine the different expectations of four key members of APEC: the United States, Japan, ASEAN, and China.

The United States

As the richest and most powerful member, the United States clearly has a special role in APEC. Members of APEC owe the success of the grouping in large part to the support given by Washington, whose interests in APEC stem from the expectation that the group performs certain important functions. These include:

• the promotion of trade and investment liberalization;

- the prevention of the establishment of an East Asian economic bloc dominated by Japan;
- greater attention to the potential market in the Asia-Pacific;
- increased American involvement in the economic activities of the world's most dynamic region;
- new means for solving the various damaging bilateral trade disputes between the United States and a number of East Asian economies;
- the establishment of a link between the market-oriented economies and the command economies in the Asia-Pacific;
- coordination of members' economic policies and the possible creation of an economic zone for the whole Asia-Pacific region. (Roth 1993, 35)

For the United States, APEC's most important function is to facilitate the process of trade and investment liberalization. In particular, the United States hopes to use APEC to open up the markets of countries, notably Japan and China, with which it has long suffered major trade deficits. To this end, Washington wishes APEC to adopt a more binding role, such as the Trade and Investment Framework agreement (TIFA), which it proposed in Williamsburg, Virginia, in early 1993. The U.S. proposal, however, was not wholly acceptable to several other members, including Indonesia, who did not want APEC to change from a loose forum for dialogue into an organization with legally binding authority. In the end, TIFA was softened to the nonbinding *Declaration on Asia Pacific Economic Cooperation Trade and Investment Framework*. Equally important, the United States views APEC as a counterweight to the European Union, and threatens to turn its back on Europe if the EU becomes an inward-looking regional bloc and fails to support the GATT/ WTO process.

Japan

Japan has been a strong supporter of APEC from the very beginning, reflecting its close economic link with other Asia-Pacific economies. As with the United States, APEC's most important function in Japan's eyes is to ensure an open and multilateral trading system to counter the threat posed by such huge trading blocs as the EU and NAFTA; APEC would safeguard Japan's trade and investment not only within the Asia-Pacific, but also in the international system as a whole, affirming Japan's status as a regional and global economic power. Through APEC, Japan also hopes to enhance its trade and investment links with others in the region, and to accelerate the opening of Asian markets through regional cooperation. Japan also hopes that APEC's multilateral setting will reduce the pressure that Washington is increasingly applying against Tokyo over their U.S.-Japanese trade disputes.

To prevent American domination of APEC, Japan favors a loose APEC structure, stressing pragmatism and flexibility and taking into account the wide variety in membership. Japan strenuously opposed efforts to change APEC from a multilateral consultation forum to a multilateral negotiating forum. Because of Japan's dependence on the world economy, it is unwilling to support preferential trading arrangements within APEC and discrimination against nonmembers, as the United States has suggested. Thus, whereas the United States was worried about free riders, Japan was concerned about supporting actions that might invite retaliation against Japan.

The ASEAN Nations

As mentioned earlier, ASEAN was initially not supportive of APEC. Not only was ASEAN worried that it would be diluted in the larger forum, but also that the larger members would dominate the APEC process. Thus, ASEAN's support of APEC was conditioned upon its status as a loose forum for consultation and upon the promise that APEC would not become a closed and inward-looking trading bloc. Along these lines, at a meeting in Kuching in Eastern Malaysia, 1990, ASEAN presented a unified position on APEC (Soesastro 1994, 27–28). The main points of the Kuching Consensus are:

- ASEAN's identity and cohesion should be preserved and its cooperative relations with its dialogue partners and with other countries should not be diluted in any enhanced APEC.
- An enhanced APEC should be based on the principles of equality, equity, and mutual benefits, fully taking into account the differences in economic development and sociopolitical systems among countries in the region.
- APEC should not be directed toward the formation of an inward-looking economic or trading bloc but should support the open, multilateral economic and trading systems in the world.
- APEC should serve as a consultative forum on economic issues and should not adopt mandatory directives for any participant's behavior.
- APEC should be aimed at strengthening the individual and collective capacity of participants for economic analysis, and should facilitate more effective mutual consultations to enable participants to identify and promote their common interests and to project those interests more vigorously in the larger multilateral forums.
- APEC should proceed gradually and pragmatically, especially in its institutionalization.

The Kuching Consensus clearly inspired the principles of APEC proposed by the EPG (Eminent Persons Group).

As noted by two leading Chinese scholars, ASEAN plays a very important checking role in APEC, making it difficult for the United States to dominate the organization. ASEAN has resisted the U.S. plan to transform APEC into an Asia-Pacific Economic Community akin to the EU. Also, ASEAN has insisted that APEC pay sufficient attention to the differences in the level of development, political systems, and cultures within the Asia-Pacific region, and has maintained that the process of trade and investment liberalization should be in accord with the actual situation of the member economies. Finally, ASEAN has opposed America's suggestion to add political and security content to APEC—all positions of "constructive significance in guaranteeing a justifiable orientation for APEC's development" that simultaneously express the opinions of APEC's developing countries, including China (Lu and Zhang 1996, 45).

Nevertheless, despite its initial caution, ASEAN has become a strong supporter of APEC, as exemplified by President Suharto's role in pushing through the landmark Bogor Declaration. The ASEAN economies have realized that global trade liberalization is inevitable, and they hope that APEC will help them to prepare for this eventuality, particularly through development cooperation. These industrializing economies hope that they can benefit from the assistance of industrialized members in such areas as human resource development, technology transfer, and the promotion of small- and medium-scale businesses.

Additionally, ASEAN believes that APEC can play an important role in preserving the multilateral trading arrangement on which its members' economies heavily depend, and that APEC can counterbalance the EU's inward-looking tendencies. Equally important, ASEAN hopes that APEC can help to balance the roles played by the United States and Japan, so that neither side will adopt policies detrimental to ASEAN's interests. Also, ASEAN regards APEC as an important network for ensuring the continuing flows of investment from Japan and the newly industrializing economies (NIEs), particularly with the rise of new economic competitors in other parts of the world (Ikrar 1994). Finally, ASEAN views APEC as an important forum for establishing economic ties with the United States, diverting some of America's attention from Latin America and Europe.

China

China joined APEC in 1991 because it believes that APEC is necessary for its economic development in at least four different ways. First, 80 percent of

China's external trade takes place with APEC members, and 90 percent of foreign investment flowing to China originates within the Asia-Pacific region. In this regard, China is in the same position as many other APEC members and has a natural interest in developing relations with the Asia-Pacific nations. Second, as its economy expands and deepens, China fully realizes the importance of participating in international and regional economic cooperation. China is keen to resume its membership in GATT/WTO and regards APEC as an important step toward global multilateralism. In fact, the importance of APEC to China is enhanced because its bid to join the WTO so far has been unsuccessful owing to U.S. opposition. Furthermore, unlike the WTO, APEC affords high independence and flexibility. China does not have to pay high fees to participate in APEC activities, as it does not have to open up its markets immediately as required by the WTO.

Third, China hopes that APEC's dispute-resolution process will ease some of China's own bilateral trade disputes with the United States, and possibly with other APEC countries, which likely will increase in frequency as China's foreign trade increases. Finally, as an emerging regional power that is often viewed with suspicion by its neighbors, China hopes that its active participation in APEC will improve its relations with other countries in the region. At the same time, China also wishes to exert its influence on APEC to create an environment favorable to Chinese interests, and to ward off the pressure and demands from the more industrialized countries. Like ASEAN, China does not want APEC to develop into a structured and binding regional organization. China also insists that APEC should not only focus on trade and investment liberalization, but also on development cooperation. (Ikrar 1994, 19–24).

It is to be expected that the other members have their own reasons for joining APEC that may not always be in agreement with one another. These differences in outlooks and expectations generate difficulties in reaching consensus. If the disillusioned party is a key player in APEC, such as the United States, the future development of APEC will be jeopardized. Nevertheless, the prospects for APEC are on the whole optimistic. Although APEC has encountered some backsliding, as when a member introduced new trade protectionism despite the pledge to liberalize, there is little doubt that APEC members are committed to achieve trade liberalization by the agreed deadlines. The desire to sustain regional economic growth and to preserve and enhance the region's position as the world's most dynamic economic center keeps member economies firmly in line, despite the absence of binding agreements. Peer pressure and demonstrated benefits of APEC membership likely will ensure adherence to the three-step proposal to achieve trade and investment liberalization.

APEC and Regional Security

Members of APEC are optimistic not only that the economic grouping will contribute to greater prosperity in the Asia-Pacific region through the increasingly free flow of goods, finances, and services among member countries, but also that APEC will contribute directly to peace and stability in the region. Although APEC does not deal with politics or security issues, the grouping is increasingly regarded as an important source of regional security. As stability is generally regarded as crucial for economic development, the presence of APEC may dampen nationalist sentiments that can lead to intraregional conflicts. More importantly, the growing economic interdependence among the members of APEC in the long run can transform international relations in the Asia-Pacific from zero-sum to positive-sum, thus making wars between the states less likely.

As Joseph Nye stated in his influential book, *Peace in Parts. Integration and Conflict in Regional Organization*, an economic or functional web of interdependence can create new relations affecting the propensity of states to resort to violence in three major ways: first, by "raising the price" of violent conflict through functional interdependence; second, by creating a common identity or community among populations in a region that makes recourse to violence seem illegitimate to leaders and important segments of the population; and third, by exploiting an existing or potential economic web of interdependence that facilitates a shift in the value of images held by political leaders of the two parties in disputes, making its "integrative solution" possible (Nye 1971, 109).

Nevertheless, as Nye warned, a common market is not a panacea for deep-rooted social or political problems. It is easy to get carried away by the bright prospects of APEC, especially by focusing only on the economic side. Political and security analysts, however, generally tend to be less euphoric than economists when evaluating the region's future direction. It is worth remembering that APEC is currently nothing more than a loose forum for economic cooperation in which commitment to any regional undertaking is wholly voluntary. The loose APEC structure is a necessary product of its diverse membership and probably can yield most of the economic objectives, but the absence of binding agreements and the lack of formal structure reflect deep-seated differences and suspicions among some of the members that are unlikely to be overcome easily, and place the burden of good behavior on the individual member states. Of equal importance, APEC needs to be seen to benefit each member equally. Unequal economic relations, in which some members feel that they are at a disadvantage when compared with the others, may actually lead to fragmentation rather than integration, with negative consequences for regional security.

An analysis of APEC's importance to regional security must take into account the political-security environment in which APEC operates. Although the prospect of global war has diminished with the end of the Cold War, and while economic cooperation largely has supplanted ideological confrontation, few talk about the peace dividends in the Asia-Pacific context. Indeed, most security analysts refer to a certain sense of uncertainty due to the "regional vacuum" resulting from the decline of the American military presence in the region, and the concurrent rise of major regional powers, notably China and Japan, whose possible regional ambitions create unease among neighboring countries. There are also several "flash points" with the potential for disrupting stability in the region, such as overlapping territorial claims in the South China Sea, the continuing tension in the Korean peninsula, and the ongoing conflict between Beijing and Taipei. Furthermore, the increase in arms acquisitions among most of the East Asian countries, spurred in part by rapid economic growth and the need to protect their growing wealth in an uncertain regional environment, adds to a general sense of uncertainty.

This regional uncertainty increases APEC's importance as a means of enhancing predictability and accountability among its members. But while some liberal scholars believe that the depth and complexity of economic interdependence between countries in APEC makes the outbreak of war very unlikely, the challenges APEC faces in this field are enormous. Buzan and Segal (1994) have argued that Asia-Pacific "econophoria" needs to be qualified for at least four reasons:

> The level of involvement in this liberal, post-modern international interdependence varies a great deal in the region and even within states such as China. Unlike the European Union, where the differences in the extent of interdependence are less pronounced, there are states in East Asia that still take a more traditional view of economic sovereignty.
>
> While East Asia has experienced rapid economic growth, interdependence within the region has failed to keep pace with the European Union. Indeed, trends suggest that the most developed states in East Asia are seeking global rather than just regional connections. There are also doubts over how evenly the mutual dependencies are distributed in the region.
>
> Economic interdependence is not necessarily a protection against tension and conflict. The U.S.-Japan relationship, both before the Second World War and recently, is evidence of this. Economic interests can be a cause for intervention rather than abstention. Political and economic cultures are less transparent in East Asia than in Western models, making conflict and misunderstanding among them more likely. (Buzan and Segal 1994)

As members of the realist school of international relations, Buzan and

Segal have little faith in the efficacy of loose regional groupings and non-binding "open-regionalism" as devices for maintaining harmonious relations between states. In their view,

> [APEC] is unlikely to become more than an unwieldy Pacific summit beloved of sherpas and journalists. Indeed, APEC can be viewed as an attempt to avoid confronting the consequences of ending the Cold War. Its objective is to keep the United States as a guarantor of Asian security, which both flatters waning American power and keeps the Asians from having to come to terms with each other. (Buzan and Segal 1994, 15)

Buzan and Segal's comments must be taken seriously to avoid complacency about development in the Asia-Pacific region. Naturally, we cannot assume linear progress from market-driven economic interdependence to the creation of a security community in the Asia-Pacific region. Thus, Buzan and Segal are quite right to suggest that one of APEC's main objectives is to keep the United States engaged in the region as mutual suspicions between countries in East Asia make many of them look to America as a basically benign regional hegemon. At the same time, however, their criticisms may also be regarded as unnecessarily harsh and Eurocentric. It is reasonable, for example, to wonder why Western Europe, with its mature regional integration, still looks to the U.S.-led NATO as its security mainstay, instead of strengthening its own Western European Union.

Although it may be true that industrialized members of APEC seek global rather than regional interaction, it is also true that all the major economic powers in APEC, including Japan and the United States, trade more with each other than the rest of the world. Thus, there clearly is a need for a more effective regionalism in the Asia-Pacific. At the same time, there is no reason why the European model of rapid institutionalization and bureaucratization should provide the only model. Given the diversity of APEC membership, containing North and South, East and West, and given the homogeneity of the European Union, the former cannot simply replicate the European experience. Like ASEAN, which despite early criticisms from European scholars regarding its lack of institutionalization has turned out to be very successful in maintaining regional stability and economic growth, APEC can only make haste slowly. Here process is as important as outcome. Besides its economic functions, APEC is an important vehicle for confidence building in the region.

Although APEC has resisted the inclusion of security issues in its agenda, the grouping can contribute to peace and stability in the region in less direct fashion. As Gary J. Smith suggests, APEC serves at least four important strategic functions (Smith 1997, 38–39):

As a Transpacific forum, APEC ties the United States firmly into the fabric of the region and enhances the chances of America's continuing engagement, both politically and security-wise, in Asia.

APEC is a means to further engage industrializing countries in multilateralism and to develop a better understanding of WTO discipline and the advantages of open investment regimes. For instance, China finds APEC a more congenial environment than the WTO for engaging the world on trade liberalization issues. Various exchanges in APEC have also helped make China more aware of the need for compromises on WTO accession issues.

APEC provides Asia-Pacific countries with the opportunity for input into major bilateral disputes that could undermine the political and economic stability of the region. Many leaders, for example, at APEC's November 1995 meeting in Osaka, spoke out about the problems for their countries and the region as a whole arising from the continuance of U.S.-Japan trade disputes.

APEC has brought together senior officials and ministers from China, Hong Kong and Taiwan. While there have been some political fights between Beijing and Taipei over Taiwan's representation and status, APEC has provided a useful vehicle for others to engage the three players together and seek to influence their behavior in positive, cooperative directions.

Ever since President Clinton initiated the first meeting of the APEC leaders in Blake Island, there has been the cultivation of strong, personal, and political ties among leaders whose political will ultimately defines APEC's direction. Annual meetings since then have created a sense of community among leaders and have become a useful occasion for interchange not only on APEC matters but other global, regional and bilateral issues that can be discussed at bilateral meetings on the margins of the APEC gathering.

Notwithstanding APEC's various positive contributions toward the political and security environment in the Asia-Pacific region, stability is not guaranteed. As Buzan and Segal point out, political and economic cultures in East Asia are much less transparent than in Western cultures and, therefore, conflicts and misunderstandings are more likely. Many East Asian countries still have authoritarian governments, so that decision-making processes are monopolized by small elite groups. In other words, decisions concerning war and peace are still determined by policymakers who are relatively unconstrained by, and unaccountable to, the wider political public as in more democratic societies. A sense of uncertainty and unpredictability in East Asia could result, as leaderships changes may lead to radical changes in policy both at home and toward other countries. Moreover, as many have pointed out, while democracies, buttressed by dense economic ties, enhance security environments, conflicts do flare up between democracies and nondemocracies, even when these two groups trade heavily, as was demonstrated by the conflicts between Germany and the Allied nations that led to two world wars.

Conclusion

Today, APEC is the most important regional grouping in the Asia-Pacific region, bringing together countries in Southeast and Northeast Asia with those from North and South America. This diversity in membership and the differences in their respective perceptions and expectations present the organization with numerous challenges, as the lack of experience in such a regionwide multilateralism, and the residue of historical misunderstandings and suspicions, act as serious obstacles to the rapid development of APEC.

Nevertheless, against the odds, APEC has progressed relatively quickly. From a modest beginning without fanfare in 1989, APEC has now developed into a widely acclaimed economic grouping, with the direct support of the members' top leaders. The very real economic interdependence that has resulted confers upon APEC the widespread support of societies at large, particularly from the private sectors of each member economy—an auspicious sign for the development of APEC, as it already has industrialized constituents. Furthermore, APEC members appear committed to achieve the set targets for trade liberalization, not only to intensify trade and investment in the Asia-Pacific region, but to ensure that the Asia-Pacific remains the primary global center for economic growth in the decades to come.

Although APEC was not conceived as a forum for discussing regional security issues, the grouping nonetheless makes important contributions to regional peace and stability. The development of complex interdependence in the region is expected to reduce, though not necessarily eliminate, conflicts. The mutual benefits of APEC cooperation would not only raise the cost of conflicts and the breaking up of interdependence, but also reduce the incentives for going to war. APEC meetings, particularly the annual conclave of the leaders, are important confidence-building measures (CBMs) in their own right, providing leaders the opportunity to discuss other issues besides trade and investment liberalization.

Nevertheless, euphoria and complacency are unwarranted. Despite APEC's bright future from a political and security perspective, the Asian side of the Pacific Rim remains turbulent. There are too many unresolved bilateral disputes that hold the potential for becoming flash points. While some of these disputes may eventually be defused, though probably not resolved, by increasing economic interdependence and active diplomacy, a number of the disputes relate to core values that cannot be easily negotiated. China's attitude toward the Taiwan independence question is a primary example. Therefore, other mechanisms are also necessary to promote peace and stability in the Asia-Pacific region. These can take the form of bilateralism, subregionalism, and supraregionalism, which may be tailored to meet specific needs involving different sets of officials and interest groups, but which, taken together, will form a network of regional interaction.

In addition, the existence of authoritarian regimes in several key East Asian countries also contributes to a degree of uncertainty and unpredictability in interstate relations, as policies are mostly dependent on the political wills and idiosyncrasies of particular leaders at any given moment. Therefore, to achieve lasting peace and stability in East Asia it is also essential to promote democracy within the region, for democracies do not go to war against each other. Here APEC can also play a contributing role. Closer economic interdependence and growing economic prosperity in the region are expected to have beneficial spillover effects onto the social and political spheres not only through the emergence of a more politically aware middle class, but also through peer pressure and demonstration effects.

Bibliography

Buzan, Barry, and Segal, Gerald. "Rethinking East Asia Security." *Survival* 36, no. 2 (Summer 1994): 3–21.

Ikrar Nusa Bhakti. "ASEAN and APEC." In Ikrar Nusa Bhakti, Dewi Fortuna Anwar, and Zainuddin Djafar, eds., *APEC: Persepsi ASEAN, Amerika Serikat dan Jepang*. Jakarta: PPW-LIPI, 1994: 19–30.

Lu Jianren, and Zhang Yulin. *Nurturing Asia-Pacific Economic Cooperation: Policies of Japan, China and ASEAN*. Beijing: Institute of Asia-Pacific Studies, Chinese Academy of Social Sciences, 1996.

Nagata, Masahoro. "Economic Aspects of APEC Viewed From Japan." *East Asian Economic Perspectives* 5 (March 1994): 8–14.

Nye, Joseph S. *Peace in Parts. Integration and Conflict in Regional Organization*. Boston: Little, Brown, 1971.

Roth, William V. Jr. "APEC Must Organize to Become an Effective Institution." In Richard J. Ellings, ed., *Americans Speak to APEC: Building a New Order with Asia. NBR Analysis*, vol. 4, no 4. Seattle: The National Bureau of Asian Research, 1993.

Smith, Gary J. *Multilateralism and Regional Security in Asia: The ASEAN Regional Forum (ARF) and APEC's Geo-Political Value*. Working Paper series, no. 97–2. Harvard University, The Center for International Affairs (February 1997).

Soesastro, Hadi, ed. *Indonesian Perspectives on APEC and Regional Cooperation in Asia Pacific*. Jakarta: CSIS, 1994.

Stubb, Richard. "Geo-Politics, Geo-Economics and the Foundation of Asia-Pacific Cooperation." Paper presented at the Conference on Economic and Security Cooperation in the Asia-Pacific: Agenda for the 1990s, Canberra, July 1990.

12

The Prospects of ASEAN
Military Cooperation

Implications for Regional Security

Bantarto Bandoro

The Association of Southeast Asian Nations (ASEAN), an indigenous regional security grouping,[1] is now entering its fourth decade of consultation and cooperation with an unchanged commitment to build a more stable and benign regional environment. The significant global changes—the end of bipolarity and the emergence of new challenges—draw ASEAN's attention to the fact that it needs to take a more proactive posture in managing and handling new international and regional problems.

Until now, cooperation has been the watchword of ASEAN. In light of the enormous changes taking place in the Asia-Pacific region, however, ASEAN cooperation has become all the more important, because member states can achieve much more jointly than individually. For example, ASEAN cooperation has been essential in handling the Cambodian conflict and the consequent refugee situation. To date, ASEAN cooperation has been successful because of the following factors. First, ASEAN is a loose regional organization that permits its members to explore areas of cooperation without any strict regulations. The process of negotiation is therefore informal, with no prescribed format for decision making. Second, ASEAN stresses consensus building in its decision making process, which provides its members flexibility in adopting decisions. Finally, awareness of the differences among ASEAN nations motivates the members to complement each other through cooperation in all realms.

Ever since its inception in 1967, ASEAN cooperation and collective actions

---

Table 12.1

ASEAN Missions

1. To enhance the welfare and security of the member states
2. To build mutual trust
3. To solve regional problems jointly
4. To collaborate with universal organizations, enhancing ASEAN's international status
5. To regulate the presence of external powers
6. To develop a genuine Southeast Asia regional order

---

are intended to achieve what may be called "regional missions" of ASEAN (Table 12.1).

These missions and commitments are executed through various treaties and agreements, which the member states then use to promote trust and stability in the region. Through such missions, ASEAN has developed into a dynamic organization that has earned respect and admiration within and outside the region.

Military cooperation is one field that can promote ASEAN cohesiveness and increases its credibility. Although military cooperation has not been a top priority, ASEAN cannot avoid it as time passes. The dramatic changes in its immediate strategic environment represent important motivations for ASEAN to develop more systematic cooperation in the military field. Although defense linkages between ASEAN and major external powers also characterize the security of Southeast Asia, such linkages should not be regarded as reliance on external powers for success in maintaining the group cohesiveness. Instead, these external linkages are ASEAN's important contribution to strengthening the regional-global linkages, and in turn enhance the global security.

This chapter assesses ASEAN's role, as an indigenous regional security organization, in enhancing peace and security in the region. Special focus will be given to the contribution of ASEAN military cooperation in confidence and trust building and regional security. This chapter inquires into the aspirations and the concerns of the Southeast Asian states with regard to military cooperation, and the shared objectives of ASEAN military cooperation. It will ask whether these objectives serve ASEAN's desires to enhance peace and stability in the region.

Post-World War II Security Organization: An Overview

Before discussing the role of ASEAN military cooperation, however, we must distinguish among three conceptions of regional security organization that have been in existence since 1945. The first, based in Chapter VIII of the United Nations' Charter, is that regional organization is a building block of world order and is part of the universal collective security system. The second, with its foundation in collective self-defense, is the containment of global security threats. In this conception, regional organizations are at the service of global powers. The third posits that the primary purpose of a regional security organization is the enhancement of the security and welfare of member states through cooperation and collective action. Such regional organizations primarily serve member states. ASEAN is perhaps suited to this third conception, because it is an intergovernmental organization devoted primarily to promoting regional peace and stability. ASEAN's principal concern has been to establish a framework for regional order (Dahl 1982, 45–66; Leifer 1989, 1–16). During its 30 years, the organization has experienced most of its successes in the political security field. Security did not formally enter the agenda until the fourth ASEAN summit in January 1992.

ASEAN as an Indigenous Regional Security Organization

Because ASEAN is classified as a security grouping, the organization represents the best medium through which to consider the scale of military cooperation in Southeast Asia. ASEAN not only embodies those aspects of cooperation among member states that already have taken place, but lies at the center of current efforts to promote regional security cooperation. As a security grouping, ASEAN has always been sensitive to its immediate strategic environment, because of the nature of its responsibilities, which include the pursuit of socioeconomic development; the elimination of threats from within and outside the region; the reduction or elimination of external power involvement in the region; and the limitation of competition and enhancement of relationships among members.

   Thus, ASEAN cannot hide from any regional problems that directly or indirectly influence the stability and security of the region, and within this context ASEAN must initiate collective efforts not only in conflict prevention but also in conflict containment and conflict resolution. The ASEAN experience in handling the Cambodian conflict suggests that it can play a valuable role in the prevention, containment, and termination of regional conflict.[2] Some members might desire more. During the conflict, a proposal was advanced that ASEAN should demonstrate its unity by conducting joint military exercises on the Thai-Cambodian borders. The emergence of such a proposal, though unfulfilled, reflects the desire of the countries in the region to embark on military cooperation as a means to cope with regional problems. Certainly, the idea of military cooperation among ASEAN member states is not unfounded, in that such cooperation can always be launched in accordance with the status of ASEAN as a regional security grouping.

Throughout its existence, the cohesiveness, solidarity, and effectiveness of ASEAN has been tested by severe security problems. To tackle these concerns, ASEAN has initiated a series of bilateral and regional actions aimed at creating a security structure benefiting individual states and the region. So far, these ASEAN initiatives support the conception of ASEAN as a security-oriented regional grouping, with a basic commitment to keep the peace and security within the region of Southeast Asia. In this capacity, it is responsible for the following tasks: to halt and bring hostilities to a satisfactory conclusion through settlement or resolution; to achieve agreement to end the use of force; and to apply long-range political and economic strategies to alter the underlying security dynamics of the conflict. Furthermore, to develop and maintain the concept of community within ASEAN, the organization stresses political will to solve regional problems through dialogue and cooperation; regional awareness to strengthen the foundation for further enhancement of security cooperation; and cooperative efforts to eliminate mistrust and suspicion.

ASEAN is aware of the fact that post-Cold War Southeast Asia faces multidimensional challenges. As the entity responsible for the maintenance of peace, security, and the welfare of the member states, ASEAN must continue to assess the fundamental changes that are taking place in the political, security, and economic realms, both globally and regionally, and to determine their impact on the region. Moreover, ASEAN must continue to develop common perceptions of the new threats and challenges to the region. This is not an easy task, but it is a necessary one. And, it must continue to discuss options for meeting those new threats and challenges.

Whether internally or with others, ASEAN military cooperation does not conflict with the stated objectives of ASEAN as a collective entity. ASEAN has its own mechanisms to facilitate such cooperation,[3] which form the basis for and supports the role of ASEAN military cooperation in enhancing regional security and stability. However, ASEAN defense cooperation so far has been conducted on a bilateral or trilateral basis rather than on an ASEAN-wide basis, an emphasis that the 1976 Declaration of ASEAN Concord stressed.[4] In fact, ASEAN statements continue to eschew any mention of turning the organization into a military alliance. Nonetheless, bilateral and trilateral approaches to regional security serve as building blocks for future accords. Thus, ASEAN's efforts to build an indigenous regional security organization are positive steps that complement and simultaneously increase multilateral cooperation.

The Role of ASEAN Military Cooperation
in Regional Security

The Treaty of Amity and Cooperation and the Declaration of ASEAN Concord, both products of the 1976 Bali Summit, provided the instruments for ASEAN's management of regional order. The concord constituted ASEAN's first statement regarding security cooperation, and it provided for continuing cooperation outside ASEAN between the member states on security matters, in accordance with their mutual needs and interests.

This military cooperation among ASEAN members clearly reflected the concern of member countries with insurgencies. At the time, bilateral border security cooperation existed between Indonesia and Malaysia, and between Malaysia and Thailand, and normally involved a combined task force headquarters as well as the combined and unilateral operations. By early 1977, all members of ASEAN had entered bilateral agreements that led to the exchange of security intelligence and that facilitated regular discussion of subversion and insurgencies. This military-to-military contact among ASEAN member countries reflects regional awareness that ASEAN was the appropriate vehicle for handling security problems.

Exchange of military training represents another aspect of ASEAN military cooperation. Widespread regional concerns with strategic development led to bilateral air and sea military exercises. Member states also entered agreements to carry out joint sea patrols against illegal activities such as piracy and smuggling between the Philippines and Indonesia; Singapore and Indonesia; Thailand and Indonesia; and among Malaysia, Indonesia, and Thailand. The bilateral Indonesia-Malaysia training program is the most comprehensive.

The ASEAN member states have agreed that there is no need to make ASEAN a military grouping per se. Firm and strong bilateral relations among ASEAN members are a sufficient foundation for multilateral cooperation. Nonetheless, military cooperation within ASEAN is valuable because it advances nonmilitary goals, such as transparency and confidence building. Furthermore, existing bilateral and trilateral cooperation may pave the way for actual concerted ASEAN defense strategies, if they should become necessary. Thus, in the long run, better military cooperation programs will lead to improvements in regional security.

For this to happen, however, ASEAN countries must strive to maximize their bilateral understanding of and familiarity with each other's defense establishments. Against this background, Prof. Mochtar Kusumaatmadja proposed to develop an ASEAN military capability in which the cooperation program of the Indonesian, Malaysian, and Singaporean armed forces would form the core of a multilateral ASEAN defense effort. This proposal, which would make these three countries primarily responsible for security planning in Southeast Asia, permits other ASEAN members to join the multilateral effort once they are prepared to do so. Development of these bilateral and trilateral military links among ASEAN members has progressed nicely and has resulted in greater understanding and familiarity among the regional states.

This greater cooperation has augmented ASEAN's capability to develop collective action against external or internal threats in times of need. A former Malaysian defense official once claimed that, given the degree of interoperability achieved among ASEAN member forces through bilateral exercises, there is nothing to prevent ASEAN from acting collectively, assuming the political will to do so. If the need develops for an ASEAN military force, it could take place almost overnight (Karniol 1993).

Challenges to Continued ASEAN Cooperation

Despite the progress in ASEAN military-to-military contacts, further development of regional security cooperation remains circumscribed by the following factors. The various intramural disputes and tensions within ASEAN, illustrating deep-seated tensions and suspicions among ASEAN members, have widely been considered obstacles to the development of ASEAN security cooperation. A further obstacle to ASEAN military cooperation has been the divergent strategic perspectives among its members, especially during the last two decades. Additionally, according to Acharya (1997, 62), there is a sense that existing bilateral mechanisms are adequate to meet the primary goal of greater trust and misunderstanding among ASEAN armed forces, which share a culture of secrecy. These obstacles are reflected in the very limited actual defense cooperation that has occurred among ASEAN members. Although multitude defense links appear to exist through various bilateral and trilateral exercises, in reality these exercises do not contribute significantly to the enhancement of member defense capabilities (Acharya 1993).

Ever since the 1980s, the region has experienced a proliferation of agreements, but it is difficult to discern which of the proliferation agreements on various forms of defense cooperation among ASEAN members are actually significant from a defense standpoint. The development of defense links within ASEAN has been more in the nature of confidence building than in functional operation toward practical objectives. In fact, the history of ASEAN military cooperation reveals that much of the cooperation has been aimed at inducing greater transparency and understanding among the cooperating states. For example, in 1991, General Hashim Mohammed Ali, then Chief of Malaysia's Defense Force, explicitly stated that one of the main aims of

Table 12.2

Desirable Actions by ASEAN Nations

1. Publishing the defense policies of individual ASEAN countries.
2. Enhancing existing military exchanges in training and promoting new venues for training in the defense field.
3. Establishing a defense and security networking center so that it can grow into a multilateral cooperation scheme.
4. Establishing a center for security and defense cooperation.
5. Promoting cooperation among the general staffs of the armed forces and the defense departments of ASEAN countries.

ASEAN defense and security cooperation is to reduce conflict and to facilitate confidence-building measures (Ali 1991). Singapore's defense minister also has spoken explicitly of the confidence-building role of intra-ASEAN military cooperation (*Strait Times*, August 25, 1992).

The ASEAN military cooperation forms part of regional efforts to build confidence and mutual trust and should become one of the pillars for the stability and security of the region. In this regard, ASEAN leaders should direct their defense programs and postures toward one that would prevent the region from becoming an area of confrontation, through a variety of actions (Table 12.2).

The above actions serve as insurance for the countries in the region that the development of intra-ASEAN defense ties will not lead some member states to view others as potential adversaries or threats to stability. By increasing familiarity and mutual understanding among the ASEAN member countries, these measures can promote more integrated cooperative efforts in security and defense, simultaneously increasing ASEAN's credibility as a collective security entity capable of defending its own interest and promoting ASEAN's status vis-à-vis the great powers. This direction of development does not violate the stipulation that ASEAN will not become a military pact. Rather, by creating a security community,[5] ASEAN can generate a sense of security among its members, enabling it to face new challenges in the region as well as low-level problems of security. Such actions, it is hoped, will induce greater transparency among ASEAN member nations in each other's defense policies and plans, thus facilitating crisis management.

Although the military component in ASEAN interaction is as important as other components, ASEAN cannot rely on military power alone to handle regional problems or threats. Continued ASEAN military-to-military contact must lead to the establishment of a more integrated defense posture. By using all of its resources to improve the quality of defense programs and joint exercises, ASEAN can create not only a surprise-free future in the region, but also a future that would guarantee national security.

The goal of increasing security cooperation necessarily has resulted in an increase in the number and complexity of joint military exercises. Because of anticipated serious regional challenges, ASEAN military cooperation should be promoted in a more orderly manner and in a more proactive fashion. Statements of ASEAN military leaders, which have stressed the importance of enhancing military cooperation, indicate the need for more regular security consultation, dialogue, and transparency in the future. The transition to more formal and multilateral cooperation is not guaranteed. ASEAN first must resolve many of the prevailing problems among its members.

Challenges from Outside the Region

The early 1990s demonstrated an increased willingness to strengthen further the process of security dialogue within ASEAN. This willingness has resulted not only from member awareness of the increasing volatility of the regional strategic environment and a desire to have some influence over the emerging pattern of regional security cooperation, but also from changes in U.S. regional policy and attitude. After the end of the Cold War, the United States began to focus on establishing multilateral security fora to help "manage or prevent emerging concerns" (quote from Winston Lord, then U.S. Undersecretary of State for East Asian and Pacific Affairs, in *Far Eastern Economic Review*, April 15, 1993, 10). Although ASEAN welcomes this challenge, it cannot hide from the fact that changing great power relations, particularly involving China, pose powerful concerns for the security of the region. Therefore, ASEAN must prepare for the possibility that any vacuum created by the withdrawal of one great power will be filled by another great power. Given these uncertainties and challenges, stronger cooperation in the defense field is necessary to provide a web of defense relations that eventually could turn into more formal defense coordination among the countries concerned.

Although ASEAN has recognized the importance of military cooperation as a means of building confidence and trust, its members cannot ignore the need to develop defense links with external powers, primarily with the United States. This is most evident with regard to Thailand and the Philippines, both of which have security treaties with the United States. It is also evident in the joint exercises and military assistance by the United States, which have benefited Malaysia, Singapore and Indonesia. In addition, because ASEAN maintains good relations with Australia, it is also possible that ASEAN could develop closer defense cooperation with Australia, but this of course cannot be based on the Five Powers Defense Arrangements (FPDA) framework. One analyst anticipates that if the United States were to withdraw completely from the Western Pacific, ASEAN might consider a more formal defense arrangement with the countries in the Southwest Pacific (New Zealand and Papua New Guinea) (Wanandi 1996, 189).

ASEAN maintains good relations with Japan, and both have recognized the importance of maintaining security and stability through dialogue and other cooperative efforts. Establishing defense linkages between the two entities is not impossible, because such links are the product of mutual recognition of mutual economic and security interests. For example, ASEAN should seek cooperation with Japan in the area of technology transfer and the supply of equipment that could assist ASEAN in safeguarding the sea lanes of communication in Southeast Asia, because the sea lanes are vital to Japanese security interests. Although ASEAN opposes any Japanese attempt to police the Southeast Asia sea lanes, it is prepared to cooperate with Japan because it cannot bear the financial burden alone.

Although cooperation between ASEAN and Japan on specific defense matters has been slower to develop, there have been signs in the early 1990s that some types of subregional security and defense dialogue are emerging between certain ASEAN countries and Japan. This has become evident in the series of visits by Japan Defense Agency officials to the ASEAN countries, which represents considerable progress in preparing the conditions for a more systematic security cooperation between ASEAN and Japan. At the same time, however, it is still difficult to point to specific matters of cooperation and defense linkages. The ultimate outcome of Japan's attempt to build subregional security and defense linkages with ASEAN remains unclear, and will depend on the changes in the strategic environment and the extent to which domestic opinion within ASEAN nations permits their policymakers to respond to Japan's initiatives. Given the historical record of Japan's policy in the region, domestic opinions within ASEAN member states are not prepared for an extensive new Japanese security role in the region. This suggests a limited security option for Japan, at least for the time being. One analyst believes that Japan should avoid a direct military role in the region, and instead should extend its defense links to Southeast Asia by agreements on the exchange and training of ASEAN military personnel (Sudo 1991).

External defense links can act as a means of building confidence by creating channels of communication and information exchanges, a role that also could be attributed to bilateral cooperation among ASEAN members (Huxley 1993, 66–67).[6] Military cooperation between ASEAN member countries and defense linkages with external powers are a fact of life in the region. These interactions are a function of the interdependence of a regional system and are directed toward making the region more stable and beneficial to the cooperating states. Both ASEAN members and external powers have some expectations with regard to their military cooperation (Table 12.3).

Table 12.3

ASEAN Member Expectations

1. Maintaining regional stability and a healthier climate of interactions.
2. Clearing up misperceptions and developing rapport and networks that would be useful in defusing tensions.
3. Sustaining a multilateral system that promises to produce order and security.
4. Sustaining the already well developed and widely understood regional arrangement for cooperation and for resolving conflict.
5. Cultivating awareness in the ASEAN countries of the importance of eliminating competition among themselves, which emerged from the process of interactive weapons acquisition.
6. Promoting the development of greater arms transparency in the region.
7. Promoting the development of the Asian Regional Forum into a more important and respected platform for multilateral security dialogue and cooperation.

The ASEAN expectations of military cooperation are shaped primarily by the attitude of its members toward the question of how to manage regional issues. There seems to be in existence a commitment and willingness of ASEAN to employ its own resources to solve regional problems. Furthermore, ASEAN has been able to demonstrate to the outside world its ability to cope with major changes taking place in the various political, security and strategic fields. The annual ministerial meetings have always presented proposals to take bold initiatives in enhancing and strengthening security cooperation, including the military component. ASEAN military-to-military contact has been in existence since the 1970s, and it now seems to be acquiring greater intensity. Although military cooperation thus far has been bilateral or trilateral only, the abolishment of military blocs and alliances provides ASEAN with an open opportunity to engage in multilateral defense cooperation.

ASEAN's principal concern has been to establish a framework for regional order, of which multilateral defense cooperation can become an important component. Concerted ASEAN efforts in the field of security, including military agreements, reflect the desires of the regional states to place a greater emphasis on the aspect of organization-as-actor rather than on the actor-in-organization. Member states are primarily concerned with the impact of mistrust and misperception on regional stability and security, and if these impacts are not appropriately managed, the prospect of conflict arises. Consequently, ASEAN needs to increase its activity in the security area to promote cooperation and instill a pattern of constructive behavior (Table 12.4).

Table 12.4

Aspirations of ASEAN Regional States

1. Enhancing mutual understanding and trust.
2. Promoting greater transparency and strengthening the commitment among cooperating actors to maintain peace and stability in the region.
3. Creating a strong foundation for dealing with future security challenges.
4. Maintaining the emerging sense of community and shared interests, standing the region in good condition to address regional challenges.

Table 12.5

Recommended Policies for ASEAN Security

1. Increase activity in the military realm.
2. Improve the quality of defense programs through regular interaction and dialogue at the highest level of the military establishment.
3. Create a subsection in the ASEAN-Senior Officials' Meeting that deals exclusively with military matters.
4. Create a sound and strong basis for a more multilateral framework for military cooperation.
5. Expand defense linkages that encompass a wider region of the Asia-Pacific.
6. Set a new regional security agenda that accommodates the concerns and preferences of cooperating states.

Conclusion: ASEAN Military Cooperation—The Road Ahead

Over the past thirty years, ASEAN's strong regional performance has primarily been attributed to its strong commitment to maintaining cooperation in all fields. Its future success, however, requires additional vigilance. As a regional security entity, ASEAN ideally should rely on its own resources to ensure security and stability; this points to the importance of exploring venues that enable greater interaction and networking among officials of the member states. Furthermore, the end of the Cold War has paved the way for a broader discussion on security problems and requires ASEAN to take a more proactive stand in managing new security issues. ASEAN is not in a position to ignore the security dimension of international politics. Confidence building, mutual trust and military transparency are now gaining increasing importance in the defense community, and ASEAN must take collective steps to realize these concepts (Table 12.5).

ASEAN is not totally insensitive to the new vulnerabilities or threats created by the end of the Cold War, which have become more complex. They originate both from within and outside the region and are not confined to politics and the military. Thus, ASEAN's approach to security problems has become more difficult, especially because it has expanded to include nine members. A more diverse ASEAN will complicate military cooperation, and will require bilateral confidence building with new members through regular contact and exchange of defense information. On a regional level, ASEAN should encourage its new members to attend all meetings that specifically discuss defense matters.

Moreover, ASEAN will continue to face pressures and confront fundamental changes at the regional and international level. These changes might accelerate the development of a multilateral framework for defense cooperation. Because of ASEAN's pledge to remain a nonmilitary organization, however, this multilateral cooperation would take place outside ASEAN and would involve the armed forces of the ASEAN member countries. Thus, common sense dictates that the development of ASEAN military cooperation must progress on three levels. First, productive and constructive dialogue is a prerequisite for a better understanding of defense policy and plans and must continue. Second, the parameters of ASEAN military cooperation must be expanded because the security of Southeast Asia and the broader Asia-Pacific region has become more integrated. Finally, active cooperation on specific military programs and issues is essential.

All of these developments are possible and will proceed in tune with the perceived desires and needs of the cooperating states. But there can be no progress in these endeavors without consensus and a strong political will.

Notes

1. In this chapter, ASEAN is referred to as a regional security organization. It is a formal, intergovernmental organization among geographically proximate states in a region that is internally and externally recognized as distinct. At least one of the purpose of ASEAN should be the maintenance of peace and security in the region.

2. For further analysis of ASEAN's role in the resolution of the Cambodian conflict, see Alagappa (1993).

3. These mechanisms and guidance are the ASEAN Ministerial Meeting (AMM); the ASEAN Post Ministerial Conference (ASEAN PMC); and the ASEAN Regional Forum (ARF).

4. See Section E, Declaration of ASEAN Concord 1976.

5. On the differences between a security community and a defense community, see Acharya (1991).

6. Despite these defense links, however, ASEAN hopes to create an understanding on the part of the external powers (particularly the United States) that these defense links are not meant to draw ASEAN into alliance relationships.

Bibliography

Acharya, Amitav. "Defense Cooperation and Transparency." In Bates Gill and J.N. Mak, eds., *Arms, Transparency and Security in South-East Asia*. New York: Oxford University Press, 1997: 49–62.

————. "A New Regional Order in Southeast Asia: ASEAN in the Post Cold War." *Adelphi Papers* no. 279, 1993.

————. "Association of Southeast Asia Nations: Security Community or Defense Community?" *Pacific Affairs* 64, no. 2 (Summer 1991): 159–78.

Alagappa, Muthia. "Regionalism and the Quest for Security: ASEAN and the Cambodian Conflict." *Journal of International Affairs* 46, no. 2 (Winter 1993).

Ali, H.A. "Prospect for Defense and Security Cooperation in ASEAN." Paper presented at the Conference on ASEAN and the Pacific Region: Prospects for Security Cooperation in the 1990s. Manila: June 5–7, 1991.

Dahl, Arnfin Jorgensen. *Regional Organization and Order in Southeast Asia.* London: Macmillan, 1982.

Far Eastern Economic Review, April 15, 1993.

Huxley, Tim. *Insecurity in the ASEAN Region.* London: Royal United Services Institute for Defence Studies, 1993.

Karniol, Robert. "The Jane's Interview." *Jane's Defence Weekly*, December 18, 1993, p. 32.

Leifer, Michael. *ASEAN and the Security of Southeast Asia.* New York: Routledge, 1989.

Sudo, Sue. "Japan and the Security of Southeast Asia." *Pacific Affairs* 4, no. 4 (1991): 333–44.

Strait Times, August 25, 1992.

Wanandi, Jusuf. *Asia Pacific After the Cold War.* Jakarta: CSIS, 1996.

13

Europe and Asia

Is ASEM a Model for the Future?

François Godement

Introduction

Time and again, Europe-Asia relations have been described as the "missing side" of a triangle that also includes the historical transatlantic and the blooming transpacific relationships. The level of this discourse can only grow as the United States, thanks to the so-called New Economy and its Schumpeterian computer-based cycle, increases its international preeminence where most observers thought it would diminish. Yet the advent of the single unified market in 1993, and the decision to create a single European currency before the year 2000, along with the rise in cross-trading between Europe and Asia, have also pushed Asians to aim for some form of coordination with Europe.

Needless to say, the great Asian financial crisis of 1997 will motivate Asia further to open up new relationships with Europe. Although Asia's security ties to the United States have remained remarkably stable, the informal peg of most Asian currencies to the dollar, without any regional system or even anchor, has turned into a disaster. Europe's currency system, with the introduction of the euro single currency, seems an attractive complement to transpacific relations.

Although Europe's institutional integration looks like an eternal, but progressing, work in process, Asia has just entered the first stage of regional integration, though the economic indices are far more advanced than overt policies would tend to indicate. Whereas Europe has aimed at a single market model, unexpectedly led by market forces and working for the benefit of the consumer, Asia has created an undeclared single production zone that largely targets the global market outside Asia (Hatch and Yamamura 1996).

Given this ambiguity of purpose between regional integration and global aim, it is not surprising that the initiative for better (and, first of all, greater) relations between Europe and Asia came from Asia itself; and within Asia, from the smaller club of the Association of Southeast Asian Nations (ASEAN), whose trading window opens as much toward Europe as to the United States; and within ASEAN, from Singapore, a city-state in the tradition of high antiquity emporiums, whose lifeline rests on global and open trading, and from its Prime Minister Goh Chok Tong, who first suggested a dialogue among heads of government of Asian and European countries (Goh 1997).

The other half of the initiative did come from some of Europe's leaders, however, and in particular from French President Jacques Chirac, a long standing Asia buff who is obsessed with the attraction of major Asian civilizations and traditions. After decades of European antidumping and "rabbit hutch" speeches, a fundamentally positive attitude about Asia was something new for Europe's governments and politicians even though commercial relations had developed beyond that stage. President Chirac's quick response to the proposal for the Asia-Europe Meeting (ASEM) had been preceded, however, by such policy moves as the European Commission's adoption of an Asia policy document,[1] as well as by German and British government-level initiatives aimed at Asia.

The Rationale Underlying ASEM

In both Asia and Europe, there may have been other, partly hidden, assumptions or motivations in forging this relationship. Whether the United States was regarded as a power on the wane in Asia (as many expected in the late 1980s) or as the towering force defining international issues over the Asia-Pacific, Asian policymakers may have sought a complement or a counterweight at times. This was tangible particularly in Dr. Mahathir Mohammed's policy propositions, from the original project of an Asia-only community (East Asian Economic Community, or EAEC) to his enthusiastic endorsement of ASEM, whose Asian leg just happened to coincide with the grand plan for EAEC. It cannot have escaped Europeans that a direct political presence and stronger geopolitical ties with Asia would enable Europe to compete economically with the United States in Asia without challenging the fundamental American alliance. And for both, a minimal purpose underlying ASEM may have been to "keep the United States honestly international" (Segal 1997) on issues as diverse as trade policies and sanctions, high-tech deals, and political relations. None of these speculations, we hasten to add, figured in the Europe-Asia official language and surrounding rhetoric at the birth of ASEM. Indeed, while some Asians possibly sought to balance the Asia-Pacific Economic Cooperation (APEC) group with its unmistakable leadership and free market stance, some Europeans may have felt that ASEM at least represented a possible bargaining chip with APEC in the future.

Underlying assumptions and open-ended strategies may have been less important, therefore, than the process itself of setting up a relationship. Indeed, ASEM achieved a brilliant start in March 1996 in Bangkok with its inaugural meeting, which involved heads of states and governments as well as the President of the European Union (EU). While some observers did note a lack of clear-cut objectives, others observed that the Pacific Basin community had taken all of 17 years to produce the first APEC summit, whereas Europeans and Asians were apparently willing to jump the gun and mobilize their heads of states and governments much sooner. As a consequence of this top-down approach, government machines have had to follow suit, producing a bewildering array of bureaucrats' meetings with strange acronyms for names. To cite a few, customs administration chiefs from Europe and Asia have already met twice since the spring of 1996; ministers of finance, economy and foreign affairs have also met; and there already are at least two formats for business roundtables.[2]

To date, in the smaller scene of cultural institutions and think tank networking, there exist at least three avenues of cooperation: CAEC (Council for Asia-Europe Cooperation, linking up a dozen think tanks from Asia and Europe, and founded in May 1996); the Asia-Europe Foundation (ASEF) launched in February 1997 and based in Singapore;[3] and a practice of forums encouraged by the European Union's DG1 (responsible for external relations), the first of which took place in Venice in January 1996, the second in Manila in December 1997. In this area, although official support is an important component, private initiatives are flowering, and they indicate that ASEM is beginning to extend beyond mere government-to-government rhetoric.

Another measure of ASEM's initial success can be found in the large number of countries that have asked, directly or indirectly, to join the process. Such countries as India, Australia, Pakistan, New Zealand, Russia and Iran cannot all be wrong about the future trend of Euro-Asian relations if they want to climb on board. From the outset, ASEM has faced the type of "widening or deepening" debates that the EU knows well. These requests are a tribute to ASEM, but they also pose a strong risk for diluting the process of solidifying a relationship that has just begun (Godement 1996).

Although the "widening" discussion has been delayed until the next Asia-Europe Meeting in London in May 1998, the founding members of ASEM will have to adopt rules to justify their choices for future membership.[4] It is already becoming clear that each member stands on its own, and not as a member of the European Union or ASEAN, for example. This may rule out "automatic membership" for new or coming ASEAN nations such as Vietnam, Laos, Cambodia, or Myanmar (formerly Burma). It also appears that the pressure for membership by India, Australia and New Zealand will be hard to resist; thus, the initial restricted geographical definition of Asia will pass away quickly, even though some of the Asian members may appreciate their first experience of an Asia-wide forum that does not include the United States. Much will also depend on bargaining or quid pro quo processes.

At the European level, a commission that felt pangs of anxiety because it was not invited to participate in the APEC process must have concluded, at least initially, that Australia and New Zealand required no reciprocity for their membership in ASEM. Conversely, India's participation (and Pakistan as a logical or unavoidable extension) would be favored both at the level of the European Union and by individual countries such as France. Geography, a long history of development assistance to India, and a proximity of European and Indian political cultures at a time when so much was made of Asiatism dictated sympathy for this large South Asian nation. The inclusion of Russia and Iran, for very different reasons, would be troublesome to almost everyone. Furthermore, the inclusion of Central European countries, completely logical for Asian members of ASEM, would confuse EU member states that recently adopted the principle of enlargement to six more countries from Eastern Europe.[5] These member states are still sorting out the issues of who may join the EU, and, more importantly, when membership may be extended.

At the same time, the members of ASEM have sought to dispel the notion that ASEM represents a region-to-region format. From a formal standpoint, there is neither an "Asian" nor a "European" side to ASEM; the European Union is present only side by side with EU member countries, and there is no ASEAN presence as such. Membership is on a country-by-country basis, and entry into ASEAN or the EU will not therefore automatically qualify a country for participation in ASEM. On the one hand, this has done much to reassure larger Asian countries, such as Japan, that ASEAN would not acquire leadership over yet another multilateral forum initiated by some ASEAN member countries; and it also affords Europeans some elbow room for mutual competition. On the other hand, membership in ASEAN does have some consequences for participation in ASEM, as the strained relationship between European countries and ASEAN concerning Burma's entry into ASEAN and its consequences for ASEM continues (Hiebert 1997).

Another and more deceptive measure of ASEM's success may lie in the sniping it has occasionally received from some high-level American experts.

The comments of Dr. Zbigniew Brezinski, who formalized in the past the concept of a triangular relationship (among the United States, China, and the USSR), are instructive. Brezinski argued to Ambassador William Bodde, the former head of the newly created APEC secretariat from 1993 to 1995, that ASEM without the United States was destined to remain "impotent" (Brezinski 1996). Bodde had recently painted a portrait of Europe's economic and technological decline, and concluded that American leadership, commitment to APEC, and military presence were essential to Pacific stability; he did not see fit to mention the existence of ASEM (Bodde 1997). But today, as APEC and other transpacific instruments of cooperation take a back seat to the International Monetary Fund in addressing the Asian financial crisis, these assurances regarding Pacific leadership ring more hollow than six months ago.

Although think tanks or U.S. government officials sporadically return to the idea of transatlantic relations, they devote a much higher proportion of their time and energy to Asia-Pacific linkages. This does not reflect so much a downgrading of Europe's importance for the United States as a feeling that Europe can be taken for granted. As a consequence, on the whole, U.S. evaluations tended to underestimate the potential for ASEM—indeed, for any European exercise toward Asia. Officials and others focused their attention on European based developments only when these posed immediate challenges to the U.S. leading role or to U.S. commercial interests. For example, with regard to European policies toward China, particularly China's entry into the World Trade Organization (WTO), experts were more likely to seek ideas for a cooperative approach among Europeans and Americans toward Asia. "The United States and Europe should strive to support each other whenever possible in order not to permit China to play one trading partner off against the other," concluded one such study (Stokes 1997), recommending coordination in the automotive and aerospace industries.

If Euro-Asian relations were definitely a link that America did not miss very much, trade competition, and its unavoidable corollary, political jockeying for advantage, is perhaps an issue likely to irritate and stimulate Washington. In recent years, a few centers, such as the East-West Center in Hawaii, have taken a longer-term approach toward encouraging a triangular (Europe-Asia-United States) approach.[6] But apart from these occasions, ASEM was largely greeted by silence, while expert articles and specialized literature on Asia-Pacific regional groupings number in the thousands.

Security Off the Agenda?

Today, ASEM faces much more difficult circumstances than it confronted at its birth. Beginning in 1992, the anxieties over the coming European unified market, followed by the last negotiating stages of the Uruguay Round and the founding of WTO in late 1993, have motivated trading nations of Asia, and especially Southeast Asia, both to seek insurance against the formation of regional blocs that would limit free trade, and also to counterbalance the United States and the predominant weight of the North American Free Trade Agreement (NAFTA). While many of these discussions took place within APEC, it is significant that Singapore, a small country with an evident vested interest in global free trading, and which from time to time has considered joining NAFTA, led the pack in promoting the idea of ASEM.

The Asia-Europe Meeting benefited from the Clinton administration's Asia policies, which at midterm were usually regarded as weak and indecisive, if not incoherent: both regional leaders and former figures in the Bush administration usually joined in criticizing the Clinton administration. Asia felt that APEC sought a grandiose commitment to free trade for the entire region that many of its member countries could not afford. It felt bewildered by U.S. human rights pronouncements that sometimes seemed to undermine the old tenets of stability and bilateral alliance. Finally, it was worried by inconclusive policies toward China that might leave the rest of Asia facing a rising and angry regional power in the not so distant future.

Asian countries therefore looked for other insurance policies. One of these policies was regional dialogue, well exemplified by the ASEAN Regional Forum (ARF), that was designed to assuage China while, it was hoped, bringing it to the conference table on such issues as the South China Sea. Another was ASEM, which might one day serve to regulate commercial disputes and to mitigate the impact of trade policies and unilateral sanctions. In addition, although the U.S. economy had begun to recover and its exports were gaining strength, these developments had not yet been termed part of a "new business cycle" that would restore American superiority in cutting edge technologies and international predominance.

Analysts of Asia's strategic problems still pointed to the possibility of a waning American military presence, and the risks that such a "black hole" would entail. The idea of ASEM thus originated as a reinsurance policy by ASEAN nations that, from a political and strategic point of view, wished to draw Europe in. One irony, in this respect, is that the founding meeting of ASEM took place in March 1996, just as a show of force by the U.S. Eighth Fleet in and around the Taiwan Strait reassured most concerned parties about the American capacity and will to defend its Asian allies. After March 1996, ASEM occupied the role of a less political international roundtable, where China was not faced with the political and strategic requests and complaints that the United States regularly takes up with Beijing.

Political and security considerations did form part of the early rationale for ASEM, as the Maastricht Treaty and the CSFP (Common Security and Foreign Policy) made security and foreign policy a legitimate area of action for the European Union. There were differences, however. ASEM's political and security role is generally regarded as the product of British and French insistence. For example, Mr. Hervé de Charette, the former French Foreign Affairs minister, pleaded for a political role for ASEM at the ASEM foreign affairs meeting in February 1997. Asian participants were much more focused on taming the "values" debate between Asian and European countries and coming to terms with Europeans on human and social rights, preferably on Asian rather than Western ground (Hiebert 1997). But most of all, participants were concerned with economic issues, with maintaining access to European markets and perhaps undercutting the potential for U.S. trade sanctions based on commercial quarrels.

In the sense of "economic security," many European nations are interested in Asia's well-being, and in solving crises with likely consequences beyond the regional level. Thus, support for the Korea Energy Development Organization (KEDO), the energy substitution scheme for North Korea's nuclear plants, has grown slowly from a limited basis to the EU level as a whole, although some Northern European nations were reluctant to endorse any form of nuclear development. In the wider sense of forming policy regarding Asia, there is less cohesion among European countries. Germany, with its wealth of foundations, its high level political debates within the Bundestag and its main political parties, and its diversity of current affairs research centers, is probably the European country best suited to the policy-making task. Nonetheless, its low profile in the area of security and strategy, as well as its recurring wish to benefit from neutral policy stances, prevents German policy from exerting significant influence on other European countries.

In addition, Northern European nations go much further in terms of neutralism and pacifism, and therefore do not constitute a coherent base of action with Germany. Britain and France are the only European nations that possess the integrated chain from constitutional entitlement to global responsibility in the United Nations,[7] along with a modest but genuine military capacity to "think Asia" in their security policies, and not only in the sales of weapons, as some other European countries tend to do.

On the Asian side, the use of ASEM as a forum for political and security organization entailed two issues. First was the overwhelming fear that the Europe-Asia dialogue would inevitably entail intervention into "internal affairs"—whether East Timor, Myanmar's human rights and political situation, or China's stand on reunification. Second was the trend toward using Europe as a testing ground for policy positions before proposing them to the

United States. Thus, Prime Minister Mahathir sought to embrace ASEM as an occasion for a dialogue with European leaders, despite Europe's sins as a former colonizer. Chinese Premier Li Peng, albeit more discreetly, also used the occasion of the Bangkok summit for a high-profile appearance. The Bangkok ASEM declaration opened with a clear statement on political and security ties between Asia and Europe, much like the one that Japan, a decade earlier, had fought hard to obtain from the G-7 leaders at Williamsburg. One can presume that in May 1997 Southeast Asia and Korea, at least, saw the advantages of engaging the political leaders of Europe in an expression of solidarity with the region. Hence, the complexity of ASEM's role is evidenced by ambiguity: Although neo-nationalists and Asianists who seek to distance themselves from a relationship with the United States have courted a Europe-Asia relationship, so have genuine internationalists and globalists such as former President Kim Young-sam of South Korea or Philippine President Fidel Ramos.

But ASEM's situation fundamentally changed in 1996–1997. First of all, an apparently endless cycle of productivity gains and prosperity has raised American self-confidence to new levels. This has affected policies toward the Asia-Pacific, and it has strongly influenced Asian perceptions about the United States. Asians have been reassured about the U.S. military commitment to the region, following the strong U.S. demonstration in March 1996 around Taiwan, and American insistence on maintaining U.S. bases in Okinawa.[8]

Second, and conversely, Europe is temporarily at least receding from strong policies and actions outside Europe, which are weakening on the eve of the crucial decisions regarding the euro currency. As Europe is absorbed by the task of working toward its own unification, the magnitude of the problems to be solved—to which several changes of governments can attest—predictably will distract European leaders from any commitment to external partners, including ASEM. Although there are credible signs of Europe's newfound interest for Asia's security and stability, such as its participation in KEDO,[9] food aid to North Korea, and involvement with the ASEAN Regional Forum, the trend favors stronger U.S. involvement to ensure Asia-Pacific security in the foreseeable future.

Finally, the growing financial and monetary crisis in Southeast Asia, which also has weakened Northeast Asian economies, is now leading to questions on both sides of the ASEM relationship. Needless to say, the crisis is a historical event even if one does not subscribe to "end of growth" or "end of the miracle" views. It highlights, among other things, the lack of any regional collective apparatus or capacity to respond to precisely such a crisis. As recently as early 1997, the United States, Australia, New Zealand, Japan, Hong

Kong and Singapore met through their financial officials to improve their mutual cooperation: Today, this group is nowhere to be seen. Although it does not signify "the end of growth," the crisis has fundamentally weakened ASEAN's philosophy of benign consensus and preservation of the status quo as a way to manage collectively ASEAN's own economic interests and regional strains. The extraordinary efforts its members have made to internationalize their economies are being negated today by their lack of institutional arrangements for economic security—and that, too, is politics.

The lack of a coordinated European response to the Asian crisis is equally bothersome, given the growing economic ties between the two regions. Because European export statistics still include intra-European trade, Asian trade only appears to account for 9 percent of European trade. Aggregate European exports to Asia , however, have been growing at a pace of 17.5 percent annually since 1980 and roughly equaled U.S. sales to Asia in 1997. Furthermore, European banks have lent surprisingly large amounts of capital to some of the troubled Asian economies, particularly South Korea and Indonesia. According to the Bank of International Settlements, European banks held 42.2 percent of all international commercial loans to Asia, with Japan second at 32.3 percent and U.S. banks a distant third at 11.2 percent (Bank of International Settlements 1997, 12). The prospect of default by some key debtors is one that should unsettle the European financial community.

With the prospect of International Monetary Fund (IMF) credit lines that would be drawn on them, major European governments have probably been worried about the Asian economic crisis since the summer of 1997. But because the first Western reactions concerning the crisis focused on the American perspective, European governments abstained from much comment. Since then, however, Europe appears to be attempting to minimize the impact of the Asian crisis on the European economy.

In recent Asian expressions about ASEM, particularly those from Southeast Asia, a new sense of pace has begun to appear. After the Bangkok declaration, which many Asians consider primarily an agreement not to disagree openly or to clash on sensitive issues, we are reminded that all dialogue— from ASEAN to ASEM—takes time. Personal contacts, informal discussion of issues, and the creation of a positive climate would constitute significant achievements, and could take some years. Under the "Asian way," as embodied in the Bangkok declaration, there is no obligation or promise to achieve concrete results. Although not explicitly stated, there is a sense, as in APEC's short history, that the economic and trade pillar is a potentially less threatening ground for ASEM coordination than the political and security aims that were emphasized so clearly in the initial Bangkok statement. Furthermore, the themes of monetary stability and international currency ties are fast developing into an intermediate ground for agreement. Although some European economists have tried to sell the benefits of the euro as the world's second currency and its potential as a reserve currency, few politicians are following suit. They know only too well that the euro is not yet in place and that trust is a long-term proposition in monetary matters.

Current ASEM developments therefore have steered away from political and security commitments. Instead, private infrastructure funds, cross-trade and investment ties, concrete follow-up on the peninsular train idea proposed in Bangkok,[10] and the initial actions of the newly created Asia-Europe Foundation, a quasi-intergovernmental body aimed at fostering cultural exchange rather than think-tank activities, all point to an apolitical stage in ASEM's development. That this trend permits Europeans simultaneously to involve themselves with China and to ignore the problems around it is in fact an accrued benefit for European leaders who neither agree nor disagree completely with U.S. policy toward China. Those leaders merely seek to occupy the honest salesman niche, a role that German Chancellor Helmut Kohl, if not his more militant Foreign Affairs Minister Klaus Kinkel, used to play to perfection.

This trend has an unhappy consequence for Taiwan. Although Taiwan clearly cannot count on the collective voice of ASEM in case of an external crisis given China's importance to both Asian and European members, it is not clear how Taiwan should treat an eventual membership or association with ASEM. Given the trend toward economics-based organization, there is no more reason to exclude Taiwan from ASEM than from APEC or, for that matter, from the Asian Development Bank (ADB). But under the terms of the Bangkok declaration, China's long-standing refusal to engage in any international security discussion in the presence of Taiwan realistically precludes such a bid.

The Case for European Involvement in Asia's Security

Europe has different, and not necessarily overlapping, reasons to become involved in Asia-Pacific security. As Sir Leon Brittan announced in February 1997, "Our interest in East-Asia is no longer just a commercial one" (Islam 1997). One reason is the historical linkage between the two regions, which dates from the intermediate missile (SS-20) controversy with the Soviet Union resulting in a common G-7 stand with Japan at the Williamsburg summit. The decline or disappearance of any significant Russian threat to Eurasia, of course, has removed this initiative. Since then, Europeans have tended to become involved piecemeal in Asia's international crises and settlements. For example, Europe became involved in the dispatch of soldiers and technicians through the UN peacekeeping mission (UNTAC), and provided large amounts of international economic aid to Cambodia between 1991 and 1993, in addition to the intense diplomacy that preceded the second Paris conference in August 1991. In the Korean peninsula, most European nations and the EU itself have joined in financially supporting KEDO after the October 1994 Geneva agreement, and have more recently extended food aid to North Korea under EU auspices.[11]

In addition, European countries have undertaken other, less obvious forms of military commitments such as naval exercises and training, mainly by France and Great Britain. Although some may regard these commitments as part of an arms sales drive or an after-sales service, they still imply a commitment to the region's security and to regional partners. In recent years, Britain has carried out numerous naval exercises, either with its main ASEAN partners, or in the South China Sea. France does the same, usually at times of major military exhibitions or fairs in the region. Both countries have defense cooperation agreements with ASEAN nations and, in conjunction with Germany, now hold regular security consultations with Japan. More recently, French President Chirac's visit to China resulted in a "global partnership" agreement paving the way for renewed military and strategic consultations, which had disappeared after the 1989 Tiananmen Square incident. The extent of this partnership, however, remains a topic of intense debate.

Nonetheless, the rationale for European intervention extends beyond these disparate elements. United Nations responsibilities (France and Britain), involvement in the Five-Power Defense Agreement[12] (Britain), and military presence in the Indian Ocean and the South Pacific (France maintains 16,000 troops in these areas),[13] provide both the motivations and the means to maintain at least a minimal security presence. The quest for energy security, and therefore for protecting shipping lanes as well as preventing conflict around potential oil fields, is a preoccupation shared by Europeans. Britain and France's permanent membership in the UN Security Council, as well as their participation in the Joint Policy Declaration on Korea, would result in their inevitable involvement if a substantial crisis broke out on the Korean peninsula. The Taiwan Strait presents a far more complex situation, as no European country has defense agreements with Taiwan and few would challenge China's contention that it is an internal matter. Despite this, France, with its extensive agreements to transfer weapons and technologies to Taiwan, could not look the other way if a conflict erupted.

Much of this potential or actual involvement forms the fundamental reason why Britain and France seek to join the ASEAN Regional Forum (ARF), which seems to have usurped the security dialogue from both APEC and ASEM. Although ARF membership is sometimes regarded as divisive among

Europeans, it need not be. Many European policy processes are developing today on both "first tier" and "second tier" levels, with the view that other European nations may join later if given the opportunity. Just as a "monetary core" for Europe has been discussed, there could conceivably be talk about "security cores," possibly with Britain and France as the Asian core.

It is important, however, to view these concepts and potential actions as works in progress. With regard to Asian security, there does not exist in Europe the same type of public opinion linkage as in the United States that has endured ever since the start of the Cold War. The paucity of economic ties in the past and the often negative views about Asian societies have not been conducive to common security. Democratization in Asia, and the achievement of more balanced trade relations have started to improve public opinion. At the declaratory level at least, reaction to the Taiwan crisis of March 1996 is instructive.

The popular European belief that the United States provides 100 percent of Asia's security is basically correct, but also is politically complacent and even dangerous. Europeans must come to terms with the notion that better relations with Asia can only be forged through political and security involvement in the broader sense.[14] Although Europeans cannot and will not encourage a power balance in Asia, focusing instead on trends and institution building, they must bring their own mix of conflict resolution diplomacy— often used within Europe—and their willingness to volunteer forces for international peacekeeping. Beyond playing no role in the architecture of security treaties that America has developed throughout the region, Europe must also move beyond a traditional role as a complementary provider of weapons,[15] toward being a new participant in Asian security.

In this respect, the curved path that ASEM has been following ever since its inception is perhaps more indicative of its problems than of the solutions it seeks. The remarkable stress on political links, security, and stability at the Bangkok meeting in 1996 probably signified more of a personal commitment by European leaders to stop questioning the status of various Asian regimes than a well-considered plan for involvement in Asia. In this respect, the present fallback on economic, trade, and cultural issues, and the focus on arcane senior officials meetings and businessmen roundtables, represents a realistic first step toward stronger interregional ties. It seems likely, however, that as these ties expand, there will be a natural move to include explicit security and political aspects of the Europe-Asia relationship.

Notes

1. The European Union document "New Strategies for Asia" was approved by the European Council in Essen in December 1994.

2. The first Business Forum was held in Paris in 1996, the second in Thailand in 1997. Upcoming Business Forums are planned for Korea (1999) and Singapore (2001). Another format for improving economic relations is the ASEM Economic Minister's Forum, which was held for the first time on September 27–28, 1997, in Japan.

3. The ASEF is the first institution to be established under the ASEM process, which purpose is to "promote better mutual understanding between Asia and Europe through greater intellectual, cultural and people-to-people exchanges." For further information, see "The Asia-Europe Foundation Ministerial Declaration," February 15, 1997.

4. This point was stressed on the occasion of the Foreign Ministers' meeting held in Singapore on February 15, 1997.

5. Hungary, Poland, Czech Republic, Slovenia, Estonia, Cyprus. Negotiations started in 1998 under the British presidency.

6. On the continuing central role of the United States and the necessity to strengthen triangular relations, see Shin and Segal 1997.

7. European nations are the largest contributors to the UN's peacekeeping operations budget.

8. American bases in Okinawa are the bedrock of U.S. defense policy in Asia. The Guidelines adopted between the United States and Japan in September 1997 confirm the U.S. military commitment in the Asia-Pacific region.

9. The EU is now a member of the Executive Board of the KEDO, together with the United States, Japan and South Korea.

10. The peninsular train project conducted by Malaysia has been actively debated among Asian countries. The European side should participate in negotiations in the near future.

11. The first pledge to the KEDO is estimated at $90 million, and European food aid to North Korea amounts to $69 million, which is likely to be the most generous response to the appeal of the UN World Food Program.

12. The FPDA links Britain with former colonies in Singapore, Malaysia, Australia, and New Zealand.

13. The EU should deepen relations with the South Asian Association of Regional Cooperation (SAARC). See also Rüland 1996.

14. On security relations between Asia and Europe, see Regaud and Stares 1997.

15. European arms transfers to the Asia-Pacific have sustained a market share of more than 20 percent since 1992.

Bibliography

Bank of International Settlements. *The Maturity, Sectoral and Nationality Distribution of International Bank Lending.* Basel, Switzerland, July 1997.

Bodde, William. "Europe, the U.S. and the Coming Asia-Pacific Century." *Trends,* May 31–June 1, 1997.

Brezinski, Zbigniew. "Summit of Impotence in Bangkok." *Washington Times,* February 25, 1996.

Godement, François. "Don't Crowd the Asia-Europe Summit." *Trends,* February 24–25, 1996.

Goh Chok Ton. "The Road to Greater Understanding." In *Cultural Rapprochement Between Asia and Europe.* Leyden and Amsterdam: Lecture Series no. 7, IIAS, 1997.

Hatch, Walter, and Yamamura, Kuzo. *Asia in Japan's Embrace: Building a Regional Production Alliance.* Cambridge: Cambridge University Press, 1996.

Hiebert, Murray. "Small Talk." *The Far Eastern Economic Review*, February 27, 1997, p. 22.

Islam, Shada. "Strategic Largesse." *The Far Eastern Economic Review*, June 5, 1997, p. 21.

Regaud, Nicolas, and Stares, Paul. "An Initial Assessment." In *France and Japan in a Changing Security Environment* (Vol. 1). Paris: Les Cahiers de l'Ifri no. 21, 1997.

Rüland, Jürgen. "The Asia-Europe Meeting: Towards a New Euro-Asian Relationship?" Universität Rostock: Rostocker Informationen zu Politik und Verwaltung, Heft 5, 1996.

Segal, Gerald. "Thinking Strategically About ASEM: The Subsidiarity Question." In *Europe-Asia: Strengthening the Informal Dialogue.* Paris: Les Cahiers de l'Ifri, no. 19, 1977.

Shin, Dong-Ik, and Segal, Gerald. "Getting Serious About Asia-Europe Security Cooperation." *Survival* 39, no. 1 (Spring 1997): 138–55.

Stokes, Bruce. "Integrating China into the Global Trading System: An Opportunity for US-EU Cooperation." New York: Council on Foreign Relations, May 28, 1997.

Part III

Flash Points and CBMs

14

China-ROK Relations and the Future of Asian Security

A Developing Continental Power Balance?

Kang Choi and Taeho Kim

More than a decade into the post-Cold War era, Asia is still in search of a new regional strategic structure that can cope with the emerging challenges to its stability and prosperity. While the new regional strategic structure is in the making, it will be shaped primarily by two critical factors: (1) sustainability and level of U.S. engagement in the Asia-Pacific region, and (2) the rise of the People's Republic of China (PRC).

Probably the most far-reaching development for Asia's new strategic environment has been the drawdown of 30,000 American troops from the Asia-Pacific region between 1990 and 1992. Although the United States decided in 1995 to freeze the level of American forces in the region at 100,000 personnel, and reiterated its intention to maintain that level in the Quadrennial Defense Review in May 1997, regional perceptions of U.S. security commitment and credibility will significantly affect the strategic calculus of individual regional states as well as the overall regional power balance. At the same time, there is a widespread perception that the stability and prosperity of Asia increasingly will hinge upon the future capability and behavior of China, potentially the most influential nation in the region. Beginning in the late 1980s, China's growing military and economic capability have been the focal point of Asian and global debate, especially the strategic implications of China's rise and how the international community can cope with its consequences.[1]

To be sure, China has long been central to East Asian and global security, but its importance has taken on a new relevance in the post-Cold War era in light of the shifting balance of power in East Asia and China's ever-growing regional and international profile. In particular, given China's power potential, continuing influence on North Korea, and growing bilateral ties with South Korea, China will doubtless continue to play a major role in Korean affairs.

To assess the strategic implications of China's rise for the Korean peninsula and for the Asia-Pacific region, this chapter takes stock of the China factor in the strategic calculus of the Republic of Korea (ROK), as well as the evolving bilateral ties between the ROK and China in the 1990s in light of the ROK's security interests. First, this chapter looks into the continuing security challenges from North Korea and explores the future role of the United States and China in Korean unification, a major event that is likely to reorder the regional power balance and affect the relationships among the major regional powers. Then, it specifically addresses various policy measures the ROK and the United States can take, individually or jointly, to cope with the challenges of an ascendant China for peninsular and regional security.

China's Post-Cold War Security and the Korean Peninsula

Only since the end of the Cold War have Chinese leaders adopted truly region-specific policies. A confluence of several developments inside and outside China has contributed to the birth of its new Asian identity. First, the demise of the Soviet Union and the ensuing end of superpower rivalry have meant that China is no longer vulnerable to a direct attack by a superior force or to a superpower condominium. The end of the strategic triangle and China's "swing value" has allowed Chinese leaders and strategists to conceive of its security in more regional terms.

Second, China's decision to adopt a new Asian stature is evident in the context of its post-Tiananmen offensive against the West. The post-Tiananmen Western economic and military embargoes against China not only delayed the pace of the Four Modernizations drive, but also, in the eyes of many Chinese leaders, heightened the danger of a Western "peaceful evolution" against Communist rule in China. To handle a Western pressure after Tiananmen effectively, China gradually but unmistakably has expanded its economic and diplomatic relations with the Asian countries, including the normalization of relations with Indonesia, Singapore and South Korea.

Third, not only has China's reform drive since the late 1970s required it to cultivate amicable relations with its Asian neighbors, but the dynamic Asian economy has gained importance to China's domestic agenda of economic development and prosperity. The centrality of Asia to China further has been underscored by the growing economic importance of China's coastal cities, which serve not only as an engine of growth for the entire country but also as a critical conduit for foreign capital, advanced technology and managerial know-how.

Aside from the Taiwan and the South China Sea issues, which China believes involve its territorial sovereignty and national unity, Chinese strategists point to the Korean peninsula as a potential flash point that could draw China into an unwanted conflict. Not only is the Korean peninsula one of the world's most militarized areas, but its future has been clouded by North Korea's nuclear gambit, the sudden death of Kim Il Sung, and the ensuing political, economic and social uncertainties in North Korea.

While China and North Korea no longer maintain the traditional "lips to teeth" relationship, Chinese leaders do have significant security concerns over the sudden collapse of the North Korean regime, which would involve large numbers of refugees, armed conflicts, and production disruptions in China's heavily industrialized Northeast region. After all, North Korea is the neighbor located closest to China's capital, Beijing, and China still sees North Korea as its strategic *cordon sanitaire*. On the economic and diplomatic fronts, their relations are constrained by different national interests, North Korea's economic plight, and North Korea's self-imposed diplomatic isolation after the death of Kim Il Sung.

China still seems to exert continuing economic and diplomatic, if not military, leverage vis-à-vis North Korea.[2] Owing partly to its economic and diplomatic needs, North Korea more often than not adhered closely to Chinese advice. Notwithstanding their continued (though diminished) mutual visits and verbal diplomatic support, however, PRC-North Korean relations have clear limitations, primarily because of their divergent policy priorities and national interests. An increasing gap between official rhetoric and objective reality has been apparent to both sides, as exemplified in such prominent cases as the entry of both North and South Korea into the UN, the Sino-South Korean normalization, and China's open disagreement with North Korea's repeated attempts to replace the current Armistice Agreement with a peace treaty with the United States.

At the same time, further isolation of North Korea from the outside world would be detrimental to China's interests in continued stability on the Korean peninsula. Thus, China has vigorously pursued a geoeconomic strategy toward Seoul, while maintaining a geostrategic policy toward Pyongyang (North Korea's capital), which Chinese leaders believe to be in China's best interests, at least for the time being.

The Continuing North Korean Challenges to
South Korean Security

Peaceful unification of the Korean peninsula remains an avowed national objective of the ROK. To make it come true, the ROK has pursued a set of consistent security goals. The first and foremost security goal is deterrence of the North Korean armed aggression against the South. Ever since the end of the Korean War in 1953, the ROK has faced a clear and present military threat from North Korea, which never has relinquished its intention and strategy to communize the entire Korean peninsula by force. Since 1962, at a time when the so-called *Four-Point Military Guidelines* were adopted,[3] North Korea has continuously beefed up its military capabilities to such an extent that it is now virtually self-sufficient in arms production and has stockpiles of war matériel that could last for six months.[4] At present, North Korea has deployed 10 army corps including approximately 60 divisions and brigades in the forward area south of the Pyongyang-Wonsan line to launch a surprise attack without additional war preparation. These troops are well equipped, and most of them are mechanized for fast-moving military operations along the 155-mile DMZ (Demilitarized Zone), which lies 30 miles north of Seoul, capital of the ROK and a home for 12 million people.[5]

In addition to its conventional military threat, North Korea's stockpile of weapons of mass destruction (WMDs) has increased in recent years. Although the October 1994 Agreed Framework has frozen its nuclear program for the moment, it has not yet clarified North Korea's past nuclear activities amid the continuing concern that North Korea has already extracted some amount of plutonium sufficient to manufacture one or two nuclear weapons. North Korea also has eight facilities capable of producing various chemical agents, and the amount of chemical agents possessed by North Korea is estimated to be in the range of 2,500 to 5,000 tons.[6] North Korea's missile capability is also on the rise. Ever since North Korea imported Scud missiles from Egypt in the early 1980s, it had begun to produce its own variants. North Korea is now believed to have the capacity to produce 80 to 120 Scud-B and Scud-C missiles annually. Furthermore, North Korea has developed the Rodong-1 missile, whose maximum range is about 1,000 km to 1,300 km. And North Korea is developing the next generation of missile systems named Taepodong-1 and -2. All these missiles can carry chemical or nuclear warheads.[7] It is also rumored that Pyongyang has a plan to use shorter-range missiles such as Scud-B and Scud-C along with long-range large-caliber artillery pieces against Seoul in the very beginning of a war so as to turn the South Korean capital into ashes. And longer range missiles are very likely to be used to prevent the involvement of external powers such as the United

Table 14.1

Military Balance Between South Korea and North Korea

Classification		South Korea	North Korea
Troops	Army	560,000	996,000
	Navy	66,000	48,000
	Air Force	63,000	103,000
	Total	690,000	1,147,000
Army	Corps	11	20
	Divisions	50	54
	Brigades	21	99
	Tanks	2,150	3,800
	Armored vehicles	2,250	2,270
	Field artillery	4,800	11,200
Navy	Combatants	180	430
	Support vessels	40	340
	Submarines	5	40
Air Force	Tactical aircraft	550	850
	Support aircraft	180	510
	Helicopters	630	310
Reserve forces		3,080,000	6,550,000

Source: The ROK Ministry of National Defense, *Defense White Paper 1997–1998* (Seoul: MND, 1997).

States and Japan in case of another Korean contingency; that is, North Korea might threaten to use its longer-range missiles against Japan to weaken the allies' determination to wage war.[8]

Judging from North Korea's huge military capabilities as well as its force deployment and configuration (Table 14.1), it seems possible that North Korea has the capacity to materialize its goal of communizing the entire Korean peninsula by force, if there is no outside involvement. More alarming and dangerous than its current military capability is the North Korean leadership's belief that it can unify the South by force, if two conditions are met: no outside involvement and domestic turmoil in the South. And the North Korean people are believed to have subscribed to the thesis of the inevitability of war between the South and the North, and they allegedly believe that war may be a better choice than dying by famine.[9]

The possibility that North Korea could mount a full-scale aggression toward the South—out of its overkill capability or desperation—cannot be ruled out. To dissuade North Korea from embarking on any future military adventure, the ROK is thus required to maintain a highly reliable and credible deterrent posture by securing its own military capabilities and maintaining a robust ROK-U.S. security alliance.

Additionally, there always exists a chance for North Korea's misjudgment of the situation and, for that matter, for South Korean determination and deterrence failure. Early warning time is very short—perhaps less than 24 hours. Even worse, given the North Korean mode of force deployment, war or attack without warning is possible. While the ROK and the United States have introduced "flexible deterrence options" (FDOs) and "force enhancement" (FE) to strengthen their combined defense/deterrence posture, it seems that FDOs and FE may not provide military assets strong enough to dissuade North Korea from aggression. In fact, not all military assets, especially the ground forces, required for the defense of the South would be available in time and be in place. If a contingency occurred in another part of the world, such as the Middle East, the available military assets would be further drawn down.

In such a situation, deterrence might fail and North Korea would invade the South. If so, the next security objective of the ROK must be to defend its homeland by blocking the progress of the North Korean force as much as possible near the Demilitarized Zone (DMZ), to repel and destroy the North Korean armed forces, and to recover the territory north of the DMZ by all means available to realize the goal of unification. In other words, should North Korea invade the South, the security objective of the ROK would not be the restoration of the previous status quo or another armistice agreement, but the elimination of the source of the threat and the achievement of Korean unification—nothing less.

There exist two obstacles in pursuing this objective: the destruction caused by war and the fear of the expansion of war. These two factors could press the ROK and its allies to terminate hostilities through negotiation and to return to the status quo ante. But compared to the expected cost and burden of the continued presence of threat after the restoration of the status quo through negotiation, those dangers might be relatively acceptable. The ROK might not be able to afford to live with its enemy, who invaded not once but twice, and it might not allow the continuing division of the peninsula any more. Although it may not be the most desirable way to realize unification, it could be the ROK's inevitable choice to secure the condition of everlasting peace and stability on the peninsula as well as in Northeast Asia.

There could also be external pressure for the termination of the war by negotiation, either if the conflict bogged down and casualties sharply increased, or if the possibility of expansion of war increased as the Combined Forces Command/United Nations Command (CFC/UNC) forces crossed the DMZ and advanced northward. It is uncertain whether China would get involved in a second Korean War as it did in 1950. The form, scope, and level of China's involvement would be determined by a combination of factors, including the combat situation, China's relations with both Koreas and the United States, and its strategic calculation of the expected outcome of the unfolding situation. One thing is for sure: China could well take advantage of the situation for its own interests and try to utilize this opportunity to maximize its influence over the Korean peninsula, even if China's move could have tremendous ramifications for the ROK and the United States. To prevent China's possible involvement and to materialize the ROK's security objective, the ROK and the United States must engage China in peacetime as well as throughout the entire process of a North Korean contingency action.

In recent years, a totally new kind of North Korean threat has emerged: the possibility of the North's sudden collapse or implosion. The ROK's security objective with regard to this threat is its prevention, or the minimization and isolation of the collateral consequences of the collapse or implosion inside North Korea. The ROK's objective, should this occur, is not to take advantage of the situation to realize its goal of unification. In a word, stabilization of the North Korean situation through close cooperation and coordination with the concerned states including China is the immediate security objective should the North collapse.

For the past seven years, the North Korean economy has consecutively recorded negative growth rates, an average of −4.5 percent annually. It is clear by now that North Korea cannot revive its economy by itself. It requires, among others, economic reform and a massive influx of foreign assistance. Fearing the political ramifications of a systemic economic reform, the current North Korean leadership is highly reluctant to launch a systemwide economic rebirth. However, without such reform, the North will not be able to attract foreign investors and assistance which it urgently needs to revive its faltering economy.[10] (See Table 14.2.)

Most North Korea specialists believe that food shortage is severe and pervasive, especially in rural areas, and that it is one of the most important and influential factors that could bring down the current North Korean regime. Since 1992, while the demand for food in North Korea has increased approximately 1.4 percent each year, the rate of food sufficiency has dropped to less than 70 percent. To worsen matters, consecutive floods in 1995 and 1996 and severe drought in 1997 have seriously damaged the harvest, and its nationwide food rationing system is in limbo in most areas.[11]

In recent years, a significant increase has occurred in the number and social status of North Korean defectors and escapees, as most vividly exemplified by the defection of the Korean Workers' Party (KWP) International Secretary Hwang Jangyop. It is also believed that the number of dislocated North Korean people is on the rise. This may be a prelude to widespread discontent and possible disorder within North Korean society. In

Table 14.2

Comparison of Economic Growth Rates Between South Korea and North Korea

Year	South Korea	North Korea
1985	6.6	2.7
1990	9.6	-3.7
1991	9.1	-6.2
1992	5.0	-7.6
1993	5.8	-4.3
1994	8.4	-1.7
1995	8.7	-4.5
1996	7.1	-3.7

Source: Bank of Korea (BOK) data.

North Korean society, people are grouped into three classes, according to the ruling regime's view of their political reliability: the core class (5.98 million, 28 percent); the sympathetic or ambivalent class (9.62 million, 45 percent); and the hostile class (5.77 million, 27 percent). Those who belong to the hostile class are destined to suffer and remain most disadvantaged in almost every dimension of their social life.[12] When the chips are down, they probably constitute the first segment that might fight against the current North Korean leadership and initiate the endgame of the North Korean regime. To cope with such problems, the Kim Jong Il regime has recently tightened the power of central government and police organs. The regime also has strengthened ideological education. It remains to be seen, however, how much longer the current leadership can hold North Korean society together without satisfying basic demands for daily needs and physical survival.

Currently and in the shorter term, the core power group of North Korea primarily comprises the first generation of revolutionaries and the Korean War veterans—"the Reds." And both the influence and the status of the Korean People's Army (KPA) have been strengthened since the death of Kim Il Sung; the current Kim Jong Il regime depends heavily on the military for its continued rule.[13] At the same time, however, the surge of technocrats and internationalists among its power elite also should be noted. More than 50 percent of Politburo members are technocrats and most secretariats of the KWP have technocratic backgrounds. Their power base and influence are still relatively weaker than those of the "Reds." But with limited reform and increasing contact with the outside world, the influence of these technocrats is likely to increase over policy formulation, decision making, and implementation. Consequently, there might arise debates and possibly struggle for policy and power within the power elite groups.

These factors could become a deadly binary that might cause the collapse or implosion of North Korea. If a precarious situation begins to unfold, the following developments could occur: a massive influx of North Korean refugees into the South, armed clashes between the North and the South along the DMZ, loss of control of weapons of mass destruction (WMDs), and neighboring countries' involvement. Under such circumstances, the ROK's immediate security objective, as discussed earlier, is to minimize and isolate the collateral consequences of the incident and to stabilize the North Korean situation by any and all means, not to "march north to realize its ultimate goal of unification."

The final security objective of the ROK is to stabilize the military situation, to reduce tensions, and to establish a peace framework to manage the transitional period peacefully and effectively. According to the Armistice Agreement, both sides have agreed to respect and honor the terms of the agreement as a framework for peace and stability until it is replaced by "an appropriate agreement for a peaceful settlement at a political level between both sides."[14]

Moreover, in the Basic Agreement and the Protocol on North-South Reconciliation, both Koreas agreed to abide by the Armistice Agreement until "a solid state of peace has been established between the North and the South."[15] Recently, however, North Korea has attempted to scrap the Armistice Agreement and has intentionally created numerous military tensions over the Korean peninsula. On April 4, 1996, for example, North Korea announced that it would no longer uphold its duties concerning the maintenance and control of the DMZ, to which it committed itself under the Armistice Agreement. North Korea also said its army would take self-defensive measures within the DMZ, which means that the status of the DMZ no longer could be maintained.[16] After the announcement, North Korea intentionally violated the provisions of the Armistice Agreement for a week, thus heightening tension on the Korean peninsula. Another example is the well-known submarine incursion of September 1996, when a group of North Korean commandos was infiltrated ashore in the South, followed by a series of violations of the DMZ in 1997. These provocations are in clear violation of the Armistice Agreement and the spirit of the Basic Agreement.

Despite such a stark military reality on the Korean peninsula, no crisis management mechanism exists today. The Military Armistice Commission (MAC), the North-South Joint Military Commission,[17] and the North-South Military Subcommittee within the framework of the North-South High-Level Talks have all ceased to function. Thus, an armed clash might escalate easily and heighten tensions owing to the absence of a crisis prevention and management mechanism. Or, in the worst case, such an incident could be used as a pretext for further North Korean military adventurism.

In response to North Korea's attempt to abolish the Armistice Agreement, the United States and South Korea, at the Cheju Summit Meeting of April 16, 1996, proposed the "Four-Party Talks" or a "two-plus-two formula," in which the two Koreas remain the key participants while the United States and China play supporting roles. The objectives of the Four-Party Talks are (1) to reduce tensions; (2) to build confidence between the two Koreas; and (3) to produce a peace mechanism.[18]

In sum, the security objectives of the ROK are (1) to deter North Korean armed aggression; (2) to defend the South and to recover the northern part of the Korean peninsula should deterrence fail; (3) to minimize and isolate the side effects of the collapse or implosion of North Korea and to restore order and stability in North Korea; and (4) to stabilize the military situation and to reduce tensions on the Korean peninsula by introducing an alternative peace mechanism and realizing arms control. To materialize these objectives, the ROK must mobilize and secure the support of related parties to the fullest extent possible. And each related party's importance and role, either positive or negative, must be assessed against these national security objectives. China, one of the signatories of the Armistice Agreement, must be regarded and included as one of the most important outside players in Korean affairs, especially from the military-security perspective. With the normalization of diplomatic relations between the ROK and China in 1992, the importance and influence of China in Korean affairs has been redefined and revisited.

The China Factor in South Korea's Strategic Calculus

For most of the Cold War, relations between China and South Korea were locked in mutual hostility and suspicion. The Chinese intervention in the Korean War, the bipolar configuration of the world's power structure, and China's continuing rivalry with the Soviet Union for influence in North Korea made Chinese-ROK relations a negligible factor for three full decades after the cessation of hostilities on the peninsula. As China recognized North Korea as the only Korean state on the peninsula, there were no contacts between Seoul and Beijing until the late 1970s.

Relations between China and South Korea began to develop in the economic and trade spheres. After China launched its reform and open-door policy in 1978, unofficial and indirect trade between China and South Korea began, albeit slowly. From each side's viewpoint, the other seemed an attractive trading partner. To China, South Korea appeared to be a model of rapid economic development and industrialization. From South Korea's standpoint, China with its 1.2 billion people was doubtless a huge potential market. By 1988, indirect trade between the two countries exceeded $3 billion. With the expansion of the trade relationship, both countries found other benefits and potentials in their bilateral ties. China regarded South Korea as a stepping stone to expand its diplomatic influence in the region in the aftermath of China's post-Tiananmen diplomatic isolation and to counterbalance America's ever-increasing dominance in the Asia-Pacific region.

To the ROK government, normalizing relations with China was a diplomatic tour de force. First and foremost, the Sino-South Korean normalization helped culminate its "Northern Diplomacy" and symbolized South Korea's victory in its decade-long diplomatic competition with North Korea. Furthermore, the ROK hoped to bring China's influence on North Korea to bear in facilitating a North-South Korean dialogue, opening up North Korean society, and restraining North Korea's provocative actions. Less immediate but still important considerations were the economic and political benefits that flowed from strengthened relations with China.

After the normalization in August 1992, however, it soon became clear to ROK policymakers and strategists that the two specific sets of goals of its China policy—one for facilitating inter-Korean relations and the other for improving bilateral ties with China per se—remained largely independent of one another. Moreover, most Korean observers concluded that there had been no appreciable progress in its political or security relations with North Korea or with China. Given these circumstances, the ROK's strategic environment reflects continued concerns about the security challenges posed by North Korea, but in the context of increased uncertainties regarding future American and Chinese roles in the region.

Notwithstanding the extraordinary changes in the wake of the Cold War and the brief thaw on the peninsula, including the North-South High-Level Talks, the crux of the South Korean security challenge—namely a land-based military threat from North Korea—remains remarkably unchanged. Indeed, the future of the peninsula has been clouded further by North Korea's continuing military threat and the increasing uncertainty of the current North Korean leadership. The key element of continued stability and peace on the Korean peninsula is the robust ROK-U.S. security alliance and its reliable combined defense posture. To make the situation in the Korean peninsula more stable and conducive to peaceful unification, it is necessary and desirable for the ROK to secure cooperation and assistance from all concerned states. Among these, China stands out prominently, next to the United States.

From the ROK's perspective, Chinese cooperation and constructive engagement in Korean affairs are among the essential elements in materializing the aforementioned security objectives; China, the only major source of external help for North Korea as well as the latter's external strategic center of gravity, can play either a negative or a positive role. To deter North

Korea's possible armed aggression toward the South, it is necessary, if not sufficient, to mobilize and secure Chinese pressure on North Korea because, in addition to the ROK's deterrent capabilities, Chinese political/diplomatic pressure on the North could discourage it from launching further military adventures.

In case deterrence fails, the defense of South Korea and an effective execution of military operations and their objectives require both the ROK and the United States to prevent China's future direct or indirect involvement. China, which always has sought a buffer state in its periphery, will not simply sit and watch the disappearance of such a valuable buffer as North Korea. The first Chinese response to a second Korean War might be the call for an immediate cessation of hostilities and the resolution of the situation through negotiation. China also might oppose the execution of all the previous UN resolutions since 1950 concerning the Korean peninsula. As a consequence, timely formation and response of allied forces might be hindered, while Seoul would suffer severely from the North Korean attack. At the same time, however, the possibility of Chinese military involvement might increase as the CFC/UNC forces successfully defended the South and marched north. China retains its treaty of friendship and cooperation with North Korea, which has a provision for China's automatic engagement in case of an external attack against North Korea. China can utilize this provision as a pretext for its military engagement. Or North Korea might invite China to get involved militarily as it did in 1950.

Such a Chinese move, the fear of Chinese military involvement, and the consequent outbreak of war might cause the allied force to settle the situation short of the accomplishment of the ultimate goal—destruction of the North Korean armed forces and full recovery of the northern part of the Korean peninsula, which means the continued division of the peninsula. For a full recovery of the northern part of the Korean peninsula and to minimize the damage of war, the ROK and its allies must try to prevent Chinese military involvement or threat of engagement under any circumstances by all means, even before the actual occurrence of a second Korean War.

If the North Korean regime were to collapse, Chinese involvement could take many forms. First, China, which shares a 1,300 km border with North Korea, would be greatly affected by the massive influx of North Korean refugees. The number of people living in the areas near the border totals about 6.5 million and represents more than one-quarter of the total North Korean population (Table 14.3). China and North Korea are separated by two rivers: the Abrok (or Yalu) and the Tuman (Tumen). Their width varies from 10 to 900 meters. Four bridges span the Abrok River and eight span the Tuman River. Unlike the DMZ, there is no minefield or barbed wire, and

Table 14.3

Demographics of North Korea

Area	Province or City	Population (in millions)
Northern Area	Pyong'ahnbuk-do	2.496
	Ja'kang-do	1.218
	Yangkang-do	0.673
	Hamkyungbuk-do	2.084
Middle Area	Pyong'ahnnam-do	2.853
	Hamkyungnam-do	2.023
	Nampo	0.801
	Pyongyang	3.334
Southern Area	Hwanghaenam-do	2.052
	Hwanghaebuk-do	1.612
	Kangwon-do	1.571
	Gaesung	0.384
Total		

Source: Kim Dong-Sup, "Talbuk Nanmin Daeryang Tan" [If a massive North Korean exodus takes place], Jukan Chosun [Weekly Chosun] November 13, 1997, p. 43.

border control is relatively loose. People in this area probably would be able to cross the border with few difficulties.

In the event of this contingency, the influx of massive numbers of North Korean refugees would create various problems for China. China might set up refugee camps along the border to receive the influx.[19] Or the Chinese leadership might consider the option of closing the border to stem the incoming human tide. In the worst case, China might decide to cross the border in the name of humanitarian relief and remain there until social order is restored. This implies further that China might be in a position to establish an alternative buffer state in the North and to prolong the division of the Korean peninsula by removing South Korea's initiative in dealing with the North Korean implosion or social collapse. The ROK must prevent this. Thus, Chinese involvement must be confined and directed to complement South Korea's leading role; hence, close coordination is necessary among all concerned parties in dealing with the North Korean issue.

To bring North Korea out of international isolation, to urge it to initiate reform and an open-door policy, and to materialize the Four-Party Talks, Chinese cooperation and assistance are also necessary. In the Four-Party Talks framework, North and South Korea are the key participants, while the United

States and China play a supporting role.[20] There were three rounds of preliminary negotiations among the four parties.[21] At the third round of negotiations, all parties agreed to have a four-nation peace conference, which convened December 9, 1997, in Geneva. The Geneva conference was followed by two further rounds of talks in 1998, but with few major breakthroughs. At the third round, it was agreed to set up committees to discuss confidence building measures and the establishment of a peace regime on the Korean peninsula. This is the beginning of a long road, and quite a few obstacles lie ahead. While South Korea is supposed to play a leading role in producing a regime of peace, it needs all the support possible from the other two participants—the United States and China—to secure and strengthen its position vis-à-vis North Korea.

From South Korea's perspective, the success of the Four-Party Talks depends on two critical factors: how much and how far the United States and South Korea can maintain and coordinate their respective common position; and how much closer they can bring China to their common circle; U.S. support can be taken as a given, whereas that of China can change. Actually, it is possible to say that the Four-Party Talks is "a two-plus-one-plus-one formula" (the United States and the ROK plus North Korea plus South Korea), not necessarily "a two-plus-two formula" (North and South Korea plus the United States and China). In other words, China occupies a "swing position" in the Four-Party Talks. Thus, to minimize any negative influence from China, to encourage China to be a constructive participant, and to strengthen China's position vis-à-vis North Korea, the ROK and the United States should approach China with a common stance.

In sum, the China factor has found a new niche in the South Korean strategic calculus ever since the end of the Cold War. In a sense, China has replaced the former Soviet Union and gained substantive significance and influence, following only the United States. While it is certainly not desirable to overestimate the significance and influence of China in dealing with the Korean issue, underestimating it would be equally detrimental.

The United States, China, and the Korean Peninsula

Korea's twentieth-century history has long been likened to a shrimp among whales, whose geostrategic and economic interests converge on the Korean peninsula. It is thus reasonable to assume that when the chips are down, large states in the region will attempt to direct the course of Korean unification such that the outcomes are congruent with, or at least not inimical to, their respective national interests.

By dint of its global reach and security alliance with the ROK, including the presence of the U.S. forces in Korea (USFK) and an integrated command structure, the United States continues to be the most important outside actor on the Korean peninsula. The United States is also involved in a wide range of issues that touch upon the unification question, including nuclear weapons, missile proliferation, a peace treaty and regional security. Recently, the significance of the U.S. factor in Korean unification has been enhanced further by a historical irony—North Korea's desire to establish direct bilateral economic and diplomatic ties with the United States to overcome its economic limitations and possibly to ensure its long-term survival.

American support for South Korea's unification plans—which envision a unified state featuring democracy, a market economy, and human dignity—remains firm and has been reconfirmed during a series of summit meetings. Additionally, South Korea has officially supported a continued U.S. military presence on the Korean peninsula, whether divided or unified.[22] The United States has confirmed its own postunification military interests in a February 1995 Department of Defense report entitled *United States Security Strategy for the East Asia-Pacific Region.* "Even after the North Korean threat passes, the United States intends to maintain a strong defense alliance with the Republic of Korea, in the interest of regional security."[23] There has been some discord between the United States and South Korea in dealing with the North Korean nuclear issue and the so-called soft-landing of North Korea, whereby it does not collapse abruptly. This, however, does not necessarily signify the weakening of the U.S.-ROK security alliance. Rather, it indicates that the U.S.-ROK alliance remains strong and mature enough to weather such differences. It seems safe to assert that Washington and Seoul will remain united in dealing with not only the Korean issues including unification but also other regional security issues in the foreseeable future.

At the same time, however, China shares a 1,300 km border with North Korea. As noted earlier, not only does China maintain a geostrategic interest in North Korea but it is acutely aware of the potential dangers of a renewed conflict on the peninsula. For the sake of external stability and China's economic modernization, Chinese leaders have consistently called for a reduction of tensions on the peninsula. It has not failed, however, to turn an external crisis into an opportunity to advance its own national interests. The North Korean nuclear issue provides an illustration.

Throughout the course of the various crises and tensions surrounding North Korea's presumed nuclear weapons development program, China has benefited from the subtle use of its images and roles—as perceived by Washington, Seoul, and Tokyo. The shared perception among the three capitals has been that China's high stakes in peninsular stability as well as its security and economic ties with North Korea leave it uniquely positioned to persuade

Pyongyang to forgo the nuclear option. In a lichee nutshell, China has adopted a complex web of policy measures to turn the situation into an opportunity to enhance its status and prestige in the emerging new international and regional order and to strengthen its bargaining position vis-à-vis that of the United States, South Korea and Japan, while allowing North Korea to continue in its diplomatic negotiations with the United States. Additionally, China has argued consistently for a dialogue among related parties, rather than overt pressure on North Korea, to find solutions to the North Korean issues including the nuclear question.

In the years to come, China's strategy toward the Korean peninsula shall be driven by two fundamental objectives: maintaining a stable and friendly buffer state and reducing or balancing America's dominant position in Korean as well as regional security affairs. Toward both ends, the Beijing leadership has pursued a "two-Korea" policy. China hopes to balance both its geostrategic interest in North Korea and its geoeconomic and geopolitical interests with South Korea, whose $20 billion trade with China in 1996 dwarfs the $570 million trade between North Korea and China. If U.S.-North Korean contacts should become more frequent and closer, China may try to promote its friendly relations with South Korea to enhance its position to influence both Koreas and to counterbalance the continuing American influence in Korean affairs. The forthcoming Four-Party Talks would become a test of such Chinese intent and strategy. The United States and South Korea must be ready to minimize China's negative involvement by maintaining closer cooperation and coordination not only with North Korea but also with China.

ROK and U.S. Policy Options Regarding China

Regional perceptions of and reactions to China's diplomatic and military behavior have not been uniform. Each regional actor's relations with China are shaped by a wide array of factors, including geographical proximity, historical and cultural inheritance, territorial disputes, and economic relations. Moreover, the strategic calculi of various Asian states often has been influenced significantly by their respective security relations with the United States. The interplay of these factors informs each Asian state's threat assessment of China's military capability and intention.

In the case of South Korea, there is no doubt that combined ROK-U.S. deterrence against possible North Korean military adventurism remains the primary goal for the foreseeable future. As long as the North Korean military threat persists, any ROK and U.S. efforts to engage China should complement the goal of deterrence. Additionally, the ROK and the United States should seek to bring China's influence on North Korea to bear in achieving the three countries' common interests on the peninsula—namely continued peninsular stability, improved North Korean-South Korean relations, and North Korea's economic reform. Mutual understanding among the three countries could not only offer a potential solution and productive result of the Four-Party Talks but also ultimately create favorable conditions for peaceful unification of Korea.

For its part, South Korea needs to chart out a long-term, comprehensive strategy toward China that envisions postunification relations between Korea and China. Economic cooperation, augmented by increased diplomatic and cultural contacts, is essential for the expansion of bilateral ties. Military-to-military relationships need to be set up as well. Given the current and expected influence of the military in China's domestic and external policies, it seems only prudent for the ROK to foster personal ties and eventually institutional relations with the Chinese military. A longer-term relationship rather than policy expediency must be a guiding principle in Sino-South Korean relations.

Regarding unification, South Korea needs to set forth a realistic and feasible unification plan clearly and make credible that Korean unification is beneficial to all of Korea's large neighbors, including China. In addition, South Korea needs to formulate in due time a panoply of confidence- and security-building measures (CSBMs) specifically designed to address China's potential concerns. These include a unified Korea's intention to promote friendly relations with China; the creation of a buffer zone in and joint development of Chinese-Korean border areas; and the establishment of a three-way security dialogue among China, the United States, and a unified Korea.

From the vantage point of the mid-1990s, one useful way to assess future East Asian stability is to inquire into the health of Sino-U.S. relations. Ideally, an improved relationship between the United States and China, especially renewed security cooperation, would contribute to regional stability and to the attainment of U.S. objectives in East Asia. In reality, however, the prospects for a cooperative Chinese-U.S. relationship remain unsettled for the immediate future, even after Chinese President Jiang Zemin's visit to the United States in October 1997.[24] Few of their outstanding issues, including the Taiwan issue and human rights, show signs of early or conclusive resolution. And there seem to exist fundamental differences between the two countries in terms of political systems, social values, strategic objectives, and conditions for regional peace and stability. Although a future contingency pitting the United States and Chinese militaries against each other remains remote, each side already may regard the other as a long-term security risk to its national interests. At the least, China's defense modernizations are geared toward safeguarding regional interests from the extensive reach of the remaining superpower.

Furthermore, China has criticized the U.S.-Japanese security alliance for its suspected intention to strengthen and prolong the regional security structure centered on the alliance. China, and for that matter South Korea as well, is quite critical toward the expansion of Japan's regional security role, which is clearly stated in the revision to the U.S.-Japan Defense Cooperation Guidelines of September 1997. China is particularly sensitive to the new guidelines' call for "appropriate measures to be taken in response to [situations in areas surrounding Japan] and for the two countries to support each other as necessary in accordance with appropriate arrangements."[25] Two areas under consideration are the Taiwan Strait and the Korean peninsula. Japan's role in both cases could trigger a very strong reaction from China.

From the South Korean perspective, with respect to a contingency on the Korean peninsula, it is desirable and necessary to secure Japan's rear area support for U.S. forces, but there exists a danger that China might use such action by Japan to justify its direct military involvement. Given that Japan sent minesweepers to Korea during the Korean War upon the request of the United States,[26] China fears it could occur again. From the ROK's viewpoint, this fear must be averted, especially if it leads to Chinese military involvement in Korean affairs.[27] Both close consultation and cooperation not only between South Korea and the United States, but also between South Korea and Japan are necessary. Chinese suspicion and misunderstanding of the intent of the United States and Japan as well as South Korea must be minimized through a common approach by the three countries toward China.

Viewed in this light, future directions for America's China policy seem clear. First, the United States should pursue the strategy of "comprehensive engagement," especially in areas of mutual benefits. Second, America's China policy must be firmly linked to its overall Asia policy, carefully weighing the costs and benefits of the former to the latter. Third, the U.S. military establishment needs to promote regular and frequent contacts with China's People's Liberation Army, including high-level visits, functional exchanges, and defense technological cooperation.[28] Fourth, in addition to its bilateral security alliances, the United States must utilize multilateral security dialogue and cooperation to reassure China.

Conclusion

Peace and stability on the Korean peninsula as well as in Northeast Asia will be shaped increasingly by the degree to which the Northeast Asian states can cooperate over North Korean issues. The U.S.-ROK security alliance is *the* backbone of the ROK's security objectives. The importance and significance of the China factor—North Korea's external strategic center of gravity—

cannot, however, be underestimated. Although China, like other nations, has limited influence over North Korea, it is important to remember that China can exert either a positive or negative impact upon the course of events depending upon its strategic calculation. Currently, China is believed to have more potential for negative influence. If China plays a pivotal or catalytic role in the Four-Party Talks process, the course and pace of the talks could change significantly. For this reason, China should be brought into the circle of the United States and the ROK to set out a common ground for peace and stability on the Korean peninsula.

To do so, the ROK and the United States should approach China with common positions. There should be neither gaps nor policy differences between the United States and the ROK in dealing with North Korea and China. Thus, the first priority of the ROK and the United States is to draw a road map that would bring stable peace and then peaceful unification to the Korean peninsula. While both countries share the goal of peaceful unification, the ROK and the United States have not clearly established a common plan and division of labor to make it materialize. Only when such a common stance, policy coordination, and strategic cooperation are established can the ROK and the United States deal effectively with North Korea and China. Chinese dominance over the Koreas as well as regional affairs cannot be allowed to take place. We should encourage China to play constructive, not abortive, roles and move Chinese influence toward a positive direction. Continued U.S. engagement with China and expansion of bilateral ties between the ROK and China will be an important step on the long road to a stable Asia-Pacific, as China can become an additional asset in materializing peace and stability in the region.

Again it must be emphasized that the maintenance of a robust ROK-U.S. security alliance is the key building block of peace and stability on the Korean peninsula and that China can play a catalytic role. In the meantime, to meet future challenges to the alliance, the ROK and the United States must work together to adjust the role, mission, and structure of the ROK-U.S. alliance, one based not on time constraints and expediency but on a realistic assessment of the situation and strategic concerns and interests of both parties.

Notes

1. For further analysis on the China debate, see David Shambaugh, "Containment or Engagement of China? Calculating Beijing's Response," *International Security* 21, no. 2 (Fall 1996): 180–209; Denny Roy, "The China Threat Issue: Major Arguments," *Asian Survey* (August 1996): 758–71.

2. Ever since the collapse of the Soviet Union in 1991, China has become the number one trading partner of North Korea. In addition, China is the major supplier of North Korea's two strategic materials—petroleum and food.

3. The *Four-Point Military Guidelines* stress (1) arming the entire population; (2) fortifying the entire country; (3) instilling leadership potential in all military personnel; and (4) modernizing all troops.

4. *The Korea Herald*, July 11, 1997, p. 2.

5. Ministry of National Defense, the Republic of Korea, *Defense White Paper 1996–1997* (Seoul: MND, 1996), pp. 55–67.

6. Ibid., p. 61.

7. The Institute for Foreign Policy Analysis, *A Study on Exploring U.S. Missile Defense Requirements in 2010* (April 1997), p. 33.

8. *The Korea Herald*, July 11, 1997, p. 2.

9. *Dongah Ilbo*, July 16, 1997, p. 5.

10. *Joong-ang Ilbo*, July 15, 1997.

11. Although the average North Korean adult is supposed to receive 600 g of grain for daily subsistence, this amount reportedly has been cut to 150 g.

12. *Jukan Chosun* (Weekly Chosun), November 13, 1997, p. 43.

13. *Sisa Jeonal*, July 24, 1997, pp. 56–60.

14. Paragraph 62 of Article V, "Miscellaneous," of the Armistice Agreement, ROK Ministry of National Defense, *Defense White Paper 1991–1992* (Seoul: MND, 1992), p. 311.

15. Article 5 of the Basic Agreement reads: "The two sides shall endeavor together to transform the present state of armistice into a solid state of peace between the South and the North and shall abide by the present Military Armistice Agreement (of July 27, 1953) until such a state of peace has been realized." And Article 20 of the Protocol on North-South Reconciliation reads: "The South and the North shall sincerely abide by the Military Armistice Agreement until a solid state of peace has been established between the South and the North." See ROK Ministry of National Defense, *Defense White Paper 1991–1992* (Seoul: MND, 1992), pp. 219, 225.

16. *The Korea Herald*, April 5, 1996.

17. The North-South Joint Military Commission was supposed to hold its first meeting in November 1992. Because of the North Korean nuclear issue, the meeting was canceled and has never taken place.

18. *The Korea Herald*, April 17, 1997.

19. China is rumored to have set up a plan to establish several refugee camps along the border to receive and isolate North Korean refugees.

20. Paragraph 4 of the ROK-U.S. Joint Announcement reads: "[T]he South and North Korea should take the lead in a renewed search for a permanent peace arrangement. . . ." *The Korea Herald*, April 17, 1996.

21. Before the convening of the Geneva conference, three rounds of preliminary negotiations took place in the United States in August, September and November 1997. The key stumbling block in these negotiations was North Korea's demand to discuss the withdrawal of U.S. forces from Korea, to which the United States and South Korea objected. In the third round, North Korea dropped its demand in return for assurances that it would be able to raise the issue at the Geneva conference. *The Korea Herald*, November 27, 1997.

22. The ROK Ministry of National Defense, *Defense White Paper 1995–1996* (Seoul: MND, 1995), pp. 118–20.

23. U.S. Department of Defense, Office of International Security Affairs, *United*

States Security Strategy for the East Asia-Pacific Region (Washington, DC: U.S. Department of Defense, February 1995), p. 10. An excellent analysis on the future security alternatives of the ROK-U.S. alliance is available. See Jonathan D. Pollack and Young Koo Cha et al., *A New Alliance for the Next Century: The Future of U.S.-Korea Security Cooperation* (Santa Monica, CA: RAND Corporation, 1995).

24. For a comprehensive but focused discussion on the different internal political dynamics in Washington and Beijing, see David Shambaugh, "The United States and China: A New Cold War?" *Current History* 94, no. 593 (September 1995): 241–47. See also Ronald N. Montaperto, "Managing United States Relations with China: A View from Washington." Paper presented at the First KIDA/INSS Workshop on "The ROK-U.S. Security Alliance and the Regional Powers over the Next Ten Years," KIDA, Seoul, Korea, April 15–16, 1996.

25. *The Japan Times*, September 24, 1997.

26. For details, see Yoichi Hirama, "Japan's Value in the Korean War." Paper presented at the Third Korea-Japan Security Shuttle, Ritz-Carlton, Seoul, Korea, December 1, 1997.

27. The issue of noncombatant evacuation operation (NEO) also is very sensitive —as sensitive as the possibility of the dispatch of Japanese minesweepers.

28. For a fuller discussion of the so-called three-pillars of Sino-U.S. security cooperation, see Thomas L. Wilborn, *Security Cooperation with China: Analysis and a Proposal* (Carlisle Barracks, PA: U.S. Army War College Strategic Studies Institute, November 25, 1994).

Bibliography

Board of National Unification, ROK. *Tongil Baeksu 1995* [Unification White Paper 1995] (Seoul: BNU, 1995).

Dongah Ilbo [Dongah daily] (Seoul, Korea). July 11, 1997, p. 2.

Hankuk Eunhang [Bank of Korea]. *Bukhan Kyungje Gipyo* [Economic data on North Korea] (Seoul: Hankuk Eunhang, 1992).

Hirama, Yoichi. "Japan's Value in the Korean War." Paper presented at the Third Korea-Japan Security Shuttle, Ritz-Carlton Hotel, Seoul, Korea. December 1, 1997.

Institute for Foreign Policy Analysis. *A Study on Exploring U.S. Missile Defense Requirements in 2010*. Washington, DC: IFPA, 1997.

The Japan Times.

Joongang Ilbo [Joongang daily] (Seoul, Korea). July 15, 1997.

Jukan Chosun [Weekly Chosun]. November 13, 1997, p. 43.

The Korea Herald (Seoul, Korea).

Ministry of National Defense, the Republic of Korea. *Defense White Paper, 1994–1995, 1995–1996, 1996–1997* (Seoul: Ministry of National Defense).

Pollack, Jonathan D., and Young Koo Cha et al., *A New Alliance for the Next Century: The Future of U.S.-Korea Security Cooperation*. Santa Monica, CA: RAND Corporation, 1995.

Roy, Denny. "The China Threat Issue: Major Argument." *Asian Survey* (August 1996): 758–71.

Shambaugh, David. "Containment or Engagement of China? Calculating Beijing's Response." *International Security* 21, no. 2 (Fall 1996): 180–209.

————. "The United States and China: A New Cold War?" *Current History* 94, no. 593: 241–47.

Sisa Jeonal [Journal of current issues]. July 24, 1997, pp. 56–60.

U.S. Department of Defense, Office of International Security Affairs. *United States Security Strategy for the East Asia-Pacific Region.* Washington, DC: U.S. Department of Defense, February, 1995

Wilborn, Thomas L. *Security Cooperation with China: Analysis and a Proposal.* Carlisle Barracks, PA: U.S. Army War College Strategic Studies Institute, November 25, 1994.

15

The Challenge of Cross-Strait Relations

The Strategic Implications of the Missile Crisis

Michael Y.M. Kau

For nearly five decades, the cross-Strait relationship between China and Taiwan has been marked by a constant mixture of tension, hostility, and controlled interactions. The militant rhetoric of "liberation by force" or the patriotic appeal for "peaceful unification" notwithstanding, Beijing never tried to project its military power and security threat directly on Taiwan before 1995. Even during the Quemoy-Matsu crises of 1953 and 1958, which involved large-scale artillery shellings of the off-shore islands and actual combat engagements of jet fighters and naval warships from both sides, the People's Liberation Army (PLA) always carefully controlled the zones of military conflict and engagement close to the mainland shores.

The missile crises of 1995 and 1996, however, marked a new departure of great significance. The series of "missile tests" and successive waves of "military exercises" of the combined forces in and around the Taiwan Strait, which occurred on and off between July 1995 and March 1996, clearly were designed to project China's military power and security threat onto Taiwan itself. It was the first time that the People's Republic of China (PRC) explicitly tried to demonstrate its military capabilities and political will to use force, if necessary, on the Taiwan (ROC) side of the Taiwan Strait.

This chapter focuses its analysis on two areas: First, the process and motives underlying Beijing's strategy of coercion in the broad domestic and international contexts of the Taiwan issue; and second, the long-term strategic implications of the crisis on the future development of cross-Strait relations and on the security environments of the Asia-Pacific region.

The Missile Crises of 1995 and 1996

In mid-July 1995, the PLA announced its intention to conduct a series of missile tests targeting the waters just north of Taiwan. Between July 21 and July 26, the Chinese launched four short-range ballistic missiles (M-9s) into the target area, 90 miles off the northern coast of Taiwan. This missile firing was followed by successive waves of large-scale military exercises along the Fujian coast throughout the summer months. Over 150,000 PLA troops from the combined forces were mobilized for the operations, which featured prominently amphibious beachhead landing maneuvers backed by jet fighters, naval frigates, heavy artillery and field tanks. On March 8 and 13, 1996, four more M-9 missiles were fired. This time they were targeted only 30 miles from Taiwan's two major harbors, Kaohsiung in the south and Keelung in the north. Immediately after this second round, the PLA again carried out massive war games, this time with the drama of live ammunition for two weeks lasting through March 25 (Kau 1996b).

While the PLA's military exercises were underway, Beijing's propaganda machine was simultaneously mobilized to deliver a barrage of vicious attacks focusing specifically on Taiwan President Lee Teng-hui and on Taiwan's present political development. Beijing accused Lee and the Kuomintang (KMT) "mainstream leadership" of a hidden political agenda. In Beijing's view, Lee's push for democratization, constitutional reform, and pragmatic diplomacy were all aimed toward "Taiwan independence." Moreover, Beijing also believed that Lee colluded with the Democratic Progressive Party (DPP) in an attempt to split Taiwan from the motherland and achieve the goal of "two Chinas" or "one China, one Taiwan" (Kau 1996b). Insisting on upholding the "one China" principle, Beijing proclaimed that if Taiwan should declare independence, the PLA would not hesitate to use force to protect the territorial integrity and sovereignty of the Chinese motherland. Beijing also asserted that as Taiwan was a "province" of China, the Taiwan issue was a "purely domestic affair" and delivered warnings that no foreign power would be allowed to interfere. China's mass media reports also made absolutely clear the exact purpose, target and audience of the military exercises (*Chung-kuo shih-pao*, February–March 1996).

In response to Beijing's mounting threat, Taipei also mobilized its armed forces for a red alert contingency. Taipei, however, stressed prudence and restraint, cautioning against any provocative actions, yet there were signs of stress and anxiety among the public, and the stock market tumbled sharply.

When the presidential campaigns in Taiwan gained momentum in the spring of 1996, Beijing intensified its military pressure. Taipei was confronted with the sensitive issue of whether or not to postpone the direct popular elections that were originally scheduled for March 23. After serious deliberation, Taipei decided to go ahead with the original schedule despite the political tension, lest Beijing would perceive the change as a sign of weakness and vacillation. Thanks to the PRC's naked military threat, the issue of cross-Strait relations indeed became the hottest issue for the presidential candidates throughout the campaign.

The impact of the Strait crisis went beyond the territorial boundary of Taiwan. The military tension in the Taiwan Strait quickly became the focus of worldwide attention and concern. Commercial flights and shipping were rerouted for safety considerations, calling into question the important issue of security in international airspace and sealanes. Asian leaders began to speculate aloud on the possible impact of a military conflict in the Taiwan Strait on the region's economy and stability.

In the United States, after months of prolonged and spirited public debate, congressional hearings, and editorial discourse, President Clinton decided to take action. On March 10, 1996, he ordered two U.S. Seventh Fleet aircraft carrier battle groups, under the *USS Independence* and the *USS Nimitz*, to the coastal waters of Taiwan to "monitor" the development of the crisis. Obviously, the U.S. action was designed to demonstrate both the resolve and the capability of the United States to resist China's use of force against Taiwan. Prime Minister Ryutaro Hashimoto of Japan also publicly expressed his concern over the crisis, sending a tacit message signaling Japan's willingness to cooperate with the United States and support its effort (*Lien-ho pao* [United Daily], January–March 1996).

On March 23, the presidential elections in Taiwan ended with a landslide victory for Lee Teng-hui. On March 25, Beijing declared the "completion" and "success" of its military exercises and missile tests. Subsequently, as the tension in the area subsided, the U.S. battle groups also departed the Taiwan Strait.

The Crux of the Problem: The Bilateral Context

During the days of KMT authoritarianism, all public policies in Taiwan, especially those politically sensitive ones, belonged in the exclusive domain of the corporatist state. There was hardly any debate before the public; no dissent was tolerated. As far as the KMT's basic policy toward mainland China was concerned, the position was simple and clear. The government insisted on a "one China" doctrine, claiming that the ROC government remained the sole legal government of all of China and that Taiwan was part of China. The two sides of the Taiwan Strait, they argued, ultimately should be reunited (Tien 1989).

As no debate or challenge was permitted in the political arena on such a fictitious claim, mainland policy was essentially a "nonissue" under authoritarian rule. Moreover, because the two sides of the Taiwan Strait were totally segregated politically and economically during the Cold War era, the fiction and the reality simply did not intersect. Consequently, there was no need even to try to sort out the fiction from the reality (Kau 1991; Kau 1992).

During the second half of the 1980s, however, the process of democratization brought about competitive party politics and the freedom of speech in the political arena. The end of the ban on economic and social contacts across the Taiwan Strait in 1987 quickly intensified Taiwan's "indirect" trade, investment, and tourism with the mainland (Clough 1993). As more and more people traveled across the Strait, they inevitably began to question the political fiction of "one China," and found the need to redefine for themselves their ethnic identity and political loyalty in light of the new realities—who they are and what they are in relation to the two political entities that compete for their political loyalty and ethnic identity (Lin 1993).

Political democratization further offered a timely opportunity to air and debate the bigger and more sensitive political issues of national identity and the long-term future of Taiwan. Is Taiwan part of China? Are Taiwanese Chinese? Should Taiwan be independent from China or be unified with the mainland? Is there one China? Are there two Chinas? Or, is there one China and one Taiwan? As the process of democratization lifted the lid of authoritarian repression, all these long-suppressed, sensitive issues quickly surfaced and took center stage. Moreover, they became closely intertwined with the domestic power struggle, factional politics and policy debate of Taiwan (Tien 1996; Cheng and Haggard 1992).

The deepening of cross-Strait economic and social interactions also created legal and political problems at the formal, official government-to-government level. It became necessary for the governments on both sides of the Taiwan Strait to define each other's legal status and administrative jurisdiction. Should they treat each other as two "equal political entities," or should Beijing be considered the central government and Taipei the "local authorities?" Are their relationship and respective status hierarchical or parallel? Are their interactions in the realm of "domestic affairs," "international affairs," or "quasi-international relations?" Should the discussions between the two sides be "direct," "indirect," or "quasi-direct" (Copper 1996)?

The past 10 years have witnessed constant debate and controversy over Taiwan's mainland policy among the major players of Taiwan politics. Three distinct policy positions are now relatively well articulated by the three major contending political parties in Taiwan (Feldman 1991).

To the right of the policy spectrum is the position advocated by the New

Party (NP) and the "non-mainstream faction" of the KMT. They essentially support the traditional "one China" doctrine, insisting that Taiwan is part of China and should be reunited with the motherland in due course. They favor broadening and deepening the "three links" (trade, shipping, and communication) at a faster pace and advocate changes in the current policy from allowing only "indirect" contacts to allowing "direct" links. They believe these functional activities will strengthen ties across the Taiwan Strait, promoting the strong socioeconomic foundation needed for political unification in the future. Because this position is about the same as that advocated by Beijing, its supporters are often identified as the "pro-unification faction," advancing the PRC's "united front" strategy in Taiwan. In addition, because the policy is largely advocated by the mainlander old guard and the second-generation mainlander activists, the position is also known as the "mainlander position" (Tien 1996).

To the left of the policy spectrum is the Democratic Progressive Party (DPP). By and large, DPP leaders espouse a strong and clear stand for "one Taiwan, one China." Some would advocate that Taiwan should seek complete and *de jure* independence from China by declaring "Taiwan independence." Arguing on historical, political, and economic grounds, they stress that Taiwan has its own national identity and is fully equipped with all the essential elements required for an independent state, not to mention its exceptional economic strength. As long as Beijing respects this basic premise of national independence, Taiwan should open up direct interactions immediately with the mainland in all areas on an equal and friendly basis (Huang 1992).

Before Taiwan can attain this goal of independence, however, the DPP stresses caution in dealing with the "tricks and traps" of both the Chinese Communist Party (CCP) and the KMT. The DPP opposes "party to party" negotiations between the CCP and the KMT, because it fears that the interest of the Taiwanese people might be sold out. To protect a small Taiwan against the threat of a giant China, the DPP emphasizes the strategy of "internationalizing" the issue of Taiwan in the world community. The DPP believes Taiwan's active international participation, especially its admission to the United Nations (UN), is critical for the island's security and survival. Continuing domestic democratization and the expansion of the DPP's political role will make it impossible for the KMT, particularly its non-mainstream wing, to attempt any secret deal with the PRC (Yang 1997; Democratic Progressive Party 1994).

The policy position of the KMT's "mainstream faction" predictably falls somewhere in the middle of the spectrum. The "Guidelines for National Unification," officially adopted by the Presidential Commission on National Unification and endorsed by the Executive Yuan in March 1991, tries to steer a middle course between the policies advocated by the NP and those of the DPP. Articulating a three-phase, gradualist approach, the guidelines call for "indirect" and "unofficial" interactions to build confidence and mutual interest across the Taiwan Strait during the first phase. Beijing's "positive response" during this stage could be tested by three interrelated conditions: its willingness to respect Taiwan as a separate, independent, and equal "political entity" in the international arena under the abstract principle of "one China," to stop obstructing Taiwan's international participation and formal diplomatic ties, and to renounce the use and threat of force against Taiwan. To Taiwan, these conditions constitute the very basis for its security and survival (Huang 1991).

Once these three conditions for confidence-building, mutual respect, and peaceful coexistence have been met and verified, Taiwan would move into the second phase of "direct" interactions and "official" contacts, including government-to-government negotiations on economic and other areas of cooperation. In the third and final phase, both sides would enter negotiations about the framework and timing of ultimate unification. Under this KMT approach, there is no "fixed timetable" for the progression of the phases; all depends on Beijing's good behavior and deeds.

The KMT rejects Beijing's "one country, two systems" formula because it treats Taiwan as a "local government," and the "two systems" are unequal ones. Instead, the KMT advocates "one China, two [equal] political entities." In essence, the KMT's gradualist approach represents an attempt to strike a balance between the two extreme positions of unification and independence. While holding out the hope of unification in the distant future under specified conditions, the KMT formula stresses the existing objective realities of the separation and independence of the two sides. By insisting on the absence of a fixed timetable, the government will be able to control the pace and scope of interactions in accordance with internal sociopolitical developments on the two sides of the Taiwan Strait (Kau 1992).

Significantly, there appears to be an increasing convergence between the DPP and KMT approaches to mainland policy in recent years. The DPP leaders seem to have come to realize that the high-pitched rhetoric of "declaring Taiwan independence" may be too provocative not only to Beijing but also to the average voter in Taiwan, who tends to favor political stability, given Beijing's repeated threats to use force under certain circumstances (Yang 1997). The two parties reached a consensus at the National Development Conference in December 1996, in which the DPP endorsed the KMT position that the ROC on Taiwan has been "independent" ever since 1912 and there is no need to "declare independence" redundantly. Instead, Taiwan simply needs more diplomatic recognition and international participation. The two parties share the basic position that the sovereignty and the jurisdiction of the PRC always has been and still is limited to the mainland, not including Taiwan, because since its founding in 1949, the PRC never has exercised its sovereignty or jurisdiction over Taiwan for even a single day. Therefore, Taiwan is not and never has been part of the PRC (National Development Conference Secretariat 1997).

At the same time, the KMT's mainstream faction is moving closer to some aspects of the DPP position concerning the Taiwan issue. For many years, until 1991, the KMT government was officially opposed to the idea of seeking UN admission or adopting the concept of "divided nation" and "dual recognition" (Ministry of Foreign Affairs, ROC 1997; Hu 1993). But as Taiwan became more democratized and its citizens more conscious of the nation's need for dignity and participation in the international arena, the KMT was forced to reexamine and adjust its foreign policy stance. As the formula of "one China, two political entities" could not easily be understood and supported by the international community, the government was forced to move to the bolder formula of de facto "two Chinas," patterned after the pre-1989 "two Germanys" and the current "two Koreas" (Wu 1995). As the recent National Development Conference shows, the trend toward bipartisan cooperation in the area of mainland and foreign policy is quite evident. The DPP fine-tunes its basic policy on Taiwan independence from the left to the center, and the KMT adjusts its strategy to mainland affairs from the center to the left.

Although Beijing's policy posture toward Taiwan underwent a fundamental change in the 1970s, moving from "liberation by force" to "peaceful unification," its basic political objective remained unchanged. In early 1984, Deng Xiaoping offered Taiwan the "Hong Kong model" of "one country, two systems." Beijing pledged that Taiwan could maintain its own political, economic, and social system after unification. But Beijing also insisted that Taiwan should function only as a Special Administrative Region (SAR) under the PRC central authorities in Beijing. In January 1995, Chinese President Jiang Zemin set forth a "six-point" proposal, urging negotiations to terminate the "state of hostility" between the two sides and exchanges of two-way visits between top leaders. Nevertheless, he also insisted that all this take place under the principle of "one China" with Beijing as the central government (Shinn 1996).

Constant appeals for "peaceful unification" notwithstanding, Beijing never stopped (1) attempting to isolate Taiwan in the international arena; (2) threatening Taiwan with the use of force under certain conditions; and (3) treating Taiwan as a renegade province of the PRC. Beijing was suspicious that Taiwanese President Lee Teng-hui had a hidden political agenda, viewing all his efforts at democratization and pragmatic diplomacy as a disguise to promote and lay down foundations for "two Chinas" or "Taiwan independence." In the eyes of Beijing, the DPP advocates an open, clear-cut solution toward Taiwan independence, while the mainstream KMT is engaged in a hidden, creeping one. Beijing felt that the latter was worse than the former, and that it should be stopped at any cost, including threats or the use of force (Su 1998). Despite the deepening economic and trade ties across the Taiwan Strait, the political gap proved hard to bridge. In fact, Taipei now perceives the deepening of economic relations as an alarming political liability, as Beijing might exploit Taiwan's increasing economic dependency on the mainland for political gains.

The Crux of the Problem: The International Context

The long-troubled cross-Strait interaction has its roots not only in the bilateral relationship between Beijing and Taipei but also in the broader contexts of the Cold War and international intervention. The Communist victory over the Chinese Nationalists in 1949 marked the beginning of China's formal split into two parts, with the PRC controlling the mainland and the ROC ruling Taiwan. The outbreak of the Korean War and the dispatch of the U.S. Seventh Fleet to the Taiwan Strait signified the beginning of the "internationalization" of the Taiwan issue.

The complete separation and perpetuation of the two governments and two territorial jurisdictions along the Taiwan Strait notwithstanding, the political and legal fiction of "one China" was maintained by the two sides for ideological and political reasons. First, both sides perceived each other as "passing phenomena," a lingering remnant of the Chinese civil war yet to be settled. Mao Zedong expected to liberate Taiwan in due course, while Chiang Kai-shek dreamed of a counterattack to recover the mainland. Second, in engaging each other in competition for international recognition and acceptance in the world arena, both sides found it expedient to uphold the principle of "one China" for the purpose of excluding the opponent in the game of diplomatic recognition and international participation under the principles of international law and the practice of world diplomacy (Kau 1992).

During the heyday of the Cold War struggle between East and West, to isolate and contain Communist China constituted a top priority in U.S. global strategy. It was, therefore, not only logical but also essential for the United States to side with Taiwan's "one China" policy to achieve U.S. strategic objectives against China. Throughout the 1950s and 1960s, Washington recognized Taipei as the "sole, legal government of China," signed a Mutual Security Treaty with Taiwan, and supported the ROC government as the representative of all of China in the UN. The ROC even occupied one of the five permanent-member seats with veto power at the UN Security Council (Kau 1992).

As the structure of the international system began to change in the 1960s, however, so did the tripartite relationship. The worsening of the Sino-Soviet conflict provided the United States with a window of opportunity to sway the PRC away from the Communist bloc and toward the Western side. Taking advantage of such an opportunity required the United States to allow its diplomatic support for Taiwan to wane. In 1971, the ROC was expelled from the UN, with tacit U.S. approval, and in the following year U.S. President Richard Nixon undertook his historic journey to China and signed the famous Shanghai Communique. It was at this time that the United States took a major turn in "acknowledging" Beijing's "one China" position:

> The United States acknowledges that all Chinese on either side of the Taiwan Strait maintain there is but one China and that Taiwan is a part of China. The United States Government does not challenge that position. It reaffirms its interest in a peaceful settlement of the Taiwan question by the Chinese themselves. (Lasater 1993)

In 1978, President Jimmy Carter further moved to normalize relations with the PRC by accepting China's "three conditions" with regard to the existing U.S. ties with Taiwan: (1) breaking off diplomatic relations; (2) terminating the Mutual Security Treaty; and (3) ending the American military presence. To compensate for the broken promises of the traditional U.S. political and security commitments to Taiwan, the U.S. Congress adopted the Taiwan Relations Act (TRA) in April 1979. The act declared:

> It is the policy of the United States [among other things]:

> to make clear that the United States decision to establish diplomatic relations with the People's Republic of China rests upon the expectation that the future of Taiwan will be determined by peaceful means;

> to consider any effort to determine the future of Taiwan by other than peaceful means, including by boycotts or embargoes, a threat to the peace and security of the Western Pacific area and of grave concern to the United States;

> to provide Taiwan with arms of a defensive character; and

> to maintain the capacity of the United States to resist any resort to force or other forms of coercion that would jeopardize the security, or the social or economic system, of the people on Taiwan. (Hickey 1994)

It is not difficult to understand why the PRC insisted on a rigid "one China" position in dealing with the United States in 1978. Such a policy would clearly strengthen Beijing's claim of sovereignty over Taiwan and enable China to exert more political and legal pressure to isolate Taiwan in the world arena (Simon and Kau 1992).

Accompanying the PRC's rigid "one China" policy was its equally rigid objection to the "two Chinas," "one China, one Taiwan," and Taiwan independence policies. Although China pledged "peaceful unification" as a "fundamental policy" of the nation, it refused to renounce the right to use force against Taiwan under certain circumstances. Beijing insisted that the unification of Taiwan with the motherland was a "purely internal matter" to China, and it would not tolerate any interference by "foreign forces." Because Beijing asserted that the Taiwan issue was an extremely sensitive and emotional matter that involved the sacred questions of sovereignty, territorial integrity, and national honor, foreign powers tended to shun the issue because they simply did not want to be perceived by Beijing as hostile or unfriendly (Su 1998).

For the United States, acquiescing in China's "one China" policy on the one hand, and living up to the commitment of its security guarantee to Taiwan on the other, clearly has been difficult. Washington must walk a tightrope between the demands of the three Joint Communiqués, which stressed U.S. adherence to the "one China" principle, and the commitments of the TRA, which promised continued U.S. security support for Taiwan. When the gap between the fiction of "one China" and the reality of "two Chinas" was too wide to be reconciled with coherence, the virtue of "creative ambiguity" was contrived and came into play. This virtue of ambiguity, however, at times became the worst source of confusion and conflict among the three parties (Chang and Lasater 1993; Kau and Marsh 1993).

Beijing's Calculus of Military Coercion

Throughout the past decade, the trend of Taiwan's domestic democratization and constitutional reform and its foreign policy pursuit deeply bothered Beijing leaders. They were particularly suspicious of President Lee Teng-hui's personal motives and political objectives. Lee's policy was often characterized by the PRC media as one "for unification in name, but for independence in substance." Beijing also was annoyed by Lee's stubborn refusal to openly endorse Beijing's version of the "one China" principle and of Washington's security commitments to Taiwan (Lee 1995; Su 1998).

Evidence to date supports the hypothesis that the 1995–1996 missile coercion by Beijing was designed to achieve two major short-term political objectives: (1) to influence the outcome of the ongoing presidential campaign in Taiwan at the time; and (2) to test the political resolve of Washington's concern for Taiwan's security (Kau 1996a).

After witnessing President Lee Teng-hui's triumphant June 1995 visit to his alma mater, Cornell University, Beijing became convinced that Lee must be prevented from winning a second term and that the United States must be deterred from supporting Taiwan's political causes. Beijing conveniently turned Lee's private visit to Cornell along with the enthusiastic support of the U.S. Congress into evidence of Taiwan's provocative move toward independence with the tacit support of Washington. The PRC leadership apparently concluded that Taiwan's "pragmatic diplomacy" should be stopped and that the best way to achieve its goals was a dramatic show of force (Kau 1996a).

The strategy followed the simple logic that prosperous middle-class voters in Taiwan, by nature, preferred stability and prosperity over uncertainty and war, and that a vivid show of force could be a most effective demonstration of Beijing's political will and its military capabilities. The dramatization of the threat of war could intimidate moderate voters into shunning Lee Teng-hui, the KMT candidate, whom Beijing considered provocative, and Peng Ming-min, the DPP candidate, who openly advocated Taiwan independence. The fears of a military attack by the PRC could then be translated into votes for Lin Yang-kang or Chen Li-an, two independent candidates who openly advocated compromise and accommodation and who were favored by the New Party (NP) and Beijing (Su 1998; Kau 1996a).

Beijing was painfully aware that, since 1950, the United States has held the key to Taiwan's security through formal or informal security arrangements. Washington, however, never clearly established the parameters of its commitment after the ending of formal U.S. diplomatic recognition and termination in 1979 of the United States-Taiwan Mutual Security Treaty. In fact, as discussed earlier, Washington deliberately tried to maintain a sense of "ambiguity" on the issue to placate and engage the PRC (Lasater 1993). As the official U.S. position professed to adhere to the "one China" principle of the three communiqués, on the one hand, and abide by the 1979 Taiwan Relations Act (TRA) for Taiwan's security, on the other, Beijing could have perceived that Washington's stand on Taiwan was indecisive and wavering. With appropriate coercion, Washington might be persuaded to shift its stance and direction. Beijing's military calculus apparently believed that a dramatic show of force by the PLA might dissuade the United States from protecting Taiwan for fear of war with China. The costs of fighting such a war with the PRC, in human and economic terms, would be too frightening for the American people to accept. Without U.S. intervention, China was convinced, its strategy of military intimidation toward Taiwan could prevail (Paal 1998).

Beijing's political calculus, however, involved a number of serious miscalculations. The atmosphere of national crisis in Taiwan resulting from the PRC's military threat, in fact, prompted voters to rally behind the defiant Lee, who vowed to fight back against Beijing's naked bullying. In a four-way competition, Lee achieved a smashing victory by collecting 54 percent of the popular vote, surpassing the combined votes for the other three candidates. In Washington, the response to Beijing's intimidation strategy was equally defiant. Citing American interest in a "peaceful settlement" of the Taiwan issue as stated in the three communiqués as well as "grave concern" for Taiwan's security as expressed in the TRA, the Clinton administration ordered two aircraft carrier battle groups to the waters surrounding Taiwan. There is no doubt the arrival of the U.S. forces played a critical role in moderating Beijing's militant adventurism.

The Long-Term Implications of the Missile Crisis

The evidence is conclusive that the PRC's military coercion of 1995 and 1996 failed to achieve its twin objectives of destroying President Lee Teng-hui's leadership in Taiwan and blocking U.S. intervention in Taiwan's security crisis. Worse still for Beijing, its militant strategy also backfired against the PRC's longer-term and broader interests in pursuing peaceful unification with Taiwan and promoting China's positive image in the Asia-Pacific as a responsible and constructive power.

Before the outbreak of the missile crisis in July 1995, the image of a "China threat" already loomed large in the minds of many Asian people, especially those in the neighborhood of Taiwan and China. Such suspicions remained largely abstract and speculative, deriving principally from historical legacies of the Middle Kingdom and the growing economic and military might of the PRC. The recent missile intimidation against Taiwan, however, greatly solidified that image and rendered it a vivid sense of reality.

In Taiwan, public opinion on the issue of unification versus independence shifted dramatically after the missile crisis. For the first time, the number of people favoring Taiwan independence surpassed those favoring the status quo (*Chung-kuo shih-pao*, June 30, 1996). Moreover, the National Development Conference held in December 1996 and the fourth round of constitutional reform just completed in August 1997 demonstrated that the opposition DPP had begun to take an active interest in cooperating with Lee Teng-hui to strengthen, through constitutional amendment, the power and leadership of the presidential office to forge a bipartisan united front and national solidarity against Beijing's mounting political and security threat (National Development Conference Secretariat 1997).

Although Taipei continued to urge Beijing for an early resumption of contacts and negotiations between the two quasi-official organizations—the Association for Relations Across the Taiwan Strait (ARATS) of Beijing and the Straits Exchange Foundation (SEF) of Taipei—which Beijing suspended unilaterally in July 1995, the government also introduced a new policy of "chieh-chi yung-jen" (be cautious and patient) in expanding Taiwan's investments in and trade with the mainland. Economic interests, President Lee insisted, should not outweigh security interests. Beijing could easily exploit Taiwan's economic dependence on the mainland to undermine the island's economic and political security (*Chung-kuo shih-pao*, Dec. 7, 1997). The evidence is clear that Beijing's strategy of coercion and intimidation not only has further alienated Taiwan's trust and confidence in the PRC but also has set back Beijing's professed cause of peaceful unification.

Regional reaction to the military crisis over the Taiwan Strait from Asia Pacific countries was equally negative, pointing to some far-reaching implications for the future development of regional security arrangements. The strong response of the United States, which dispatched aircraft carrier battle groups to the Taiwan Strait, needs no elaboration. The Japanese government expressed its concern publicly and urged Beijing to exercise restraint and discipline. From Southeast Asian nations, public criticisms were typically muted, but privately they aired their concern just the same. Although the modality of reactions varied, the essence of anxiety was similar.

The missile crisis strongly sensitized the region to the fact that China is a big power and gaining strength each day. The crucial question is: What if the PRC's militancy and assertiveness were repeated elsewhere in the region? Historically, the PRC had used force in the Korea peninsula and in several border disputes with the former Soviet Union, India and Vietnam. More recently, the PRC has used force in dealing with the disputed islets and reefs in the South China Sea (Paal 1998). Although Beijing tried to assure its neighbors that the case of Taiwan was entirely different—a "purely internal matter"—it could not easily explain away the nagging question whether, if Beijing could use force against its own compatriots in Taiwan, it could be trusted not to use the same method against others in the name of its vital national interests. China's behavior toward Taiwan could be easily perceived as a barometer for its behavior elsewhere.

In response to a rising China and its potential as a security threat, two distinct approaches are discernible in the region. Emphasizing the Asian style of informal consultation, dialogue, networking, confidence-building, and consensus-formation, the Association of Southeast Asian Nations (ASEAN) approach seeks to engage and integrate the PRC into the institution-building process of the Asia-Pacific community. It is hoped that China will be socialized into the cooperative norms and accommodative behavioral patterns of the regional community and become a constructive and responsible member. For example, ASEAN made tremendous efforts to invite the PRC to become a dialogue partner of the ASEAN-PMC (Post-Ministerial Conference) process and to join the ASEAN Regional Forum (ARF), the Council for Security Cooperation in the Asia Pacific (CSCAP), and the Asia-Pacific Economic Cooperation (APEC) forum (Evans 1997; Ramnath 1996). The ASEAN approach refuses to demonize the PRC: The more China is perceived and treated as a threat or aggressor, the more China is isolated and contained, the more likely it is to realize its potential. "Demonization" of China, according to the ASEAN view, would inevitably fall into the trap of a self-fulfilling prophesy.

The Northeast Asian countries emphasize a different approach. The traditional alliance and deterrence structures are still deemed crucial for the region's peace and stability, even after the end of the Cold War. Recognizing that "uncertainty and instability" still exist and that the region's cooperative security mechanisms and regimes are still wanting, proponents of the alliance approach stress the critical significance of the alliance structure, such as the United States-Japan and the United States-South Korea security treaties, and the forward deployment of U.S. forces in the region. While "constructive engagement" and "community building" are worth trying in their own right, they are no substitute for power balancing and deterrence in the real security environment of the world (Cossa 1998; Matsunaga and Singh 1996).

It is worth noting that since 1993, American and Japanese military planners and security experts have been working together to update and enhance their bilateral defense cooperation. In 1995, while the American side was pursuing its East Asian Strategic Review (EASR), its Japanese counterpart completed the revision, for the first time since 1976, of Japan's National Defense Program Outlines (NDPO). These two efforts essentially formed the basis of the Clinton-Hashimoto Joint Declaration on United States–Japan Security Alliance for the Twenty-first Century, issued in Tokyo on April 17, 1996 (originally scheduled for November 1995 but postponed). Aside from reaffirming the role of the U.S.-Japanese alliance as the "cornerstone" of Japanese security and renewing their commitments to enhance and deepen bilateral defense cooperation, the Joint Declaration envisioned that the significance of the U.S.-Japanese security alliance would extend beyond Japan's own national security and play a greater role in the peace and security of the Asia-Pacific region (Yamamoto 1998).

To serve that vision, Washington and Tokyo worked closely to review and enhance the United States-Japan Defense Cooperation guidelines, first adopted in 1978. The new 1997 Guidelines provide that defense cooperation between the two countries covers not only aggression directed against Japan per se but also conflicts "in areas surrounding Japan that will have an important influence on Japan's peace and security." In other words, the new guidelines now cover conflicts that occur outside Japan's geographical scope. Furthermore, the Guidelines specified 40 types of security support that Japan would provide to the United States. In times of conflict, Japan would, for the first time, join naval blockades of third countries, conduct aerial surveillance and minesweeping, repair U.S. warships and aircraft, and carry out search and rescue operations at sea. In peacetime, the two sides shall conduct joint exercises, engage in intelligence exchanges, and hold defense consultations. There is no question that the revised Guidelines will give Japan its highest military profile in the Asia-Pacific region since World War II (Yamamoto 1998).

Ever since the release of the Interim Report on the Review of the Guidelines in June 1997, controversies have erupted over the meaning of the undefined "areas surrounding Japan." This vague geographical reference was particularly sensitive in the wake of the recent Taiwan Strait crisis. Do the "areas" include the Taiwan Strait? Does this mean that in the case of war in or around the Strait, the Japanese Self Defense Force (SDF) should join forces with the U.S. Seventh Fleet to fight the Chinese PLA? Recently, the Japanese mass media revealed that during the missile crisis in the Taiwan Strait, the Japanese government did formulate "contingency plans" in consultation with the United States. It is generally understood that the recent "enhancing" and "updating" of U.S.-Japanese security cooperation was part of an ongoing cooperative process, and not specifically in response to the recent Taiwan Strait crisis. There is no doubt, however, that the newly enhanced Guidelines will take on new political significance and strategic weight in light of the missile crisis.

Concluding Remarks

In hindsight, the verdict on Beijing's missile intimidation is clear. Under the prevailing political environments and security structures of the region, the PRC's strategy not only failed to achieve its short-term political objectives but also backfired on its long-term international image and security aspirations as a constructive and responsible member of the Asia-Pacific community. The missile strategy clearly failed to weaken Lee Teng-hui's leadership in Taiwan. In addition, Washington took the position that the PRC's attempt to use force to change the status quo in the Taiwan Strait was unacceptable and that the United States would not relinquish its strategic leadership and credibility in the world in fear of China.

The longer-term implications of the crisis are equally damaging to Beijing. In Taiwan, the PRC's military intimidation caused further alienation and fear among the Taiwanese people. It has even prompted a realignment of Taiwan's domestic political forces against the PRC threat. Under Beijing's security assault, the DPP and KMT leaders put aside some of their bitter ideological and political differences and forged a united front of national solidarity to resist Beijing's coercive pressure. With greater unity and solidarity, Taiwan will be able to deal with Beijing with strength. In the future, Taiwan is likely to liberalize its economic interactions with the mainland further for confidence building and mutual interest. But in the areas of national security and international participation, Taipei is bound to remain unyielding as a matter of national survival.

In the Asia-Pacific region, China's military intimidation against Taiwan clearly solidified its negative image as a "bully" and potential threat, prompting a fresh sense of urgency and realism on the questions of how to "engage" and/or "deter" China and how to make China a cooperative and responsible member of the regional community. Two distinct approaches have arisen: the Southeast Asian approach, which emphasizes engagement and integration; and the Northeast Asian path, which stresses alliance and deterrence. Although the styles and methods vary, the ultimate goals of making China behave are essentially the same. In fact, the two approaches could complement each other and progress simultaneously.

In light of the lessons of the missile crisis, Beijing's viable options for the Taiwan problem are rather limited indeed. Beijing certainly could try its coercive diplomacy and military intimidation again. Under the prevailing security environments in Asia today, however, it is doubtful that the outcome could be any different. Conversely, if Beijing could set aside its old mindset and strategy of coercion and threat in favor of the pragmatism and rationality of peaceful coexistence and co-prosperity, it is certain that a peaceful solution to the cross-Strait challenge would be more likely in the foreseeable future. Such an act of foresight and wisdom, if taken, is bound to make China's quest for genuine respect and leadership in the region more possible.

Bibliography

Chang, Parris H., and Lasater, Martin L. *If China Crosses the Taiwan Strait.* Lanham, MD, and London: University Press of America, 1993.

Cheng, Tun-jen, and Haggard, Stephan, eds. *Political Change in Taiwan.* Boulder, CO: Lynne Rienner, 1992.

Clough, Ralph N. *Reaching Across the Taiwan Strait.* Boulder, CO: Westview Press, 1993.

Copper, John F. *Taiwan: Nation-State or Province?* Boulder, CO: Westview Press, 1996.

Cossa, Ralph A. "Security Cooperation in Northeast Asia." Paper presented at the 12th Asia Pacific Roundtable, Kuala Lumpur, Malaysia, May 31–June 4, 1998.

Democratic Progressive Party. *Charter and Platform*. Taipei: Democratic Progressive Party, 1994.

Evans, Paul M. "Assessing the ARF and CSCAP." Paper presented at the Inaugural Conference of Asia-Pacific Security Forum, Taipei, Taiwan, September 1–3, 1997.

Feldman, Harvey J., ed. *Constitutional Reform and the Future of the Republic of China*. Armonk, NY: M.E. Sharpe, 1991.

Hickey, Dennis Van Vranken. *United States-Taiwan Security Ties*. Westport, CT: Praeger, 1994.

Hu, Jason C. "The Case for Taiwan's U. N. Representation." Paper presented at the Atlantic Council, Washington, DC, 1993.

Huang, Kun-huei. *The Key Points and Content of the Guidelines for National Unification*. Taipei: Mainland Affairs Council, 1991.

Huang, Teh-fu. *Min-chu-chin-pu tang yu T'ai-wan ti-ch'u cheng-chih min-chu-hua* [The Democratic Progressive Party and political democratization in Taiwan]. Taipei: Taiwan Elite Press, 1992.

Kau, Michael Ying-mao. *Taiwan: The National Affairs Council and Implications for Democracy*. Hearing Before the Subcommittee on Asian and Pacific Affairs, Committee on Foreign Affairs, U.S. House of Representatives. Washington, DC: U.S. Government Printing Office, 1991.

———. "The ROC's New Foreign Policy Strategy." In Denis Fred Simon and Michael Ying-mao Kau, eds., *Taiwan: Beyond the Economic Miracle*. Armonk, NY: M.E. Sharpe, 1992: 237–56.

———. "The Power Structure in Taiwan's Political Economy." *Asian Survey* 36, no. 3 (March 1996a): 287–305.

———. "China's Campaign of Intimidation Will Not Cow Taiwan." *International Herald Tribune*, July 29–30, 1996b, p. 4.

Kau, Michael Ying-mao, and Marsh, Susan H., eds. *China in the Era of Deng Xiaoping*. Armonk, NY: M.E. Sharpe, 1993.

Lasater, Martin L. *U.S. Interests in the New Taiwan*. Boulder, CO: Westview Press, 1993.

Lee, Teng-hui. *Ching-ying ta-Tai-wan* [Developing the great Taiwan]. Taipei: Yuanliu, 1995.

Lien-ho pao [United daily], Taipei.

Lin, Wen-cheng. *Political Integration and Democratization: The Case of Taiwan*. Unpublished Ph.D. dissertation. Medford, MA: The Fletcher School of Law and Diplomacy, 1993.

Matsunaga, Nobuo, and Singh, Jasjit, eds. *Enhancing Peace and Cooperation in Asia*. New Delhi: Institute for Defense Studies and Analyses, 1996.

Ministry of Foreign Affairs, ROC. *The Necessity to Review the UN General Assembly Resolution 2758*. Taipei: 1997.

National Development Conference Secretariat. *National Development Conference Resolutions*. Taipei: 1997.

Paal, Douglas H. "The United States and China." Paper presented at the 12th Asia Pacific Roundtable, Kuala Lumpur, Malaysia, May 31–June 4, 1998.

Ramnath, Thangam, ed. *The Emerging Regional Security Architecture in the Asia-Pacific Region*. Kuala Lumpur, Malaysia: ISIS, 1996.

Shinn, James, ed. *Weaving the Net*. New York: Council on Foreign Relations, 1996.

Simon, Denis Fred, and Kau, Michael Ying-mao, eds. *Taiwan: Beyond the Economic Miracle*. Armonk, NY: M.E. Sharpe, 1992.

Su, Ge. *Mei-kuo tui-Hua cheng-ts'e yu T'ai-wan wen-t'i* [American China policy and the Taiwan issue]. Beijing: Shih-chieh chih-shih, 1998.

Tien, Hung-mao. *The Great Transition: Political and Social Change in the Republic of China.* Stanford, CA: Hoover Institution Press, 1989.

Tien, Hung-mao, ed. *Taiwan's Electoral Politics and Democratic Transition: Riding the Third Wave.* Armonk, NY: M.E. Sharpe, 1996.

Wu, Jaushieh Joseph, ed. *Divided Nations: The Experience of Germany, Korea, and China.* Taipei: Institute of International Relations, 1995.

Yamamoto, Yoshinobu. 1998. "Security Cooperation in Northeast Asia." Paper presented at the 12th Asia Pacific Roundtable, Kuala Lumpur, Malaysia, May 31– June 4, 1998.

Yang, Maysing, ed. *Taiwan's Expanding Role in the International Arena.* Armonk, NY: M.E. Sharpe, 1997.

16

Confidence-Building Measures in the South China Sea

Chien Chung

Introduction

In post-Cold War Asia, hundreds of coral reefs, sand cays, and tropical islets in the South China Sea have emerged as new flash points of low-intensity, regional armed conflict. On-line surveillance by low-orbit space satellites has revealed that research ships, reconnaissance aircraft, and troop supply convoys from neighboring countries have been strengthening their territorial control and searching for oil and gas resources under the vast ocean sea-bed.

The trouble looming in this region of the South China Sea stems from territorial, jurisdictional, and sovereign dispute involving seven neighboring countries: Brunei, the People's Republic of China (PRC), Taiwan, Indonesia, Malaysia, the Philippines, and Vietnam. The situation is further complicated by the expansionism and regionalism practiced by the PRC and the Association of SouthEast Asian Nations (ASEAN), respectively, in the strategic South China Sea, through which at least several hundred commercial ships pass each day. Because each claimant has been busy maintaining its military presence, a full-scale economic development in the disputed waters has been either delayed or hampered. To reduce the tension and eventually diffuse the conflict, confidence-building measures (CBMs), such as shelving the territorial sovereignty issue, should be established—only after that can the South China Sea be effectively developed jointly by the claimants into a zone of peace, freedom, and neutrality (Song 1995).

All the claimants around the South China Sea have expressed their willingness to resolve the disputes on the basis of international law, particularly the United Nations Convention on the Law of the Sea (UNCLOS). The 1982 UNCLOS has become one of the most important legal instruments to establish order in the oceans, including the South China Sea. All claimants except the Republic of China (ROC) have adopted the various provisions of the UNCLOS, either nationally or regionally. But because claimants are implementing the provisions in their own way, however, differences in interpretation or application of UNCLOS provisions may lead to eventual conflict. Accordingly, it is important for the South China Sea countries, especially those having ratified UNCLOS, to discuss and exchange views on how each one plans to implement the provisions. In this way, mutual understanding can be enhanced and misapprehension prevented (Song 1995).

Moreover, the South China Sea countries, both claimants and nonclaimants, have launched dialogues designed to increase the prospects for peace and cooperation in the region. Principles for a code of conduct in the South China Sea may be agreed upon between various parties in the future. It is also true that the claimants' endeavors to establish CBMs in the South China Sea and to transform it into an area of active cooperation have been accorded worldwide appreciation as a good example of preventive diplomacy. Moreover, these efforts are vitally needed, and the continued prosperity of this region depends in large measure on the maintenance of peace and stability in the South China Sea. For that matter, global security and economic growth cannot be assured unless the guns remain silent in this highly strategic corner of the world. (Morris 1993).

This chapter will review the origins of territorial, jurisdictional, and sovereign disputes, the navigational freedom and security of sea lanes of communication, and the rich hydrocarbon resources in the South China Sea. It will discuss various CBMs designed to resolve disputes as well as to seek ways to promote cooperation through dialogue, both formal and informal, bilateral and multilateral. Finally, it will suggest possible ways to build up mutual confidence among claimants in the disputed waters in the context of a new order established in the impetus of change in the South China Sea security environment.

The Security Environment in the South China Sea

Issues involving territorial disputes and sovereignty claims have been major causes of regional conflict and international tension. In the South China Sea, such causes are further complicated by the strategic importance of the sea lanes of communication and the huge oil and natural gas resources therein. There are various potential disputes in the South China Sea region that may lead to low-intensity armed conflict or even high-intensity conventional war.

These include territorial, political, and jurisdictional disputes. Thus, CBMs in the South China Sea region must be established effectively so as to avoid potential armed conflict.

Territorial disputes over the islets in the South China Sea have arisen where ownership of these islets is claimed by two or more countries. The potential conflict therefore may be bilateral or multilateral in nature (Valencia 1988). Disputes over the Paracel and Spratly Islands and more recently over the Scarborough Reef in the South China Sea have seriously hindered the creation of a security environment in this region. Brunei, the PRC, and the ROC, Indonesia, Malaysia, the Philippines, and Vietnam claim either part or all of the islets, reefs, and the attendant maritime area. The sea-bed around the Spratly Islands, together with the Paracel Islands and Scarborough Reef, is thought to contain rich oil and gas resources. Claimants have tried to bolster their sovereignty claims in many ways, including occupying and fortifying islets by military force; building up submerged rocks and shoals, erecting markers, or even using military force to resolve the disputes.[1] Troops of competing claimants have occupied the features in a patchwork pattern, and armed conflict, which will only encourage new political and economic divisions, may occur again (Greenburger 1992).

A second source of potential armed conflict in the South China Sea may be either political or strategic (Valencia and Marsh 1986). In addition to the claimants' interests in the islands themselves, disputes could arise over the navigational interests and the security of the sea lanes of communication. Recently, political and security relations between the South China Sea nations have improved considerably, as have relations between ASEAN and non-Southeast Asian countries around the South China Sea. ASEAN is increasing in strength and is expanding its activities and membership, and the increased cohesion among Southeast Asians provides a strong impetus for more cooperative efforts.[2] Nonetheless, political and security relations between the South China Sea countries and the great powers outside the region remain uncertain, particularly in view of both existing conflicts and potential conflicts in the region. Potential conflict in the South China Sea could arise from the redistribution of the roles of the major powers in the area, especially that of the United States, Japan, Russia, and certain European nations.

A possible, but sensitive, source of cooperation arises from the shared exploitation and utilization of resources, either in the form of fisheries or minerals (Valencia 1985, 80–83). Perhaps the most significant minerals beneath the sea-bed of the South China Sea are the hydrocarbon resources. Up to 17 percent of the world's remaining recoverable crude oil is believed to be deposited under the South China Sea (Du 1994). Claimants have established scientific stations on the reefs, incorporated the claimed areas into nearby provinces, published maps showing claims, released historical documents to substantiate claims, allowed tourists and journalists to visit the disputed islets, and even granted concessions to oil companies in claimed areas. In addition, coastal countries have been willing to cooperate in the management of the living resources, in the conduct of marine research, in protecting and preserving marine environments, and in inviting other regional or nonregional organizations as non-South China Sea countries to participate in the joint venture.

These multiple sources of conflict are the concern of all countries in the region and therefore require discussion by all concerned, as they could lead to conflict on a global scale. In addition, the nature of these conflicts may disturb the interests of nonregional countries and invite the involvement of non-South China Sea nations. For these reasons, resolving the issues of potential multiple conflicts in the South China Sea is a most challenging problem.

Territorial Disputes in the South China Sea

In the 3.6 million km² South China Sea, seven countries are engaged in either bilateral or multilateral sovereignty disputes over islets, reefs, banks and shoals. Currently, the disputed portions in the South China Sea having economic and strategic importance are the Pratas Islands, the Paracel Islands, Macclesfield Bank, Scarborough Reef, and the Spratly Islands, as illustrated in Figure 16.1. The most complicated dispute is over the Spratly Islands and its attendant maritime area, where the competing claimants include Brunei, the PRC, the ROC, Indonesia, Malaysia, the Philippines, and Vietnam.

The People's Republic of China

The People's Republic of China has made sweeping claims to most of the South China Sea, often illustrated by a map showing a U-shaped historical claim line that encompasses much of the continental shelves (Figure 16.2A). In particular, China claims all the islets and submerged features of the Spratly Islands (Nansha Qundao) on the basis of historical discovery and use (Chen 1993). Although the claim is based on grounds of ancient exploration, China's modern claim stems from 1950, when the People's Liberation Army (PLA) took over part of the Paracel Islands (Xisha Qundao) from the retreating Nationalist troops.[3] In a brief but decisive battle, the PLA drove away all the South Vietnamese occupants of the Paracel Islands and subsequently

Figure 16.1 **Disputed Waters in the South China Sea**
(Major sea-lanes of communication are indicated by dashed lines; areas where
the Taiwanese merchantmen and trawlers were interdicted by the People's
Liberation Army [PLA] naval gunboats between 1992 and 1997 are marked by
stars.)

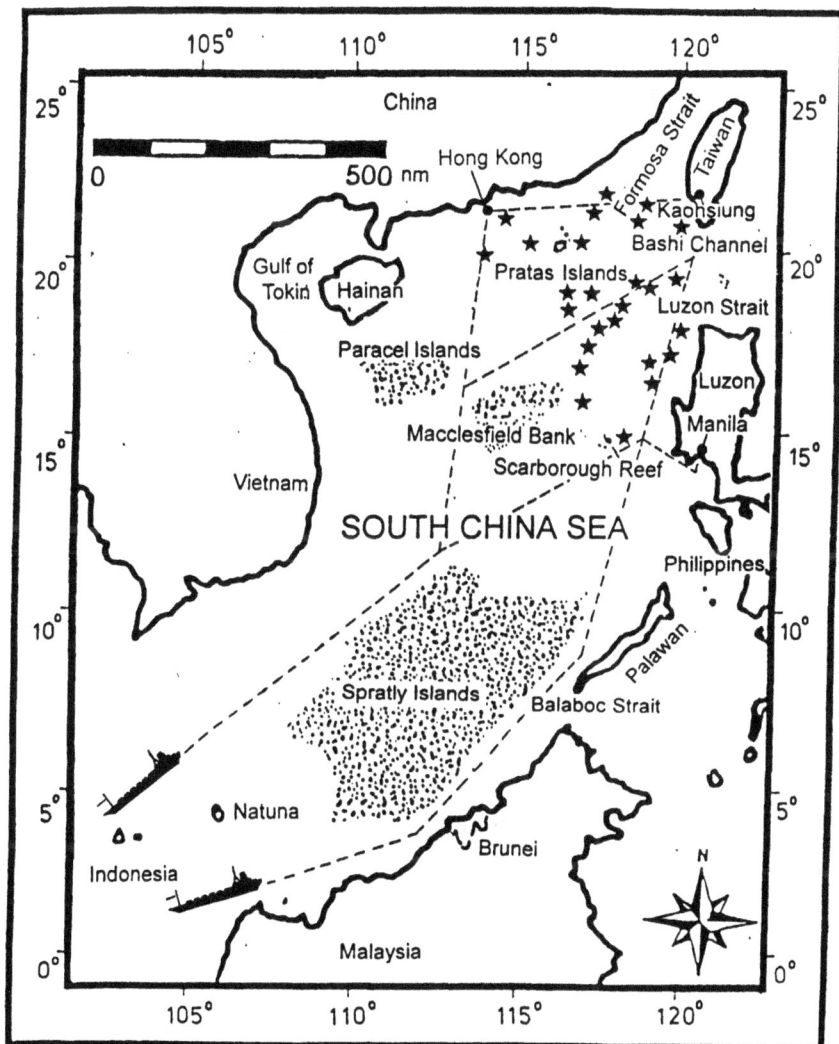

acquired control over the islands in January 1974, despite the long-standing
claims of Vietnam and Taiwan. China has recently fortified the Paracel Islands,
and satellite photos have revealed that the PLA had constructed a 2,700-
meter runway and a deep-water harbor on the Woody Islet (Yongxing Dao).

Ships and aircraft of the PLA's South Sea Fleet have been stationed there since 1994.

In late 1987, China began to install troops on some unoccupied reefs in the Spratly Islands. A naval skirmish with Vietnamese forces ensued when the PLA landing party stormed the Johnson South Reef (Chiqua Jiao) on March 14, 1988. Within a year, the PLA occupied seven reefs and rocks in the Spratly Islands, and constructed a naval depot on the Fiery Cross Reef (Yongshu Jiao) with a 300 meter pier capable of handling 4,000-ton landing ships, a helicopter pad, and an oceanographic observation station (Gallagher 1994).

In 1994, PLA naval militia occupied the Mischief Reef (Meiji Jiao) in the Spratly Islands, only 124 nautical miles from the Philippines' Palawan Island. In February 1995, the Philippines accused China of occupying its territory, a charge that soon escalated into a regional incident. This incident brought the PLA into conflict with not only the Philippines but also Taiwan and Vietnam: The unfortunate Mischief Reef (da Vanh Khah in Vietnamese, Meichi Chiao in Taiwanese, Panganiban in Filipino) is claimed by all these countries.

The Republic of China

Taiwan (ROC) has South China Sea claims identical to those of China. Nationalist troops took over some islets in the South China Sea after the end of World War II and withdrew to Taiwan in 1950. In 1956, the Nationalists returned to the Spratly Islands, and they arrested but immediately released settlers from the Philippines who had settled on the islands. The troops stationed themselves on the Itu Aba Islet (Taiping Tao), the largest islet in the Spratly Islands, which is also claimed by Vietnam, the Philippines, and China. This fortified islet has enough water and food for a garrison of up to 800 troops, and it has direct postal and satellite communication links between Taiwan and the personnel stationed on the islet (Valencia 1995, 8–24). Taiwanese authorities planned to build airstrips, harbors, lighthouses, and resort hostels on this tropical paradise.

Taiwan also stationed troops on the Pratas Islet (Tungsha Tao), which is also claimed by China. Although the modernized ROC armed forces are more than capable of using force to gain some control over the Spratly Islands, using the 1,750 meter runway on the Pratas Islet as a staging base, it nevertheless has refrained from using force to resolve island-related disputes. At the height of the Mischief Reef incident, Taiwan recalled three police patrol vessels heading for the area in the face of protests from both Vietnam and the Philippines, thus immediately diffusing the tension that could have led to an international armed conflict.[4]

Figure 16.2 **(A) Historical Waters Claimed by both the PRC and ROC in the South China Sea, and (B) Exclusive Economic Zone (EEZ) Claimed by Vietnam, the Philippines, Malaysia, Brunei, and Indonesia.**
(Their claims not only overlap one another, but are also well within the area of the historical waters claimed by the PRC and the ROC.)

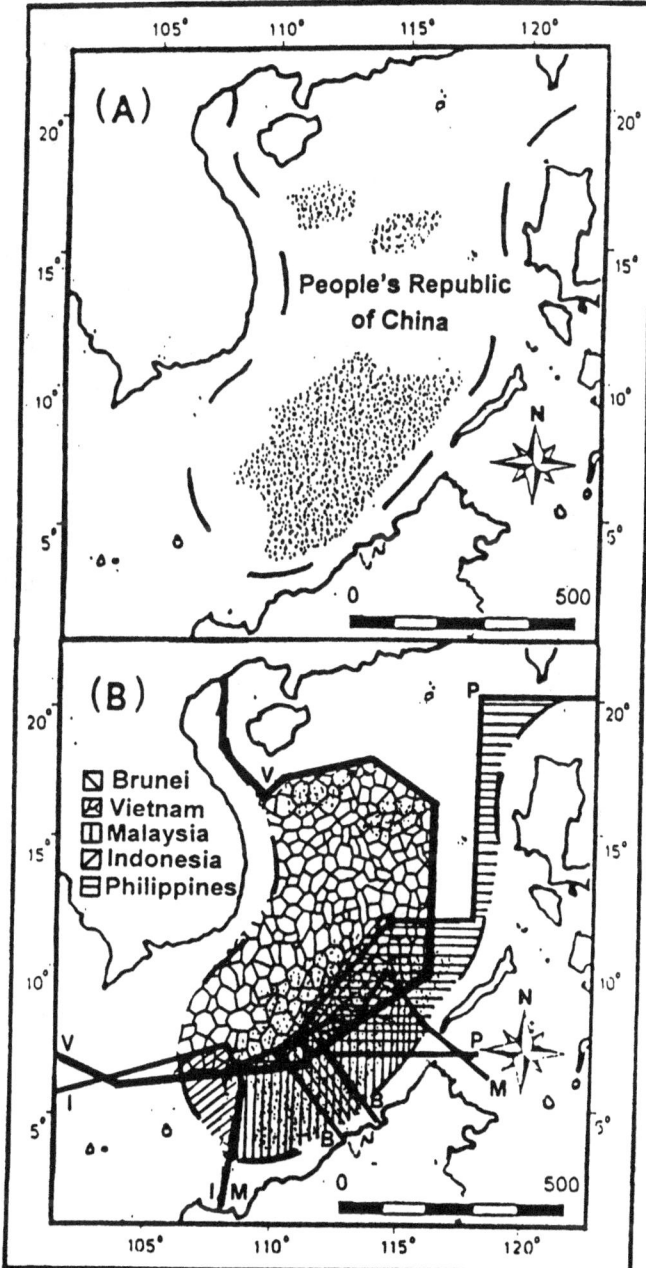

Vietnam

Vietnam has fewer claims in the South China Sea than China and Taiwan, but it claims both the Paracel and Spratly Islands on the same basis of historical discovery and use (Figure 16.2B). Military occupation by French colonial troops dates back to 1933, and Vietnamese settlers subsequently landed on both the Paracel Islands (Quan Dao Hoang Sa) and the Spratly Islands (Quan Dao Truong Sa). After a brief Japanese occupation during World War II, French colonial forces retook the islands and subsequently were replaced by the South Vietnamese Army. In January 1974, the Chinese expelled the Vietnamese from the Paracel Islands, but Vietnam dispatched more troops farther southward on the islets scattered among the Spratly Islands. Today, Vietnamese forces occupy more than 24 islets in the contested islands.

To augment its settlement in the South China Sea, Vietnam has constructed research stations, an airstrip, and a fishing port on the Spratly Islet (Dao Truong Sa). In December 1992, Vietnam invited foreign journalists to visit this fortified islet, which the Philippines, China, and Taiwan immediately protested (Smith 1992). Vietnam also constructed a lighthouse and a scientific station on the Amboyna Cay (Dao An Bang), which is also claimed by Malaysia, the Philippines, China, and Taiwan.

Vietnam is also engaged in a dispute with China concerning the maritime boundary of the Gulf of Tonkin, an important area in the South China Sea. Vietnam lacks the naval and air superiority to enforce its claims in the South China Sea. In addition, as the Vietnamese armed forces are primarily a coastal-defense force, they lack the capability to project force into the South China Sea or farther afield and would be overwhelmed in any island conflict with either China or Taiwan. Although Vietnam joined ASEAN in July 1995, it cannot rely on ASEAN for help in resolving this dispute.

The Philippines

The Philippines claims a smaller portion of the South China Sea and only a portion of the Spratly Islands (Kalayaan Group). The Philippines has justified its claim to this area by arguing that it is vital to its security and economic survival, that the area does not legally belong to any other country, and that claims by other nations had been abandoned (Valencia 1993). The Philippines announced its intention to annex the Kalayaan Group as early as 1946, and subsequently sent settlers to some islets. They were driven off by a Taiwanese naval task force. It was not until 1970 that the Philippines military began to occupy the northeastern portion of the Spratly Islands, and today they have fortified nine islets and reefs to protect their strategic interest in the attendant maritime area (Figure 16.2 B).

During the Mischief Reef incident, the Philippines reinforced its defense forces in the fortified Thitu Islet (Pagasa) (*Japan Times* 1995a). Nonetheless, a similar incident in the near future would not lead to a major armed conflict, because the Philippines is the country least prepared militarily to defend or assert its interests against the competing claimants of Vietnam, Malaysia, China, and Taiwan. Despite its inferior military capabilities, the Philippines continues to exercise its jurisdiction over the Kalayaan Group by conducting elections among settlers, developing tourism, and building lighthouses in the Reed, Nares, and Seahorse Banks at the corners of the Kalayaan Group as a legal basis for claiming sovereignty (Reuters 1995b).

Malaysia

Malaysia claims nine features outright in the southern Spratly Islands because they fall within its continental shelf boundary. The southernmost territory claimed by both China and Taiwan, James Shoal (Zengmu Ansha), is also situated on Malaysia's continental shelf and only 63 nautical miles from the Sarawak coast. To back up its claim, Malaysia has sent troops to occupy five features since 1977; its maritime boundary in the southern part of Spratly Islands is illustrated in Figure 16.2B.

In 1991, Malaysia announced that the occupied islet of Swallow Reef (Terumbu Layang Layang) had been converted into a tourist resort for divers, and that the airstrip on the islet was capable of handling small civilian aircraft (*Far Eastern Economic Review* 1991). To promote tourism, Malaysia's government officials and journalists visited the 17-room resort hostel, prompting the competing claimants to protest. The promotion of tourism on Swallow Reef—the only islet that has been opened to international visitors so far among the disputed islands in the South China Sea—demonstrated Malaysia's intention to prove that the reef can sustain economic life by itself, and thus can fulfill the minimum requirement of UNCLOS to generate its own 200-nautical mile (nm) Exclusive Economic Zone (EEZ).

Brunei

Brunei claims an EEZ in the form of a corridor extending to the south of the Spratly Islands, and beyond its coast to include the Rifleman Bank (Defense Mapping Agency 1991) (Figure 16.2B). Brunei's claim not only overlaps with the historical waters of Taiwan and China, but also contains the unoccupied Louisa Reef, which has been given different names by three other claimants (Terumbu Semarang Barat Kecil by Malaysia, Nantong Jiao by China, and Nantung Chiao by Taiwan). In addition, Brunei's extended maritime boundary also overlaps with those claimed by the Philippines and Vietnam, resulting in six competing claims in a remote corner of the South China Sea.

Indonesia

Indonesia has a more direct stake in the South China Sea dispute because the historical waters boundary claimed by both China and Taiwan apparently encompasses Indonesia's Natuna attendant maritime area, a region as large as 75,000 km^2. Although Indonesia neither claims nor occupies any reefs or rocks in the Spratly Islands, its maritime boundary in the South China Sea also overlaps with those claimed by Vietnam (Figure 16.2B). These disputes, despite Indonesia's intention to broker a resolution, remain unsettled (*Japan Times* 1995b).

Today, up to 65 islets, reefs, and rocks in the South China Sea are occupied by military troops flying different national flags. Table 16.1 lists the occupied portions and their concomitant territorial disputes.[5] There are, however, more than a hundred unoccupied reefs and rocks not listed in Table 16.1. These may someday be fortified by a claimant's military troops, thus worsening the already volatile situation in the South China Sea.

The Sea-Lanes of Communication in the South China Sea

China is one of the littoral countries of the South China Sea. The vast historical waters it claims not only contain rich mineral and fishery reserves but also offer advantages for transportation and trade. Safeguarding the sea-lanes of communication in the South China Sea is a vital interest for China and other concerned countries. Once each nation realizes the importance of maritime interests, freedom of navigation and the security of the sea-lanes of communication in the region become major issues involving both competing claimants with territorial disputes and the major powers that utilize the South China Sea for various strategic purposes.

Recently, China has shifted its naval strategy from coastal defense to offshore defense, upgrading its green water fleet into a blue water task force. The explicit task for the PLA navy is "deterring and defending against enemy invasions from the sea, fighting a local war on the sea, ensuring national reunification with Taiwan, maintaining territorial integrity, in pursuit of maritime interests, and promoting peace in the world" (Cheng 1992). Its task specifically covers both the South China Sea and the Taiwan Strait, and its navy can be used to protect China's merchant marines; the same naval task force can also be used for interdiction and surveillance of the sea-lanes of communication within its historical waters of the South China Sea. This dual-use strategy also includes blocking the potentially hostile global naval forces of the United States and Russia, as well as the regional naval forces of India and Japan, from approaching its seaports that face the South China Sea. When the PLA's navy completes its modernization about 2010, it may have the capability to control not only the key international shipping lanes in the South China Sea, but also those choking points surrounding the South China Sea, such as the Taiwan Strait, Bashi Channel, Luzon Strait, Balaboc Strait, and the Strait of Malacca, thereby enhancing China's power and influence (Liao 1995).

Importance of the Sea-Lanes of Communication

The most frequently used routes for trade and communication among Europe, the Middle East, and the Far East are the sea-lanes that stretch from Singapore to the Bashi Channel in the South China Sea; up to 700 ships pass through these sea-lanes daily. En route to their final destination, some of the commercial ships make a port of call around the South China Sea, such as Hong Kong and Manila (Figure 16.1).

These sea-lanes of communication are used not only by the South China Sea countries but also by others. For instance, tankers transport 70 percent of Japan's crude oil through the South China Sea, making these shipping lanes strategically sensitive. In addition, Taiwan very much depends on the safety of the sea-lanes in the South China Sea—a situation that fully demonstrates their significance in maritime security (Lin et al. 1995). Taiwan is a model of rapid economic growth, experiencing an average annual growth rate of more than 8 percent over the past three decades. During that time, Taiwan converted itself from an agrarian state into an industrialized nation with a gross domestic product (GDP) per capita exceeding $12,000 in 1996. Taiwan's economic structure is such that 81 percent of its GDP comes from foreign trade. Most of its export and import goods, up to 150 million tons each year, are shipped by merchant marines, while only 0.8 million tons of cargo are transported by air. Furthermore, 75 percent of this sea cargo is shipped via the shipping lanes in the South China Sea.

Perhaps the most sensitive cargo upon which Taiwan depends is crude oil. Because Taiwan has no recoverable oil reserves, every single drop of crude oil used has to be imported. Each day Taiwan imports an average of 588,310 barrels of crude oil, 98 percent via the shipping lanes in the South China Sea (67 percent comes from the Middle East, 12 percent from Africa, 2 percent from the North Sea, and 17 percent from Southeast Asian countries). Any disruption or even delay of these shipments could have a catastrophic impact on Taiwan's economy (Chung 1994b).

Table 16.1

Occupied Features with Territorial Dispute in the South China Sea[a]

Location (latitude, longitude)	English	Chinese	Vietnamese	Filipino	Malaysian	Area (km²)	Present occupants[c] (yr)
	Pratas Islands		—[a]	—	—	1.14	
20°43'N,116°44'E	Pratas Islet		—	—	—	1.14	ROC(46)
	Paracel Islands		**Hoang Sa**	—	—	7.62	
17°04'N,111°28'E	North Reef		Bai Da Bac	—	—	—	PRC(50)
16°59'N,112°16'E	Tree Islet		Cay	—	—	—	PRC(50)
16°59'N,112°13'E	West Sand Cay		Tay	—	—	—	PRC(50)
16°50'N,112°20'E	Woody Islet		Phu Lam	—	—	1.88	PRC(50)
16°40'N,112°44'E	Lincoln Islet		Linh Con	—	—	1.60	PRC(50)
16°34'N,112°39'E	Pyramid Rock		Thap	—	—	—	PRC(50)
16°32'N,111°36'E	Pattle Islet		Hoang Sa	—	—	0.31	PRC(74)
16°31'N,111°35'E	Robert Islet		Huu Nhat	—	—	0.30	PRC(74)
16°28'N,111°44'E	Drummond Islet		Duy Mong	—	—	—	PRC(74)
16°28'N111°42'E	Duncan Islet		Quang Hoa	—	—	0.28	PRC(74)
16°27'N111°41'E	Palm Islet		Chim Yen	—	—	0.06	PRC(74)
16°27'N,111°36'E	Antelope Reef		n.a.	—	—	—	PRC(74)
16°27'N,111°31'E	Money Islet		Quant Anh	—	—	0.36	PRC(74)
16°03'N,112°27'E	Bombay Reef		Con Bong Bay	—	—	—	PRC(50)
16°03'N,111°46'E	Pasu Peak Reef		Bach Quy	—	—	0.40	PRC(50)
15°47'N,111°12'E	Triton Islet		Tri Ton	—	—	1.24	PRC(50)
	Macclesfield Bank						
15°06'N,117°50'E	Scarborough Reef		—	—	—	—	

Coordinates	Spratly Islands	Truong Sa	Kalayaan			
				n.a.	2.08	P(71)
11°28'N,114°21'E	Northeast Cay	Song Tu Dong	Parola			
11°26'N,114°20'E	Southwest Cay	Song Tu Tay	Pugad	—	0.187	V(74)
11°23'N,114°18'E	South Reef	Nam	n.a.	—	0.132	V(88)
11°05'N,115°01'E	West York Islet	Ben Lac	Likas	—	—	P(71)
11°03'N,114°17'E	Thitu Islet	Thi Tu	Pagasa	—	0.157	P(71)
10°54'N,114°06'E	Subi Reef	Su Bi	n.a.	—	0.326	PRC(88)
10°52'N,114°55'E	Irving Reef	Ca Nham	Balagta	—	—	P(78)
10°49'N,115°51'E	Flat Islet	Binh Nguyen	Patag	—	—	P(70)
10°45'N,115°49'E	Nashan Islet	Vinh Vien	Lawek	—	—	P(70)
10°44'N,114°31'E	Lankiam Cay	Bo Loai Ta	Panata	—	0.063	P(78)
10°43'N,114°20'E	Loaita SW Reef	Loai Ta Nam	n.a.	—	—	P(78)
10°41'N,114°25'E	Loaita Islet	Hon Loai Ta	Kota	—	0.101	P(71)
10°24'N,114°34'E	Petley Reef	Nui Thi	n.a.	—	—	V(88)
10°23'N,114°28'E	Sandy Cay	Son Ca	Truman	—	0.051	V(73)
10°23'N,114°21'E	Itu Aba	Ba Binh	Ligaw	—	0.498	ROC(46)
10°21'N,114°42'E	Eldad Reef	Uncoy	Erenesto	—	—	V(88)
10°12'N,114°13'E	Gaven Reef	Ga Ven	Citizen	—	—	PRC(88)
10°11'N,114°22'E	Namyit Islet	Hon Nam Yit	Binago	—	0.076	V(74)
10°01'N,113°52'E	Discovery Great Reef	Lon	Paredes	—	—	V(88)
10°01'N,114°02'E	Discovery Small Reef	Nho	n.a.	—	—	V(88)
9°55'N,114°29'E	Hughs Reef	Ba Bau	n.a.	—	—	PRC(88)
9°54'N,114°35'E	Gralarson Reef	Sinh Tonh Dong	n.a.	—	—	V(78)
9°53'N,114°27'E	Kennan Reef	Ken Nan	n.a.	—	—	PRC(88)
9°52'N,114°19'E	Sin Cowe Islet	Sinh Tonh	Rurok	—	0.016	V(73)
9°52'N,115°31'E	Mischief Reef	Vanh Khan	Panganiban	—	—	PRC(94)
9°45'N,114°15'E	Collins Reef	Co Lin	Mabini	—	—	V(88)
9°45'N,114°21'E	Lansdowne Reef	Len Bao	n.a.	—	—	V(88)
9°43'N,114°18'E	Johnsons Reef	Gac Ma	n.a.	—	—	PRC(88)
9°40'N,113°02'E	Fiery Cross Reef	Chu Thap	Katigingan	—	—	PRC(88)
8°58'N,113°44'E	Pearson Reef	Phan Vinh	Hizon	—	0.0005	V(87)
8°55'N,112°24'E	London Central Reef	Truong Sa Dong	Gitna	—	—	V(88)

(continued)

Table 16.1 (continued)

Location (latitude, longitude)	Names given by claimants[a]					Area (km²)	Present occupants[b] (yr)
	English	Chinese	Vietnamese	Filipino	Malaysian		
8°52'N,112°13'E	London W. Reef		Da Tay	Quezon	—	—	V(88)
8°52'N,114°39'E	Tennent Reef		Tien Nu	Tennent	—	—	V(88)
8°50'N,113°59'E	Alison Reef		Toc Tan	De Jesus	—	—	V(88)
8°50'N,112°34'E	London E. Reef		Dong	Silangan	—	—	V(88)
8°47'N,114°1'E	Cornwallis S. Reef		Nui Le	n.a.	—	—	V(88)
8°47'N,112°50'E	Cuarteron Reef		Chau Vien	Calderon	—	—	PRC(88)
8°38'N,110°55'E	Spratly Islet		Truong Sa	Lagos	—	0.148	V(73)
8°38'N,110°40'E	Ladd Reef		Da Lat	n.a.	—	—	V(88)
8°22'N,115°10'E	Commodore Reef		Cong Do	Rizal	Laksamana	0.0006	P(80)
8°13'N,113°15'E	Barque Canada Reef		Thuyen Chai	Magsaysay	Perahu	—	V(87)
7°59'N,113°56'E	Mariveles Reef		Ky Van	Mariveles	Mantanani	—	M(86)
7°56'N,111°43'E	Bombay Castle Reef		Vung May	n.a.	n.a.	—	V(89)
7°53'N,112°55'E	Amboyna Cey		An Bang	Kalantiyaw	Amboyna	0.015	V(75)
7°38'N,113°56'E	Ardasier Reef		Bai Kleu Ngua	Antonio Luna	Ubi	—	M(86)
7°38'N,113°48'E	Dallas Reef		Kleu Ngua	—	Laya	—	M(87)
7°25'N,113°50'E	Swallow Reef		Hoa Lau	—	Layang Layang	0.062	M(77)
6°57'N,113°30'E	Royal Charlotte Reef		Sac Lot	—	Barat Besar	—	M(87)

[a]Data updated from the compilation in note 23.
[b]Local names for the feature from multiple claimants are given; both the PRC and the ROC claim Chinese features.
[c]Occupants: ROC, Republic of China on Taiwan; PRC, People's Republic of China; M, Malaysia; P, Philippines; V, Vietnam.
— Indicates the country has no claim.

Taiwan's long-time adversary, the People's Republic of China, can cut off the sea-lanes stretching from the seaports of Taiwan through the Spratlys and beyond to the mainland. Despite the formidable firepower of its modernized navy and air force, Taiwan cannot flex its muscles at anytime and anyplace beyond the area 200 nm off the coast of Taiwan. The PLA navy in the South China Sea, in contrast, can use wolf pack tactics to harass the Taiwanese merchant marines in the sea-lanes at any time (Chung 1996a, 1996b, 1996c).

These concerns about the security of the sea-lanes are based on several incidents over the past several years. Between 1992 and 1996, 134 Taiwanese fishing boats and merchant marines were harassed, inspected, detained, rammed, and fired upon by PLA naval vessels in the northern part of the South China Sea. These interdictions were clustered in a triangular area bounded by Hong Kong, Manila, and Kaohsiung (Figure 16.1). In only a very few cases did Taiwan's navy arrive in time to chase away the harassing PLA naval gunboats. The worst incident occurred on January 27, 1996, when the Panamanian-registered merchant *Ocean Glory No. 9* was chased and machine-gunned by a Chinese gunboat 45 nm off the southern tip of Taiwan in the South China Sea (*United Daily News* 1996b). The severity of the incident is not mitigated by the gunboat's flight to the mainland coast prior to the arrival of two guided-missile destroyers of the Taiwanese navy.

In addition, the Taiwanese trawler *Yung Fa Chen No. 1* was rammed and inspected by a PRC gunboat on January 21, 1997. As the harassment occurred 90 nm off the Pratas Islet, well beyond the reach of Taiwan's navy, no rescue team could be organized to approach the trawler in time (*United Daily News* 1997a). And during the night of July 13, 1997, the Taiwanese trawler *Chi Hong Ching No. 37* was surrounded by four PLA naval gunboats 160 nm south of the Pratas Islet; at gunpoint, Taiwanese fishermen were forced to give up their food, drinking water, and cash in exchange for their immediate release.

Whether this systematic harassment of Taiwanese merchant vessels in the South China Sea is the coordinated effort of the central government in Beijing or just the undisciplined behavior of local warlords remains to be seen. It is also possible that trigger-happy low-level functionaries initiated these incidents without the knowledge or consent of their superior commanders. Whatever the case, these incidents clearly indicate that China has the capability, experience, and the will to interrupt Taiwan's sea-lanes of communication in the South China Sea whenever it chooses. To cope with this explicit threat, Taiwanese President Lee Teng-hui announced that the government will accelerate the naval buildup program so that its fighting ships can escort Taiwanese merchant vessels throughout the South China Sea to ensure the security of the sea-lanes of communication.[6]

Freedom of Navigation

Taiwan is not the only state whose shipping lanes in the South China Sea have been threatened by China. Other South China Sea countries, particularly those with territorial disputes with China, have expressed their concerns over freedom of navigation. Even nonclaimant states such as Singapore have expressed grave concerns to China for the safety and freedom of navigation endangered by the increasing harassment in sea lanes. The prime minister of Singapore, for example, has warned China that its increasing military assertiveness and concomitant economic development in the South China Sea have aroused feelings of great unease in the region (Reuters 1995a).

Although the Chinese PLA is using its antiquated gunboats to threaten the safety of the sea-lanes of communication, it is well on its way to developing a blue-water navy, projecting its firepower into the entire South China Sea and beyond. The PLA navy is building new destroyers and frigates equipped with advanced radar, missiles, and electronic gear, and purchasing two *Soveremenny*-class missile destroyers and four *Kilo*-class advanced submarines from Russia (Sharpe 1997, 113–40). When the 300 Russian Su-27 long-range fighter-bombers it has ordered become combat-ready about 2000, the military balance in the South China Sea will be altered decisively. Already, the PLA has based a rapid-response force on Hainan Island, a force capable of undertaking multiple landings against atoll garrisons with guaranteed success.

The aggressive actions of the PLA in the South China Sea have rattled other claimants and have drawn the attention of the United States and even Russia. These countries all depend on clear and secure shipping lanes for communication between European and Asian trade partners. For the first time, the notion of a credible "China threat" to the region is gaining currency. As a consequence, a small-scale regional arms race is underway. Malaysia has considered acquiring more MiG-29 fighter aircraft's from Russia; approval was granted in October 1996 for the acquisition of two uncompleted *Meko*-class 3,360-ton frigates from Argentina. Vietnam has rearmed its air force with a few Su-27 advanced fighter-bombers, in addition to licensing the production of two Russian designed BPS-500 class missile corvettes. The Philippines plans to purchase second-hand F-5E interceptors (at bargain-basement prices) to strengthen its air defense, while its navy just completed the acquisition of three *Peacock*-class 700-ton corvettes from the United Kingdom.[7] Recently, Indonesia decided to purchase 12 Russian-made Su-30K fighter-bombers, which will be deployed at Ujung Pandang in Sulawesi to protect its oil fields in the South China Sea (*China Times* 1997b, Reuters 1997b). Even the 800-man Brunei navy has ordered three 1,500-ton missile corvettes from a Scotland shipyard.

These claimants have faced off against Chinese and Taiwanese vessels in the South China Sea on a number of occasions. On March 23,1995, Malaysian navy patrol boats opened fire on a Chinese trawler off Sarawak, injuring four crew members (*China News* 1995). On July 7, 1996, Malaysian gunboats again opened fire on a Taiwanese fishing boat, *Chih Chi No. 16*, 150 nm off the Swallow Reef (*China Times* 1996). In December 1995, Vietnamese patrol boats and PLA naval vessels confronted each other near a Chinese drilling platform on the Vanguard Bank of the Spratlys (*United Daily News* 1996).

The most violent of these incidents was the gun battle between a Philippine patrol boat and Chinese vessels (*China Post* 1996). In the early hours of January 22, 1996, a Philippine naval patrol boat, *PG-381*, spotted two suspicious ships 11 nm off the Luzon coast on the South China Sea side. Although the *PG-381* fired a warning shot to stop the ships for inspection, the two vessels, later identified as an armed trawler from China and a PLA navy gunboat, tried to ram the Philippine boat. A battle ensued for about 90 minutes as the two sides engaged in heavy gunfire. The engagement broke off only when the *PG-381* ran out of fuel while in pursuit, and the weapons of the Chinese vessels became either jammed or were knocked out. Six months prior to this conflict, however, China and the Philippines had announced a code of conduct renouncing the use of force to settle disputes. Before making the announcement, the Chinese foreign minister remarked that China had always attached great importance to the safety and freedom of navigation in the South China Sea, and that there were unlikely to be any problems in this regard (Richardson 1995).

The most feared scenario in the South China Sea is the one in which the frequency and the scale of violent incidents increase, endangering freedom of navigation along strategic sea-lanes, and eventually involving the United States and Japan. For these reasons, China is unlikely to move in an exceptionally aggressive manner, although it quite possibly will conduct naval maneuvers with the intention to test and warn other concerned countries. External powers like the United States and Japan have clear security and economic interests in maintaining freedom of navigation in the South China Sea.

In June 1995, the American assistant secretary of defense stated that "if military conflict occurred in the Spratlys and interfered with freedom of the seas, [the United States] would be prepared to escort and make sure that free navigation continues" (Holloway 1995). For economic and security reasons, the United States requires free, flexible, and, for its nuclear submarines, undetected passage in the South China Sea. Recent events, such as the Taiwan Strait crisis in March 1996, have led it to alter its policy from passive neutrality to active neutrality. China's accelerating economic and military modernization make it more reliant on the shipping lanes in the South China Sea for trade and communication. If such strategic importance becomes acute, border disputes, verbal warnings, military posturing, and the decisive use of force toward Japan-Taiwan-ASEAN-United States coordination on security matters may follow. China might quickly seek a settlement by a preemptive, surgical strike with conventional forces.

As the PLA navy ventures farther offshore it is bound to enter the Indian and Japanese maritime spheres of interest. Thus, although the U.S.-Japanese security relationship remains strong, Japan has insisted on building up its own navy and air force with long-range escort capabilities to protect its maritime trade routes. Inevitably, because the PLA will also encounter American naval forces, the United States is drawn into the imbroglio. In fact, in joint naval exercises with some ASEAN allies in the South China Sea, the U.S. navy has cast China as the adversary and worried about a possible escalated conflict with China over the Spratlys in the near future.[8] The freedom-of-navigation issue in the South China Sea and the territorial dispute over the Spratlys have both been raised repeatedly in the ASEAN Regional Forum (ARF)—a loose grouping of 19 Pacific countries including Japan, China, the United States, and the European Union (EU)—which had been formed to discuss and enhance regional security in East Asia. In July 1997, the ARF found its collective voice on this issue by "expressing serious concern over the recent developments, which affect peace and stability in the South China Sea," and by urging promotion of CBMs and trust among the concerned parties (*China Post* 1997c).

Hydrocarbon Resources in the South China Sea

The South China Sea disputes concern not only the islands' strategic significance and sovereignty claims thereto, but also their rich reserves of both living and nonliving resources, in particular crude oil and natural gas. Securing the petroleum supply is a top priority, especially for those oil-hungry countries in the region. As the huge deposits of crude oil and natural gas in the South China Sea attract both competing claimants and major powers, future energy shortages and crises will certainly turn the South China Sea into a flash point.

World Energy Supply and Demand

Primary energy, defined as commercially available coal, crude oil, natural gas, hydroelectricity, and nuclear power, is indispensable for industrialization and economic development. Although hydroelectricity and nuclear power provide us with a renewable but limited source of energy, the bulk of the energy that the world consumes relies on the hydrocarbon resources of coal, oil and natural gas. In 1995, the world consumed primary energy at the rate of 172 million barrels of oil equivalent per day (mmboe/d), the majority in the form of hydrocarbons: crude oil (40 percent), coal (28 percent), and natural gas (23 percent); nuclear power (7 percent) and hydroelectricity (2 percent) contribute only a minor part (Energy Resources Council 1996).

The supply of hydrocarbon resources is limited, because the proven reserve of economically recoverable hydrocarbon resources, including the newly discovered Central Asia oil and gas fields, is estimated as 1,007 billion barrels of crude oil, 1,039 billion metric tons (tonnes) of coal, and 138 trillion cubic meters (m^3) of natural gas. If the world consumption rate were to remain at the current level, the remaining hydrocarbon resources could only last another 40 years for oil, 62 years for gas, and 229 years for coal.

The refined products of crude oil are burned directly by the end users, and most of them lack adequate substitutes. In the foreseeable future, aircrafts will continue to rely on jet fuel, ships on heavy oil, motor vehicles on gasoline, and diesel engines on diesel oil. The rapid depletion of irreplaceable crude oil will lead to an energy shortage as early as 2010. Although some scholars optimistically predict that ships and even cars may someday be powered by electric batteries, batteries must be recharged via the electricity supplied by power plants, many of which must burn oil to generate electricity (Fried and Trezise 1993).

Energy security has been a major issue for all concerned countries ever since the first oil crisis in 1973. In recent years, however, it has received less attention as oil prices stabilized and supplies seemed more secure. But as we look toward the next century, we cannot be smug. Many experts predict that the world is likely to become increasingly dependent on crude oil, and will rely more and more on crude oil produced from the politically volatile Middle East. Given current trends, some contend that another oil price hike will result from this coming energy shortage, followed by armed conflict to secure the remaining oil fields. Microeconomic model analysis demonstrates that a doubling of oil prices owing to an energy shortage would cut the U.S. gross domestic product (GDP) by about 5 percent after a period of 18 months. The recession that would occur in the United States would have a devastating impact on the world's economy (Clawson 1996, 3–10).

In view of the critical supply-and-demand situation for oil, the world urgently seeks an unexplored, potential rich oil reserve to gain enough time to develop such alternative energy sources as solar power and nuclear fusion. The only places with such potential are the hydrocarbon resources in the South China Sea.

Potential Reserves in the South China Sea

The potentially rich deposits of hydrocarbon resources in the South China Sea are a major factor underlying territorial disputes in the region. It is unclear how large the oil and natural gas reserves are, although the China National Offshore Oil Corporation (CNOOC) has estimated that the economically recoverable oil reserve within the historical waters claimed by China contain about 205 billion barrels of oil.[9] If this is the case, the South China Sea deposit would account for 17 percent of the world's remaining reserves. In the Spratlys region alone, the estimated quantity of recoverable oil and gas ranges from 7.7 billion to 136 billion barrels of oil equivalent. The discrepancy among various estimates is due partly to the fact that government officials tend to overestimate the size of the deposit to emphasize its strategic significance, whereas oil companies often maintain a low profile and downplay the potential size of reserves, hoping for more lucrative contract terms. This posturing may explain the difference between the estimates of government officials, who are relatively optimistic (Wu 1991), and some large oil companies, which are always pessimistic (*Asian Oil and Gas* 1992).

Independent nonregional scientific institutions may provide more reliable estimates. The Lamont Doherty Geological Observatory and the German Geological Survey both agree with Chinese government officials about the potential for huge reserves in the Spratlys. The Russian Research Institute of Geology of Foreign Countries estimated that the portion of South China Sea claimed by Vietnam could contain up to 6 billion barrels of oil equivalent, of which 70 percent could be natural gas. In the disputed area of the Vietnamese Big Bear (Dai Hung) oil field, 130 nm off the Mekong Delta in the South China Sea, the recoverable oil reserve was estimated at up to 0.8 billion barrels of oil (*Far Eastern Economic Review* 1995). And just north of the energy-rich Zengmu Basin in the Spratlys, the Chinese WAB-21 block, which covers 25,000 km^2 of the Vanguard Bank (Wan'an Tan), the Prince Consort Bank (Xiwei Tan), and the Prince of Wales Bank (Guangya Tan), has recoverable oil reserves estimated at approximately 2 billion barrels of oil by Crestone ("Active Exploration Prospects" 1994).

Another disputed issue concerns the technical difficulties involved in deep sea drilling. Although most of the confirmed oil and gas reserves in the South China Sea lie less than 100 fathoms under the continental shelf, others lie beneath the 500-fathom sea-bed in the Spratlys region. Oil companies can establish drilling platforms in the atolls, shallow shoals, and banks, but they face a deep-water drilling challenge in other oil fields. To make deep water drilling economically feasible, the size of oil and gas reserves must be large enough to justify the expenditure, perhaps totaling 1 billion barrels of oil equivalent at a lift cost of half the market price, or $9 per barrel in early 1998. One oil concessionaire has already conducted subcommercial discovery drilling in the sea bed 700 fathoms below sea level at the Northwest Palawan Basin off the northern tip of the Spratlys region, setting a record for deep sea drilling in Asia (*Offshore* 1995). Elsewhere in the world, Shell Oil has conducted exploratory drilling in 1,300 fathoms of deep water in the Mississippi Canyon, and it expects to produce crude oil commercially from such depths in the near future.

Even if the CNOOC's estimate only reflects half the actual amount of oil and gas reserves in the historical waters claimed by China, these huge reserves could only satisfy world demand for an additional four years. By the time we turn our focus from the oil-depleted Middle East to the South China Sea, perhaps about 2010, deep-sea drilling technology will have matured and the relevant difficulties overcome, enabling exploitation of the huge deposits of crude oil deep below the South China Sea.

China's Energy Strategy

China is the world's second largest energy consumer after the United States, and the third largest energy producer after the United States and Russia. In absolute terms, China appears to have an abundance of hydrocarbon resources, but on a per capita basis, its energy resources are well below the world average (Russell 1995). China's energy strategy has long been characterized by a policy of self-sufficiency and the coexistence of both large- and small-scale production and consumption. China has repeatedly expressed the importance of developing its own energy resources, including those within the historical waters of the South China Sea, and it plans to satisfy most, if not all, of its future energy demands. Its policymakers consider this self-sufficiency policy key to its successful future economic development (*Seattle Post-Intelligencer* 1994).

In 1995, primary energy consumption in China amounted to 17.4 mmboe/d, while domestic production amounted to 16.7 mmboe/d. Its energy imports of about 0.7 mmboe/d consisted almost exclusively of crude oil and refined products. China is the world's largest coal producer, with raw coal production of 1.29 billion tons in 1995 and proven coal reserves of about 144.5 billion tons in that year. It also has huge but largely undeveloped natural gas resources, with proven natural gas reserves estimated at 1.7 trillion m^3. Natural gas production was 0.02 trillion m^3 in 1995; commercial gas supplied from the oil and gas fields accounts for 69 percent of China's total domestic production (British Petroleum 1997).

The size of the oil reserves claimed by China differs from the estimates of independent sources elsewhere. The 1994 official estimate of China's total overall oil resources amounted to 686 billion barrels (*Annual Report of Chinese Petrochemistry* 1994). Although China never releases the highly classified figures of its domestic proven oil reserves, experts from British Petroleum estimate such reserves at 24 billion barrels, not including reserves in the South China Sea. Throughout the 1980s, China was a net oil exporter, with exports peaking at 0.73 million barrels of oil per day (mmbo/d) in 1985. Its oil surplus has been shrinking throughout the late 1980s and early 1990s. In 1993, China became a net oil importer for the first time (*Wall Street Journal* 1993). Starting at 0.20 mmbo/d in 1993, net oil imports dropped momentarily to less than 0.10 mmbo/d in 1994, but shot up to 0.23 mmbo/d in 1995 and climbed to 0.37 mmbo/d in 1996. The figures may increase further to 0.49 mmbo/d in 1997 (*South China Morning Post* 1997a).

China's domestic crude oil production faces a precarious situation. In northern China, production from the well-known Daqing and Shengli oil fields is stagnating, Huabei oil production is declining, and Liaohe field production is increasing only slowly. Although these four oil fields accounted for 81 percent of China's annual domestic production in 1986, they accounted for only 67 percent in 1996. In the near future, China hopes for additional production from the Xinjiang and Tarim fields in western China, some offshore fields, other marginal oil fields in southern China, and possibly from the South China Sea. Future crude oil production is estimated between 3.2 and 3.45 mmbo/d in 2000, between 3.25 and 3.6 mmbo/d in 2005, and between 3.35 and 3.75 mmbo/d in 2010 (Chao 1995).

Meanwhile, demand for petroleum products, including the direct burning of crude oil, is expected to outpace domestic production, growing at an average annual rate of 4.4 percent under the base-scenario (*New York Times* 1994). Accordingly, China is expected to increase its net oil imports to 0.76 mmbo/d in 2000, 1.9 mmbo/d in 2005, and 2.9 mmbo/d in 2010. By 2014, China's recoverable crude oil deposits will be totally exhausted, so every single drop of crude oil demanded that year, estimated at about 7.6 mmbo/d, will have to be imported if no proven reserves are discovered domestically.

Because China has been importing crude oil and refined products from the Middle East and Southeast Asian states, the sea-lanes of communication in the South China Sea have become the lifeline for its rapid economic development. By 2010, half of its oil demand, and by 2015 all of its oil demand, will be transported via the shipping lanes in the South China Sea, and China will face two critical issues: the stability of foreign oil supplies and the security of the shipping lanes. By 2010, the main suppliers to China—Iran, Iraq and Libya—will reduce their oil production rate owing to the depleting oil deposits and/or raise prices because of the high cost of recovering oil from more inaccessible reserves. And even as China secures its foreign oil supplies, it will face concerns about the safety of the shipping lanes between the Persian Gulf and its seaports facing the South China Sea. Hostile navies can easily cut off China's supply lifeline anywhere in the Indian Ocean, the South China Sea, or in the choking points of the Strait of Malacca and the Luzon Strait.

Because the substantial increase of onshore oil production on the mainland is highly unlikely, China must either reduce its oil consumption or increase its offshore oil production to promote its self-reliant, self-sufficient energy strategy and rapid economic growth. In China, petroleum consumption growth has been closely correlated with economic growth over the past two decades. This trend will remain the same in the near future because of the rapid expansion of its motor transportation and petrochemical industries. The relative demand for various petroleum products in China between 1997 and 2010 is expected to remain quite stable among diesel fuel (37 percent), gasoline (24 percent), fuel oil (15 percent), and jet fuel (4 percent) for transportation, liquid propane (10 percent) and naphtha (6 percent) for the petrochemical industry, and the remaining 4 percent for other industries (Fesharaki and Wu 1997). Transportation and industry demands for petroleum products cannot be replaced by other primary energy sources such as coal, gas, hydroelectricity, and nuclear power. The need for crude oil in China is critical, and, needless to say, reducing oil consumption is impossible.

The only way for China to maintain both its economic development and self-sufficient energy strategy is to secure the potential oil fields in the South China Sea, particularly those situated within its claimed historical waters. If the CNOOC estimate is correct, the huge deposits of crude oil within its claimed boundary, totaling 205 billion barrels, is nearly ten times its current proven reserve. If China secures its historical waters and confirms the mentioned figures, crude oil production in the South China Sea will allow China to fulfill its self-reliance targets for at least another century, although other states will face an energy crisis and fight for economic survival. Conceivably, China will have to compete with other countries, especially those energy-hungry states, who have already delved into the disputed waters to explore and even recover oil and gas from the South China Sea.

Energy Exploration in the South China Sea

Despite China's threats to Taiwan, and its treatment of Taiwan as one of its own provinces, the cooperation between the CNOOC and the Taiwanese China Petroleum Corporation (CPC) has resulted in joint exploration of the East China Sea and the northern part of the South China Sea. The joint venture, which is operated by the U.S.-based Chevron Oil Corporation, requires the firms involved to invest through Taiwan's subsidiary in Panama to avoid Taiwan's ban on direct investment in China (Associated Press 1995). Already, representatives from both CNOOC and CPC have targeted areas off Hainan Island, Hong Kong, and Pratas Islet for joint exploration (*World Journal* 1994).

China has also ventured into the Spratlys region, and reportedly has constructed its own exploratory well, the Nanyang No. 1, on the Fiery Cross Reef. China also has granted oil concessions to the Benton Oil and Gas Company and the Crestone Energy Corporation, both American firms with plans for seismic survey and drilling in the disputed areas (*China News* 1997). The CNOOC has also drilled several test wells in the Gulf of Tonkin more recently, but Vietnam immediately protested China's exploration because the drilling took pace in Block-113 of Petrovietnam (*South China Morning Post* 1997a). Compared with other claimants' efforts in the South China Sea, China's exploration and production efforts are too little, too late.

The most active claimant is the Philippines, which enjoys the support of the major powers outside of the South China Sea region. Since 1970 the Philippines has granted oil concessions to AMOCO, Salen, and Philippine Oil Development to drill wells on the Reed Bank. More recently, the Kirkland Oil Company, Alcorn and Occidental Petroleum received geophysical survey and exploration contracts from the government of the Philippines covering the entire Kalayaan Group. To halt Chinese advancement in this area, the Philippine navy destroyed the Chinese survey markers erected on the Pennsylvania Reef, First and Second Thomas Shoals, while simultaneously protesting China's permanent occupation of the nearby Mischief Reef (*China Post* 1997b). The Chinese naval militia built new structures, however, and the most recent seesaw has taken place on the Sabina Shoal, only 65 nm off Palawan Island of the Philippines.[10]

The disputes between China and the Philippines gradually spread beyond the Kalayaan or Spratlys region. Recently, the Scarborough Reef, 200 nm north of the resource-rich Reed Bank, became the focal point of territorial dispute (*China Times* 1997a). The Scarborough Reef, claimed by the Philippines, China and Taiwan, is located directly on the strategic shipping lanes in the South China Sea, and is an atoll covering 160 km², with several rocky reefs scattered on the ring, an ideal location for an oil exploration drilling platform. The Philippine navy first landed on the Scarborough Reef on May 20,1997, destroyed the Chinese survey markers, fired warning shots to the nearby Chinese fishing boats, and arrested 21 Chinese fishermen. The government of the Philippines subsequently announced that a lighthouse would be installed on the Scarborough Reef for navigational safety (Reuters 1997a). Because the Reef (Minzhu Jiao in Chinese) is too distant from the

PLA's naval base in Hainan Island (520 nm due west), the PLA cannot exercise force over the Scarborough Reef without first securing a staging point somewhere in between, such as the occupation of the Addington Patch (Anding Lianjiao in Chinese) in Macclesfield Bank.

The other South China Sea claimants also have a great military and economic stake in the South China Sea. Vietnam's government is constantly aware of sovereignty concerns and of the need for oil, particularly in the Gulf of Tonkin, the Paracel Islands, and the Spratly Islands. Recently, Petrovietnam has awarded exploration rights to the U.S.-based Conoco Incorporated for a disputed area in the Spratlys region (*Far Eastern Economic Review* 1997), while the nearby Big Bear, West Diamond, Red Orchid and West Orchid fields of Petrovietnam, all located in the disputed waters, had already experienced annual oil and gas production of approximately 20 mmboe. Meanwhile, Malaysian PETRONAS was granting concessions for deep water drilling around the southern Spratlys region. The Indonesian government has decided to build a 750 nm natural gas pipeline, transporting the gas lifted from ESSO's Natuna gas field in the disputed waters back to Java.[11] To protect its gas field in the South China Sea, Indonesia will set up surface-to-air missile launchers and a radar warning system on the drilling platforms in the Natuna gas field (*Liberty Times* 1997a).

About 120 oil and gas wells have been drilled under the auspices of non-Chinese claimants within China's historical waters boundary, and the total annual output for both oil and gas in this disputed area exceeds China's annual net imports.[12] The granting of oil and gas concessions in disputed areas is a common but provocative means for claimant states to assert their jurisdiction over portions of the South China Sea. Chinese PLA leaders have argued that, whereas China is unable to exploit its oil and gas inside its territorial waters, militarily weaker countries are taking advantage of the PRC's tolerance and restraint by quietly plundering the oil and gas in the South China Sea. PLA planners have used this argument to justify military modernization in general and larger budgets for its navy in particular to secure the oil and gas fields in the South China Sea in the near future (Ba 1994).

Collective Efforts to Build the Security Environment

Although territorial disputes, competing maritime claims, historical mistrust, and increasing military presence all dim the prospects for establishing security structures to avoid potential conflicts in the South China Sea, the post-Cold War era has given the world the opportunity to build lasting peace collectively for the first time. The only effective way to conduct CBMs is through joint management to induce demilitarization, and to diffuse the accumulated tension from the disputes over the ownership of hydrocarbon resources and competing sovereignty claims.

The potential conflicts in the South China Sea are primarily multilateral. Fortunately, multilateral negotiations tend to be more effective than do bilateral negotiations, which tend to be disadvantageous to the smaller power. Multilateral negotiations may force the major power to yield. Furthermore, when more than two countries claim the same territory or feature, bilateral negotiations are inappropriate to resolve conflicting claims: Any agreement between two claimants in such a case might violate the rights of other claimants. Effective joint management in the disputed waters must be multilateral in nature.

To build a collective security environment in the South China Sea, a stable administrative decision-making structure that is perceived as fair and equitable to all competing claimants must be established. Any multilateral negotiations to resolve the conflicting claims over the resource-rich islets and attendant maritime areas must take into account the need to allocate fair benefits among large and small claimants, to acknowledge the interests of nonclaimants around the South China Sea, and to accommodate the interests of maritime powers outside of the South China Sea region. The intentions of each concerned country, in particular the major powers, must be understood before a realistic plan for a collective security environment in the South China Sea can be undertaken.

China and the South China Sea

China is the dominant regional power and has the most extensive claims in the South China Sea. Any solutions to the disputes must consider its interests, though not necessarily fulfill or satisfy its demands. China usually takes both hard and soft lines in its territorial disputes with other claimants, however, and there is a widening gap between its words and its deeds in the region. Discerning its intentions and interests has become more difficult, if not impossible.

To make positive contributions to the security environment in the South China Sea, China urges that all concerned states should be treated as equals, based on the "five principles of coexistence":

> No state should interfere in the internal affairs of other states; disarmament and arms control should be carried out in a fair and reasonable manner; efforts should be made to end arms races and prevent nuclear proliferation; no state should seek hegemony or spheres of influence, nor organize or join any military bloc directed against other states; and territorial disputes,

border disputes and other differences among regional states should be settled peacefully without the use of force. (Garett and Glaser 1994)

At the same time, however, China has developed a "three no's" policy to deal with the South China Sea issue: no specification of claims; no multilateral negotiations; and no internationalization of the issue, including no involvement of outside powers (Jiang 1995). Thus, China prefers to develop joint efforts with each competing claimant bilaterally. In particular, China is more than willing to negotiate and even to participate in bilateral joint development of the disputed areas over which it has no firm control, such as the Spratly and Pratas Islands. China refuses to negotiate, let alone participate, in any joint development of the disputed areas where it exercises firm control, such as Hainan Island and the Paracel Islands. Only when other economic or political interests override its narrow concerns of sovereignty claims may China be willing to compromise and to cooperate.

With its size and its growing economic, political, and military power, China insists on bilateral negotiation with each smaller competing claimant under its favored terms. From China's perspective, any multilateral discussions or internationalization of disputes could derail its strategy of defusing tension through improved relations with other claimants, while postponing settlement of the unification issue with Taiwan (Hargett 1997). At the same time, however, unilateral or bilateral exploration and development dominated by China in the disputed waters certainly could trigger an armed conflict, disrupting relations in the region. China must be made aware that a multilateral joint development scheme would legitimize its presence peacefully in the South China Sea.

The United States and Japan

The United States is the key player in the South China Sea despite the fact that it is located outside the region. The United States is also the dominant military presence in the South China Sea, and has bombed, strafed and undertaken amphibious attacks on those islets held by Japan during World War II.[13] Nonetheless, the United States is trying to stay out of the South China Sea disputes. Its official policy is as follows:

> The United States urges peaceful settlement of the issue by the states involved in a manner that enhances regional peace, prosperity and security; it strongly opposes the threat or use of military force to assert any nation's claim to South China Sea territories and would view any such use as a serious matter; it takes no position on the legal merits of competing sover-

eignty claims and is willing to help in the peaceful resolution of the competing claims if requested by the parties; and it has a strategic interest in maintaining maritime lines of communication in the region and considers it essential to resist any maritime claims beyond those permitted by UNCLOS. ("United States Government Policy," 1994)

In accordance with this policy, the United States advocates the peaceful development of natural resources while maintaining the freedom of navigation in the region. The United States has also informed all U.S.-based oil companies of the competing claims and of the risks of conducting on-site activities in the disputed waters before multilateral joint development is established in the South China Sea.

Despite America's professed neutrality, internationalization of the South China Sea issue is inevitable because of the strategic significance of the Spratlys, which sit astride the vital sea-lanes, the interest in hydrocarbon resources, and the U.S. defense agreements with some claimants. The United States could be dragged into armed conflict in the South China Sea by its allies if it were invited in, either by passive or by active arrangement, as in the Vietnam War. As a matter of fact, the Philippine government asked the United States, with which it has a mutual defense commitment, to assist militarily in the 1995 Mischief Reef incident and the 1997 Scarborough Reef conflict (*United Daily News* 1997b).

American policy implies that it will support any broad, formal multilateral negotiations on the South China Sea issues and may even try to play the role of mediator. In the event of conflict, U.S. military forces would become involved somehow to protect the sea-lanes of communication, at least to protect U.S. national interests. The United States has repeatedly urged China to enhance transparency in its South China Sea policy and to build the confidence of its neighbors such that others will not assume the worst and that potential armed conflict can be avoided.

Another maritime power outside the region, Japan, does not claim or own any islets, reefs, or shoals in the South China Sea. It was the only state with previous claims in the region that has annexed and used economic development of all disputed areas, including the Paracel, Pratas, and Spratly Islands in the South China Sea, before and during World War II. But because Japan's oil imports must pass through the South China Sea, it is in a position to rapidly expand its navy beyond the traditional 1,000 nm patrol range for security reasons. The United States-Japan Treaty of Mutual Cooperation and Security could be expanded to include the escort and protection of the shipping lanes in the South China Sea (Lee 1997). Japan is concerned that what it perceives as China's expansionism will threaten its shipping lanes and erode its economic establishment in the Southeast Asian region. As a result, Japan may envision itself as a check on China's ambitions, through either economic sanctions or military deterrence, or both.

Other South China Sea Countries

In response to China's advancements in the South China Sea, the 1992 ASEAN Post Ministerial Conference in Manila announced its first formal declaration on the issue of regional security. This ASEAN Declaration on the South China Sea urged all competing claimants to settle their disputes peacefully and called for regional cooperation in furthering the safety of navigation and communication, pollution prevention, search and rescue, and in combating piracy and drug smuggling in the South China Sea. China opposed this declaration.[14] ASEAN was dragged into another fight with its giant neighbor to the north during the Gulf of Tonkin incident in 1997. Vietnam, a member of ASEAN since 1995, used the incident to seek ASEAN's support in a territorial dispute with China outside of the Spratlys. Although ASEAN members condemned Chinese drilling in Vietnamese waters, some of them signaled to Vietnam that it would be on its own if it became involved in an armed conflict with China (*South China Morning Post* 1997b). Today, China finds itself occupying a defensive position against a loosely united ASEAN, which strives for unity while its members have different intentions for their separate economic and strategic interests.

The South China Sea issues also found their way onto the ARF agenda. Although the urgent situation in the Spratlys was raised in each annual forum, China predictably reemphasized that it would only negotiate with each competing claimant on an individual basis. The ARF's only contribution to preventing armed conflict was a 1994 proposal for volleyball matches among troops flying different national flags in the Spratlys (*International Herald Tribune* 1994). As a further compromise with China, the ARF agreed that it would only serve as a consultative forum and would not discuss any direct solutions to the South China Sea issues.

Although Taiwan has been denied the right to attend most international activities at China's insistence, it nevertheless contributes positively to a more realistic solution to the South China Sea disputes. Taiwan President Lee Teng-hui has proposed multilateral joint development of the disputed areas, and competing claimants have been invited to pool funds to establish an international firm that would exploit resources throughout the South China Sea.[15] China, however, has rejected this proposal, as expected, and the other claimants have not responded officially as none of them have diplomatic relations with Taiwan.

Of all the claimant countries, Indonesia has advanced further than any other in establishing a framework for coping with China. It strongly supports multilateral regional security dialogues and urges all concerned parties to work within the framework it has provided. Indonesia's ongoing efforts to work out a peaceful solution to the South China Sea disputes, stressing joint resolution of the issues and development of the disputed areas, rather than uni-lateral assertion of sovereignty claims, are perhaps the only lasting attempts to build the security environment so far. Because of its abundant resources and strategic location, Indonesia has been considered a potential great power that could have been in a position to dominate the world in 2050 if the government were managed by a highly educated and efficient team (Cronin 1996, 3–6).

The Philippines has proposed that the disputed waters be demilitarized and be declared a marine reserve. It also proposed that each disputed islet be placed under the stewardship of the claimant state geographically closest to it. China rejected this proposal out of hand. In November 1994, the Philip-pines even proposed a meeting among the garrison commanders of different governments stationing troops in the Spratlys to discuss the possibility of establishing radio communication for conflict prevention. The Philippine proposal was kindly turned down because of concerns that the multilateral military intelligence activities might be getting out of control.[16] Despite these unsuccessful attempts to achieve multilateral cooperation, the Philippines enjoys considerable external support against China: Although the Philippines is militarily by far the weakest littoral country, it has the most influence regarding intervention from and backup by the United States. In fact, China's advances in the South China Sea will only bring the Philippines and the United States closer.

Malaysia is a stronger military power than the Philippines, but it lacks military ties with the United States and has turned down an American re-quest for bases and joint naval exercises in the South China Sea. Although wary of China, whose nearest occupied feature lies right on its doorstep, less than 250 nm off Sarawak, Malaysia is reluctant to allow the United States to pre-position military installations off its coast for fear of antagonizing China. Similarly, energy-rich Brunei has no desire to irritate China because it has sufficient oil reserves to last at least 20 years and enough natural gas to last 40 years, even without further discoveries in its EEZ (Exclusive Economic Zone) in the South China Sea (*World of Information* 1993, 37–40).

Vietnam and China have agreed to settle their disputes peacefully and to increase the pace of the settlement process. Vietnam has now ratified the UNCLOS and it is willing to take its territorial disputes with China to the International Court of Justice in an attempt to seek international support, including U.S. assistance, to restrain China from military action (and possibly even to embarrass China). In addition, Vietnam has joined ASEAN and has normalized relations with the United States, giving it additional sources of support in the event of a crisis with China.

Some South China Sea countries that are ASEAN members have become indirectly involved in the disputes, although they have no sovereignty claims in the area. Although Thailand and Singapore are not claimants, both nations are concerned about the freedom of navigation in this region and have offered to mediate the disputes. Laos (a new member of ASEAN) and Cambodia have backed Indonesia's efforts to find solutions for the South China Sea disputes.

Confidence-Building Measures

Several official multilateral meetings have convened to discuss the South China Sea conflicts, including the ARF (since 1994) and the ASEAN Post Ministerial Conference (since 1991). Progress leading to effective solutions has been slow. To augment these official fora, "track two," nongovernmental multilateral meetings have been specifically designed to foster a security environment in the region.

The Council for Security Cooperation in the Asia-Pacific (CSCAP) was established and its first annual meeting held in June 1993 (*Indonesian Quarterly* 1993). This nongovernmental organization (NGO) was created to reduce the risk of potential conflict in the region (Wanandi 1994). The NGO meetings are actually a novel way to prevent conflict and to build confidence among participants. Thus, some experts have suggested that the establishment of CSCAP is a confidence-building measure by itself, despite the fact that conflict reduction cannot be achieved without the consent of government officials (Evans 1994).

Up to 17 countries have participated in CSCAP meetings concerning navigational safety, military transparency, security environment and confidence building in the Asia-Pacific region, but no specific solutions to the South China Sea disputes have been developed to date (Lin 1997a). The Indonesia-supported Workshop on Managing Potential Conflicts in the South China Sea, however, has been one of the most active meetings to craft solutions for South China Sea disputes.

Workshop on Managing Potential Conflicts in the South China Sea

The goal of the Workshop on Managing Potential Conflicts in the South China Sea (hereinafter Workshop) is to establish cooperation on broad initiatives so as to build sufficient confidence to undertake multilateral joint development in the South China Sea region. The main purposes of the Workshop process are:

    a. to promote confidence and a conducive atmosphere in the South China Sea area in which the countries in the region could solve their problems through dialogue and mutual understanding in the interest of the region as a whole;

    b. in this spirit, to encourage the parties to any dispute to seek ways and means to settle their disputes by peaceful means; and

    c. to develop specific cooperative efforts or projects on which all participants could cooperate or learn how to cooperate no matter how small or insignificant the activity, in view of the fact that the South China Sea countries seemed to have more experience in confronting each other rather than in cooperating with each other. (Shepard 1995)

The Workshop was conducted on an informal basis, and participants acted in their individual capacities. This informality has both advantages and disadvantages: Although issues can be discussed frankly and solutions debated freely, the concerned countries do not have to honor the Workshop recommendations and can even insist on policies that contradict the Workshop's conclusions. The Workshop and its ad hoc meetings are hosted by Indonesia, and supported by regional authorities as well as by other states, such as Australia, the United States, and Japan, and by the European Union (EU), the Office of the Secretary General of the United Nations, and the Canadian International Development Agency (CIDA) in affiliation with the University of British Columbia at Vancouver.

The Workshop's predecessor, the project on Managing Potential Conflicts in the South China Sea, was launched in 1989, and the First Workshop was convened in Bali in 1990. This initial meeting was in the nature of an exploration, and only participants from ASEAN states were invited. The first meeting recommended a second Workshop, with participants invited from the entire region. Cambodia was excluded pending the settlement of its internal peace process. The Second Workshop took place in Bandung in 1991, and demonstrated the value of informal processes dedicated to the advancement of cooperation in the South China Sea, regardless of the resolution of sovereignty and jurisdictional issues. The Workshop was not merely "academic"; participants searched for practical and realistic opportunities to pursue cooperation, build confidence, and avoid conflict. The Workshop's most significant contributions, however, lie in its intellectual atmosphere and creative suggestions for multilateral resource development regimes.

This Second, quasi-diplomatic Workshop was attended by participants from Brunei, China, Taiwan, Indonesia, Laos, Malaysia, the Philippines, Singapore, Thailand, Vietnam, and resource personnel from CIDA. Most of the participants were foreign ministry officials, and a few were academics. The multilateral invitation-only Workshop covered a broad range of South China Sea topics. Despite their closed, informal and nongovernmental status, each Workshop resulted in statements for public release. One key product of the Workshop was the July 1991 Bandung statement, which advised against the use of force to settle territorial and jurisdictional disputes. Where conflicting claims exist, states should consider the possibility of cooperating for their mutual benefit, including joint development. Self-restraint should be exercised to avoid complicating the situation of conflicting claims.

Up to and including the Fourth Workshop in Surabaya, participants were given opportunities to exchange views on their respective national positions regarding the territorial claims in the South China Sea, first on the Spratly and the Paracel Islands, but later limited to the Spratlys alone. Participants were increasingly reluctant to discuss these matters even in an informal meeting such as the Workshop process, mainly because of the sensitivity of the issues. Some participants believed that the Workshop should not deal with territorial issues at all, and that these should be left to the countries concerned. For example, at the end of the Third Workshop in Yogyakarta in 1992, participants were unable to agree upon fundamental matters such as the boundaries in disputed waters. In view of this, the presentation of views concerning the Spratlys and other disputed areas was practically terminated at the Fifth Workshop in Bukittinggi.

The Workshops did discuss several CBMs in more detail, however, particularly during the Fifth Workshop in Bukittinggi and the Sixth Workshop in Balikpapan. Participants agreed that CBM discussions should promote a cooperative atmosphere for avoiding conflicts in the South China Sea area and for clearing up the various misunderstandings that still prevail among participants. Taking note of the members' efforts to pursue bilateral dialogues, the Workshops sought ways to continue these dialogues with more rigor so that the results of the dialogues could form the basis for developing an agreement or mutual understanding on a multilateral level at a later stage. Although the bilateral dialogue process has produced some CBMs in the form of bilateral codes of conduct, the problems in the region are primarily multilateral. Moreover, once the parties have entered into a bilateral code of conduct, the code still must be implemented and re-presented at a regional or multiple level.

Multilateral issues were discussed in more detail in the latest Workshop held in Batam, which hosted more than a hundred participants, including

Table 16.2

Workshops on Managing Potential Conflicts in the South China Sea, 1990–1997

First Workshop	1990/1/22–1/24	Bali, Indonesia
Second Workshop	1991/7/15–7/18	Bandung, Indonesia
Third Workshop	1992/6/28–7/2	Yogyakarta, Indonesia
Fourth Workshop	1993/8/23–8/25	Surabaya, Indonesia
Fifth Workshop	1994/10/26–10/28	Bukittinggi, Indonesia
Sixth Workshop	1995/10/09–10/13	Balikpapan, Indonesia
Seventh Workshop	1996/12/14–12/17	Batam, Indonesia
Eighth Workshop	1997/12/2–12/6	Puncak, Indonesia

representatives from Cambodia. At this meeting, participants from all concerned countries, including China and Taiwan, agreed to establish technical working groups, in the hope that the slowly evolving web of activities will constrain aggressive behavior by claimants and thus reduce potential conflict. Participants also identified a number of projects for regional cooperation; it is thought that confidence-building efforts can eventually lead to regional cooperation in ocean management (see Table 16.2 for list of first eight Workshops).

Technical Working Groups of the Workshop

The Workshop spawned Technical Working Groups (TWGs) on marine scientific research, safety of navigation, shipping and communication, marine environmental protection, legal matters, resource assessment, and means of development in the South China Sea. Each TWG proposes group experts meetings (GEMs) with specific focal points. Dozens of proposals and ideas, ranging from the very simple to the very complex, have been advanced, covering almost the entire range of technical and legal subjects in ocean management and cooperation (Table 16.3). The list of participants runs into the hundreds, and well over a thousand person-days have been devoted to this work.

Marine Scientific Research

The Marine Scientific Research (MSR) project is the most advanced of all the Workshop proposals. At the Third Workshop in Yogyakarta, participants decided to create the TWG-MSR, which held its first meeting in Manila in 1993. This meeting identified numerous areas for cooperative research and selected three topics as the focus of the second TWG-MSR meeting in

Table 16.3

Technical Working Group (TWG) and Group Experts Meeting (GEM) under the Workshops on Managing Potential Conflicts in the South China Sea, 1993–1997

Group	Meeting	Location	Dates
Marine Scientific Research in the South China Sea	1st TWG	Manila, Philippines	1993/5/31–6/2
	2nd TWG	Surabaya, Indonesia	1993/8/23
	3rd TWG	Singapore	1994/4/25–4/29
	4th TWG	Hanoi, Vietnam	1995/6/27–6/30
	5th TWG	Cebu, Philippines	1996/7/14–7/17
	1st GEM	Cebu, Philippines	1996/7/18–7/20
Safety of Navigation, Shipping and Communication in the South China Sea	1st TWG	Jakarta, Indonesia	1995/10/3–10/6
	2nd TWG	Brunei	1996/10/29–11/1
	1st GEM	Kuching, Malaysia	1997/6/12–6/15
	2nd GEM	Singapore	1997/5/7–5/10
Marine Environmental Protection in the South China Sea	1st TWG	Hangzhou, PRC	1994/10/6–10/8
	2nd TWG	Haikou, PRC	1997/10/14–10/15
	1st GEM	Phnom Penh, Cambodia	1997/6/9–6/11
Legal Matters in the South China Sea	1st TWG	Phuket, Thailand	1995/7/2–7/6
	2nd TWG	Chiang Mai, Thailand	1997/5/13–5/17
Resource Assessment and Ways of Development in the South China Sea	1st TWG	Jakarta, Indonesia	1993/7/4–7/5

Surabaya in 1993. The selection of focal points was based primarily on cost. These topics were developed into the following proposals in the third meeting of TWG-MSR in Singapore in 1994: the Proposal for Regional Cooperation in the Field of Marine Scientific Data and Information Network in the South China Sea; the Study of Tides and Sea Level Change and Their Impact on Coastal Environment in the South China Sea as Affected by Potential Climate Change; and The Proposed Collaborative Research Project on Biological Diversity in the South China Sea.

The Biological Diversity proposal was finalized and endorsed by the Fifth Workshop in 1994, and was then submitted to the United Nation Development Program (UNDP) for financial support. The other two proposals were finalized in the fourth meeting of TWG-MSR in Hanoi in 1995 and endorsed at the Sixth Workshop the same year. In particular, the proposal selected 27 sea level and tidal monitoring stations in Brunei, Cambodia, the PRC and ROC, Indonesia, Malaysia, the Philippines, Singapore, Thailand, and Vietnam as symbols of CBMs. The first group experts meeting to make recommendations on the most effective method of implementing these project proposals was held in Cebu right after the fifth meeting of TWG-MSR.

Safety of Navigation, Shipping, and Communication

The Safety of Navigation, Shipping and Communication (SNSC) project is strategically significant. During the first TWG-SNSC meeting in Jakarta in 1995, four topics for potential cooperation were identified: education and training of mariners; exchange of hydrographic data and information; contingency plans for pollution; and unlawful activities at sea and search-and-rescue at sea.

The TWG-SNSC concluded that the exchange of data and information regarding unlawful activities should be enhanced in the region. The Regional Piracy Center of the International Maritime Bureau was identified as a focal point for the regional collection of information. In the second meeting of TWG-SNSC in Brunei in 1996, participants agreed that Singapore should prepare a proposal outlining a regional ship reporting mechanism permitting participants to forward information to the authorities. During that session, participants also agreed to continue working on the ways and means to enhance safety of navigation, shipping, and communication in the South China Sea.

Marine Environmental Protection

Forty-eight participants from South China Sea nations attended the first TWG session of Marine Environmental Protection (MEP) in Hangzhou in 1994.

Participants, in their individual capacities, expressed their common interest in protecting the marine environment in the entire South China Sea region and their willingness to develop cooperation in this area. They considered the following topics in depth: exchanging information on the impacts of environmental threats; establishing a network among scientists involved in marine pollution control; developing an information exchange mechanism in relation to climate change; establishing a regional monitoring system of ocean observation; developing ecosystem study training programs; assessing marine, coastal, and wetland ecosystems; and studying the upwelling phenomena and their importance to the ecosystem, health and fisheries.

During the first TWG-MEP, participants agreed to give priority to developing a marine monitoring network and a regionwide observation system, which can meet regional requirements and contribute to the Global Ocean Observation System. Attendees also advocated appropriate cooperation with other TWG programs in MSR and SNSC, in the area of marine pollution prevention and control, and they recommended discussing these proposed coordinations with the respective government authorities for possible implementation.

The second TWG-MEP meeting and the first GEM-MEP conclave are expected to convene in 1998 in China and Cambodia, respectively.

Legal Matters

Perhaps the best hope for avoiding armed conflicts over territorial disputes and sovereignty claims in the South China Sea lies in the TWG-LM. The first one took place in Phuket in 1995, with 63 participants from the South China Sea nations. The primary task of the TWG-LM was to discuss legal issues arising from proposals for cooperative regional efforts to produce concrete, practical, policy-oriented ideas and concepts. Although the TWG-LM was explicitly forbidden to discuss claims and sovereignty issues, it did address the role of international law such as the UNCLOS in resolving the territorial disputes.

During the initial TWG-LM meeting, which found an urgent need for legal cooperation, the participants discussed the following common concerns: implications of UNCLOS; legal aspects of cooperation in MSR, SNSC, and MEP; resource assessment and ways of development (RAWD); and the establishment of priorities for the future work of TWG-LM. Specifically, the TWG-LM identified numerous legal issues in SNSC, including the prevention and rapid mitigation of oil spills, piracy, transportation of hazardous cargo, abandoned installations and structures, and safety of lives at sea. Participants agreed that international law, including UNCLOS, can facilitate cooperation as well as CBMs in the South China Sea; that provisional agreements for cooperation are possible, desirable, and required despite unresolved territorial and jurisdictional issues; and that the second TWG-LM should be convened in 1998.

Resource Assessment and Ways of Development

Both living and nonliving resources, in particular the hydrocarbon deposits in the South China Sea, have been identified as a potential area of cooperation ever since the First Workshop in 1990. The TWG-RAWD was established during the Third Workshop in 1992, and the initial TWG-RAWD meeting was convened in Jakarta the following year. The first TWG-RAWD session considered 33 proposals for cooperation over marine living resources and nonliving resources, including hydrocarbon and mineral deposits. Proposals prepared for the meeting included an overview of hydrocarbon potential; cooperative studies of hydrocarbon resources; a regional project on offshore mineral exploration; marine biology and resource development; regional fisheries stock assessment; and the creation of a marine park in the Spratly Islands area.

The first TWG-RAWD meeting included a proposal for joint offshore mineral exploration in parts of the South China Sea, under the joint auspices of the Committee for the Coordination of Joint Prospecting for Mineral Resources in Asian Offshore Areas (CCOP) and other NGOs. It also included a proposal for joint hydrocarbon resource study. Several discussants suggested moving toward cooperation even in the more sensitive areas, possibly through a stage-by-stage approach. For example, joint development of offshore petroleum in the absence of a boundary has been taking place since 1976. Indeed, joint development is becoming increasingly popular: In the South China Sea region, Malaysia-Thailand, Malaysia-Vietnam, and China-Taiwan have undertaken some sort of joint resource development. Other potential schemes are known to be under negotiation between other countries.

The participants agreed to recommend that joint development activities should commence with data exchange and analysis, including assessment of the mineral potential of the areas selected, and that this information should lead to a data map showing hard mineral resource potential. The goal of these activities is to promote a better understanding of these resources, without prejudicing territorial or jurisdictional claims. A proposed team of experts composed of geologists and geophysicists would collect available data from countries and regional organizations such as CCOP, undertake analysis and interpretation of basin configuration, suggest better means of estimating the hydrocarbon resources of the region, and recommend future joint efforts. The multiple claims area was suggested as a potential target for this activity.

There was some discussion about whether the "multiple claims area" was the appropriate venue for such an activity, and how to identify that "area." Although many boundary issues in the South China Sea are purely bilateral, others are more complex. Restricting joint activity to the multiple claims area, and restricting participation in any activity to those claimants, would deny the participation of a great number of regional authorities with interests in the South China Sea.

After discussion, the first TWG-RAWD meeting agreed to recommend:

- a joint preliminary study of a suitable sedimentary basin in the South China Sea area, with prejudice to claims of any kind
- the collation, exchange, and interpretation of the available geological, geophysical and geochemical data that exist in each participating country or that could be accessed easily from other sources
- maintaining the longer-term view of using an appropriate evaluation technique for resource assessment
- identification of national focal points, with Indonesia as the focal point coordinator
- the promotion of tourism and the creation of a marine-park or marine protected area.

Although Resource Assessment was one of the leading TWGs identified by the Workshop, it stalled completely after the first TWG-RAWD meeting. Nonetheless, its purpose is as important now as it was when the TWG-RAWD was first created. The Workshops have not pursued the TWG-RAWD for logistical reasons: Although the subject matter is important, it is undoubtedly sensitive. Even so, it is possible to proceed carefully without giving rise to undue alarm among the participants.

Confidence-Building Measures by the Workshop

Seven Workshops, ten TWGs meetings, and two GEMs have already taken place, and at least another seven relevant meetings were planned for 1998 (Tables 16.2 and 16.3). In addition, over 18 project proposals have been submitted and reviewed by the Workshops.[17] The participants generally agree that all activities of the Workshop constituted CBMs, and that the discussions augur well for solving potential conflicts and maintaining peace in the South China Sea region. The Workshop will continue to engage in constructive discussions on CBMs.

As a CBM measure, however, the Workshop process is not without its problems. For example, the Workshop is the only concrete multilateral process in which representatives from both China and Taiwan are engaged in discussions about security issues in the South China Sea. Nonetheless, the Workshop has limited utility as a forum for China-Taiwan cooperation. Although the Workshop has recognized that all participants, including those from Taiwan, are entitled to host a GEM or TWG meeting in the context of the Workshop process, China has repeatedly opposed the proposals that Taiwan host the relevant meetings in Taiwan.[18] Furthermore, during the Workshop process, competing claimants in the South China Sea disputes have undertaken some actions that might destabilize the CBMs generated by the Workshop. More significantly, participants have been unable or unwilling to agree unanimously to more CBMs, such as demilitarization or military transparency, and have failed to make any progress toward a solution to the territorial disputes by clarifying the nature or specific terms of their claims.

Because of the failure to move efficiently toward a multilateral solution, the future of the Workshop has been called into question. Some participants even believe that the "Workshop" has become a "Talk-shop," a diversion holding out the false promise of cooperation and allowing some claimants, such as China, to consolidate and strengthen their military positions. A more optimistic view holds that the NGO Workshop process is right on track, and that its slow process and limited progress should not be a cause for disappointment. Indeed, the Workshop is the only process that is geared specifically toward solving the South China Sea disputes, and it has made significant progress with regard to promoting cooperative efforts and encouraging claimants to solve their own problems through dialogue. As the Workshop has more to contribute to CBMs, participants should stay the course, using the Workshop to manage the potential conflicts in the South China Sea region and participating in opportunities for multilateral joint development.

Conclusions

The security environment in the South China Sea depends on diffusing the tension of multilateral territorial disputes, on the safety of the sea-lanes of communication, and on the distribution of resources among competing claimants. Various confidence-building mechanisms to resolve disputes and promote cooperation through dialogue, formal and informal, bilateral and multilateral, have been initiated in the last decade of the twentieth century. Among the official "track-one" conferences, and the nongovernmental "track-two" meetings, the most effective forum for accommodating all South China Sea claimants—including China and Taiwan—is the Workshop on Managing Potential Conflicts in the South China Sea.

The Workshop process has induced the countries in the South China Sea to do their best to avoid escalating conflicts. Although the underlying conflicts have not been resolved, there is now a better understanding that they should not erupt into armed conflict. The countries around the South China Sea are becoming more aware of the dangers of such a conflagration to their individual stability and economic development. Efforts to create conditions conducive for dialogue have also met with considerable success, and dialogues increasingly are taking place among the parties concerned. The South China Sea nations must continue their efforts in this area because failure to resolve problems still poses a threat to the region.

The other purpose of the Workshop, encouraging cooperation among the South China Sea countries, is the most active. This cooperation has resulted in several project proposals. The three projects on marine scientific research—namely biological diversity, sea level and tide monitoring, and database and networking—are the most advanced. In addition, four more areas for cooperation are also being closely developed with regard to safety of navigation—specifically, education and training of mariners, illegal acts at sea and search and rescue, pollution control and abatement and contingency planning, and hydrographic survey and mapping. The Workshops hope to make progress on these four projects of cooperation in the near future.

Another result of the South China Sea discussions has been the attention given to promoting confidence building measures in this region. In fact, CBMs have been a Workshop issue ever since the beginning of the Workshop process. Although some Workshop participants believe the Workshop is itself a CBM, others have suggested the development of CBMs that are external to the Workshop process.

These efforts at resolving the South China Sea disputes are laudable, but insufficient. Despite these attempts to improve cooperation and diminish conflict, tensions in the South China Sea are slowly but progressively worsening because of the forthcoming worldwide energy shortage and ever-expanding energy demand. The Workshop process alone is too slow, and perhaps too late. Lasting improvement in the South China Sea requires the participation of official organizations, as well as NGOs. In the meantime, a new "track three" process may be helpful. The Asia-Pacific Security Forum adds more fuel for building confidence measures that may eventually lead to a multilateral joint development of the South China Sea, which will transform the region into a zone of peace, freedom, and neutrality.

Notes

1. China and Vietnam had engaged each other twice in the South China Sea: a major battle took place in the Paracel Islands during January 11–20, 1974, and

another minor skirmish occurred in the Spratly Islands on March 14, 1988. (*The War History of People's Liberation Army* 1989, 590–592).

2. Laos and Myanmar joined ASEAN on July 23,1997; other members of ASEAN are Brunei, Indonesia, Malaysia, the Philippines, Singapore, Thailand, and Vietnam.

3. The PLA had landed on the Woody Islet of the Paracel Islands in the South China Sea in June 1950, a month after Nationalist troops withdrew to Taiwan; other islets of the Paracel Islands were occupied by French troops dispatched from colonial Indo-China. (Compilation of the South China Sea files 1995).

4. The police patrol vessels of the 7th Peace Preservation Police Corps, National Police Administration of the Ministry of Interior, are under the operational control of the ROC navy in time of crisis.

5. Updated from the compilation by C. Chung (1994a).

6. The ROC naval buildup program mentioned here is the Kwang Hwa V project of ten 1,500-ton corvettes equipped with ship-to-ship, ship-to air missiles, and advanced antisubmarine warfare equipment (*United Daily News* 1997c).

7. The Hong Kong-based flotilla was sailed to the Philippines by its British crews when the colony was handed over to the PRC on July 1,1997.

8. In a hypothetical naval engagement with the PLA navy in 2006, the U.S. task force fights a bloody battle in the South China Sea, but the Spratly Islands dispute remains unresolved. (Borik 1995).

9. The largest hydrocarbon reserve is in the Zengmu Basin at the southern part of the Spratly Islands; the recoverable oil and gas deposits there are estimated at about 104 billion barrels of oil equivalent, or more than half of the potential size deposited within the historical waters claimed by both the PRC and ROC; see the table in Du 1994.

10. Clusters of Chinese survey markers were found on the atoll of Sabina Shoal in the Dangerous Ground of the Spratly Islands; they were destroyed by Philippine marines (*China Post* 1997b).

11. The ESSO Natuna gas field is located 60 nm deep inside the historical waters boundary claimed by both the PRC and the ROC; the natural gas delivered to Java, with proven reserves of 2.6 billion barrels of oil equivalent, will be burned in 8,000 MW power plants to generate electricity for Indonesians (*Liberty Times* 1997b).

12. The official figures quoted by the PRC, "stolen" by other claimants in the entire region within the historical waters boundary in the South China Sea, was 0.66 mmboe/d; see the tables in Du 1994, and Sheng 1994.

13. The U.S. naval task force TF38 and the 5th Army Air Force had bombed and strafed the strategic Paracel, Pratas, and Spratly Islands in the first half of 1945 in order to neutralize the Japanese weather and radio stations there and to interdict Japanese shipping lanes in the South China Sea. A U.S. Marines search party landed on the Pratas Islet on May 29, 1945, demolishing a Japanese oil dump and barracks (Morrison 1959, 157–177; USAF Historical Division 1953, 490–492).

14. Immediately after the ASEAN declaration, the PLA publicly redeployed its submarines from the North Sea Fleet to the South China Sea, patrolling the disputed waters as far as the James Shoal area.

15. President Lee has urged that the claimants and other concerned countries be invited to invest a combined $10 billion in a South China Sea Development Company and has called on the disputants to put aside their claims to the disputed areas in favor

of the project, in which the profits of the joint venture would be used for development elsewhere (Lin et al. 1995; *Liberty Times* 1994).

16. The Philippine government also proposed a basketball match among garrison troops in the Spratlys; the first match had been proposed to take place at the headquarters of the Philippine West Command in Puerto Princesa in Palawan Island.

17. Meeting reports and project proposals of the Workshop on Managing Potential Conflicts in the South China Sea are available from: South China Sea Informal Working Group, c/o Center for Asian Legal Studies, University of British Columbia, Vancouver V6T 1Z1, Canada, or by e-mail at: scs@law.ubc. ca.

18. Beginning in the Fifth Workshop held in 1994, representatives from the ROC on Taiwan offered to host the TWG-SNSC meeting in each annual Workshop. The offer has been opposed by representatives from the PRC each year (Lin 1997b).

Bibliography

"Active Exploration Prospects." Pamphlet prepared by Crestone for distribution. Washington, DC: Crestone Energy Corp., 1994.

Asian Oil and Gas. "Spratlys: Only Modest Oil and Gas Potential" (September 1992): 12.

Annual Report of Chinese Petrochemistry. Beijing: National Information Center (August 30, 1994) (in Chinese).

Associated Press. "Taiwan, China to Look for Oil," August 31, 1995.

Ba, A.D. "Oil and the South China Sea: Prospects for Joint Development." *American Asian Review* 12, no. 4 (1994): 1–10.

Borik, F.C. "Sub Tzu and the Art of Submarine Warfare—A Brief Analysis of the Spratly War." *Naval Institute Proceedings* 121, no. 11 (November 1995): 64–72.

British Petroleum. *British Petroleum Statistical Review of World Energy.* London: British Petroleum, June 1997.

Chao, C.L. "Prospects of China's Oil Demand and Supply." *Energy Quarterly* 25, no. 3 (July 1995): 1–14 (in Chinese).

Chen, H.Y. "A Comparison between Taipei and Peking in their Policies and Concepts Regarding the South China Sea." *Issues and Studies* 29, no. 9 (1993): 22–57.

Cheng, C. "The Expansion of the PLA Navy." *Mainland China Studies* 26, no. 12 (1992): 69–71 (in Chinese).

China News. "China Warned over Spratlys, Vietnam Calls on Beijing to Stop Drilling Near Disputed Island Chain." March 17, 1997, p. 4.

———. "Malaysian Navy Opens Fire on Chinese Fishing Boat." March 26, 1995, p. 7.

The China Post. "Philippines Reports Gun Battle with PRC." January 27, 1996, p. 1.

———. "PRC Ships Ignore Protest, Stay by Spratly Islands." May 2, 1997a, p. 1.

———. "RP Destroys Beijing's Structures in Spratlys." July 1, 1997b, p. 2

———. "Japan Urges Watch on PRC." July 26, 1997c, p. 1.

China Times. "After Bombardment by a Malaysian Gunboat at Spratlys, Our Fishing Boat Is Missing." July 9, 1996, p. 7 (in Chinese).

———. "Tension Mounts on the Scarborough Reef between China and the Philippines." May 14, 1997a, p. 10 (in Chinese).

————. "Indonesia Announces Purchase of 12 Russian-Made Su-30K Fighter-Bombers." August 6, 1997b, p. 10 (in Chinese).

Chung, C. "Economic Development of the Islets in South China Sea." Paper presented at the South China Sea Conference. Washington, DC: American Enterprise Institute, September 7–9, 1994a.

————. "Energy Demand in Taiwan and Air-Sea Blockade by the PRC." *National Policy Dynamic Analysis* 102 (December 27, 1994b): 14–15 (in Chinese).

————. "Strategic Importance of the South China Sea Islets." *Defense Technology Monthly* 140 (1996a): 81–88; 141 (1996b): 81–87; 142 (1996c): 81–85 (in Chinese).

Clawson, L. *Energy and National Security in the 21st Century.* Washington, DC: National Defense University Press, 1996.

Compilation of the South China Sea Files in the Ministry of Foreign Affairs. Taipei: Ministry of Foreign Affairs, 1995, pp. 27–747 (in Chinese).

Cronin, M. ed. *2015: Power and Progress.* Washington, DC: National Defense University Press, 1996.

Defense Mapping Agency. *Sailing Directions for the Central Part of the South China Sea.* Publication 161. Washington, DC: U.S. Government Printing Office, 1991.

Du, S. "Estimate of Oil and Gas Deposits and Extraction in the South China Sea." Paper presented at the Workshop of the South China Sea. Taipei: Chinese Society of International Law, June 27–28, 1994 (in Chinese).

Energy Resources Council. *Energy Policy for the ROC on Taiwan.* Taipei: Ministry of Economic Affairs, 1996.

"Estimate of Oil and Gas Deposits andExtraction in the South China Sea." Paper presented at the Workshop of the South China Sea. Taipei: Chinese Society of International Law, June 27–28, 1994 (in Chinese).

Evans, P.M. "Managing Security Relations after the Cold War: Prospects for the CSCAP." *The Indonesian Quarterly* 22, no. 1 (1994): 62–68.

Far Eastern Economic Review. "Malaysia Plans Airstrip on Disputed atoll." September 12, 1991, p. 14.

————. "Oily Claims." March 30, 1995, p. 4.

————. "Drawn to the Fray—Fuel for Dispute." April 3, 1997, pp. 14–16.

Fesharaki, F., and Wu, K. "Overview of China's Energy Demand and Supply with a Special Focus on Oil Sector Development." Paper presented in the International Conference on the PRC Political Economy: Prospects Under the 9th Five-Year Plan. Tainan: National Cheng Kung University, June 7–8, 1997.

Fried, E., and Trezise, P. *Oil Security: Retrospect and Prospect.* New York: The Brookings Institution, 1993.

Gallagher, M.G. "China's Illusory Threat to the South China Sea." *International Security* 19, no. 1 (1994): 169–94.

Garett, B., and Glaser, B. "Multilateral Security in the Asia-Pacific Region and Its Impact on Chinese Interests: Views from Beijing." *Contemporary Southeast Asia* 16, no. 11 (1994): 14–34.

Greenburger, R.S. "Dispute Underscores Necessity in Asia for U.S. Presence." *Asian Wall Street Journal*, August 3, 1992, p. 1.

Hargett, J.M. "The Return of Hong Kong and the Future of Taiwan: Some Random Thoughts." Paper presented at International Conference on Relations Between Taipei, Hong Kong, and Beijing. Taipei: Tamkang University, July 4–5, 1997.

Holloway, N. "Jolt from the Blue." *Far Eastern Economic Review*, August 3, 1995, pp. 22–23.

The Indonesian Quarterly. "Announcement: Establishment of the Council for Security Cooperation in the Asia-Pacific" 22, no. 1 (1993): 69–70.

International Herald Tribune. "Beijing Snubs Summit Plan; War Fears Mount in Row over South China Sea Resources Carve-Up." July 27, 1994, p. 1.

Japan Times. "Philippines to Boost Forces on Spratlys." February 16, 1995a, p. 4.

————. "Indonesia Calls for Peaceful Solution to Six-Nation Dispute over Spratlys." February 18, 1995b, p. 4.

Jiang, S.Q. "A Balanced Diplomacy: Beijing's Handling of the South China Sea Territorial Dispute." Draft paper. Washington, DC: Washington Center for China Studies, 1995.

Lee, M.C. "Analysis of Japanese Policy Toward South China Sea Conflicts." *National Policy Dynamic Analysis* 171 (August 19, 1997): 10–11 (in Chinese).

Liao, W.C. *China's Blue Waters Strategy in the Twenty-first Century.* Taipei: Chinese Council of Advanced Policy Studies, Occasional Paper Series, 1995.

Liberty Times. "President Lee: Claimants Should Organize a Firm to Develop the South China Sea." November 9, 1994, p. 4 (in Chinese).

————. "Australia Will Assist Indonesia Deploying Missiles in the South China Sea." August 1, 1997a, p. 6 (in Chinese).

————. "Gas from the South China Sea for Electricity May Invite Trouble." August 6, 1997b, p. 6 (in Chinese).

Lin, C.Y. "Asia-Pacific Security Dialogue: Mechanism and Future Trend." *National Policy Dynamic Analysis* 171 (August 19, 1997a): 2–3 (in Chinese).

————. "Taiwan and the Workshop." *Liberty Times*, December 26, 1997b, p. 19 (in Chinese).

Lin, C.Y. et al. "South China Sea Policy for the ROC." *National Policy Dynamic Analysis* 128 (December 26, 1995): 2–9 (in Chinese).

Morris, E. "Choppy Seas for ASEAN's Security Quest." *Jane's International Defense Review* 26, no. 11 (1993): 876.

Morrison, S.E. *History of U.S. Naval Operations in WWII.* Boston: Little, Brown, 1959.

New York Times. "OPEC's Lonely at the Tap, but China's Getting Thirsty." April 3, 1994, p. 1.

Offshore. "Oxy Abandons Bantac off Filipino Palawan." (February 1995), p. 10.

Report of the First Workshop on Managing Potential Conflicts in the South China Sea, Denpasar, Indonesia, January 22–24, 1990.

Report of the Second Workshop on Managing Potential Conflicts in the South China Sea, Bandung, Indonesia, July 15–18, 1991.

Report of the Third Workshop on Managing Potential Conflicts in the South China Sea, Yogyakarta, Indonesia, June 28–July 2, 1992.

Report of the Fourth Workshop on Managing Potential Conflicts in the South China Sea, Surabaya, Indonesia, August 23–25, 1993.

Report of the Fifth Workshop on Managing Potential Conflicts in the South China Sea, Bukittinggi, Indonesia, October 26–28, 1994.

Report of the Sixth Workshop on Managing Potential Conflicts in the South China Sea, Balikpapan, Indonesia, October 9–13, 1995.

Report of the Seventh Workshop on Managing Potential Conflicts in the South China Sea, Batam, Indonesia, December 14–17, 1996.

Report of the Fifth Meeting of the Technical Working Group on Marine Scientific Research in the South China Sea, Cebu, Philippines, July 14–17, 1996.

Report of the Second Meeting of the Technical Working Group on Safety of Navigation, Shipping, and Communication in the South China Sea, Bandar Seri Begawan, Brunei Darussalam, October 29–November 1, 1996.

Report of the First Technical Working Group Meeting on Marine Environmental Protection in the South China Sea, Hangzhou, China, October 6–8, 1994.

Report of the First Technical Working Group Meeting on Legal Matters in the South China Sea, Phuket, Thailand, July 2–6, 1995.

Report of the First Technical Working Group Meeting on Resource Assessment and Ways of Development in the South China Sea, Jakarta, Indonesia, July 4–5, 1993.

Reuters. "Singapore Leader Warns China on Military Ambitions." May 13, 1995a.

———. "Philippines to Build Lighthouses on the Spratlys." June 14, 1995b.

———. "China Warned Philippines Not to Erect Lighthouse on the Scarborough Reef." May 25, 1997a.

———. "Indonesia to Offer Goods for Russian Planes." August 25, 1997b.

Richardson, M. "China Takes Softer Stand in Dispute on Spratly Isles." *International Herald Tribune*, July 31, 1995, p. 1.

Russell, N. "Energy Prospects in China." In Clawson, L., ed., *Energy and National Security in the Twenty-first Century.* Washington, DC: National Defense University Press, 1996: 37–56.

Seattle Post-Intelligencer. "China's Energy Crisis: More Resources Needed to Power Economic Growth." April 17, 1994, p. 4.

Sharpe, R., ed. *Jane's Fighting Ships 1997–98.* Surrey: Jane's Information Group, 1997.

Sheng, L.J. "China's Policy Toward the Spratly Islands in 1990s." Draft paper. Canberra: Strategic and Defense Studies Centers, Australian National University, 1994.

Shephard, A. "Maritime Tensions in the South China Sea and the Neighborhood: Some Solutions." *Studies in Conflict and Terrorism* 17, no. 2 (1993): 181–211.

———. "Oil on Troubled Waters: Indonesian Sponsorship of the South China Sea Workshop." *Studies in Conflict and Terrorism* 18, no. 1 (1995): 1–15.

Smith, C. "The Spratly Spats." *Vietnam Investor* 1, no. 13 (October/November, 1992): 1.

Song, Y.H. "Territorial Disputes in the South China Sea and the Asia-Pacific Security." Paper presented at the International Conference on Asia-Pacific Collective Security in the Post-Cold War Era. Taipei: Institute for National Policy Research, April 12–14, 1995.

———. "Impact of the Adoption of UNCLOS by the South China Sea Claimants." *National Policy Dynamic Analysis* 171 (August 19, 1997): 8–9 (in Chinese).

South China Morning Post. "China-Vietnam Oil Row Fuelled by Economics." March 21, 1997a, p. 9.

———. "Crises ASEAN Must Face." April 10, 1997b, p. 21.

United Daily News. "Chinese Navy Has Threatened Vietnamese Patrol Boats in the South China Sea." January 27, 1996a, p. 3 (in Chinese).

————. January 28, 1996b, p. 1 (in Chinese).

————. "Taiwanese Fishing Boat Was Rammed by the PRC Gunboat off the Pratas Islet." January 22, 1997a, p. 5 (in Chinese).

————. "The U.S. Urges Not to Solve the Scarborough Dispute by Force." May 30, 1997b, p. 9 (in Chinese).

————. July 28, 1997c, p. 3 (in Chinese).

"United States Government Policy on the Spratly Islands and the South China Sea." Statement handed out at the South China Sea Conference, Washington, DC, September 7, 1994.

USAF Historical Division. *The Army Air Forces in WWII*, Chicago: United States Air Force, 1953.

Valencia, M.J. *South-East Asian Seas: Oil Under Troubled Waters*. Oxford: Oxford University Press, 1985.

————. "The Spratly Islands: Dangerous Ground in the South China Sea." *Pacific Review* 1, no. 4 (1988): 382–95.

————. "Spratly Solution Still at Sea." *Pacific Review* 6, no. 2 (1993): 155–70.

————. *China and the South China Sea Disputes*. IISS Adelphi Paper no. 298, Oxford University Press, 1995.

Valencia, M.J., and Marsh, J.B. "Southeast Asia: Marine Resources, Extended Maritime Jurisdiction and Development." *Marine Resource Economics* 3, no. 1 (1986): 3–27.

Wall Street Journal. "China's Oil Needs Outstrip Its Supply." September 14, 1993, p. 1.

Wanandi, J. "The Future of ARF and CSCAP in the Regional Security Architecture." Paper presented in the ASEAN-ISIS 8th Asia Pacific Roundtable on Confidence Building and Conflict Reduction in the Pacific. Kuala Lumpur, January 5–8, 1994.

The War History of People's Liberation Army. Beijing: Military Science Publishing, 1989 (in Chinese).

World of Information: Asia and Pacific Review 1993/94. London: Kogan Page and Walden, 1993.

World Journal. "China and Taiwan to Begin Joint Exploration of Offshore Oil and Gas." March 13, 1994.

Wu, J.M. "The Geological and Structure Features of Nansha Islands and Their Prospect for Hydrocarbon Potential." Guangzhou, South China Sea Institute of Oceanology, *Geological Research of South China Sea Series* 3 (1991): 24–38 (in Chinese).

17

China and Confidence-Building in East Asia

Richard L. Grant

For two decades, beginning in the 1970s, Asia-Pacific security arrangements focused in general on containing and deterring the Soviet Union. Militarily, the United States provided the principal counterweight to Soviet power, and strategically the United States, Japan and China, together with other countries in the region, cooperated against Soviet assertiveness.

The collapse of the Soviet Union in 1991 radically altered this picture. Today, only one country retains superpower status in the region and globally: the United States. The unique status of the United States has raised fears that America might unilaterally attempt to impose its will on the region. In the meantime, other countries, free from the constraints of the Cold War, are seeking to promote their national interests in new and sometimes more vocal ways. This has led some to fear that regional instability, in the form of territorial disputes or arms races, could emerge in East Asia.

Others have longer-term fears about the durability of the U.S. commitment to the region or about the future intentions of East Asia's other two major powers, Japan and China. These uncertainties, among others, have led to calls for the creation of new security mechanisms to promote stability in East Asia. Already, since 1994, a regionwide government-to-government security dialogue has been taking place under the auspices of the ASEAN Regional Forum (ARF). This arrangement has been informally undergirded by the nongovernmental, track-two Council for Security Cooperation in the Asia-Pacific (CSCAP), as well as a host of other official and unofficial groups, primarily under the ASEAN umbrella, that meet to discuss and to coordinate cooperation in numerous areas.

High on many lists of security-enhancement mechanisms are confidence-building measures (CBMs). These can include general, declaratory measures, such as pledges of nonuse of force or the creation of zones of neutrality, or more specific steps, such as regular meetings of defense ministers, annual defense white papers, greater military transparency, and prior notification of military exercises.

The ARF organized a conference on CBMs in March 1997, which met in Beijing and was co-hosted by China and the Philippines. The participants at this meeting discussed such CBMs as security dialogues, exchange of military data and personnel, and the publication of national defense papers (Sutter 1997a, 10). But although China co-chaired this meeting, Beijing remains ambivalent about, if not hostile to, many efforts to develop a comprehensive set of CBMs in East Asia. This chapter assesses perceptions of China and its attitudes toward regional security, as well as Chinese perceptions of these very issues.

The "China Threat"

In today's post-Cold War environment, there are many who fear that China will emerge as a new regional hegemon in East Asia, using its economic weight and modernized military to impose its will on its neighbors and threaten regional stability. Some analysts point to China's unprecedented economic development during the last 18 years and to signs that this dynamism will continue well into the next decade, arguing that Beijing inevitably will seek expanded influence as a result. These analysts also point to China's military modernization, including weapons purchased from Russia such as 72 Su-27 fighter-ground attack aircraft, 50 T-72 tanks, and several *Kilo*-class submarines, as a clear sign of China's potential to become a military threat (Goldman 1997, 6).

For these analysts, one of the most compelling arguments for establishing a comprehensive set of CBMs in East Asia is to ensure that China does not destabilize the region. This argument, however, fuels Chinese skepticism over the desirability of participating in CBMs, for if they are promoted as a means of "containing" China, then the CBMs quite understandably lose their attraction to the Chinese. It is therefore worth downplaying the notion of a "Chinese threat" from the outset, making it easier to demonstrate that CBMs exist for the benefit of all participating states.

Moreover, although China is modernizing its military forces, most analysts believe that its true potential to threaten its neighbors is quite small. The People's Liberation Army (PLA) continues to rely on outdated technology and would only be able to transport three divisions to Taiwan (Godwin 1996). China's fighter aircraft and frigate forces remain at the same levels as in the 1980s, and there are serious doubts over the state of China's defense technological base (Frankenstein 1996). Most analysts do not believe that China could deploy a blue-water navy for at least two decades (Ferdinand 1997, 9).

In addition to its current inadequate military forces, China historically has not acted as a military aggressor except when its vital national interests, particularly its territorial sovereignty, are threatened. By way of example, one might regard the so-called ancestral instructions by Zhu Yuanzhang, founder of the Ming Dynasty:

> Remote separation by mountains and seas marks all the overseas states such as Vietnam, Korea, Thailand, India and Japan . . . Acquisition of their lands would not add to our supplies, and subjugation of their peoples would not augment our subjects. If they dare to make disturbances on our border areas, misfortune would befall them. Given their not making trouble, misfortune would similarly visit us if we should rashly attack them. I am worried that my descendants, relying on China's riches and strengths, would wantonly dispatch troops to cause bloodshed out of greed. . . . Such kinds of action should be absolutely forbidden. (Jin 1997, 3).

This fourteenth-century quote continues to reflect Beijing's strategic view of the world, and could be summed up colloquially as "Don't mess with us, and we won't mess with you!" The problem for many outside China is the definition of "us." And the problem for many within China is the difficulty in understanding how China's neighbors perceive Beijing's actions to defend China's territorial sovereignty, as China perceives it.

The Absolutes of Sovereignty

Chinese attitudes toward sovereignty must be framed in a historical context. To the Chinese, Western attitudes and behavior have been a festering affront ever since the mid-nineteenth century. Initially, they resulted in territorial concessions of Hong Kong and Macao under outside military pressure. Foreign occupation followed, first by Japanese troops, and continued after 1949 until the early 1970s, when most of the major powers embarked on isolationist policies. For China, the return of Hong Kong was a major step toward redressing the wrongs of history, a process that Mao Zedong initiated by restoring Chinese control over most of China's territory in 1949. The reversion of Hong Kong, Macao, and eventually Taiwan, will complete this process for the mainland Chinese.

The lengths to which China will go to ensure that its sovereignty will not be violated are extreme. China will sacrifice economic interests that the outside world views as essential in order to protect its self-defined territorial interests. For example, if Taiwan does move down the road to independence, China will take countervailing military action, even at enormous military, diplomatic, and economic cost. China demonstrated the strength of its commitment to the "one China" policy by launching large-scale military exercises in the Taiwan Strait in late 1995 and early 1996, during the prelude to legislative and presidential elections in Taiwan.

Because China views cross-Strait relations as an internal matter, it gives little consideration to the international repercussions of its actions. The alarm the 1995 military exercises caused throughout the region fueled the beliefs of "China threat" proponents and forced others to ask whether China might take similar action with regard to its claims in the South China Sea. For these reasons, CBMs, particularly those that enhance transparency of military doctrines and capabilities, would play a useful role, reassuring and clarifying China's intentions. Nonetheless, China continues to resist these types of CBMs, viewing them as interference in their internal affairs and a means of exposing military vulnerabilities to the outside world.

China and Territorial Disputes

Territorial disputes historically have been one of the greatest sources of tension—and not just in East Asia. China has always been sensitive to the integrity of its borders, dating from before Emperor Zhu's time and continuing today. In fact, since World War II, China has engaged in border skirmishes with Russia, India and Vietnam. But today, nearly all of these border territorial disputes have been settled peaceably. Most strikingly, nearly all the disputed border areas between Russia and China were resolved between 1991 and 1994, and both sides have pulled their forces 100 km back from their respective borders. In 1996, Russia, China, Kazakhstan, Krygyzstan and Tajikistan agreed to a series of multilateral confidence-building measures, including advance notification of military exercises, observer participation in exercises, and reductions in military force (Goldman 1997, 5).

Clearly, China is willing to resolve territorial disputes and to engage in concrete confidence-building measures when it believes such measures will advance its national interests. In the case of its shared borders with Russia and the central Asian republics, China realized that a multilateral approach would help secure its need for agreed borders, lower tensions, and, not incidentally, to control migrant populations. If China can engage in such activities to secure disputed land borders, it may be reasonable to hope that Beijing might enter into similar agreements to resolve maritime territorial disputes, particularly in the South China Sea.

Here, on the surface, China's record is less promising than its recent agreements with Russia, the central Asian republics, India, and Vietnam. In 1992, China passed a territorial law that laid claim to large swathes of the South China Sea, including areas also claimed by Vietnam, the Philippines, Malaysia, and Brunei. The ASEAN countries regard these disputes as the most important security issue in their relations with China, and they have sought to present China with a united front so as to engage China in multilateral dispute resolution. The ASEAN members seek to preserve stability and to limit or perhaps forestall permanently any change in the territorial status quo in the South China Sea. They hope to promote confidence, first by engaging in multilateral discussions to promote scientific, technical, and economic cooperation, and eventually by using these advances to resolve the sovereignty question (Wanandi 1996, 10).

Moreover, ASEAN has developed a number of mechanisms to further its approach. Beginning in 1990, Indonesia, which is not party to the South China Sea dispute, has organized a series of nongovernmental workshops to promote dialogue among the disputants. ASEAN has also sought to raise the issue within the ARF and CSCAP. China, however, has only been a grudging participant in these discussions. In addition, China has taken separate actions that appear to be attempts to resolve disputes with each individual country concerned.

While China has indicated its willingness in principle to participate in the ASEAN multilateral process, it has been extremely unwilling to discuss the military issues that arise from the South China Sea dispute. Moreover, China has taken military action, such as occupying Mischief Reef (claimed by the Philippines), and engaging in naval skirmishes with Vietnam, that indicate its desire to settle claims on its own terms. China also has provocatively engaged in oil exploration and fishing activities in disputed areas.

Encouragingly, however, China has entered into one bilateral confidence-building agreement with the Philippines. In 1996, the two countries agreed to a military code of conduct in the South China Sea that includes military exchanges, communications mechanisms for forces deployed in the area, and joint research on maritime science and cooperation on piracy control. This agreement might be expanded to include the other parties to the South China Sea territorial dispute.

China's Overall Approach to Confidence-Building Measures

In principle, China does not oppose confidence-building measures in East Asia. But for the historical reasons discussed earlier, the Chinese leadership remains extremely wary of any steps that they believe infringe on China's territorial rights. The Chinese, along with many others in the region, also are skeptical that models developed in the European context apply to East Asia. First, Beijing considers the Euro-Atlantic model irrelevant to Asia because it arose in the context of the Cold War, in which two powerful blocs were pitted against each other. This dichotomy does not exist in Asia, and China would be loath to support the development of institutions that would create one, particularly if it resulted in support for a U.S.-Japanese alliance against China.

Second, a key component of the Euro-Atlantic experience was the incorporation of human rights issues into the confidence-building process via Basket III of the Council on Security Cooperation in Europe (CSCE). China and most other East Asian nations do not consider human rights an appropriate subject for regional security discussions. Finally, Beijing would be loath to engage in any CBM process in which it was not a full and founding participant. This resistance to imposed regimes renders China highly skeptical of any initiatives proposed by the United States.

But as we have seen from the discussion of territorial disputes, China is not wholly averse to the use of CBMs. In general, Beijing places great importance on regional and global stability, and the avoidance of conflict. First and foremost, the Chinese consider a peaceful East Asia a prerequisite to its continued economic development. This concern recently was evident during the flare-up over the Senkaku/Diaoyu Islands, to which both China and Japan lay claim. Following the construction of a lighthouse on the islands by a Japanese right wing group, vociferous protests took place in Hong Kong and Taiwan, but the response from Beijing was much more muted; demonstrations were not permitted and the official government response was low-key. While restrictions on protests may have been linked to concerns over internal political stability, the overall response was also motivated by a desire not to alienate the Japanese, who are the largest provider of aid to China.

The Chinese approach to confidence-building is based on the basic principles of peaceful coexistence, including favoring voluntary measures; exhibiting a preference, although not an absolute one, for bilateral rather than multilateral mechanisms; supporting general measures that will promote peace and stability; and advocating a step-by-step approach to conflict resolution. China also believes it can make positive contributions to confidence building through its own actions and policies. For example, China has without a doubt contributed to stability on the Korean peninsula. It has done so not by applying pressure on North Korea, but by encouraging Pyongyang (the North Korean capital) to open up, reform economically, and to participate in four-party talks with China, South Korea, and the United States. Beijing also consults and cooperates with the United States, South Korea and Japan in efforts to engage North Korea in negotiations. Finally, Beijing views the good relations it has developed with South Korea not merely as a model that the United States and Japan could follow in possible future relations with North Korea, but also as a signal to other East Asian nations that China is capable and willing to engage in productive ties with smaller nations on a basis of equality (Sutter 1997b, 3).

Because of China's approach to confidence-building, the ASEAN approach, rather than that of the United States, is most likely to meet with success. China is likely to resist suggestions from the United States for a detailed confidence-building agenda and will respond more positively to calls for dialogue and cooperation. Initially wary of, if not hostile to, ASEAN attempts to develop a multilateral political and security dialogue, China became a full dialogue partner to the ASEAN Post Ministerial Meetings in 1995 and now participates in the ARF as well. In response to concerns within the ARF about a lack of transparency regarding its military capabilities and intentions, China published a defense white paper in 1996. Although this white paper falls far short of providing the kind of detailed information that other nations would provide, it is nonetheless an important first step. As noted earlier, China agreed to co-host an ARF meeting on confidence-building measures in March 1997.

More generally, China is engaged in discussions with ASEAN on a wide range of issues. In 1994 China and ASEAN created two joint committees on economic and trade cooperation and another on scientific and technical cooperation. The level of activity between China and ASEAN is so great that in February 1997, ASEAN and China created a joint cooperation committee to identify possible joint projects and to coordinate the ASEAN-China senior official talks, the work the two joint committees created in 1994, and the activities of the ASEAN Committee in Beijing (Lee 1997, 18).

Notwithstanding its preference for ASEAN-style dialogue, China does not reject all "hard" confidence-building measures proposed by the United States. China welcomes military-to-military cooperation, which the United States has resumed after temporarily suspending it following the 1989 Tiananmen Square tragedy. Senior Chinese military officials, including Liu Huaqing, the Vice Chairman of the PLA Military Commission, have visited the United States. American military officials have reciprocated, including General John Shalikasvili, then-Chairman of the Joint Chiefs of Staff. For the first time since 1989, the U.S. Navy made a port of call to Shanghai, and for the first time ever, the Chinese Navy called at San Diego. China has also resumed exchanges of personnel at military staff colleges in the United States.

These types of actions should be expanded to include other countries as well. It should be noted, however, that suggestions that China participate in such activities on a multilateral basis, perhaps initially jointly with Japan and the United States, have not received a warm response from the Chinese (Sutter 1997a, 3).

Conclusion

Although China is not wholly adverse to the development of confidence-building measures, its enthusiasm will remain limited. It will prefer a gradual approach, stressing the general over the specific, and bilateral over multilateral initiatives, and will resist fiercely any initiative that it believes violates its sovereignty. For example, China has entered into CBMs with Russia, India, the Philippines, and to a limited extent, the United States. It has now become more comfortable with the ARF process, and is making a contribution to stability in Northeast Asia. It has indicated sensitivity to concerns about its military capabilities and intentions.

Beijing has also demonstrated a willingness to participate in global confidence-building initiatives, including the Comprehensive Test Ban Treaty and adherence to, if not participation in, the Military Critical Technology Regime (MCTR). The prospects for a positive Chinese response to future confidence-building measures are good, provided that China believes that such measures are in its national interest and contribute to regional peace and stability.

Bibliography

Ferdinand, Peter. "China—The Emerging Giant." Paper presented at the 13th Conference of the UK-Japan 2000 Group, 1997.
Frankenstein, John, and Bates Gill. "Current and Future Challenges for Chinese Nuclear Force Modernisation: Limited Deterrence versus Multilateral Arms Control." *China Quarterly* 146 (June 1996): 394–427.
Goldman, Stuart. *Russia-Chinese Cooperation: Prospects and Implications.* Congressional Research Service, Report for Congress, January 1997.
Godwin, Paul. "From Continent to Periphery: PLA Doctrine, Strategy, and Capabilities Towards 2000." *China Quarterly* 146 (June 1996): 464–87.
Jin Dexiang. "Yellow Peril—A Hoax Then and Now." *Contemporary International Relations* 7, no. 7 (July 1997).
Lee Lai To. *The China Factor in ASEAN Security.* Conference paper, Ost-West Kolleg. Germany, March 1997.
Sutter, Robert. *Asian-Pacific Security Arrangements: The US-Japanese Alliance and China's Strategic View.* Congressional Research Service, Report for Congress, March 1997a.
———. *Korea: Improved South Korean-Chinese Relations—Motives and Implications.* Congressional Research Service, Report for Congress, July 1997b.
Wanandi, Jusuf. *Southeast Asia-China Relations.* Chinese Council of Advanced Policy Studies, December 1996.

18

Confidence-Building Measures in the Taiwan Strait

Cheng-yi Lin

In the post-Cold War era, the national security policies of Taiwan and China have followed different paths. By the late 1980s, as martial law was lifted and regulations concerning contact with the mainland relaxed, the Republic of China (ROC) on Taiwan began to modify its national security policy to a strictly defensive posture. Beijing, however, refuses to renounce the use of force to settle the Taiwan issue. As a result, Taipei not only must raise Beijing's costs of a military coercion of the island, but also must prepare to deal with nonmilitary pressure, military shows of force, and other kinds of harassment from China. In the diplomatic arena, Taipei seeks to maintain a substantial number of formal diplomatic relations, for fear of being downgraded to the status of another Special Administrative Region (SAR) of the People's Republic of China (PRC). According to one of a series of public opinion polls (National Sun Yat-sen University, February 1997), only 25 percent of people on the island regard cross-Strait relations as more important than Taiwan's diplomatic standing, and about 75 percent of the respondents believe that the PRC has been taking a hostile stand toward the ROC since June 1995.

In response to a June 1995 visit by Taiwanese President Lee Teng-hui to his alma mater, Cornell University, Beijing decided to suspend cross-Strait dialogue and to launch a series of military exercises near Taiwan. Beijing regards Taipei's move to break out of diplomatic isolation as a plot to create "two Chinas" or "one China, one Taiwan," and demands that Taipei suspend its pragmatic diplomacy as one precondition to improving cross-Strait relations. Beijing blames Taipei for initiating the current cross-Strait crisis by challenging the status quo, in effect since 1979, and recently has displayed a greater inclination to use coercive means to bring Taipei back to the "one China" principle. Beijing has also effectively restricted Taiwan's international activities to nongovernmental economic and cultural exchanges, and claims that those "spaces" are sufficient for Taiwan.

China has signed two separate confidence-building measures (CBMs) agreements in the military field to stabilize its border areas. The first was with Russia, Kazakhstan, Kyrgyzstan and Tajikistan in April 1996; the second was with India in November 1996. China also regards Taiwan as a major security threat, however, and tensions in the Taiwan Strait have escalated since June 1995. For Beijing, Taiwanese acceptance of China's nationalism, and U.S. rejection of Taiwan's arms acquisitions and visa applications for high-ranking officials are examples of viable CBMs. But because Beijing argues that CBMs can only be negotiated between sovereign states, it has suggested that the most useful form of CBMs is for other countries to "properly handle the Taiwan question"(Liu 1995, 134; Chalmers et al. 1995).

Ever since President Lee's visit to Cornell University, the United States has called for the resumption of cross-Strait dialogue. For example, Secretary of State Madeleine Albright advised that "[Taiwan and China] should do all they can to build confidence and avoid provocative actions and words" (Albright 1997). An interesting dialogue between Congressman Matt Salmon (R.-Arizona) and Assistant Secretary of State Winston Lord at a U.S. congressional hearing indicated the imperative need for CBMs between Taiwan and China:

> Salmon: Well, what actions has President Lee or the mainstream government of Taiwan done to show them that they are pursuing independence? To me, it is just a comedy of errors, and I would like your comments. Why is the leadership in China misreading so badly? Is it that they are getting erroneous information? What is the problem?

> Lord: [P]art of it is miscommunication, part of it is historical distrust, part of it is jockeying, but nevertheless, the more they can talk directly . . . the better off everyone will be. (U.S. Congress 1996a, 23)

Beginning in the early 1990s, Taiwan and China have concentrated on extending the economic aspect of CBMs, based on Taipei's expectation that cross-Strait security relations would thereby be ameliorated. For some theorists and practitioners, these economic interactions and human exchanges belong to the category of the low politics of functionalism rather than true CBMs. For lack of political negotiations on a government-to-government level, however, Taiwan and China could begin only with the nonmilitary dimensions of CBMs. These measures have helped to stabilize the situation in the Taiwan Strait, particularly after the suspension of cross-Strait dialogue. But because Taiwan-China confrontations have been regarded as one of the principal flash points in the Asia-Pacific ever since the March 1996 Taiwan Strait crisis, Taipei and Beijing need to focus primarily on security-oriented CBMs in addition to economic and other functional CBMs.

Nonmilitary CBMs in the Taiwan Strait

One theory posits that the development of economic and social cooperation between states is a prerequisite for the ultimate solution of political conflicts without resort to war. In other words, the social and economic effects of mutual cooperation spill over to facilitate the settlement of security issues. Taiwan has employed this functionalism as an approach to the PRC conflict. Functionalists in Taiwan firmly believe that as economic, social and cultural differences across the Taiwan Strait diminish, the conditions for peaceful reunification will gradually improve.

In February 1991, the ROC government adopted the "Guidelines for National Unification" (Guidelines), which envisage a three-phase process of reunification beginning with exchanges and reciprocity, followed by increased mutual trust and cooperation, and ending with consultation and unification (Mainland Affairs Council 1996a, 25–29). Rejecting Beijing's proposal for direct party-to-party talks regarding reunification, Taipei insists that cultural exchanges must come first, followed by bilateral trade and, finally, by direct political contacts. It is clear from the Guidelines that Taiwan's policy to refrain from official contacts with the PRC unless and until Beijing renounces the use of force as a means for unification, as well as its other efforts to isolate the ROC in the international arena.

The prospects for cross-Strait relations certainly appeared promising in the first half of 1995, when leaders for the two sides issued their blueprints for improvement of relations. PRC President Jiang Zemin's eight-point proposal of January 30, 1995, urged that a cross-Strait summit take place on Chinese soil and suggested that "talks be initiated and an agreement be reached on officially ending the state of hostility between the two sides of the Taiwan Straits under the principle of one China"(*China Daily* 1995). ROC President Lee Teng-hui responded on April 8, 1995, by issuing a six-point proposal to "pave the way for peace talks on ending the state of hostility." President Lee also urged Beijing to consider that "both sides should be assured of the ability to join international organizations on an equal footing," and that leaders of both sides may "meet on international occasions" (*Free China Journal* 1995b). But although Jiang stated that "Chinese should not fight their fellow

Chinese," Beijing did not forswear the use of force against "foreign forces attempting to interfere in China's reunification and advancing Taiwan independence." Even so, President Lee Teng-hui pledged that the "Chinese should help their fellow Chinese to serve their mutual interests in trade and business," and he expressed Taiwan's willingness "to provide agricultural expertise to help farmers on the mainland."

Lee Teng-hui's visit to Cornell University, however, had a tremendous and immediate impact on Beijing's policy toward Taiwan. What concerned Beijing the most was Taipei's commitment to the "one China" principle. The PRC conducted several rounds of military exercises near Taiwan to intimidate Taiwan's voters as they chose a new legislature in December 1995 and a new president in March 1996. President Lee Teng-hui and Peng Ming-min together seized 75 percent of the popular vote, however, an indication that the majority of Taiwanese were not intimidated by Beijing's coercion. Nevertheless, the PRC did not totally fail in its coercive campaign against Taiwan. Beijing demonstrated that it had the capability to set the agenda in Taiwan's first direct presidential election, as cross-Strait relations became the dominant issue in the presidential race. All presidential candidates pledged to seek better relations with China after the election and urged Beijing not to intervene in Taiwan's election. At the same time, all promised that if elected they would seek a peace accord with the PRC.

Informal Relations

Despite their lack of official contacts, Taiwan and mainland China have developed a number of informal relations since 1987. Tourism, trade, investment, and cultural and sports exchanges are increasing rapidly. The private but government-endorsed Straits Exchange Foundation (SEF) was established in Taiwan to handle bilateral issues in conjunction with its PRC counterpart, the Association for Relations across the Taiwan Strait (ARATS). The first high-level, semi-official meeting between Koo Chen-fu, Chairman of SEF, and Wang Daohan, Chairman of ARATS, took place in Singapore in April 1993. Taipei described the Koo-Wang meeting as "nongovernmental, administrative, economic, and functional in nature," but the key to the breakthrough of this meeting was that "both sides agreed to express the meaning of 'one China' in each side's own words" (Koo 1996, 6). Altogether, four agreements were signed between the SEF and the ARATS:

1. Agreement on Use and Verification of Certificates of Authentication Across the Taiwan Strait.
2. Agreement on Matters Concerning Inquiry and Compensation for [Lost] Registered Mail Across the Taiwan Strait.

3. Agreement on the System for Contacts and Meetings Between SEF and ARATS.
4. Joint Statement of Koo-Wang Talks. (Straits Exchange Foundation, 1993, 43–51)

In establishing regular communication channels, the SEF and the ARATS agreed in principle to "hold a meeting once every six months" at the vice-chairman or secretary-general level, concerning the business of the two organizations, and that these meetings would alternate between Taiwan and China, "or in a third place settled on through discussions." Deputy secretaries-general of the organizations would hold meetings quarterly. They are designated "as liaison persons for emergencies," and "should contact each other and take appropriate measures in such cases." In the fourth agreement, the SEF and the ARATS "concur in the necessity of strengthening economic exchanges" and "agree to actively promote mutual visits and exchanges of young people, the press, and science and technology exchanges" across the Taiwan Strait. The SEF and the ARATS also named topics to be addressed in the future, including joint efforts to quash marine smuggling and robbery, repatriation of illegal migrants, resolution of marine fishing disputes, protection of intellectual property, judicial cooperation, and cooperation in exploitation of energy and resources (Straits Exchange Foundation 1993, 28–31).

Ever since the historic Koo-Wang talks, at least three rounds of negotiations at the vice-chairman level and seven rounds of negotiations at the deputy secretary-general level have taken place between the SEF and the ARATS (Table 18.1). The vice chairmen of the two organizations, Chiao Jen-ho of the SEF and Tang Shubei of the ARATS, issued statements in February and August 1994. In the August 1994 joint statement, the SEF and the ARATS announced a preliminary agreement regarding the return of air hijackers and illegal immigrants, and the resolution of fishing disputes (*Free China Journal* 1994). No agreements on these issues had yet been signed when the third round of the Chiao-Tang talks ended in Beijing in January 1995, however, because of disagreement over a provision allowing personnel on official vessels to carry out "on-the-spot settlements" in fishing disputes (*Free China Journal* 1995a).

Regarding joint cooperation on energy exploration, representatives of the Chinese Petroleum Corporation of Taiwan (CPCT) and the PRC's China National Offshore Oil Corporation (CNOOC) met in Singapore in April and October 1994 to discuss the possibility of a joint venture for commercial interests, disregarding political and sovereignty issues. In August 1995, the two corporations held a conference on cross-Strait oil technology in Taipei, despite heightened tensions between Taipei and Beijing over President Lee's

Table 18.1

Cross-Strait Talks Since April 1993

Major issues: Repatriation of hijackers and illegal immigrants and handling of fishing disputes

At the vice-chairman level
Chief negotiators: Chiao Jen-ho (SEF); Tang Shubei (ARATS)

Round	Place	Time
1	Beijing	February 1994
2	Taipei	August 1994
3	Beijing	January 1995

At the deputy secretary general level
Chief negotiators: Shi Hwei-you (SEF); Sun Yafu (ARATS)

Round	Place	Time
1	Beijing	August 25–September 3, 1993
2	Xiamen	November 2–7, 1993
3	Taipei	December 18–22, 1993
4	Beijing	March 24–31, 1994
5	Taipei	July 30–August 7, 1994
6	Nanjing	November 21–28, 1994
7	Beijing	January 21–28, 1995

Source: Straits Exchange Foundation, *Jiaoliu* (Intercourse), various issues.

visit to the United States. In July 1996, the CPCT-affiliated Overseas Petroleum Investment Corporation and the CNOOC formally signed a two-year agreement in Taipei on seismic and oceanographic survey for joint exploration off the Zhujiang (Pearl River) Delta near Tungsha (Pratas) Island in the northern boundary of the South China Sea (*Jiaoliu* 1996; *Asian Wall Street Journal* 1995b).

Those who deem better cross-Strait relations a prerequisite for Taiwan's security would like to see Taipei cooperate with Beijing in the South China Sea as a way to build confidence in the Taiwan Strait. They believe talks with China concerning the development of resources in the South China Sea could improve mutual trust between Taipei and Beijing. Beijing has also demonstrated its interest by offering to provide the garrison on the Taiping Island (Itu Aba) in the Nansha (Spratly) Islands with desalinized water and other supplies, and by suggesting a joint survey and development of natural resources in the region (Gao 1994, 354; *Zhongguo shibao* 1995). But Beijing's shift from a peaceful reunification policy to a militant strategy that combined a media criticism campaign with coercive military pressure has forced Taipei to rule out the option of siding with the PRC, not only in the Nansha

(Spratly) Islands, but also in the Tiaoyutai (Senkaku) Islets, vis-à-vis other claimants.

Economic Policies

Taiwanese President Lee Teng-hui had expressed an interest in opening direct commercial links across the Taiwan Strait, although he urged the PRC to sign a peace accord before Taiwan would do so (*China Post* 1996a, 1996b; *Asian Wall Street Journal* 1996). In his May 1996 inaugural address, President Lee took a step further:

> In the future, at the call of my country and with the support of its people, I would like to embark upon a journey of peace to mainland China taking with me the consensus and will of the 21.3 million people. I am also ready to meet with the top leadership of the Chinese Communists for a direct exchange of views in order to open up a new era of communication and cooperation between the two sides and ensure peace, stability and prosperity in the Asia-Pacific region. (Mainland Affairs Council 1996b, 45)

The idea of a summit meeting between the heads of Taiwan and China was endorsed subsequently by Taiwan's National Development Conference in December 1996. The ruling Kuomintang (KMT), the opposition Democratic Progressive Party (DPP), and the New Party reached a consensus at the conference, stating that "efforts should be made to facilitate the opportune moment for the leaders of both sides to meet and create a new era of cross-Strait cooperation." In the meantime, representatives of the KMT and the opposition parties recommended that the private sector (e.g., the Straits Exchange Foundation) establish a Cross-Strait Forum in which "a wide array of representative figures from various sectors of each side are invited to exchange general views in a personal capacity on how to peacefully solve cross-Strait issues, without pre-set positions."

Tensions in the Taiwan Strait slowed the growth rate of bilateral trade between Taiwan and China; for example, it stood at 19.4 percent in 1994, but dropped to 8.2 percent in 1995 and 6.0 percent in 1996, as cross-Strait trade totaled $22.5 billion in 1995, and $23.8 billion in 1996 (*Zhongguo shibao* 1996). Taipei was forced to regulate the flow of investment to China and called on local firms to focus on investing in the island. President Lee urged Taiwan's business sector to realize that "national survival and development are more important than business opportunity" and to refrain from challenging the government policy of "staying the course with all deliberate speed." Taipei's restrictions on investment in China caused a 10.9 percent slide in investment in China between 1996 and the first half of 1997 (*Straits Times* 1997c).

Development of cross-Strait relations, however, did not come to a complete standstill. In March 1997, a Taiwanese jet airliner was hijacked to China, but was quickly returned. The hijacker, Liu Shan-chung, an unemployed journalist, was denied his request for political asylum and handed over to Taiwan in May 1997. In return, Taipei reversed its policies regarding hijackers and repatriated two convicted hijackers to China in July 1997 (*International Herald Tribune* 1997; *Free China Journal* 1997b; *Straits Times* 1997d). After two years of resisting Taipei's offshore transshipment scheme, Beijing allowed its first merchant vessel to call on Kaohsiung in April 1997. For Taipei, the shipments are not "direct" because cargo is not allowed to enter Taiwan's customs and can only be reloaded for onward shipment to third countries (*Asian Wall Street Journal* 1995a; *Straits Times* 1997a, 1997b). For years, Taipei had indicated its willingness to conduct negotiations through the SEF and the ARATS regarding air and sea links between Taiwan and Hong Kong after July 1, 1997. Beijing rejected Taipei's proposal but, out of practical necessity, backed Hong Kong's Cathay Pacific Airlines and Shipowners' Association to reach agreements, respectively, with Taipei Aviation Association and the SEF in July 1995 and May 1997 (*Lianhebao* 1995; *Free China Journal* 1997a). Coming during the period of suspension of cross-Strait dialogue, all these breakthroughs indicate that unilateral CBMs can invite opposing parties to adopt reciprocal measures and thus can constitute a process of tacit bargaining.

After President Jiang Zemin's state visit to the United States, on November 6, 1997, the ARATS sent a letter inviting SEF Vice Chairman Chaio Jen-ho to attend a seminar on the prospects for cross-Strait economic relations in Xiamen in December. Taipei appreciated the invitation but suggested that SEF Chairman Koo Chen-fu lead a delegation to visit the mainland. Taipei also urged Beijing to resume the Koo-Wang talks without any preconditions. The ARATS declined Taipei's proposal, blamed the SEF for politicizing the event, and announced on November 13, 1997, the postponement of the seminar (*Straits Times* 1997e). The surprise victory of the Democratic Progressive Party (DPP), however, in Taiwan's local elections on November 29, 1997, may become a nightmare for Beijing. China can no longer engage in wishful thinking that the KMT will remain in power forever. Instead, Beijing will be forced to devote more energy to contacts and communication with the DPP and be prepared to negotiate with its leaders.

Security-Oriented CBMs in the Taiwan Strait

Although the large gap in military capability between Taiwan and China makes it hard to establish CBMs in the Taiwan Strait, Taipei is paying more attention to this aspect of its security. Taipei has adopted a nonoffensive

Table 18.2

Defense Share of Total ROC Government Budget, 1987–1996

1987	50.8%
1988	49.2%
1989	47.7%
1990	35.2%
1991	31.8%
1992	27.7%
1993	25.3%
1994	24.3%
1995	24.5%
1996	22.8%

Source: The Republic of China Yearbook 1997 (Taipei: Government Information Office, 1997), p. 124.

strategic posture, proposed a peace agreement with China, pledged not to acquire nuclear weapons, thinned out troops stationed on the offshore islands, and adopted other security-related CBMs to increase transparency on national defense.

Taipei has stated that its defense goal is to protect Taiwan, Penghu (the Pescadores), Kinmen (Quemoy), and Matsu, rather than to adopt an offensive posture toward China. Under the ongoing arms replacement program, ROC defense spending has increased in absolute terms despite the end of the Cold War and the changed focus of Taiwan's military strategy and defense priorities. The proportion of the budget devoted to defense expenditures has decreased, however, as has the defense share of the gross domestic product. ROC defense expenditures fell below 40 percent in 1991 and below 30 percent of the government budget in 1992. Since 1992, the ROC government has decreased defense expenditures to approximately 25 percent of the budget, or about $10 billion (Table 18.2). In 1996, Taiwan's total armed forces stood at 459,000 (*Lianhebao* 1996). Under the Plan of Restructuring of Defense Organizations and Armed Forces and the so-called elite troops policy, the ROC's armed forces will fall to a maintenance level of 400,000 by the year 2003. Taipei currently believes that 400,000 is the minimum size force needed to support a defensive deterrence strategy.

In May 1992, Cheyne Chiu, then President Lee's close aide and presidential spokesman, suggested that Taiwan and China sign a nonaggression agreement (FBIS-China 1992; Hickey 1997, 49–50). Despite Beijing's shift from a peaceful reunification policy to a militant strategy toward Taiwan, Taipei has continued to propose negotiating a peace accord with China. For leaders in Taipei, the experiences of such divided nations as Germany and Korea, particularly policies against mutual exclusivity in the international arena and the renunciation of the use of force against each other, could be adopted as principles of cross-Strait relations.

Dual-System Models

In November 1972, the Federal Republic of Germany and the German Democratic Republic initialed the Basic Treaty, with the two governments pledging (1) to maintain good-neighborly relations on the basis of equal rights, including inviolability of borders and noninterference in the affairs of the other; (2) to solve disagreements through peaceful means and to abide by the principles of the United Nations Charter, including respect for independence, the right of self-determination, and the protection of human rights; and (3) to exchange permanent representatives, and to move forward with economic, scientific, and cultural cooperation (Balfour 1982, 239–240).

In the case of the two Koreas, Seoul and Pyongyang signed an Agreement on Reconciliation, Nonaggression, and Exchange and Cooperation in 1991, consisting of (1) respect for each other's political and social systems, and noninterference in each other's internal affairs; (2) nonuse of force, peaceful resolution of disputes, and prevention of accidental armed clashes; and (3) family reunion and increased trade, travel, and education contact (Rudolph 1993, 30).

In comparison with the divided nations of Germany and Korea, the sharp inequalities between the PRC and ROC in terms of territory (270:1) and population (60:1) suggest that it is almost impossible to maintain a pluralistic two-Chinas environment. Taiwan's leaders doubt the credibility of Beijing's commitments, given the dominant bargaining position of the PRC. Taipei is also discouraged by having to negotiate from a position of weakness. Although the two Germanys and Koreas renounced the use of force in the form of either a treaty or an agreement, the PRC will not commit to refraining from the use of military means against Taiwan to achieve any future reunification.

Following the model of the German Basic Treaty and other CBM agreements, the KMT Central Policy Council commissioned a study of a cross-Strait peace accord in 1996, including the substance of such CBMs as nonuse of force, transparency of defense budget, a ban on military exercises in the Taiwan Strait and its proximity, noninterference in each other's internal and external affairs, and the establishment of permanent representative missions in each other's capitals. The draft peace accord states that peaceful reunification of China is a common wish of the Chinese people on both sides of the Taiwan Strait, and separatist activities should be diminished. In fact, Taipei could argue for a quid pro quo: Beijing would renounce the use of force in exchange for Taipei's agreement to refrain from seeking independence. For Taipei and Beijing, these kinds of declaratory CBMs could be most beneficial in resolving long-standing points of contention (*Zhongyang ribao* 1997; Manning and Montaperto 1997, 3).

Facing the PRC's missile threat, Taiwan's legislators and members of the National Assembly have advised the government to reconsider a nuclear option for Taiwan's ultimate defense. President Lee at first responded that Taipei "should restudy the question from a long-term point of view," but he later concluded that Taipei would not pursue a nuclear option (*Ziyou shibao* 1995; *Yazhou zhoukan* 1996; Hickey 1997, 42–46). Not only have the major political parties in Taiwan reached a consensus against going nuclear, but the Ministry of National Defense and Atomic Energy Council also have consistently rebutted foreign media reports about a secret nuclear program in Taiwan (*China Post* 1996c; *Qingnian ribao* 1996b).

CBMs in the Taiwan Strait Area

Even though there is little chance that the PRC will use nuclear weapons against Taiwan, Beijing's refusal to renounce the use of force still causes Taipei to worry about the worst possible scenario: that Beijing will cross the nuclear threshold to bring Taiwan back to the motherland. Taipei's concern is not altogether groundless. For example, Chinese disarmament ambassador Sha Zukang told *Newsweek* magazine in August 1996 that China would not give up the right to use force to settle the Taiwan issue, and even stated that the Chinese policy against first strikes with nuclear weapons "does not apply to Taiwan." Soon after this chilling remark, Beijing issued a statement that the report was inaccurate (*Straits Times* 1996a; 1996b). This misunderstanding demonstrates the necessity of a joint declaration prohibiting the use of nuclear weapons, or affirming nonattack on opposing nuclear facilities, in any future cross-Strait peace accord.

Taipei regards the Quemoy and Matsu Islands as its first defense perimeter. In the 1958 Taiwan Strait crisis, then U.S. Secretary of State John Foster Dulles probed the possibility of an agreement between Taiwan and China aimed at demilitarizing the offshore islands. The ROC president, Chiang Kai-shek, rejected the proposal on the ground that the loss of Quemoy would naturally lead to the loss of Taiwan; he was forced, however, to withdraw 15,000 troops from Quemoy (*Foreign Relations of the United States* 1996, 157–158, 485, 536). To defuse the 1958 Taiwan Strait crisis, Mao Zedong decided not to fire on even-numbered days against Quemoy's airfields, beaches, and wharves if the ROC resupply convoy to the island lacked an American escort. President Dwight D. Eisenhower later described this fire pattern as a Gilbert and Sullivan war (Eisenhower 1965, 304). Oddly enough, this fire and cease-fire pattern was maintained for 20 years, until Beijing established diplomatic relations with the United States.

After the repeal of the Formosa Resolution in 1974 and the normalization of relations between the United States and the People's Republic of China in 1979, civilian and military analysts in Taiwan and the United States questioned the wisdom of maintaining one-fifth of Taiwan's best troops on the offshore islands. They argued that from a military perspective, the ROC would pay a high price for defending the offshore islands because "[t]he troops garrisoned there would be sacrificed in any determined invasion, and their loss would significantly reduce the defense capabilities of the ROC in any subsequent invasion of Taiwan." Furthermore, they suggested that "a reduction in the force levels on the offshore islands might even lessen the possibility of PRC attack on them, since such an attack, without the potential for reducing the military capabilities of the ROC, would net the PRC only a small amount of land" (Snyder et al. 1980, 50).

In May 1990, having survived the political crisis over the upcoming presidential election that factionalized the KMT, President Lee Teng-hui called on Beijing's leaders to roll back the People's Liberation Army's deployment to 300 km from Fujian Province, which faces Quemoy and Matsu (*Lianhebao* 1990). In November 1994, Shih Ming-teh, then-Chairman of the DPP, proposed demilitarizing the offshore islands and converting them into a Zone of Peace, Freedom and Tourism and a center of cross-Strait economic interactions (*Tzuli wanbao* 1994). No positive response came from Beijing to these innovative CBM proposals.

In 1991, a group of Taiwan's scholars published a draft treaty aimed at alleviating the crisis. With respect to communications CBMs, it proposed "the establishment of a hot-line between the top leaders on the two sides" (Yu et al. 1991). For years, Taiwan's Straits Exchange Foundation has sought an effective communications link with its counterpart ARATS, such as a hotline, but the feedback has not been as positive as hoped or expected. During the March 1996 Taiwan Strait crisis, Gerrit W. Gong, director of the Asia Studies Program of the Center for Strategic and International Studies, suggested to the U.S. Congress that "the United States officially or unofficially might offer good offices to facilitate limited contact between PRC and Taiwan militaries focused on hotline and crisis management issues in the beginning" (U.S. Congress 1996a, 25). The creation of bilateral hotlines would be a first step toward a more predictable and less crisis-prone environment in the Taiwan Strait, but a formal multilateral communications network among Taipei, Beijing, and Washington could be more difficult to achieve. There is a possibility, however, that Taipei and Beijing may begin dialogue on security perceptions through their retired military officers to alleviate misunderstandings and misperceptions (*National Policy Dynamic Analysis* 1996).

Under current circumstances, it would be nearly impossible for Taipei and Beijing to adopt open CBMs in the form of a treaty, yet constraints on military activities that the PRC tacitly adopts should be encouraged. For example, People's Liberation Army's military activities usually are prevented from crossing the median line of the Taiwan Strait or affecting Taiwan's air flight routes and sea-lanes of communications to the Quemoy and Matsu Islands, as well as to the Taiping (Itu Aba) and Tungsha (Pratas) Islands in the South China Sea. Further positive responses by Beijing to Taipei's unilateral gestures are necessary, however, to the creation of a risk-reduction regime in the Taiwan Strait.

The fortifications of Quemoy and Matsu may be impressive, but a naval blockade would quickly dry up ROC firepower and force the garrison to become hostage to the PRC. Demilitarization of the offshore islands might deprive Taiwan of some strategic depth, but certain constraining CBMs covering ROC-held offshore islands and the Fujian Province might mitigate the losses. These include prohibiting large-scale military exercises, designating a keep-out zone for air combat patrols, eliminating deployment of weapons of mass destruction, and installing a hot-line between military authorities, and other measures. In fact, Taiwan already has undertaken some CBMs of this sort. Its air force has not patrolled the airspace to the west of the median line in the Taiwan Strait for a long time. In addition, Taipei has taken other steps to avoid further tensions in the Taiwan Strait, including its decisions, since the late 1980s, to redeploy additional troops from the offshore islands to Taiwan and to delay a live-ammunition military exercise on Matsu Island in April 1996 (*International Herald Tribune* 1996a).

With regard to transparency CBMs, the ROC Ministry of National Defense has published three editions of its Defense White Paper (1992, 1994, 1996), which detail its security strategy toward China. The PRC, however, only issued its first White Paper on Arms Control and Disarmament, which did not mention the Taiwan issue, in 1995 (*Beijing Review* 1995b; ROC Ministry of National Defense 1992, 1994, 1996). The ROC Ministry of National Defense also makes a practice of announcing a detailed military exercises calendar at the beginning of each fiscal year in July, to dispel suspicions and reduce uncertainties (*Qingnian ribao* 1997; *Ziyou shibao* 1997). By contrast, China only gave three days' notice before it launched missile tests in the East China Sea in July 1995 and in the Taiwan Strait in March 1996 (*Renmin ribao* 1995; *Xinhua yuebao* 1996). This short notice caused considerable inconvenience for Taipei, notably in the diversion of air traffic routes. When compared to the five and ten days' prior notification of major military exercises that China gives to

India and Russia, respectively, this short notice period indicates that Beijing, in fact, is less tolerant of its "compatriots" in Taiwan.

A Third-Party Confidence Builder?

The role of the United States in facilitating CBMs between China and Taiwan has been inconsistent at best. After the Sino-British Joint Declaration over Hong Kong in 1984, Beijing began to promote the concept of "one country, two systems" to U.S. leaders. Deng Xiaoping expressed his wish to President Ronald Reagan, via British Prime Minister Margaret Thatcher, that the United States could "do something" to help China's reunification. The Reagan administration turned down the proposal (Lasater 1989, 148). In September 1986, Deng Xiaoping revealed to Mike Wallace, on the CBS "Sixty Minutes" program, that the United States "can encourage and persuade Taiwan first to have 'three exchanges' with us, namely the exchange of mails, trade, and air and shipping services," because contacts of this kind could create conditions for Taiwan and China "to discuss the question of reunification and ways to achieve it" (*Beijing Review* 1986). After Beijing's leaders urged the U.S. government to become involved in efforts to promote China's reunification, Gaston J. Sigur, then-Assistant Secretary of State for East Asian and Pacific Affairs, argued in December 1986 that "there is a real danger that American involvement would be counterproductive" (*Department of State Bulletin* 1987a, 51).

Although the United States has thus far declined to mediate differences between Taiwan and China, mutual accommodation between Taipei and Beijing is not only desirable and necessary for the stability of East Asia, but also is one way to relieve the U.S. dilemma in future confrontations across the Taiwan Strait. Whether Washington should take a strictly neutral position, not promoting the expansion of cross-Strait relations, or whether it should actively engage in fostering an environment for rapprochement is debatable and it is difficult to arrive at a clear-cut answer. While the United States refrains from pressuring Taipei to negotiate with Beijing, Washington welcomes and sometimes even encourages Taipei to conduct direct talks with Beijing to settle their differences. In March 1987, then Secretary of State George Shultz implied that the United States would not reject the role of animator in cross-Strait relations when he declared in Shanghai that "steadfast [U.S.] policy seeks to foster an environment in which such development [indirect trade and increasing human exchanges] can continue to take place" (*Department of State Bulletin* 1987b, 10–11). Regarding the Koo-Wang talks in April 1993, then-Assistant Secretary of State Winston Lord reiterated that the United States welcomed direct talks between Taipei and Beijing on functional matters, as long as these were accomplished peacefully (*Zhongyang ribao* 1993).

The United States insists that the Taiwan issue be solved peacefully by the Chinese themselves. At the same time, Washington does not reject a role as a balancer and stabilizer in Taiwan-China military relations. For example, the United States tried to establish a linkage between improved U.S.-PRC relations and the PRC's renunciation of force against Taiwan when it decided to phase out U.S. troops on Taiwan, to establish diplomatic relations with the PRC, and to reduce U.S. arms sales to Taiwan (Harding 1992, 51, 72, 114–115; Oksenberg 1982, 188). As Taiwan gains more confidence in the military arena, Washington believes that Taipei will be more willing to expand its level of contacts with Beijing. President George Bush asserted in September 1992 that the sale to Taiwan of 150 F-16s would promote stability in the Taiwan Strait because "the United States has provided Taiwan with sufficient defensive capabilities to sustain the confidence it needs to reduce the tensions [in the Taiwan Strait]" (*Weekly Compilation of Presidential Documents* 1992, 1556–1557). Interestingly, Qian Qichen, PRC Vice Premier and Foreign Minister, and Hau Pei-tsun, then ROC Premier, both expressed the belief that Beijing and Taipei would not let the F-16 sales hinder further development of cross-Strait relations. As evidence of this cooperation, the first high-level semi-official meeting of Koo-Wang talks took place in April 1993, only seven months after the American decision to sell the F-16s (*Lianhebao* 1992; *Zhongyang ribao* 1992).

There is no doubt that the United States opposes any military solution to the Taiwan issue, but the degree to which the United States is willing to endanger its relations with the PRC to support Taiwan's defense against a PRC invasion is in question. The U.S. government clearly prefers unspecified support rather than a specified defense commitment in the event of PRC coercion against Taiwan, and maintains this "strategic ambiguity" mainly to avoid encouraging either Beijing to choose a path of military coercion or Taipei to make a unilateral declaration of independence (U.S. Congress 1996b, 16–19, 22). If Taiwan does not provoke China by declaring independence, but instead Beijing initiates the military action for any variety of reasons, then the United States would become involved in defusing the crisis (Shinn 1996, 75). While the United States would try to avoid direct military confrontation with the PRC, the U.S. naval presence in the Taiwan Strait would force Beijing to guess what actions the United States might take.

Under the initiative of Secretary of Defense William Perry, President Clinton decided to dispatch the aircraft carrier *USS Nimitz* to join the *USS Independence* near Taiwan to monitor the PRC's military activities in March 1996. Clinton's decision quickly defused the 1996 Taiwan Strait crisis and allowed Taiwan's first direct presidential election to proceed smoothly (*Jane's Defence Weekly* 1996a, 1996b). Immediately before and after this decision, U.S. National Security Adviser Anthony Lake met Liu Huaqiu, the Foreign Affairs Director of PRC State Council, on March 8, and U.S. Deputy National Security Adviser Samuel R. Burger met Ting Mou-shih, Secretary-General of the ROC National Security Council, on March 11, to counsel Beijing and Taipei against further provocative actions (*International Herald Tribune* 1996b).

It is still too early to tell whether the dispatch of U.S. aircraft carriers will become the mode of handling future Taiwan Strait crises. Even if the PRC crosses the line into military intimidation, the actions the U.S. Seventh Fleet might remain tactically ambiguous (U.S. Congress 1996a, 11–12). Although the Clinton administration played the role of good offices by conducting separate talks with Taipei and Beijing during the Strait crisis and regarded "resumption of the cross-Strait dialogue between Beijing and Taipei" as a key security objective, whether it would exert pressure on Taipei to enter negotiations with Beijing remains to be seen (*Washington Post* 1997; The White House 1997).

If and when the United States decides to mediate, it probably would damage itself by begging for concessions from both sides of the Taiwan Strait to keep negotiations alive. Beijing might reject U.S. mediation of the specific terms of reunification because it violates the principle of noninterference in Chinese internal affairs. If Washington were to offer to play the role of mediator, its offer could be interpreted as an explicit endorsement of reunification as the only option for Taiwan's future. The United States has not challenged Beijing's policy to apply the "one country, two systems" concept in determining Hong Kong's future. But with respect to the future of Taiwan, the U.S. government has taken no specific position. The Clinton administration has acted to forestall Taiwan independence and any actions that might imply Taiwan's independence as a sovereign state. At the same time, however, Taipei appreciates U.S. reaffirmation of its interest in a peaceful settlement of the Taiwan issue while declining to specify the reunification of China as a desirable goal.

Taipei might desire that the United States play the role of guarantor if a future cross-Strait peace accord were reached, but not as a mediator exerting pressure on Taiwan. Taipei's sense of insecurity, the major obstacle to peace talks, cannot be mollified in the absence of three conditions: the right to participate in intergovernmental organizations; reciprocal status in government-to-government negotiations; and PRC renunciation of the use of force. The United States would find it difficult not to sympathize with Taipei, and it would be easy to antagonize Beijing in seeking such concessions. In such a case, Washington might become the scapegoat in an abortive attempt to bring Taipei and Beijing together.

Taipei welcomes the experience of the United States as animator and messenger in supporting its membership in the Asian Development Bank and the Asia-Pacific Economic Cooperation, but U.S. support seems to be limited to regional economic/financial organizations rather than global security organizations, such as the United Nations. Washington has declined to support Taiwan's entry to the UN, because such an action "would come at great cost to [U.S.] relations with China," and "would jeopardize peace and stability in the Taiwan Strait" (Wiedemann 1995). But those advising Taipei to negotiate directly with Beijing regarding membership in intergovernmental organizations argue that as Taiwan is "a sovereign state," it does not "need the approval, nor the acquiescence, of any state" for international participation and status. Taipei also believes Beijing's policy "will not change regardless of whether we do or do not ask for U.S. help in admitting us to various international organizations." At the very least, Taipei still needs Washington's reassurance that the PRC will not be allowed to change the status quo in the Taiwan Strait by military means.

Conclusion

Suspicion and mistrust impede Taiwan and China from moving beyond the economic aspect of CBMs. Taiwan's threat perception of the PRC is based mainly upon Beijing's refusal to renounce the use of force against the island. In circular fashion, however, China's threat perception of Taiwan mostly comes from the fear that Taiwan is creeping toward de jure independence, so Beijing retains the option to use force against Taiwan.

Resisting the possibility that it will be downgraded to the status of Hong Kong, Taiwan has poured significant resources into maintaining a certain number of formal diplomatic relations and seeking entry to the UN. Although Taipei cites the case of Germany and argues that allowing Taiwan to enter the UN would help promote the reunification of China, Beijing regards Taipei's move as creating "two Chinas" or "one China, one Taiwan." For Taipei, the purpose of diplomatic initiatives is not to compete for diplomatic recognition with Beijing, but for the survival of the island. Nevertheless, Beijing regards Taiwan's defensive posture as provocative.

Through the SEF and the ARATS, Taiwan and China had conducted dialogue on cooperation in suppressing criminal activities and solving marine fishing disputes before Beijing called off the second round of Koo-Wang talks in 1995. Taipei and Beijing thus have achieved the difficult task of beginning social and economic cooperation before political and security problems are solved. What matters most, however, is the spillover effect of these discussions into tougher security issues. Despite suspension of cross-Strait dialogue, both Taiwan and China have adopted unilateral CBMs to persuade each other to cooperate for the common interest. Two years after Taiwan first proposed Special Operational and Transshipment Zones as the first step to establish direct navigational and commercial links, direct shipping between Taiwan and China began in May 1997. But in addition to trade, cultural exchange, and humanitarian CBMs, Taipei and Beijing need reconciliation, consultation, and nonaggression CBMs to maintain peace and stability in the Taiwan Strait.

Beijing has set Taipei's suspension of its UN bid as a precondition for the resumption of cross-Strait dialogue. Taipei may find it equally difficult to ask Beijing to renounce the use of force before negotiating for a peace accord. China's CBMs with Russia and India to reduce tensions and to disengage forces along disputed border are remarkable, however, and Beijing has also demonstrated its interest in the concept of multilateral CBMs. Thus, Beijing can hardly justify excluding the Taiwan Strait as a testing ground for CBMs, particularly when it regards Taiwan as one of its primary security threats. A modus vivendi to promote peace and stability in the Taiwan Strait is imperative, not only for Taipei but also for Beijing.

Bibliography

Albright, Madeleine. "American Principle and Purpose in East Asia." *U.S. Department of State Dispatch* 8, no. 3 (March/April 1997): 23–24.
Asian Wall Street Journal. "Taiwan Backs Direct Shipping to China Ports." January 6–7, 1995a, p. 1.
―――. "China, Taiwan United on Oil Exploration," August 31, 1995b, p. 2.
―――. "Our Quiet Revolution." March 27, 1996, p. 8.
Balfour, Michael. *West Germany: A Contemporary History.* New York: St. Martin's Press, 1982.
Beijing Review. "Deng on Issues of World Interest" 29, no. 38 (September 22, 1986): 4–7.
―――. "President Urges Cross-Strait Summit" 38, no. 7 (February 13–19, 1995a): 5.
―――. "China: Arms Control and Disarmament" 38, no. 48 (November 27–December 3, 1995b): 10–25.
Chalmers, Malcolm, Owen Green, and Xie Zhiqiong, eds. *Asia-Pacific Security and the UN.* West York: University of Bradford, 1995.
China Daily. "The Text of Jiang's Call for Reunification," February 2, 1995, p. 2.
China Post. "Lee Airs Views on PRC," February 24, 1996a, p. 1.
―――. "Cross-Strait Policies Outlined," February 26, 1996b, p. 20.
―――. "Military Promises Not to Use Uranium for Nuclear Weapons," August 18, 1996c, p. 11.

Department of State Bulletin. Vol. 87, no. 2119 (February 1987a.).
———. Vol. 87, no. 2122 (May, 1987b).
Eisenhower, Dwight D. *The White House Years: Waging Peace, 1956–1961.* New York: Doubleday, 1965.
FBIS-China (Foreign Broadcast Information Service, Daily Report, People's Republic of China). May 21, 1992, p. 54.
Foreign Relations of the United States. China, vol. 19, 1958–1960. Washington, DC: U.S. Government Printing Office, 1996.
Free China Journal. "Talks Break Deadlock on Hijacking, Other Issues" (August 12, 1994), p. 1.
———. "Cross-Strait Talks Near Accord, but Negotiators Come Upon a Snag" (January 27, 1995a), p. 1.
———. "Lee Maps 6-point Policy for Taiwan-Mainland Relations" (April 14, 1995b), p. 1.
———. "'Acceptable' Deal Reached on Taiwan-Hong Kong Sea Links" (May 30, 1997a), p. 2.
———. "SEF Ready to Transfer Mainland Hijackers" (June 27, 1997b), p. 3.
Gao, Zhiguo. "The South China Sea: From Conflict to Cooperation?" *Ocean Development and International Law* 25, no. 3 (July–September, 1994): 345–59.
Harding, Harry. *A Fragile Relationship: The United States and China Since 1972.* Washington, DC: The Brookings Institution, 1992.
Hickey, Dennis Van Vranken. *Taiwan's Security in the Changing International System.* Boulder, CO: Lynne Rienner, 1997.
International Herald Tribune. "Live-Fire Drill in Strait Is Postponed by Taiwan," April 3, 1996a, p. 4.
———. "U.S. Reveals Secret Taiwan Talks," May 4–5, 1996b, p. 4.
———. "Jet Airliner in Taiwan Is Hijacked to China, and Quickly Returned," March 11, 1997, p. 4.
Jane's Defence Weekly. "China Condemns USA as Taiwan Vote Nears" 25, no. 13 (March 27, 1996a): 3.
———. "Taiwan Election Ends China's Military Show" 25, no. 14 (April 3, 1996b): 4.
Jiaoliu [Interchange]. No. 29 (September, 1996): 35–38.
Koo, Chen-fu. "Relations Across the Taiwan Strait." Speech delivered at the symposium "Relations Across the Taiwan Strait" sponsored by the Institute of East Asian Studies, University of California-Berkeley, September 27, 1996.
Lasater, Martin L. *Policy in Evolution: The U.S. Role in China's Reunification.* Boulder, CO: Westview Press, 1986
Lianhebao [United daily news]. May 23, 1990, p. 2.
———. September 24, 1992, p. 2.
———. August 1, 1995, p. 6.
———. September 25, 1996, p. 4.
Liu, Huaqiu. "Step-by-Step Confidence and Security Building for the Asian Region: A Chinese Perspective." In Ralph A. Cossa, ed., *Asia Pacific Confidence and Security Building Measure.* Washington, DC: Center for Strategic and International Studies, 1995: 119–36.
Mainland Affairs Council. *Peaceful Exchanges, Friendly Interaction, Democratic Unification Toward a New Era in Cross-Strait Relations.* Taipei: Executive Yuan, 1996a.

————. *Promoting Cross-Strait Relations: The Conscious Efforts of the Republic of China Government*. Taipei: Executive Yuan, 1996b.
Manning, Robert A., and Ronald N. Montaperto. "The People's Republic and Taiwan." *Strategic Forum* (National Defense University), no. 103 (February, 1997).
National Policy Dynamic Analysis (Taipei). no. 139 (May 28, 1996): 4, 16.
Oksenberg, Michel. "A Decade of Sino-American Relations." *Foreign Affairs* 61, no. 1 (Fall 1982): 175–95.
Qingnian ribao [Youth daily news]. September 14, 1996a, p. 4.
————. September 26, 1996b, p. 2.
————. July 9, 1997, p. 3.
Renmin ribao [People's daily]. July 19, 1995, p. 1.
ROC Ministry of National Defense. *1992 National Defense Report, Republic of China*. Taipei: Li Ming Cultural Enterprise Co., 1992.
————. *1993–1994 National Defense Report, Republic of China*. Taipei: Li Ming Cultural Enterprise Co., 1994.
————. *1996 National Defense Report, Republic of China*. Taipei: Li Ming Cultural Enterprise Co., 1996.
Rudolph, Matthew C.J. 1993. "Confidence-Building on the Korean Peninsula." In Michael Krepon, Dominique M. McCoy, and Matthew C.J. Rudolph, eds., *A Handbook of Confidence-Building Measures for Regional Security*. Washington, DC: The Henry L. Stimson Center, 1993.
Shinn, James. 1996. "Conditional Engagement with China." In James Shinn, ed., *Weaving the Net: Conditional Engagement with China*. New York: Council on Foreign Relations Press, 1996.
Snyder, Edwin K., A. James Gregor, and Maria Hsia Chang. *The Taiwan Relations Act and the Defense of the Republic of China*. Berkeley: University of California Press, 1980.
Straits Exchange Foundation. *A Résumé of the Koo-Wang Talks*. Taipei: Straits Exchange Foundation, 1993
Straits Times. "N-weapons Use 'Does Not Apply to Taiwan.'" August 6, 1996a, p. 3.
————. "Our Policy of No-First Use of N-weapons Applies to Taiwan Too: China." August 7, 1996b, p. 12.
————. "Chinese Ship Sails into Kaohsiung flying Taiwan Flag." April 21, 1997a, p. 14.
————. "Taiwan to Further Expand Cross-Strait Shipping." April 22, 1997b, p. 16.
————. "Taiwan Investment Less in China This Year." July 14, 1997c, p. 13.
————. "Chinese Courts to Try Two Hijackers Sent Back from Taiwan." July 18, 1997d, p. 24.
————. "China-Taiwan Economic Ties—Seminar Off for Now." November 14, 1997e, p. 28.
Tzuli wanpao [Independence evening post]. November 1–3, 1994, p. 2.
U.S. Congress. *Crisis in the Taiwan Strait: Implications for U.S. Foreign Policy*. Hearing before the Subcommittee on Asia and the Pacific, Committee on International Relations, 104th Congress, 2nd Session, March 14, 1996. Washington, DC: Government Printing Office, 1996a.
————. *The Growth and Role of the Chinese Military*. Hearing before the Subcommittee on East Asian and Pacific Affairs of the Committee on Foreign Relations,

United States Senate, 104th Congress, 1st Session, October 11–12, 1995. Washington, DC: Government Printing Office, 1996b.
Washington Post. "Transcript of Clinton-Jiang News Conference," October 30, 1997, p. A16.
Weekly Compilation of Presidential Documents. Vol. 28, no. 36 (September 7, 1992).
White House. "A National Security Strategy for a New Century." Washinton, DC: Government Printing Office, 1997
Wiedemann, Kent. "Taiwan and the United Nations." *Department of State Dispatch,* 6, no. 34 (August 21, 1995): 655.
Xinhua yuebao [New china monthly]. April, 1996, pp. 121–23.
Yazhou zhoukan [Asia weekly]. October 14–20, 1996, pp. 43–48.
Yu, Peter Kien-hong et al. "Treaty for Alleviating the Crisis Across the Taiwan Strait." *Mao yu dun zazhi* [Spear and shield] (Taipei), no. 54 (October 15, 1991): 3–4.
Zhongguo shibao [China times]. April 18, 1995, p. 9.
———. December 23, 1996, p. 9.
Zhongyang ribao [Central daily news]. September 10, 1992, p. 2.
———. January 28, 1993, p. 2.
———. July 19, 1997, p. 10.
Ziyou shibao [Liberty times]. July 29, 1995, p. 3.
———. July 9, 1997, p. 3.

Acronyms

ABM: Anti-Ballistic Missile (Treaty)
ADB: Asian Development Bank
AELM: APEC Economic Leaders' Meeting
AFTA: ASEAN Free Trade Area
AMM: ASEAN Ministerial Meeting
APEC: Asia-Pacific Economic Cooperation
ARATS: Association for Relations Across the Taiwan Strait (PRC)
ARF: ASEAN Regional Forum
ASEAN: Association of Southeast Asian Nations
ASEM: Asia-Europe Meeting
ATBM: anti-theatre ballistic missile
CAEC: Council for Asia-Europe Cooperation
CBM: confidence-building measure
CFC/UNC: Combined Forces Command/United Nations Command (South Korea)
CFSP: Common Foreign and Security Policy (EU)
CNOOC: China National Offshore Oil Corporation (PRC)
CPC (or CPCT): China Petroleum Corporation (ROC)
CSBM: confidence- and security-building measure
CSCAP: Council for Security Cooperation in the Asia Pacific
CSCE: Council on Security Cooperation for Europe
CTB: Comprehensive Test Ban Treaty
CWC: Chemical Weapons Convention
DG I: First Directorate of the European Commission, responsible for external relations
DPP: Democratic Progressive Party (ROC)
DMZ: Demilitarized Zone (Korea)
DPRK: Democratic People's Republic of Korea
EAEC: East Asian Economic Caucus
EASR: East Asia Strategy Report (US)

EEZ: exclusive economic zone
EPG: Eminent Persons Group (APEC)
EU: European Union
FPDA: Five-Power Defense Arrangements
GDP: gross domestic product
GEM: Group Experts Meeting (Workshop on Managing Potential Conflicts
    in the South China Sea)
GNP: gross national product
GPS: Global Positioning System
HKSAR: Hong Kong Special Administrative Region
IAEA: International Atomic Energy Agency
IBRD: International Bank for Reconstruction and Development
ICBM: inter-continental ballistic missile
IMF: International Monetary Fund
IRBM: intermediate-range ballistic missile
ISG: Inter-Sessional Support Group (ARF)
ISIS: Institutes of Strategic and International Studies (ASEAN)
ISM: Inter-Sessional Meeting (ARF)
JDA: Japan Defense Agency
JSP: Japan Socialist Party
JSDF: Japan Self Defence Forces
KEDO: Korean Peninsula Energy Development Organization
KMT: Kuomintang (Nationalist) Party (ROC)
KWP: Korean Workers' Party (North Korea)
KPA: Korean People's Army (North Korea)
LACM: land-attack cruise missiles
LDP: Liberal Democratic Party (Japan)
MAC: Mainland Affairs Council (ROC)
MAC: Military Armistice Commission (Korea)
MAD: mutually assured destruction
MCTR: Military Critical Technology Regime
MFA: Ministry of Foreign Affairs (PRC)
MFN: most-favored nation trading status
MIED: Maritime Information Exchange Directory
MIRV: multiple independently targetable reentry vehicle
MOFA: Ministry of Foreign Affairs (Japan, ROC)
MRBM: medium-range ballistic missile
MTCR: Missile Technology Control Regime
NAFTA: North American Free Trade Agreement
NATO: North Atlantic Treaty Organization
NDPO: National Defense Program Outline (Japan)

NGO: nongovernmental organization
NP: New Party (ROC)
NPT: Nuclear Nonproliferation Treaty
PAFTAD: Pacific Forum on Trade and Development
PASSEX: Passage Exercise
PBEC: Pacific Basin Economic Council
PD: preventive diplomacy
PECC: Pacific Economic Cooperation Council
PKI: Communist Party of Indonesia
PLA: People's Liberation Army (PRC)
PLAAF: PLA Air Force (PRC)
PMC: Post-Ministerial Conference (ASEAN)
PRC: People's Republic of China
QDR: Quadrennial Defense Review (US)
RAN: Royal Australian Navy
ROC: Republic of China on Taiwan
ROK: Republic of Korea
SAARC: South Asian Association of Regional Cooperation
SACO: Special Action Committee on Facilities and Areas in Okinawa (Japan)
SCC: Security Consultative Committee (Japan)
SDC: Subcommittee on U.S.-Japan Defense Cooperation (Japan)
SDF: Self Defense Force (Japan)
SEF: Straits Exchange Foundation (ROC)
SEANWFZ: South East Asia Nuclear Weapons Free Zone
SLBM: submarine-launched ballistic missile
SLOC: sea lines of communication
SMIS: Strategic Maritime Information System
SOM: Senior Officials Meeting (ASEAN)
TAC: Treaty of Amity and Cooperation (ASEAN)
TMD: Theater Missile Defense system
TRA: Taiwan Relations Act (US)
TWG: Technical Working Group (Workshop on Managing Potential Conflicts in the South China Sea); further divided into TWG-LM (Legal Matters), TWG-MEP (Marine Environmental Protection), TWG-MSR (Marine Scientific Research), TWG-RAWD: (Resource Assessment and Ways of Development), TWG-SNSC (Safety of Navigation, Shipping, and Communication)
UAV: unmanned aerial vehicle
UN: United Nations
UNCLOS: United Nations Convention on the Law of the Sea
UNGA: United Nations General Assembly

UNTAC: United Nations Transitional Authority in Cambodia
USFJ: United States Forces Japan
USFK: United States Forces Korea
USSR: Union of Soviet Socialist Republics
USTR: United States Trade Representative
WMD: weapons of mass destruction
WTO: World Trade Organization
WPNS: Western Pacific Naval Symposium
ZOPFAN: Zone of Peace, Freedom and Neutrality

The Editors and Contributors

The Editors

Hung-mao Tien is Minister of Foreign Affairs of the Republic of China, as of May 20, 2000. Prior to his current appointment, he was President and Chairman of the Board of the Institute for National Policy Research. Among numerous other books, articles and edited volumes, he has published *China Under Jiang Zemin* (co-edited with Yun-han Chu, 2000), *Consolidating the Third Wave Democracies: Themes and Perspectives* (co-edited, 1997); *Taiwan's Electoral Politics and Democratic Transition: Riding the Third Wave* (edited, 1995); *The Great Transition: Social and Political Change in the Republic of China* (1989); and *Government and Politics in Kuomintang China, 1927–37*.

Tun-jen Cheng is Professor of Government and Chair of the East Asian Studies Committee at the College of William and Mary. He has been a research fellow at the Brookings Institution, a Visiting Associate Professor at the University of Michigan at Ann Arbor, and has taught at the University of California at San Diego. He has written many journal articles and book chapters in the area of political economy and democratic changes in East Asia, and edited or authored the following books: *Inherited Rivalry* (co-edited with Chi Huang and Samuel Wu, 1995), *Political Change in Taiwan* (co-edited with Stephen Haggard, 1992), and *Newly Industrializing Asia in Transition* (co-authored with Stephen Haggard, 1987). He received his Ph.D. from the University of California at Berkeley in political science.

The Contributors

Dewi Fortuna Anwar has been a researcher at the Centre for Political and Regional Studies of the Indonesian Institute of Sciences since 1983 and head of its Regional Affairs Division since 1994. During the administration of President B. J. Habibie, she served as Assistant Minister/State Secretary for Foreign Affairs. She also served as a member of the Golkar Advisory Body for Foreign Affairs and Defence, a research executive of the Centre for Information and Development Studies, and a member of the Economic Research Institute at the Indonesian Chamber of Commerce. She received her Ph.D. from Monash University's Department of Political Science and History, with the thesis, "ASEAN as an Aspect of Indonesian Foreign Policy."

Desmond Ball is a Professor in the Strategic and Defence Studies Centre of the Australian National University, of which he previously served as head from 1984–1991. He is also a founding member of the Steering Committee of the Council for Security Cooperation in the Asia-Pacific (CSCAP). Among numerous other books and articles, he has recently published monographs entitled *Building Blocks for Regional Security: An Australian Perspective on Confidence and Security Building Measures (CBMs) in the Asia-*

Pacific Region; Signals Intelligence in the Post-Cold War Era: Developments in the Asia-Pacific Region; The Transformation of Security in the Asia-Pacific Region; and *Presumptive Engagement: Australia's Asia-Pacific Security Policy in the 1990s.*

Bantarto Bandoro is a researcher and head of the Department of International Affairs at the Center for Strategic and International Studies, Jakarta and is a member of Indonesian CSCAP's CBM Working Group. In addition, he serves on the faculty of Social and Political Science of the National University, Jakarta, and lectures or teaches at several other institutions, including the Post Graduate School, University of Jayabaya; the Joint Staff and Command College; the School of Intelligence and Strategic Studies, Bogor; and the School for Foreign Service, Department of Foreign Affairs.

Kang Choi is Senior Director for Policy Planning of the National Security Council of the Republic of Korea. Prior to this post, he served as an associate research fellow at the Arms Control Research Center, Korea Institute for Defense Analyses and the Director-General of CSCAP Korea. His publications include "Military Capabilities of South Korea's Peace-keeping Forces" (forthcoming), *Inter-Korean Confidence Building* (1996), and *Land-based Confidence Building Measures in Northeast Asia* (co-authored, 1994). He received his Ph.D. from Ohio State University in political science.

Chien Chung is Professor of Nuclear Science of the National Tsing Hua University. He is also Vice-Chair of the Chinese Nuclear Medicine and serves on the faculty of the Armed Forces University, teaching warfare and science/technology. He has previously held the post of research associate at Brookhaven National Laboratory. In addition to numerous articles on nuclear science and medicine, he is also a noted commentator on national security. He received his Ph.D. from McGill University in nuclear chemistry.

Ralph A. Cossa is Executive Director of the Pacific Forum CSIS and the Executive Director of the U.S. Member Committee of CSCAP. He is also sits on CSCAP's Steering Committee and is a member of the Board of Directors of the Council on U.S.-Korean Security Studies. He served in the U.S. Air Force from 1966–1993, retiring at the rank of colonel. While on active duty, he served as a Special Assistant to Commander-in-Chief, U.S. Pacific Command (USCINCPAC), Director of USCINCPAC's Study Group, and Chief of the Policy Division in USCINCPAC's Strategic Planning and Policy Directorate. Previous assignments included duty as Deputy Director for Strategic Studies at the National Defense University. Among other publications, he is the author of *The Japan-U.S. Alliance and Security Regimes in Asia; China and Northeast Asia: What Lies Ahead*; and *United States Security Posture in the Asia-Pacific: A Changing Strategy for a Changing World*, as well as the editor of *Asia Pacific Confidence and Security Building Measures* (1995) and *The New Pacific Environment: Challenges and Opportunities* (1993).

Paul M. Evans is Professor of the Faculty of Graduate Studies at the University of British Columbia, based in the Institute for Asian Research and the Liu Centre for Global Studies. He began this position in July 1999, after serving as Professor of Political Science at York University since 1981. From 1991–1996, he also served as Director of the University of Toronto-York University Joint Centre for Asia Pacific Studies, and from 1997–1999, he was a Visiting Scholar at the Asia Center of Harvard University. He served as the co-chair of the Canadian committee of CSCAP until July, 1997, and from 1994–1998 as co-chair of the CSCAP North Pacific Working Group. Major publications include the books *John Fairbank and the American Understanding of Modern China* (1988); *Reluctant Adversaries: Canada and the People's Republic of China, 1949–1970* (co-edited, 1991); *Studying Asia-Pacific Security* (ed., 1994) and the essays "Reinventing East Asia: Multilateral Cooperation and Regional Order" (1996), "The New Multilateralism in the

Asia-Pacific and the Conditional Engagement of China" (1996), and "Assessing the ARF and CSCAP" and, with Iain Johnston, "China's Engagement with Multilateral Institutions" in forthcoming edited volumes. He received his Ph.D. in political science from Dalhousie University.

Harvey J. Feldman is Senior Fellow for China Policy at the Asian Studies Center of the Heritage Foundation and Adjunct Professor of Social Sciences at New York University. His lengthy diplomatic career included the posts of Ambassador to Papua New Guinea and the Solomon Islands, as well as numerous other assignments, notably in Hong Kong, Taiwan, and Japan, as well as at the United Nations, as Alternate United States Representative. As the State Department's Country Director for the Republic of China, he created the American Institute in Taiwan, which now carries out the essential functions of the former embassy. His publications include *Taiwan in a Time of Transition* and *Constitutional Reform in the Republic of China.*

François Godement is Senior Research Associate in charge of Asia-Pacific affairs at the Institut Français des Relations Internationales, Professor at the French National Institute of Oriental Languages and Civilizations (where he chairs the International Business Department), and Co-chair of the European Committee of CSCAP. He also serves as consultant to the Policy Planning Staff of the Ministry of Foreign Affairs. Among other publications, he is the author of *The New Asian Renaissance* (1997). He is a graduate of the Ecole Normale Superieure.

Richard L. Grant was until recently head of the Asia-Pacific Programme at the Royal Institute of International Affairs, which he joined in 1993. He formerly served as the Executive Director of the Pacific Forum/CSIS and as the Director of the Political Committee of the North Atlantic Assembly. His publications include *The Process of Japanese Foreign Policy: Focus on Asia* (1997); *The European Union and China: A European Strategy for the Twenty-first Century* (1995); *China and Southeast Asia: Looking Toward the Twenty-first Century* (1993); *Security Cooperation in the Asia Pacific* (1993); and *The 1990s: Decade of Challenge for the Asia Pacific* (1991).

Carolina G. Hernandez is founder and President of the Institute for Strategic and Development Studies and Professor of Political Science at the University of the Philippines, where she holds the Carlos P. Romulo Chair in International Relations. She is also the current Chair of the ASEAN Institutes of Strategic and International Studies (ASEAN ISIS) and Co-Chair of CSCAP. She has published widely in international, regional and Philippine journals, and she was editor of the *Philippine Foreign Relations Journal* and has edited or co-edited a number of books on politics, security, and civil-military relations.

Michael Ying-mao Kau, is Professor of Political Science at Brown University, where he has been on the faculty since 1966, and where he also directs the Mao's Writings Project and the East Asian Security Project at Brown. In addition, he is the president of the Twenty-first Century Foundation in Taipei and editor of the journal *Chinese Law and Government*. His publications focus on Chinese and East Asian politics, and include *China in the Era of Deng Xiaoping* (1993) and *Taiwan: Beyond the Economic Miracle* (1992). He received his Ph.D. in comparative politics and international relations from Cornell University.

Taeko Kim is a Senior China Analyst in the Policy Planning Directorate at the Korea Institute for Defense Analyses. He is also former associate editor of the *Korean Journal of Defense Analysis*, as well as Visiting Research Associate of the Mershon Center at Ohio State University. He is the author of numerous books, reports, and monographs, including

China's Arms Acquisitions from Abroad: A Quest for "Superb and Secret Weapons" (with Bates Gill, 1995), *The Dynamics of Sino-Russian Military Relations: An Asian Perspective* (1993), and *The ROK Defense Policy After ROK-PRC Normalization* (1993).

Cheng-yi Lin is Director of the Institute of European and American Studies at the Academia Sinica, where he has also served for many years as Deputy Director and Research Fellow. His English publications include *Taiwan's Defence Policy: Threat Assessment and Security Strategies* (1998), *The New World Order and Taiwan's International Role* (1998), *Taiwan's South China Sea Policy* (1997); *The Taiwan Factor in Asia-Pacific Regional Security* (1997); *The U.S. Factor in the 1958 and 1996 Taiwan Strait Crises* (1996); and *Taiwan's Security Strategies in the Post-Cold War Era* (1995). He received his Ph.D. in foreign fffairs from the University of Virginia.

Koji Murata is Assistant Professor of American Studies of the Faculty of Integrated Arts and Sciences of Hiroshima University, Adjunct Research Fellow of Hiroshima University's Institute for Peace Science, and a research fellow of the U.S.-Japan Project of the Washington-based National Security Archive. His publications include *The U.S.-Japan Alliance and the U.S.-South Korea Alliance: Their Origins, Dilemmas, and Structures* (1995) and *The Carter Administration's Policy to Withdraw U.S. Ground Combat Forces from South Korea: A Dilemma in Defense Commitment Towards South Korea* (1994). He received the Yomiuri Merit Award for New Opinion Leadership in 1996.

Douglas H. Paal is President and founder of the Asia Pacific Policy Center. Prior to forming the center, he was Special Assistant to Presidents Bush and Reagan for National Security Affairs and Senior Director for Asian Affairs on the National Security Council. He has also served in the State Department Policy Planning Staff, as a Senior Analyst for the CIA, and in the U.S. embassies in Singapore and Beijing. He publishes frequently on Asian affairs and national security issues.

Akio Watanabe is Professor at the School of International Politics, Economics, and Business of Aoyama Gakuin University and Professor Emeritus of the University of Tokyo. In 1994, he served as a member of the Prime Minister's Advisory Group on Defense Issues, and was the chief author of its report, "The Modality of the Security and Defense Capability of Japan: The Outlook for the Twenty-first Century." He has held numerous research and teaching fellowships at such institutions as the Woodrow Wilson International Center for Scholars; the Japanese Research Center at Beijing Foreign Languages University; and the Royal Institute for International Affairs. His other publications in English include *Japan's Dual Roles in the Asian Drama: War and Development* (1996); *The End of the Cold War and the Asia-Pacific Region* (1991); and *The Okinawa Problem: A Chapter in Japan-U.S. Relations* (1970). He received his Ph.D. from the Australian National University in international relations.

Byron Weng is Adjunct Professor of Public Policy and Administration at National Chi-Nan University. He previously served for many years as Professor and Chairman of the Department of Government and Public Administration at the Chinese University of Hong Kong. He has served, at various times, both the Hong Kong government (as a member of the Law Reform Commission and of the Central Policy Unit) and the ROC government (as a research member of the National Unification Council and as a member of the Advisory Committee of the Mainland Affairs Council). His extensive publications focus on the politics, law, and foreign policy of the PRC, Taiwan and Hong Kong, and the inter-relations between these three parts of "Greater China."

Index

Acharya, Amitav, 156, 159, 194
Ahmad, Reme, 147
Alatas, Ali, 117
Albright, Madeleine, 315
Ali, Hashim Mohammed, 194–195
Anti-ballistic missile (ABM) treaty, 74
Anwar, Dewi Fortuna, 11, 173–188
APEC. *See* Asia-Pacific Economic
  Cooperation
ARATS. *See* Association for Relations
  Across the Taiwan Strait
ARF. *See* Asian Regional Forum
Arms control, 83, 91n, 137, 141
Arms sales, 22–23, 82–83, 86, 142
Art of War, The (Sun Tsu), 15
ASEAN. *See* Association of Southeast
  Asian Nations
ASEAN Free Trade Area (AFTA), 175
ASEAN Regional Forum (ARF), 6,
  10–11, 37, 67, 95, 146, 154–155,
  207
  agenda of, 131–132, 136–137, 139–142,
    149–150
  characteristics of approach, 157–159
  China in, 160, 166–170, 254, 312
  Concept Paper, 132, 133, 134, 138, 141
  and confidence and security building
    measures (CSBMs), 133–134, 136,
    160, 306–307
  and CSCAP, 163–164
  effectiveness of, 155–157, 159–160
  establishment of, 118–119

ASEAN Regional Forum (ARF)
  (continued)
  and Europe, 212–213
  leadership of, 157
  member committees of, 50n.3
  and Mischief Reef incident, 88
  preventive diplomacy proposals of, 137,
    161–162
  second-track meetings of, 133, 160
  secretariat proposal for, 163
  Senior Official Meetings (SOM),
    132–133, 160
  and South China Sea disputes, 276, 287,
    289
ASEM. *See* Asia-Europe Meeting
Asia-Europe Meeting (ASEM), 11–12,
  158, 202–203
  and economic ties, 210–211
  membership of, 204–205
  rationale underlying, 203–206
  and security considerations, 206–213
Asian Development Bank (ADB), 95,
  211, 330
Asia-Pacific Economic Cooperation
  (APEC), 5, 11, 37, 39, 87, 165, 204,
  207, 330
  ASEAN nations in, 158–159, 173, 174,
    180–181
  Bogor Declaration, 176, 181
  China in, 173, 174, 177, 181–182, 254
  Economic Leaders' Meetings (AELM),
    175–178

For Product Safety Concerns and Information please contact our EU
representative GPSR@taylorandfrancis.com
Taylor & Francis Verlag GmbH, Kaufingerstraße 24, 80331 München, Germany